D0700052

LETTERS OF JAMES STEPHENS

Also by Richard J. Finneran

W. B. Yeats, *John Sherman and Dhoya* (Editor)
William Butler Yeats: The Byzantium Poems (Editor)
The Prose Fiction of W. B. Yeats: The Search for "Those Simple Forms"

LETTERS OF JAMES STEPHENS

edited by
RICHARD J. FINNERAN

Macmillan Publishing Co., Inc.
New York

Macmillan Publishing Co., Inc.
866 Third Avenue, New York, N.Y. 10022

Library of Congress Catalog Card Number: 74-30

First American Edition 1974

Printed in Great Britain

For E.J.F., with thanks

James Stephens

The visionary and the artist in James Stephens the world knows long since. Novel, story, hero-tale, poem, the pages sing and shine: caprice and tenderness, subtle generosities underlain by playful brutalities, extraordinary force with a winning innocence: it is a seeing power like that of a savage, a song and dance as of a child, the loving tolerance of a mystic discerning in all things, noble or trifling or ugly, always some trace of some god.

These things are known: one man would like to add to them and to the limner's presentation some inkling of the private Shēamus underneath it all.

There are writers that keep their best wine, and their merely good, for their marriage feasts; they part only for profit. Not so Shēamus; not so. He gives like the sun gladdening the place beneath all day long. It is the richest talk.

A stranger from a strange though not far land came once questing the soul and habit of Ireland and he wrote a book; Dublin a city of magicians of talk; rub the lantern and all the embroidered cloths glow around you: this innocent had met Shēamus. Shēamus fills a room; he passes for a city; he gives character to a nation; he has the vision and the report of a prophet, spellbinding, aweing, stilling doubts. The very laughingheartedest of men he is also one grim earnestness; whatever he says, he believes and whatever he believes has been grasped with an intuitional fury which leaves it henceforth the truth.

And the lavishness of him: St. Martin is immortal at cost of half a cloak: Shēamus gives whole cloaks and the purse and fountain pen in the pocket and thanks the beggar for the whine.

Note by Stephen MacKenna in William Rothenstein's *Twenty-Four Portraits, Second Series* (London: Chatto & Windus, 1923)

"... a competent critic ... should refuse to avail himself of letters from ... the person he is celebrating."

"An Essay in Cubes" (1914)

"Have you ever read Keats' letters. I'm at them, now only! They are very good, remarkable. Mine wont be, I dont write any."

To Elizabeth Bloxham, October 1938

Contents

List of Illustrations

between pages 200 and 201

Preface and Acknowledgements

For the purposes of this edition the term "letter" has been rather broadly defined; I have thus included not only letters proper but also such items as important inscriptions and the articles which Stephens published in *The Dial* under the heading of "Dublin Letter" or "Irish Letter".

This edition contains 376 letters to ninety identified correspondents. Eighteen of these were published by Stephens and are taken from printed sources. Of the remaining items – all of which are taken from manuscript sources – only eleven have been previously published in full: one each by Olivia Howard Dunbar, Richard Ellmann and James F. Carens; two by Simon Nowell-Smith; and three each by Hilary Pyle and myself (see Appendix B for the citations). Excerpts from several other letters included here have been published in various places, most notably in the works of Dunbar and Pyle.

It is not an exaggeration to say that "*et al.*" should follow the editor's name on the title-page of this volume. The number of people who have had some part in this edition runs well into the hundreds. The limitations of space will allow me to single out only a very few; I trust that the others will accept my silent thanks.

First of all I should like to express my sincere thanks to Mrs. Iris Wise (Stephens's stepdaughter) and her husband, Norman. What began as a relatively simple matter of permission to undertake this edition has developed into a warm friendship. Along the way no request has been unfulfilled and no question has gone unanswered; without that co-operation my work would have been many times more difficult, if not impossible. And the hospitality shown to me by the Wises during my visits in London (often at "Eversleigh", once Stephens's home and now theirs) has been exceptionally generous.

I should also like to acknowledge my debt to Mr. Dan H. Laurence, whom I have been fortunate to know in various ways: first as one of my instructors, then as a colleague, and always as a friend. Dan has not only continually provided me with advice on editorial matters and information on Shaw and others; equally importantly, his monumental edition of Shaw's correspondence has served as a constant model of excellence.

Mr. Alan Denson is another scholar who has been most generous in providing me with assistance on this volume. He has not only responded in full to my many queries but has also sent me a great deal of information nowhere else available – about both AE and countless other matters.

Professor Brendan P. O Hehir has with great kindness performed the indispensable task of translating Stephens's Gaelic – no easy accomplishment, since Stephens's knowledge of that language was something less than perfect, to say the least. Professor O Hehir's patience with my continual stream of queries has been equalled only by the completeness of his replies.

I am greatly indebted to the various Librarians (and their staffs) at all of the institutions listed on pp. xix–xx. Although I cannot mention them all, I would like to cite here a few who have been exceptionally helpful: Mr. John C. Broderick at the Library of Congress; Mr. Richard Cary at Colby College; Mr. Kenneth W. Duckett at Southern Illinois University; Mr. David Farmer and Mrs. Mary M. Hirth at the University of Texas; Mrs. Elsie Freivogel at Washington University in St. Louis; Mr. Donald Gallup at Yale University; Mr. K. C. Gay at the State University of New York at Buffalo; Mr. Dean H. Keller at Kent State University; Mr. Alf Mac Lochlainn at the National Library of Ireland; Mr. Peter M. Rainey at the Manuscript Division of the New York Public Library; and Mrs. Lola L. Szladits at the Berg Collection of the New York Public Library. And of course my thanks go to the staff of the British Museum, where much of the research for this edition was carried out.

Of the countless other individuals to whom I am indebted, I should like to mention the following: Professor Andy Antippas; Professor Sergio Baldi; Mrs. Aileen Bodkin; Professor Zack Bowen; Professor Birgit Bramsbäck; Mr. Garceh Browne; Professor James Carens; Mrs. Valerie Eliot; Mr. Colin Fenton; Mr. Neville Figgis; Miss Jessamine Gist; Professor George Harper; Professor Carroll Hollis; Miss Norah Hoult; Mr. Charles E. Kelly; Mrs. Mary M. Lago; Professor Fran Lawrence; Mr. Harold Loeb; Professor Patricia McFate; the late Sir Compton Mackenzie; Professor Wallace Martin; Mr. Liam Miller; Mr. Maximilian H. Miltzlaff; Professor William M. Murphy; Professor James O'Brien; Mrs. Eileen O'Casey; Mr. John O'Riordan; Professor Edward Partridge; Professor Donald Pizer; Miss

Hilary Pyle; Mr. Paul C. Richards; Professor Gerald Snare; Mrs. Dorothy Carter Snow; Dr. Michael Solomons; Dr. Walter Starkie; Professor Henry Summerfield; Mr. Colin Summerford; Mr. Herbert Weinstock; Dr. James White; and Senator Michael B. Yeats.

I am grateful to Mr. Alan Denson (yet again) for his assistance in reading the proofs; and for help in preparing the indices I should like to thank Miss Elaine Menge.

Finally, I should like to express my appreciation to the Graduate Council on Research of Tulane University for continuing financial assistance during my work on this edition.

Newcomb College, Tulane University *R.J.F.*
New Orleans, Louisiana

Editorial Policy

My basic principle has been to reproduce exactly what Stephens wrote. Where possible, I have given him the benefit of the doubt in such matters as spelling and punctuation; and errors such as repeating the last word on a page at the top of the next have been silently corrected. But there has been no attempt to regularize Stephens's idiosyncratic style. Thus, the term "*sic*" is not used: whatever errors appear in the letters are (hopefully) Stephens's own.

Since all letters are presented in full, any ellipses are by Stephens. Editorial interpolations within a letter have been enclosed in brackets. Inside addresses have been regularized to give the date and the city of origin (a precise address can be determined from the headnotes). Correspondents, cities, or dates in brackets have been determined from various sources, ranging from internal allusions to the date of a Segovia concert. The kind of stationery a letter is written on (Stephens used whatever was available) has not been indicated unless necessary to understand a reference in the letter. His occasional drawings have not been reproduced and have been cited only when alluded to in the letter.

Although Stephens had no great fondness for paragraphs, I have indented the first line of each letter. I have also often assumed, when it seemed logical to do so, that starting a new page of a letter was the equivalent of starting a new paragraph. All postscripts – which often occur at the top or side of a letter – have been placed at the end of the letter.

When the meaning was clear from the context and the equivalent words in English, Stephens's French has been neither corrected nor translated; when translated, though, it has been corrected. Stephens's Irish has always been translated and has been corrected where necessary.

In so far as has been possible, the headnotes present whatever information is necessary to understand any references or allusions in the letters. Since the letters are of course meant to be read in order, I have not continually repeated such matters as the name of the volume which Stephens is discussing; such matters are usually obvious from the date and context and can be confirmed by reference to the Index. In most cases, the allusions and references are discussed in the order in which they occur in the letter. Except for the most familiar figures (and a few minor ones who have eluded me), the dates of each person are given the first time that his name is mentioned; the same procedure applies to publication dates.

Code to Description and Location of Manuscript Material

The bracketed information above the headnote indicates the nature and location of the manuscript material, according to the following code:

A Holograph letter or postcard
T Typewritten letter
I Holograph inscription

1. Privately owned
2. Amherst College Library
3. Henry W. and Albert A. Berg Collection, The New York Public Library, Astor, Lenox and Tilden Foundations
4. Bodleian Library, Oxford University
5. British Broadcasting Corporation, Written Archives Centre
6. British Museum
7. Brown University Library
8. Bucknell University Library
9. University of California at Berkeley, General Library
10. University of California at Los Angeles, University Library
11. University of Chicago Library
12. Colby College Library
13. Cornell University Library
14. Dartmouth College Library
15. Harvard University, Houghton Library
16. Henry E. Huntington Library and Art Gallery
17. Indiana University, Lilly Library
18. University of Kansas, Kenneth Spencer Research Library
19. Kent State University Library
20. Library of Congress
21. University of London Library
22. Loyola University of Chicago, E. M. Cudahy Memorial Library
23. Macmillan & Company Ltd., London

24. University of Michigan Library
25. Mills College Library
26. National Library of Ireland
27. Newberry Library
28. New York Public Library, Manuscript Division
29. New York University Library, De Coursey Fales Collection
30. Princeton University Library
31. University of Southern California, University Library
32. Southern Illinois University, Morris Library
33. Stanford University Libraries
34. State University of New York at Binghamton Library
35. State University of New York at Buffalo, Poetry Collection, Lockwood Memorial Library
36. University of Texas, Humanities Research Center
37. University of Toronto Library
38. Trinity College Library, Dublin
39. Tulane University Library
40. University of Vermont, Guy W. Bailey Library
41. Washington University Libraries, St. Louis, Modern Literature Collection
42. Yale University, Beinecke Rare Book and Manuscript Library
43. Yeats Memorial Museum, Sligo County Library

Chronology

1880	9 February	Possible date of birth in Dublin
1882	2 February	Announced date of birth, in "County Dublin"
1886	June	Enters Meath Protestant Industrial School for Boys
1896	30 April	Leaves Meath School; employed by a Dublin solicitor, Mr. Wallace
1901	21 March	On a gymnastic team which wins the "Irish Shield"; about this time employed in a solicitor's office, Reddington & Sainsbury
1905	16 September	"The Greatest Miracle" published in the *United Irishman*
1906	?	Employed as a clerk-typist in the office of T. T. Mecredy & Son, solicitors
1907	20 April	Begins regular contributions to *Sinn Féin*
	14 June	Birth of stepdaughter, Iris; shortly thereafter forms a liaison with "Cynthia" (Millicent Josephine Kavanagh, 22 May 1882–18 December 1960)
	28 June	Is "discovered" by George W. Russell (AE) and thus gains entrance into the Dublin literary circles
1909	29 April	Acts in the Theatre of Ireland production of Seumas O'Kelly's *The Shuiler's Child*, playing Tim O'Halloran (under the name "Stephen James")
	26 October	Birth of son, James Naoise (d. 24 December 1937)
	11 & 13 November	Plays same part in a revival of *The Shuiler's Child*

1910	28, 30 & 31 March, and 2 April	Acts in the Theatre of Ireland production of Gerald Macnamara's *The Spurious Sovereign*, playing the Assassin, the Court Juggler and the Icelander (under the names "Seumas James", "Samuel James" and "Stephen James")
	November	Associated with David Houston, Thomas MacDonagh and Padraic Colum in founding and editing the *Irish Review* (published March 1911–November 1914)
1911	25 March	Acts in Padraic O Conaire's *Bairbre Ruadh*
	17–18 November	*The Marriage of Julia Elizabeth* produced by the Theatre of Ireland at the Hardwicke Street Theatre
1913	January	Receives a commission from *The Nation* (London) to write a series of short stories
	6 May	Having resigned from his position with T. T. Mecredy after the success of *The Crock of Gold*, moves to Paris "for about a year"
	26–28 June	Another production of *The Marriage of Julia Elizabeth* at the Hardwicke Street Theatre
	28 November	*The Crock of Gold* awarded the Polignac Prize; Stephens in London to receive the award from W. B. Yeats
1914	10 July	Returns from Paris to Dublin
	1 November	Returns to Paris
1915	8 July	Elected Unestablished Registrar of the National Gallery of Ireland (Registrar on 15 December 1918)
	29 July	Returns to Dublin and takes up his position at the National Gallery in August
1918	October	Serves on Executive Committee of the Dublin Drama League

1919	14 May	Marries "Cynthia" (then a widow) in London
1920	31 May–5 June	*The Wooing of Julia Elizabeth* (identical with *The Marriage of . . .*) produced at the Abbey Theatre by the Dublin Drama League
	December	One of a series of operations for gastric ulcers
1924	9 August	*Deirdre* presented the medal for fiction at the *Aonach Tailteann* festival in Dublin; Stephens assists AE in judging the competition in poetry
	9 December	Resigns from the National Gallery (effective 18 January 1925)
1925	28 January	Leaves from London on American lecture tour
	18 June	Returns to London; shortly thereafter settles into "Eversleigh" in the Kingsbury suburb of London
	30 December	Goes to America on another lecture tour
1926	April–May	Returns to London
1927	July	Developing friendship with James Joyce
	December; or January 1928	Joyce suggests that Stephens complete *Finnegans Wake* if he were unable to do so; this proposal made more formally in July 1929
1928	15 March	First B.B.C. broadcast (on Synge)
	April–May	Substitutes for Joyce as a lecturer at the Third International Book Fair in Florence
1929	May–June	Goes to Rumania and meets Queen Marie
	August	Goes to America and stays with W. T. H. Howe in Kentucky
	October	Returns to London
1930	30 April	Goes to America and stays with W. T. H. Howe in Kentucky
	August	Returns to London

1931	April	Goes to America and stays with W. T. H. Howe in Kentucky
	October	Returns to London
1932	August	Goes to America and stays with W. T. H. Howe in Kentucky
	18 September	A founder member of the Irish Academy of Letters
	November–December	Returns to London
1933	July	Goes to America and stays with W. T. H. Howe in Kentucky
	December	Returns to London
1934	August	Goes to America and stays with W. T. H. Howe in Kentucky; also goes on lecture tour
	December	Returns to London
1935	September	Goes to America on final lecture tour
	December	Returns to London
1937	27 March	Marriage of Iris Stephens with Norman Wise (b. 16 July 1907)
	18 May	Begins regular series of B.B.C. broadcasts
	24 December	Accidental death of son, James Naoise
1940	October	Moves to Woodside Chapel in Gloucestershire to escape the Blitz
1942	March–April	Awarded British Civil List Pension (of from £100 to £200)
1945	August	Returns to London
1946	November	Offered honorary degree from Dublin University (Trinity College)
1947	30 June	Receives grant from the Royal Bounty Fund, allowing trip to Dublin to receive honorary degree
	22 October	Awarded honorary D.Litt. degree from Dublin University (Trinity College)
1950	11 June	Final B.B.C. broadcast (on his childhood)
	26 December	Death at Eversleigh
1951	1 January	Funeral at the Parish Church of St. Andrew in Kingsbury
	25 January	Memorial service at St. Martin-in-the-Fields

1907 — 1915

> I have discovered a new young poet in a young fellow named James Stephens who has a real original note in him. He has had the devil of a time poor fellow works about fourteen hours a day for twenty shillings a week and is glad to get it. Was out of work for over a year once and went hungry and homeless and was saved from starving by a woman who sold fruit on a street stall. Good education for the soul sometimes but bad for the body.

AE to Katharine Tynan Hinkson, 19 December 1908 (*Letters from AE*, ed. Alan Denson)

In June 1886 a young boy named James Stephens effectively became an orphan, being placed in the Meath Protestant Industrial School for Boys in Dublin. Exactly when and where he had been born is a matter of some debate (see Appendix A). But in any event he spent most of his youth in the Meath School, leaving there in April 1896 to find employment in the office of a Dublin solicitor. For the next ten years Stephens seems to have drifted from job to job, and only occasionally does a definite fact about his life come to the surface – such as his presence on a gymnastic team which won the "Irish Shield" in 1901. On 16 September 1905 he made a tentative foray into the literary world with a short story published in the *United Irishman*; but he was not to follow up this preliminary trial until 1907, the year in which his literary career actually began.

By 1907 Stephens was regularly employed in the office of T. T. Mecredy & Son, solicitors, in Dublin. In April he contributed his first article to Arthur Griffith's *Sinn Féin*; in the next four years he was to publish over seventy items in that newspaper. At the end of June 1907 the publication of his first poem in *Sinn Féin* brought Stephens to the attention of George W. Russell (AE), who became one of his closest friends. George Moore recounts this "discovery" in *Vale* (1914):

> And every Thursday evening the columns of *Sinn Féin* were searched, and every lilt considered, and every accent noted; but the days and the weeks went by without a new peep-o-peep, sweet, sweet, until the day that James Stephens began to trill; and recognising at once a new songster, AE put on his hat and went away with his cage, discovering him in a lawyer's office. A great head and two soft brown eyes looked at him over a

typewriter, and an alert and intelligent voice asked him whom he wanted to see. AE said that he was looking for James Stephens, a poet, and the typist answered: I am he.

At about this same time, Stephens acquired a wife ("Cynthia") and a stepdaughter (Iris) when Cynthia's husband left his family (Stephens had been a boarder in their house; Cynthia's other daughter went to live with her father's family). Thus, by the end of 1907 Stephens had become a husband, a father, a writer, and an accepted member of Dublin's literary circles.

In May 1909 Stephens's literary reputation began to be established with the publication of *Insurrections.* In that same year his only child, James Naiose, was born. Late in 1910 Stephens became one of the founders and editors of the *Irish Review*, the journal in which his first novel, called "Mary: A Story", was published from April 1911 to February 1912.

Once its periodical version was completed, "Mary: A Story" was published in book form as *The Charwoman's Daughter*, thus beginning what was to be Stephens's *annus mirabilis.* The novel was immediately followed by a book of poetry, *The Hill of Vision.* The year was brought to a triumphant conclusion with the publication in October of *A Crock of Gold*, Stephens's masterpiece and the work which established him as a major writer on the Anglo-Irish scene.

Stephens's increasing royalties and a commission from the London *Nation* to write a series of short stories now allowed him to become a full-time writer, and thus he resigned from his job as a clerk-typist. Apparently seeking to widen his experience, in May 1913 he moved to Paris. Stephens clearly enjoyed life in that city, maintaining a flat there for the rest of his life and always considering it his second home. The first literary result of his Paris stay was *Here Are Ladies*, a collection of short stories published in October 1913.

Stephens had planned to follow *Here Are Ladies* with a volume of poetry, *Songs from the Clay*, in the spring of 1914. But the adverse reactions to the manuscript on the part of many of his friends – including AE – resulted in his withdrawing it, and the book was not published until March 1915. Instead, Stephens devoted his energies to completing a novel, *The Demi-Gods*, which appeared in October 1914.

By the middle of 1915 Stephens was finding it increasingly difficult to survive on his royalty income; and the Paris of the First

World War was not the most pleasant environment for a writer to live in. Thus, when a number of his friends managed to have him elected (despite. his obvious lack of qualifications) to a position at the National Gallery of Ireland, he decided to accept it. Stephens returned to Ireland in late July 1915, bringing to a close what had been the most productive and most important segment of his literary career.

To GEORGE ROBERTS

Dublin
[A/29] 3 August 1907

[George Roberts (1873–1953) was one of the founders of Maunsel & Co., the Dublin firm which published *Insurrections* in 1909. "Influenza" was never printed. Kilmashogue, a mountain near Dublin, is one of the settings in *The Crock of Gold.* The Irish writer George W. Russell (1867–1935), who used the pseudonym "AE", was one of Stephens's closest friends; I have not traced his address, which was probably connected with his work for the Irish Agricultural Organisation Society. Stephens had bought a copy of *Poems* (1893) by the English writer Francis Thompson (1859–1907).

The postcript, added on the first page of the letter, appears to have been written on Sunday, 4 August, after the weekly meeting of the Dublin Hermetic Society. James H. Cousins (1873–1956) was an Irish writer; his " 'Irish' night" was probably held in conjunction with the Oireachtas celebrations, which opened on 5 August.

Stephens was currently living at 80 Rathmines Road.]

Dear Roberts

It was decent of you to send me the letter, but you really mus'nt be doing that sort of thing. Keep your arms under the blankets, and get well as soon as you can for Heavens sake.

I was sorry to hear that you have had such a bad time. I think this beastly Influenza, is about the worst form of torture I know.

However you seem to be over the worst now, and (to judge from the last part of your note,) almost enjoying it. Perhaps your fervent brooding has something to do with it.

I wish I had done more in that line. It might have helped to dispel the hideous crowd of phantasmagorias and day-nightmares which inflicted me with continuous torment. So much so that I wrote a sonnet entitled 'Influenza' describing my agony. I would send it to you, but think it wiser to wait till you are stronger.

I went out to Kilmashogue this morning and had a most glorious time. The lights on the mountain were extraordinary. On one part in particular there was an unearthly light-green colour which I never saw before. It was as if the hill-side was *transparent*.

Russell *was* at the Hermetic on Saturday and read more of the Upanishads. He is still suffering with a heavy cold, in spite of which he tells me he addressed an open air meeting on Sunday, for *3 hours* (*think of yourself and me going to bed*). I got a copy of Thompsons Poems 1st ed. 1893 from an English bookseller for 3/6. Must stop now to catch the post

Yours
J.S.

I was *not* at the Hermetic last night; but went instead to Cousins 'Irish' night at Georges Hall [–] It was very good

J.S.

To ESTELLA SOLOMONS

[A/1] Dublin
3 June 1909

[Estella Solomons (1882–1968) was an Irish artist; her portrait of Stephens is in the Municipal Gallery of Modern Art in Dublin. *Insurrections* was published in May 1909. "Brigid Beg" ("Little Brigid") apparently refers to either "The Tale of Mad Brigid", included in *Insurrections*, or "Brigid", included in *Here Are Ladies* (1913).

Stephens was currently living at 34 Holles Street.]

Dear Miss Solomons

The Imp of Perversity appears to be dealing with our letters. Yours went to the wrong address. I posted my reply to you a week ago & miraculously found it today in my pocket[.] A resurrected letter is a hideous & monstrous thing. I am sure you felt that when your first epistle boomeranged back to you, dead & dolorous.

I am very glad indeed that you liked Brigid Beg – its a nice wee poem. & I am also very glad that you liked Insurrections, its a nice wee book. It is, I suppose, unnecessary to tell you that since the publication of my book I have felt that my brow is one admirably adapted to the wearing of laurels, & I am practicing a look of "poetic frenzy" for the use of those myri[a]d people who stare at me in the street with, more or less, reverent terror. I am, as you suggest, a great man and you'r another.

Is mise do c[h]ara
["I am, your friend"]
JAMES STEPHENS

To GEORGE PLATT BRETT (Macmillan Company, New York)

Dublin
[A/28] 4 November 1909

[George Platt Brett (1858–1936) was President of the Macmillan Company in New York. Acting on the advice of the English writers Richard Whiteing (1840–1928) and Edward Verrall Lucas (1868–1938), Brett wrote to Stephens on 22 October 1909; he asked permission to publish a book consisting of *Insurrections*, the four poems published in *The Nation* (London) earlier in 1909, and some manuscript material. Eventually, Brett ordered 500 copies of *Insurrections* from Maunsel & Co. and published an American edition, dated 1909. "The Lonely God" was included in *The Hill of Vision* (1912).

Stephens was currently living at 91 Merrion Square West.]

Dear Sir,

I have your letter naming terms for the American rights in my book *Insurrections*. I am sorry to say that my publisher here claims that these rights are his property (altho' he has allowed them to lapse) and, therefore, I do not see that I can do anything in this particular matter. I would not give additional poems when he might "bag" my profits.

I propose bringing out another volume of poems in the spring – the mss of which I have now ready. I shall be very glad to treat with you for it. The poems Mr Lucas sent you ("The Lonely God &c) will form part of this book as also those printed in the Nation & other unprinted matter which I have by me. Could you get me any serial money on the poems you have? That would retain the American copyright and in a measure prepare your market

Yours truly
JAMES STEPHENS

To GEORGE PLATT BRETT (Macmillan Company, New York)
Dublin
[A/28] 10 December 1909

[Brett wrote Stephens on 16 November 1909 to ask for additional manuscripts and to inquire about the fee for serial rights. "Change" was included in the Macmillan volume of *The Lonely God and Other Poems*. Neither of the sonnets referred to from *Insurrections* – "Seumas Beg" and "Slan Leath" – was included in *The Adventures of Seumas Beg* (1915).]

Dear Sir,

I enclose you mss of about 70 poems as detailed in list annexed. They are put together, so far, without any order & will have to be returned to me for this purpose later on, that is if we come to terms. I think you have some poems (sent you by Mr Lucas) which I may have forgotten. You have one called "Change" which I have not included in the bundle sent herewith. Please include any other you may have.

As to serial money. I usually get £2/2/- per poem over here. I do not know how American Editors pay, but I gave you carte blanche in the matter & my best thanks for your trouble. I should like you to deduct 10% for your work in this direction[.] This is I believe usual.

In the series entitled The Adventures of Seumas Beg: the 1st sonnet & the last are included in "*Insurrections*" but my present Publisher has agreed with me that these might go into the series when they were being published. I had intended doing them separately as a picture book.

Sincerely yours
JAMES STEPHENS

P.S. I shd like to hear from you as early as possible – I have other poems but think there is enough in these sent

To GEORGE PLATT BRETT (Macmillan Company, New York)
Dublin
[T/28] [April 1910]

[On 21 January 1910, Brett declined to publish the manuscript sent to him by Stephens on 10 December 1909. Brett returned that manuscript but retained the smaller one he had received from E. V. Lucas. In reply to his second request for the Lucas manuscript, Stephens received a copy of *The Lonely God and Other Poems*. The volume contained "The Lonely God", "Astray" (later called "Little Lady"), "In the High Court of Justice" (later called "The Last Judgment"), "Change", "Who'll Carry a Message?", "Secrets" (later called "When I Was Young") and "Light of Love". Macmillan had printed the book for copyright purposes (it was entered at the Library of Congress on 29 October 1909) but had not published it. In spite of this incident, Macmillan became Stephens's American publisher, beginning with *The Hill of Vision* in 1912.]

Dear Mr Brett.

In reply to my letter to your firm asking for some spare mss, which you had, I have been forwarded a small book consisting of the "Lonely God" and six other poems. On the fly leaf is printed that this book was copyrighted and published in 1909. Have you published this book or not? as your last letter to me rejected the mss which I sent you and returned some 80 poems.

I should hate the poems which are collected in this small book to go out, as the smaller poems are very bad ones – in comparison with the Lonely God.

Please let me hear from you as early as possible.

Yours sincerely.
JAMES STEPHENS

There is of course no agreement entered into between us

To JAMES SULLIVAN STARKEY

Donnybrook
[A/38] [10–16 July 1910]

[James Sullivan Starkey (1879–1958) was an Irish writer; he published under the pseudonym of "Seumas O'Sullivan". This letter was written from the house of Stephen MacKenna (1872–1934), best known for his five-volume translation of Plotinus (1917–30); MacKenna was one of Stephens's closest friends. Robin Flower (1881–1946) was an English poet; his *Eire and Other Poems* was published in 1910. Stephens's "Crooked-Heart" was printed in the *Spectator* for 9 July 1910.]

Dear Starkie

My unfortunate lady has just had a miscarriage last night – She is very gifted in ways. I am in a deuce of a hole for a few pounds – Could you in any way manage £2 for me. I wouldnt trouble you unless I was really against the wall. I had a visit from a London poet! named Robin Flower, yesterday he recited his verses to us, that may account for the happy catastrophe. I am very sorry to ask you this as I know you are as hardup as I am, but I dont like asking any one else. The Spectator owes me for last weeks issue & they will pay – sometime –

Truly yours,
JAMES STEPHENS

To [THE EDITOR OF *SINN FÉIN*] & JAMES SULLIVAN STARKEY

[Dublin]
5 November 1910

[The text is from *Sinn Féin* for 5 November 1910. In *Sinn Féin* for 8 October 1910, Stephens had reviewed *The Hours of Fiametta: A Sonnet Sequence* (1910) by Rachel Annand Taylor (1876–1960). Stephens's main objection to the volume was an excessive amount of "ornamentation": "I consider that a sonnet should be as naked as a statue. In almost all cases decoration in verse is a sign of functional debility." In the course of the review Stephens also speculated on a definition of "Decadence". Stephens's comments led J. S. Starkey to publish "Decadence: An Open Letter to James Stephens" in *Sinn Féin* for 29 October 1910. The following letter is Stephen's reply to Starkey.

Dalkey is a suburb of Dublin. Messalina (d. A.D. 48), third wife of the Roman emperor Claudius, was notorious for her immorality.]

A REPLY TO AN OPEN LETTER

My Dear Seumas O'Sullivan, –

I am sorry you are displeased by my criticism of Mrs. Taylor's poems, but otherwise am unrepentant, for to have drawn a letter from you will, in the estimation of all judicious people, amply justify the existence of any criticism and will probably set other writers to work in critical paths in the hopes of being similarly rewarded.

It is, I believe, a point of good manners that letters shall be answered, the more especially when they are written with all the circumstance of publicity by so distinguished a poet and craftsman as yourself, but in the controversy which seems imminent it is as well that the point at issue should be strictly defined, and that the argument should not draw within its tentacles any person who might not be glad of such doubtful fame. Therefore, I wish to say at once, and I am sure you will also wish it, that the subject at present under discussion is not in any way connected with the poems of any particular person, and to make it as clear as possible that Mrs. Taylor's poems are not, in any aspect, in my mind in this discussion, except so far as is necessary to refer to them to clear a misconception.

I notice with some dismay that you have "always regarded me as before all things honest". In those times of rapid living one's failings are spoken of in the market place almost before they become apparent to oneself. I, in conjunction with the remainder of humanity, must do the best I can with the sharply curtailed, indeed, stinted virtues wherewith Providence has endowed me, and as honesty at any time is an extremely variable, fluctuating virtue it is perfectly legitimate to speak of it and any individual in the past tense.

There is a story why the clothing of railway porters is usually, or unusually, ill-fitting. This legend which has a certain merit of antiquity avers that upon a day the railway staff is marshalled in a long line upon the platform, then through the station an express train rushes at great speed. The Company's tailor is in that train, and from a carriage window, as he hurtles past, he takes down the measurements of his victims. I am afraid, dear friend, that you accuse me of adopting a somewhat similar method to this in my reviews. You visualize me as one who looks stealthily and from a considerable distance at the covers of a book, and who disapproving of the binding, anathematises the contents. I plead not guilty on this count.

You say I should have reconstructed the mood out of which the poems were wrought. I do not consider it is the business of the critic to do this, but only to criticise the mood into which the poem is wrought. It is the finished performance by which the play is judged and not the rehearsals or the mood of the playwright before he began his scenario.

You say – "Surely you [meaning me] must know in your heart that the artists who have concerned themselves primarily, perhaps solely, with the idea of beauty can never, with any show of justice, be designated Decadent."

I do not designate such as Decadents, but as artists I quarrel with them. They are, as you state, only concerned with "the idea" of beauty. Of beauty itself, that flaming energetic reality, they have no knowledge, and can only approach it at all through a maze of intellectual or artistic conceivings, academic and starched imaginings which have been first clipped to scientific precision by pedants and then drilled remorselessly by madmen who are known in the dictionary as philosophers and reside, I have no doubt, in Dalkey.

You say these (the Decadent artists) "have wrought seriously to bring back from that overworld, which is their kingdom, some token of their travels there".

They never travelled in an overworld. They are under-people who do not travel at all. They live for ever in subterranean, tortuous ways, heavy with the fumes of incense and unwholesome with narcotics. They detest nectar, ambrosia is porridge to them. Their food is pills and powders, their recreation is powder-puffs and purgatives, their imaginations hachish. Their progress to art is through gluttony into satiety and the intolerable boredom of their existence is only made bearable by the exercise of a vicious and base craft which it is a sin to dignify by the honourable title of art. They are "arty" and obscene and incapable. They have not the common lay capability of grossness – their appetites are too attenuated for that. Grossness is no more than a simple and uncritical exuberance, and between it and Decadence there is the entire width of human evolution. From the childish absurdity of the one to the elaborate refinements of the other is a grave distance. The person who roysters on porter is a more estimable individual than he who gets drunk on liqueur. One can even conceive a certain respect for that primitive rascal who chased the Delight of his Soul into a corner and there lammed her with his cottonwood club into a submissive and loving pulp. But the other who sings the Canticles of Messalina – there is a pit there into which I dare not sink a shaft of language.

The Decadent, as I understand (or misunderstand) the term, is one who has departed from the broad human path of evolution to explore the secret and forbidden byeways of life – and who never comes back. That, I fancy, is his sin against humanity. He is a renegade to his kind, one who does not desert this place for that place, but who goes from Somewhere into Nowhere.

I do not know this type at all in Irish or English literature. It is common enough, I am informed, in French. My reading in that tongue has so far been confined to the very virtuous statements of the gardener's wife to the nephew of the postman, but I am willing to believe that Decadence is rampant in France, and with the over-cultivation of art, or of the Art-for-Art's-sake School it may become common in these countries also.

My dear Seumas, I do not make these trite remarks at you. I have disassociated one person already from this letter, I do hereby dissever you also from it. I would dissolve myself from it but that I do not know how. Unfortunate that I am! Behold me a Perpetual Disclaimer. It is only that having begun a letter to you, I have continued it to myself, in a poor attempt to satisfy from my own resources the queries which I had hoped someone else might have resolved for me. You might easily have done this for me, but with that tantalising waywardness which (pardon me if I again become critical) is so happy a feature of your art, you have belaboured my ignorance and yet refused me the charity which your wide reading and deep experience could so easily and graciously have nourished me with. I am still the proprietor of those abysmal ignorances and prejudices against which you have lifted up your voice and perhaps from one, who above all things yearns for wisdom and the consolations of knowledge, the plea for a little comfort from you will not still be unheeded. My ignorance is already a trifle less dense, and I do here willingly retract and take back and render null and void the word Decadence in my review of Mrs. Taylor's poems. The placing of it there was an aberration which I regret. My criticism in reality only found fault with a generosity of ornamentation which I considered excessive and making more for Art than Poetry. To that criticism I still cling and proclaim despairingly that if I am accused of anything else I deny it.

Believe me,
My Dear Seumas O'Sullivan,
Very sincerely yours,
JAMES STEPHENS.

To LORD DUNSANY

[A/3] Dublin
17 November 1910

[The Irish writer Edward John Moreton Drax Plunkett, 18th Baron Dunsany (1878–1957), sent Stephens a copy of *A Dreamer's Tales* (1910), which contains "The Hashish Man". The other Dunsany story is "The Bride of the Man-Horse", printed in *The Sketch* (London) for 1 February 1911 and included in *The Book of Wonder* (1912).

Stephens was currently living at 54 Lower Mount Street.]

Dear Lord Dunsany

Thanks for your book – It was very decent of you to send it. A few weeks ago Russell read me two stories from it. One about a hachish eater, & since then I have been on its track but had not caught up with it. I think it is (from what AE read) one of the finest books of recent years & that you really are a wonderful writer.

AE told me last night that you had written the most astonishing story he ever read. You will probably remember which he referred to – Could you let me know in what paper it will appear. I am saving up your book to read on Sunday & am very happy in the possession of it.

I am
JAMES STEPHENS

To LORD DUNSANY

[A/3] Dublin
[early December 1910]

[The "new story" was "The Bride of the Man-Horse". The stories mentioned from *A Dreamer's Tales* are "Poltarnees, Beholder of the Ocean", "Blagdaross" and "The Hashish Man". Although Dunsany published regularly in the *Saturday Review* (London) from March 1908, "Poltarnees" was first printed in the *Irish Homestead* for December 1908 (Christmas issue).

The book of poems, *The Hill of Vision*, was not published until 1912. By "repression" Stephens probably refers to the rejection of his poems by Macmillan (London) earlier in 1910. The novel, *The Charwoman's Daughter*, began to appear serially in the *Irish Review* in April 1911 (as "Mary: A Story") and was published in book form in 1912. Dunsany answered Stephens's final question by saying that he no longer wrote poetry.]

Dear Lord Dunsany

I delayed answering your letter in order that I might be able to write more fully on another matter.

If this new story is better than the hachish man it must be rather wonderful. I am very anxious to see it – You have certainly the most vividly out of the world imagination I have ever read. Its fertility seems boundless: in this book, at any rate, you give with both hands. Indeed I congratulate you most sincerely & enviously. Personally I have a theory for that kind of "getting away" rioting in spaces with queer people & making things after my own model instead of the hard & fast ones handed down to us. &, therefore, I am able to apprehend joyfully your queer stories. But I am quite unable to do it myself in prose. I have made many attempts in verse (some succeeded & some did'nt)[.]

The first story about the sea is great – I read it in I fancy the Sat. Rev. & there is another story (I am writing away from home) about what the piece of rope said & the lucifer match & the old Rocking Horse. The humour in this is delicious. I think many people will for a while miss the humour – the hachish man is packed with it, but it is so delicately introduced or injected, that it never interferes with the story – that huge Spirit who was the Soul of a star, striding tremendously away – its great! & that evil Spirit who delayed the Eater. I love those things – they give me a good feeling. I do believe you are one of the greatest living writers & are going to do amazing things. Even apart from the idea the mere writing is exquisite. That is it can be read again for its own sake independently of the story. I have been asked to write you on the subject of a magazine to be started in March next but I do not wish these two letters to be in conjunction, therefore I will delay a few days.

Yours sincerely
JAMES STEPHENS

I may have a book out early next year (poems) if the mss is accepted – it has already been repressed, to my great amazement, for the work is good. I have also finished a short novel with which I am very pleased. I am beginning to learn how to write prose. I wish I had your furious imagination. Have you written verse?

To LORD DUNSANY

Dublin

[T/3] 14 December 1910

[*The Irish Review: A Monthly Magazine of Irish Literature, Art, and Science* had four co-founders: Stephens; David Houston, a Lecturer in the Royal College of Science for Ireland and the author of *The Milk Supply of Dublin* (1918); Thomas MacDonagh (1878–1916), a prominent member of the Irish Volunteers and also a writer; and Padraic Colum (1881–1972), at the time perhaps best known as an Abbey playwright. Dunsany contributed both funds and literary work to the *Irish Review*.]

Dear Lord Dunsany

I enclose herewith Prospectus of a new Magazine to be issued in March of next year. This magazine will be conducted by Colum, Professor Houston, Thomas MacDonagh and myself and I have been charged to write you on the subject.

Last year you were thinking about partially financing a similar venture. Would you think favourably of transferring your interest to this venture? If so, the plans of the magazine would be submitted for your approval.

Independently of this we would be honoured if you could let us have some of your work for the first number. We will, as you observe from the Prospectus, print not only stories and sketches, but also short plays and articles. From the outset there will not be any possibility of paying the contributors: but the basis of the magazine will be co-operation – that is, such profits as accrue during the course of the year will be divided among the contributors according to the value and amount of their published work.

The magazine will not be allowed to get into the hands of any publishing or mercantile people. We will pay for the printing as it is done and will publish ourselves.

(Excuse me writing in typescript but I cannot find a pen).

Yours sincerely
JAMES STEPHENS

To LORD DUNSANY

[A/3]

Dublin
22 December 1910

[Dunsany sent Stephens a manuscript copy of his "The Bride of the Man-Horse" and asked about the financing of the *Irish Review.* When published in 1912, *The Book of Wonder* had as a subtitle "A Chronicle of Little Adventures at the Edge of the World". Theocritus (fl. *ca.* 270 B.C.) was a Greek pastoral poet.]

Dear Lord Dunsany

Thanks for lending me the story – I dont know whether it is the best you have done or not, but it certainly is unique – Its swiftness is amazing. It is as clean & swift & sharp as a spring morning – I hope when you are quite finished with the Edge of the World that you will have some adventures in the Morning of the World[.] You have the sharp tang of just before sunrise, the width & horizon of great spaces & the eager curiosity of those children who inhabited the Morning Land – The only example of that clear frankness which I know of in literature is Theocritus. I wish you could rewrite his odes[.] I will (if you permit) keep the mss for a few days as I wish to read it a few times again before returning[.]

These three words I think best criticise your work – Spontaneity – movement – zest – The zest is enormous. Do you know that your prose work – that is the basic feeling in it & my later verse are curiously alike – we are seeking the same thing, great windy reaches, & wild flights among stars & a very youthful laughter at the gods – We are both at that & in your proze you have undoubtedly fou[nd] it. The art behind your stories does not appear conscious, there is no chiselling or polishing or gravers work in it that I can see & yet the art is extreme – thats what I call Spontaneity[.] For my part I am hammering out with great labour a prose style. I was enamoured of the purplest patches & used to wave my arms & lips at once, also I used to make jokes that one could both hear & see from a great distance. I am only beginning to get out of these crudities & I really believe I have got a grip on something that is very like a style. You will see it in this new Review – I am giving the serial to it.

As to the Review – it will cost to publish roughly £10 per edition of 1000 copies (initial) & each subsequent edition will be about £3. £13, add £7 for all contingencies & the utmost limit of expenditure is £20. We are not going to run it with a view to profit, but we will try to make it a magazine that people will buy and read. May we place your name on the 3rd page of the Prospectus as a possible contributor – I will send you a list of the contributors in a few days. There will be little or no politics in the paper[.] I fought stubbornly against that – Indeed it will be a literary & artistic journal with very little occupations outside art. The advertisements will I expect be mostly publishers catalogues.

Yours sincerely
JAMES STEPHENS

To LORD DUNSANY

Dublin
[A/3] 1 January 1911

[The first issue of the *Irish Review* (March 1911) included the opening section of AE's "The Problem of Rural Ireland", Colum's "The Parrot and the Falcon", Stephens's "In the Poppy Field", and "A Flood" by George Moore (1852–1933). Nothing was included by the Revd. J. O. Hannay (1865–1950), who wrote novels under the pseudonym of "George A. Birmingham". W. B. Yeats (1865–1939) did not contribute until the December 1911 issue. David Houston was nominal editor of the *Irish Review* until March 1912, when he was replaced by Colum.]

Dear Lord Dunsany

We are about preparing the plans for the first two numbers of the Review – Among the contributors to the first number will be AE, Mr Geo. Moore, Mr Hannay, Colum, & myself (on the literary side) – We will try to get Mr Yeats for this number – We would be very pleased if your name might also be included as a contributor to the first number. I can quite understand that your pen may be exclusively employed & that the preparation of the series of which you wrote me will occupy your entire time, but if it is possible I would beg for a sketch, article or story from you for the start. The Editor has bidden me say that such monies as are advanced will be repaid with interest at 5%

I will return you mss. this week.

Sincerely yours
JAMES STEPHENS

To LORD DUNSANY

Dublin

[A/3] 7 January 1911

[Although the first issue of the *Irish Review* did not contain any plays by Dunsany, it did include a short story, "Alone the Immortals". The Theatre of Ireland was an amateur acting company formed by Maire Nic Shiubhlaigh and others after they left the Abbey; their first performance was in December 1906. Stephens acted in some of their plays, and *The Marriage of Julia Elizabeth* was produced by the Theatre of Ireland on 17 November 1911. Dunsany's new play was *King Argimēnēs and the Unknown Warrior*; his *The Glittering Gate* was produced by the Abbey on 29 April 1909 and at the Court Theatre in London on 6 June 1910.]

Dear Lord Dunsany

I delayed writing to you as I wanted to get full information from the Editor of funds &c to send you; but, outside of the days appointed for meeting, he is difficult to find. I have, however forwarded your cheque to him with a request to send you information & receipt &c.

I am sorry you will not be in the opening number. I have heard also of those mysterious rights accruing to strangers in the produce of one's own private head by printing without doing certain other things[.] The law regarding writers & dramatists certainly makes me veer towards those champions of the morality that slays policemen – Your rights, however, can easily be preserved either by your having them read by the Abbey people with whom you are in touch, or I could have them read by the Theatre of Ireland folk with whom I have not as yet come into conflict. I shall look with great interest to the performance of your new play – the Glittering Gate dazed most people who saw it – the "intellectuals" by the saying of the things they dared not say – the others whose souls sequeated [for "secreted"?] blasphemy – It is a brave play & its very bravery carried it safe – Bravery always does go safely – I hate those people who have a morality with a label attached. Morality must be incognito. It is'nt anything; or its the base of a nature not of a religion. I only know of one morality – & that is Energy. I call every *thing* or *thought* that acquiesces or sits down Vice & I call every thing that disobeys, & refuses, & breaks, "Virtue" & again I call

Force Virtue & Energy Vice & the latter seems to me the better of the two. The Glittering Gate is the only manifestation of Energy – that is an outbreaking power – that has ever appeared in this country or in England & I'll bet there will be periods marking from it. I take it that the job of a man who is, like you, an Artist & a Creator is to break everything within reach of his hands or feet & now & then make a cockslut of his own ideals – A city would travel as long a distance on Blasphemy & Laughter as on Prayer & Fasting & be much better to live in. Pray forgive me; but a sheet of paper dares me to fill it up

Yours sincerely
JAMES STEPHENS

I am giving poems as well as verse [for "prose"] to the Review –

To LORD DUNSANY

Dublin
[A/3] [*ca.* 27 January 1911]

[John Millington Synge (1871–1909) had been the most important – if not the most popular – playwright of the Abbey Theatre. Dunsany's *King Argimēnēs and the Unknown Warrior* was produced at the Abbey on 26 January 1911. Arthur Sinclair (1883–1951), who played the role of King Darniak, worked at the Abbey from 1904 to 1916 and was best known as a comedian.]

Dear Lord Dunsany

I have your letter – I fancy I have also to thank you for a pass to the Abbey – If anyone can take Synge's place in drama it will be yourself – not on account of this present play but the very great promise that it shows – There is real drama stuff in you & a richness & vivid life such as no other writer I know has – The first act was very fine indeed the setting good & the movement swift, but you must pardon me for saying that the 2nd act will not do at all – There is nothing happening in it. It seems to me more like a shorthand note of what had happened, than a dramatic detailing of the events – The stage is left empty too long & this is always a very risky experiment – The continuity of your story is destroyed & the audience is given time to become more self conscious than is good for them. Of course, against this there is the difficulty of having anything big happen on so small a stage as the Abbey. The first Act enthralled me & the mere phrasing of the 2nd was delightful – I am writing a first night impression & may be all wrong. The actors were not as serious as they might have been – King Darniac with battles behind him & victories in his fist was not the sleepy buffoon that Sinclair presented – The humour of your conception is excellent but should have been differently acted. Sinclair, however, can only do low comedy & subtelties are altogether outside his abilities – The general idea about the play, that I can gather, is that people are very anxious to see your next. I know I am – I have noticed that all great writers are companioned by an imp – Small writers are very perfect; but the big writer is provided with a little devil that pokes its jowl around most important corners & wants to wink at an audience & "give the show away"

I trust I have not trespassed but I was very interested –

Yours sincerely
JAMES STEPHENS

To LORD DUNSANY

Dublin
[A/3] 1 February 1911

[Fred Morrow was the Stage Manager of the Theatre of Ireland. The "new tragedy" was *The Laughter of the Gods*, included in *Plays of Gods and Men* (1917) and produced at the Punch and Judy Theater in New York on 15 January 1919. Since Stephens was corresponding with him at this time, Brown is probably Thomas Brown Rudmose-Brown (1878–1942), Professor of French at University College, Dublin. Dunsany had published a story weekly in *The Sketch* since 21 December 1910. *King Argimēnēs and the Unknown Warrior* was published in the *Irish Review* in September 1911.]

Dear Lord Dunsany

Thanks for your letter – I think the changes you have made will make the play all right. Morrow, the manager of the Theatre of Ireland, liked your play very much & did not entirely agree with my views. He is a very competent stageman so maybe I was wrong. I have been told that it went finely on Saturday night. The general opinion is that it was more than good. I hope this new tragedy will be a success – You wrote two acts in between your letter to me! Your head must be buzzing with ideas. I am sorry I cannot go for the weekend – I am managing the new Review & up to my eyes in ink & advertisements & prospectus. Houston came to me mad with amazement & delight to say you had sent him a further £50 – Brown has sent me half a dozen copies of the sketch with your stories which I am just about to read –

Yours sincerely
JAMES STEPHENS

I hope you will let us print King Argimenes[.] It should read splendidly – From memory the phrasing of the first act seemed peculiarly good

JS

To STEPHEN MacKENNA

Dublin
[A/19] 1 March 1911 [& August 1930]

[MacKenna had been employed since November 1908 as a regular writer for the *Freeman's Journal*, the leading Irish Nationalist newspaper. The Gaelic selection in the first issue of the *Irish Review* was a bilingual edition of "The Keening of Mary" by Padraic Henry Pearse (1879–1916), a writer and later one of the leaders of the Easter Rebellion; these selections continued on and off for the life of the journal. "John Eglinton" was the pen name of the Irish critic William Kirkpatrick Magee (1868–1961); his article, "Irish Books", was a rather negative sketch of Anglo-Irish literature from the novelist William Carleton (1794–1869) to Eglinton's contemporaries. *Bairbre Ruadh* ("Redhaired Barbara") was a one-act Gaelic play by the Galway writer Padraic O Conaire (1881–1928); it was first performed at the Oireachtas on 6 August 1908, where it won first prize. The production which Stephens refers to was given by the Five Provinces' Branch of the Gaelic League on 25 March 1911. "Seagdan" is probably an error for *Seaghan*, a variant of *Seán*: the reference may be to *Seàn* MacCiolte, an actor in the Theatre of Ireland who used *Seàn* Óg as his stage name. MacKenna did not contribute to the *Irish Review*.

In 1930 (dated "August" in one instance) Stephens wrote a

commentary on many of his letters to MacKenna; in each instance these remarks are presented directly after the relevant letter. The "Beau" was Thomas ("Buck" or "Jerusalem") Whaley (1766–1800), a well-known rake; in 1788–9 he fulfilled a wager to play handball against the walls of Jerusalem. Thomas Henry Huxley (1825–95) was a strong supporter of the evolutionary theories of Charles Robert Darwin (1809–82); John Tyndall (1820–93) was influential in the popularization of science. "Tennessee" refers to the trial of John T. Scopes in July 1925 in Dayton, Tennessee, for teaching Darwin's theories.]

Dear Stephen

Thanks for your letter – There has been a mistake – The Review was not intended to be sold or even exposed for sale until *this present day* but those damned book-sellers must try to steal marches on each other – They have thrown our arrangements out of gear. Yesterday a copy of the Review was sent to the Freeman, timed to arrive there on day of issue, today. I am sending another copy to the Editor now

I am glad you liked the Gaelic selection – I am told there are good things to follow – I havent read one page of the Review yet, but I know Eglinton's methods well [–] his work is often amazingly cold – All these men are anglicized – the wonder is that a literary gent of any ability or much reading can escape it – We've all been nourished on it & our traditions, models, precidents & so forth are most difficult to escape from. To break away even in thought is a very difficult thing, our literary pedigree will persist until we get new parents

I am going to act in a Gaelic play shortly (Barbara Ruadh) by Conaire – I think it is a very good way of getting quick Gaelic. Seagdan Óg also comes to lecture me & I have great hopes now of climbing to the austere heights from which one may declaim Gaelic verse & know what its about. I have been wishing I could get out to you, but it is impossible for a while –

Have you thought at all about an article or story or anything for the Review?

le meas mór
Is mise
["with great esteem, I am"]
JAMES STEPHENS

[The following are Stephens's 1930 comments:]

The "Review" mentioned here is "The Irish Review"[.] It was founded after a conversation between Padraic Colum, Tommy McDonagh, Professor Houston, and myself. Houston lived then out of town, beyond Rathfarnham in a house on the slope of the Dublin Hills. He told with some glee that his house had, in the days of yore, belonged to a famous Beau. Beau Nash, I think it was. This Beau had once in one of the Coffee Houses uttered an idle desire to play hand-ball against the walls of Jerusalem and, on one of his companions as idly defying him to do it, he promptly set out for Jerusalem, played his game of hand-ball against the walls, or a wall, and gat him home again. Dr Houston was elder by perhaps twenty years to the rest of us. He had been the favourite pupil of Huxley, when Huxley was the most famous of scientists, and he had many tales to tell of the great teacher and his circle. Time flies! Huxley & much of his science, and all of his polemics are now matters of a lost past. He and Tyndall and Darwin, and the hubbub they made, (a hubbub indeed they did make) are, perhaps, yet angrily known in the back-hills of Tennessee: are among the curiosities of science and literature, and are valid, and are wondered at, no more – in so short a time! Indeed, and today, Time works "overtime": taking upon herself what a load of matters to remember for the day, and how vast an accumulation of matters to forget within the year. It may be that the same excess of satisfactions which jades the human being will at last sate even Time, and she will cease from all her rememberings, and become a forgetter, a something that does not tell her hours any more, and needs not any more to be counted. Indeed, if we forget Time, and if she forgets herself, where is she[?] And here now am I remembering these things and those and wondering from what cause and to what effect are all these experiencings and rememberings, and whether they are as the Buddhists conceive, not nonsense, but illusion, and of value only as they serve the illusion that invented them. I have known no man who seemed to me to be wise; many who were learned, & more who, without learning, were witty: and occasionally some few who were what we may call good: in whom, that is, there was force, without harm, and without selfishness. David Houston was one of these. In all the "good" people that I have known there has always been present a tenacious memory, wedded to a slow, tenacious mind: and I have often wondered if the quality goodness is inevitably connected with a certain slowness of mental pace[.] Whether this pondering, or cautious pace is responsable for the reluctance with which young people accompany those who are "good"[.] The desire of all young people is to display an athletic ability in both body and mind. The function of goodness is to control these and make them subserve a use. But every young artist, at least, and possibly every young man is ardently in love with pure uselessness: seeing it as pure speed, and, possibly, as absolute value. We can, and must, be bored by the mind that moves too slowly. We can also be bored by the mind that moves too deeply: and we can be, as dreadfully, fatigued by the companion-mind that is quicker than ours.

To LORD DUNSANY

Dublin
[A/3] 9 November 1911

["Mary Makebelieve" is the main character of *The Charwoman's Daughter*, currently being published serially in the *Irish Review* as "Mary: A Story"; Dunsany had written to Stephens about a "sly and damnable woman" who had "called her book 'Molly Makebelieve' ". In fact, though, Eleanor Hallowell Abbott's *Molly Make-Believe* had been published in New York in 1910. It appears that Stephens was planning to call his novel either *Mary* or *Mary Makebelieve* until he learned of Abbott's work. He thus experimented with various titles – *The Charwoman's House* (15 November 1911) and *Mary: Dublin: A Story* (26 December 1911) – before deciding on *The Charwoman's Daughter* on 3 January 1912. The American edition, published not by Macmillan but by Small, Maynard & Company in Boston, was entitled *Mary, Mary*. The book of verse was *The Hill of Vision* (1912).

Dunsany's *The Gods of the Mountain* was produced at the Haymarket Theatre in London on 1 June 1911.]

Dear Dunsany

Thanks for your letter & invitation.

I am a very shy person &, moreover, so unused to visiting that I would be ill at ease – Therefore, I beg you will pardon me. I have seen the "Molly Makebelieve" advertisement you speak of and I'm rather up a tree about it. Macmillan of London & America are going to publish the book & I am getting a book of verse out in

February – There is one poem in it you will like – You are right about the English writers. If there *are* five worth a rap I'll be surprised. There is only one writer I am really afraid of & that is yourself. I do believe that you & I are the only writers doing real stuff, the artist seems to have died out of English prose & the Jerry builders reign in his stead. Poetry is in the same condition – pretentious flummery. The drama is a bit better. There at least you have some more or less worthy people to butt up against, but to have to write without decent competitors is disheartening. Have you noticed that the whole notion of "beauty" has vanished from these people, dramatists and all; thats where we come in. I reread King Argimenes in the Irish Review – Its even better than I thought before, but I did not see or hear anything of the English play you produced – were you pleased with it? I have lent your book to a good many people – they shout your praises.

Sincerely yours
JAMES STEPHENS

To MACMILLAN & COMPANY, LONDON

Dublin
[A/23] 28 February 1912

[Macmillan met this request in future editions of Stephens's work. Stephens was now living at 91 Merrion Square.]

Dear Sirs,

I have received six copies of my book "The Charwoman's Daughter" for which I am much obliged.

In the event of your printing further copies of this book I beg you will insert a blank page at the end between the last page of the story & the beginning of your advertisements. The last sentences were calculated to produce an effect of finality which is interfered with by the carrying over of the readers eye to further printed matter – I trust you will oblige me in this without inconvenience –

Yours truly
JAMES STEPHENS

To JAMES B. PINKER

Dublin

[T/15] [16 April 1912]

[The literary agent James B. Pinker (1863–1922) offered his services to Stephens on 29 March 1912. Stephens terminated their agreement late in December 1913 because of the unauthorized publication of a Tauchnitz Edition of *Here Are Ladies* (1913). From 1918 until his death, Pinker handled some of Stephens's serial rights.]

Dear Sir,

Thanks for your letter.

I have been thinking over this matter and I do not see that we could be of any particular use to each other. My output is very small and my "occasional" work almost nil. In the matter of novels Messrs Macmillan will, I think, accept whatever I offer them and Messrs Maunsel are glad to have my poems. As to occasional work, short stories, articles etc. – I made up my mind long ago that I would do none of this unless I was specially commissioned to do it. I return your agreement with many thanks.

Yours faithfully,
JAMES STEPHENS

To [JAMES B. PINKER]

Dublin

[T/15] [23–25 April 1912]

[The new novel was *The Crock of Gold* (1912). At this time the American rights were held by the Small, Maynard Company of Boston.]

Dear Sir

I return herewith your draft Agreement amended. I wish to reserve from your 1st Clause any direct *commissions* made with me by editors or publishers and all work that I do for the Irish Review (I get no money for this latter work, but I and three other writers have agreed to give work when called on until the Irish Review is in a position to pay its contributors).

I shall send you on signing the agreement a bundle of poems which you may care to start with – I am better known as a writer of verse than prose.

I have almost completed the mss of a new novel, this will certainly be completed within a few months. The American book right for this story is already arranged for, but the English, serial, and all other rights are still my property. I think the American serial rights are also my property. My agreement is to give my American publishers the first opportunity of considering my next novel.

You will see from this that my programme is a very meagre one. You, however, may be able to advise me as to work

Yours faithfully
JAMES STEPHENS

To HAROLD MONRO

Dublin
[T/36] 25 April 1912

[The poet Harold Monro (1879–1932) founded the *Poetry Review* and edited its monthly issues from January to December 1912. Stephens was the featured poet in the June 1912 issue; of the poems mentioned here, only "Pessimist" was included in the selection. The poet and novelist Richard Aldington (1892–1962) contributed a balanced but generally favourable prefatory note. The "Daisy poem" is "With the Daisies", published in *Harper's Monthly Magazine* for July 1913.]

Dear Sir,

I have your letter – Your remarks therein are very just. I think the best thing you can do is to return me the verses you dont like and I will send others. The "Three Waves" is a rotten poem. "Pessimists" is, of course, nothing more than an exercise in metrics. In the Daisy poem, I think the word which is typed as "bitd" ought to be "bi*r*d" – I am writing away from my drafts – Is the line not "Chased a bird into the sky?" The last verse of this poem gives me a pain but it wouldn't come any different: it is not a bad poem. In "Cycle" the word which you query should be written *warm* instead of warm*s*. Anyhow, post them back to me and I'll try to give you something better. I have no long poems unprinted. A guinea is a terribly solitary, unentheusiastic kind of a coin. I would prefer, if you must have a foreword, that it should be written by a stranger.

Yours faithfully,
JAMES STEPHENS

Would you post me the magazine?

To [HAROLD MONRO]

Dublin
[T/36] 27 April 1912

[The *Hill of Vision* had been published earlier in 1912.]

Dear Sir,

I have your letter and enclosures. I really feel I ought to apologise for the stuff I sent you; but you will remember that The Hill of Vision has almost cleared me out of verse which I could send you with an easy conscience. However, I have a few other verses which I enclose for your approvel. I must compliment you on an ability to touch the weak spot in a poem such as I have seldom met with. I was not complaining about the guinea I was only mourning, for I do sometimes get three guineas for one of these things. However!

Yours faithfully,
JAMES STEPHENS

I enclose six more poems. I beg you will let me know if you like or dislike these –

To [HAROLD MONRO]

Dublin
[T/36] 5 May 1912

[The first part of this letter deals with "The Last Judgment", which had been printed in *The Lonely God and Other Poems* (1909) under the title "In The High Court of Justice". The revisions made for the *Poetry Review* publication were as follows: "Chanting in fury to a holy song/Their flighty wrath" became "Chanting in fury to a flighty song/Their holy wrath"; "These vagabonds who always had been dead/E'en when alive, and massed into the space" became "(These vagabonds who always had been dead)/And packed their multitudes into the space"; and "Here they kept silence, every face intent/With a dumb grin upon the sun was bent" became "There they were silent, every awful stare,/With a dumb grin, was lifting anywhere."

"From the Golden Book", also included in the June 1912 *Poetry Review*, consists of six quatrains followed by a sestet.]

Dear Sir,

I return the two poems – I have made all the alterations you suggested. The word "flighty" is to be read in the train of "madness". I have got quit of the phrase "Even when alive" and thank you for pointing it out. In the last verse of this poem I have removed the two lines with "intent, sun and bent" and think that the new lines will meet that vacancy which you mentioned. I usually work at great heat and then rather shirk the labour of chizelling my statue. I have changed the title High Court of Justice with its humourous or grotesque implication to "The Last Judgment"[.] It is in the tradition of artists to do this subject. If, however, you do not approve please change it. The golden book poems are better as you have arranged them. The last two quatrains, as a matter of fact, were a complete poem which I had entitled "The Pendulum" – They move nicely. Will you let me see proofs?

Yours sincerely,
JAMES STEPHENS

To THE EDITOR OF *THE NEW AGE*

Dublin
9 May 1912

[The text is from *The New Age* for 9 May 1912. The letter is Stephens's response to a review of the 1912 edition of W. B. Yeats's *The Land of Heart's Desire* published in *The New Age* for 2 May 1912. The unsigned review was the work of either A. R. Orage (1873–1934), the editor of *The New Age*, or more likely, Emily Alice Haigh Thomson (1879–?), a writer and reviewer for the periodical who used the pseudonym "Beatrice Hastings".

The quotations which Stephens repeats are from Addison's *Cato*, V. i. 15–17; Dryden's *All For Love*, IV. i. 43–5; Keats's "Hyperion", I. 1–4; Milton's *Paradise Lost*, IV. 269–73; and Shakespeare's *The Tempest*, IV. i. 156–8, and *A Midsummer Night's Dream*, II. i. 146–54. The "joke which someone once made about Mr. Yeats" ran as follows: "Misled by Mr. Carpenter's apparent sympathy, Mr. Yeats was letting himself go on the subject of a Fairy Prince he had recently met in one of the seven woods of Ireland. When he had concluded, Carpenter laconically remarked: 'Well, let's hope it is not quite true'. "]

PRESENT-DAY CRITICISM.

Sir,–

Both the opening and the closing sentences of your article on "The Land of Heart's Desire" are more illuminating of your critical attitude that you may, perhaps, be prepared to admire. The opening of what purports to be a considered, literary criticism of a great poet is presented with a smirk as when a music-hall comedian announces his next eccentricity. Permit me to quote: "A short review, by request, of that affecting tragedy, 'The Land of Heart's Desire', by Mr. William Butler Yeats."

This is quite sufficiently funny to be laughed at by easy-tempered people and to be blushed for by yourself. Your closing sentences question your right to the title of critic while leaving intact that of humorist. I will also quote them:–

"A voice outside sings a song ending with words sufficiently puzzling:

> 'When the wind had laughed and murmured and sung,
> The lonely of heart is withered away.'

But it sounds pleasant and catchy."

You can scarcely have quoted these two lines without having read the lines immediately preceding them, and which constitute one of the most perfectly melodious and moving poems in the English language. Your remark, which is your criticism, that "it sounds pleasant and catchy", is a terrible comment on your own critical standard.

I do not write this in order to reason with you, but in order to protect your readers, who may fancy that the loud voice must proceed from an oracle. I might ask you are not the poets of these countries already sufficiently neglected without the critics, by justifying this neglect, creating a further artificial barrier between them and their meagre audience. I accuse you of making no reasonable effort to critically examine Mr. Yeats's poem. The critic has not only a duty towards his reader; equally imperative is his duty towards his author. The first of these, in mere justice to himself, he will perform; the second, as an artist and a gentleman, he will not neglect. In your article on Mr. Yeats you have outraged both of these decencies, and this is the more lamentable when coming from a writer of so evident vitality and ability as yourself. What wrong has

Mr. Yeats' poems done to you that you should attack him with this gratuitous effrontery? Mr. Yeats, equally with other poets, may be destructively criticised, but not by this method. Why have you chosen from his poem sentences which, when rudely snatched from their comrades, must appear weak? Why, when dealing with a fairy tale, do you submit nothing of that atmosphere which is its life and its justification? Furthermore, your method of criticism is utterly bad. It is nothing more than a machine-made, labour-saving device, unworthy of any artist and certainly unworthy of your own powers – it is to take the worst sentences of the writer under review and to contrast these with the best sentences of a dead genius. The dissertation on such a difference is not a criticism but a piece of shoddy writing unworthy of a good writer or a great paper. In this bad article you quote against Mr. Yeats some lines from five different poets, and having on these parallels condemned Mr. Yeats of uncouthness and bathos, you acclaim your own examples as "the style of Art that exalts the simple to its essential grandeur". I will take the liberty of requoting your quotations:

"Addison:

" 'If there's a Power above
(And that there is all nature cries aloud
Through all her works), he must delight in virtue.'
(Cato.)

"Dryden–

" 'Men are but children of a larger growth;
Our appetites are apt to change as theirs,
And full as craving too and full as vain;'
–'All for Love.'

"Keats–

" 'Deep in the shady sadness of a vale,
Far sunken from the healthy breath of morn,
Far from the fiery noon and eve's one star,
Sat grey-haired Saturn, quiet as a stone.'

"Milton–

" 'That fair field
Of Enna, where Proserpine, gathering flow'rs,
Herself a fairer flower by gloomy Dis
Was gathered, which cost Ceres all that pain
To seek her through the world.'

"Shakespeare–

" 'We are such stuff
As dreams are made on, and our little life
Is rounded with a sleep.' "

The three lines from Addison (I humbly crave pardon of the mighty dead) are, when presented in this dismemberment, sheer, unredeemed bathos. The three lines from Dryden seem as turgid, as flat lines as ever came by misadventure from the jaded brain of a poet, and Milton's five lines are better passed by with the reflection that if he had lost them he would never have remembered their existence.

Against a quotation from Mr. Yeats you further array one of Oberon's speeches, stating that it "has something of the matter and mood we want" – that is, the fairy matter and fairy mood. I am sorry to again quote:

" 'Well, go thy way: thou shalt not from this grove
Till I torment thee for this injury.
My gentle Puck, come hither: thou remember'st
Since once I sat upon a promontory,
And heard a mermaid on a dolphin's back
Uttering such dulcet and harmonious breath,
That the rude sea grew civil at her song,
And certain stars shot madly from their spheres
To hear the sea-maid's music.' "

And you follow this with a joke which someone once made about Mr. Yeats. Do you consider the above quotation is fairy talk? I think it is a grating, material voice striving, without even the shadow of success, to subdue its harsh worldliness to the dulcet, harmonious breath of fairyland.

There are, indeed, in this age many writers who are bad, treacherous artists, unfitted for anything but reprobation: but the number of those precious writers who may be praised is too small to be further curtailed by you, and of these Mr. Yeats is one. I write this letter, not to champion Mr. Yeats, who has an able champion in himself, but because certain inconsiderable persons have written to THE NEW AGE to publicly thank you for your transgressions. I would suggest that you should honourably apologise to Mr. Yeats and to the readers of THE NEW AGE, and so regain the approbation not of those uncouth barbarians, but of your own people, your brothers in literature.

JAMES STEPHENS.

To JAMES B. PINKER

[T/15]

Dublin
13 June 1912

[Pinker wrote on 12 June to inquire about the length of *The Crock of Gold:* it would have to be longer than *The Charwoman's Daughter* to be published at 6s. No section of *The Crock of Gold* appeared in the *English Review.*]

Dear Sir,

"The Crock of Gold" will be longer than "The Charwoman's Daughter"[.] I think it will be long enough to sell at 6/-

I am just now writing the last chapter of the book. There is one portion of it which makes a complete story in itself. I had intended typing this out and sending it to the English Review – Shall I send this to you to deal with or shall I forward it to the Review myself?

What would you estimate the length of the part of the story which you have in mss to be?

Very truly yours,
JAMES STEPHENS

You have not returned my American agreement – I think that this agreement is final & that you cannot do anything further with it – Is this not so?

JS

To JAMES B. PINKER

[T/15]

Dublin
19 June 1912

[On 18 June, Pinker told Stephens that Macmillan's offer for *The Crock of Gold* was a 20% royalty on the first 5,000 copies and 25% thereafter if the novel came to 60,000 words; otherwise, their terms were 15% on a price of 3s. 6d. The "Christmas book of verse", later entitled *The Calendar*, was never published; there is a typescript of it in the Berg Collection.]

Dear Sir,

I am very glad you have been able to give the book to Messrs Macmillan.

I quite approve of the terms you quote and have to thank you for the trouble you have taken. The book will certainly come to 60,000 words. I will be able to place the entire mss in your hands about the middle of July, possibly earlier. I would be glad to complete the agreement as early as you can manage it as I wish to draw on some of the advance royalties at once.

Yours very truly,
JAMES STEPHENS

Would you care to negotiate a little Christmas book of verse? Macmillan might take it – both here & in America, but these transactions should be separate ones –

To JAMES B. PINKER

Dublin
[T/15] 21 June 1912

Dear Sir,

Thanks for your letter.

I will send the spare copy of the Crock of Gold for America when forwarding the complete mss. I have just estimated the material I have written and find it is about 55,000 words so there will be no difficulty in bringing it up to, or beyond, the 60,000 required by Messrs Macmillan.

I shall send you the Christmas book of Verse (in duplicate) tomorrow when I get it typed. If you have any difficulty in getting a publisher for it Messrs Maunsel & Co, Dublin, will, I am quite sure, be ready to take it up.

Yours very truly,
JAMES STEPHENS

To JAMES B. PINKER

Dublin
[T/15] 23 June 1912

Dear Mr Pinker,

Herewith I enclose the little Christmas Book of Verse – The title "The Calendar" is only a provisional one. I find it very difficult to name this collection – most of the good titles seem to have been used.

Yours very truly,
JAMES STEPHENS

To HAROLD MONRO

Dublin
[A/32] [June–July 1912]

[Along with payment for his poems in the June 1912 *Poetry Review*, Monro sent Stephens copies of his *Before Dawn* (*Poems and Impressions*) (1911) and the 1912 reissue of *Judas* (1907). The passage from *Judas* is correct except for punctuation and the substitution of "&" for "and". "Scrannel pipes of wretched straw" is a quotation from Milton's "Lycidas" (l. 124). Lascelles Abercrombie (1881–1938) was an English poet and critic. "A Prelude and a Song" and "The Breath of Life" were included in *The Hill of Vision.*

Monro had evidently asked Stephens to find Dublin booksellers to distribute the *Poetry Review.* Ponsonby & Gibbs closed down soon after the First World War; Combridge and Hodges & Figgis are still in business.]

Dear Mr Monro

Thanks for your letter & for the cheque[.] That extra guinea was tremendously good of you and it came just at the moment when I wanted it badly – The Poetry Reviews arrived and this morning your two books – I notice that "Judas" was written nearly four years ago – On page 15 from the line ending "He it was" down to "enterprise" is very good verse – I have read the poem through with great interest, but I dont think it has "come off" – Blank verse is the devil. I am utterly unable to write it: you could see the blanks everywhere in my blank verse – The last eight lines on page 7 are excellent – the real thing; & on page 21

I dropped back
Like a spent swimmer whom a silent wave
Sweeps over, stifles suddenly & drowns

Thats the big stuff

Its a huge, eerie conception – I think you are going to do great things because you can think large – I know your craft must be all right from the way you spotted my misfortunes & I should have known from that, that you were a poet yourself – From Judas, which (pardon me) is poetry in the bud, I prophesy resplendencies in the blossom – I hate those lean nigglers with ten pounds worth of technique & a ha'porth of thought parading their scrannel pipes of wretched straw – I conceive that a poet should have as much brains as a philosopher & more guts than a pirate – then the breath of God (which is Imagination) will have something to blow into – All the verse I have read lately has been infected by tuberculosis, but I am told there's a man named Abercrombie who is real – The Lord send that he is so that we may all fight one another & be happy. I notice what you say about my Prelude & Song – I nail my banners to that poem & wont mind anyone – By the way the best poem in my book is, I think, The Breath of Life–

Many thanks
JAMES STEPHENS

I hope to write you about Combridge & Hodges & Figgis & Ponsonby tomorrow – My working hours synchronise with theirs so that Saturday is the only day I can really get at them [–] Ireland is a hard place to push poetry into –

To HAROLD MONRO

Rathmines, Co. Dublin

[A/10] 8 July 1912

[Monro's *Before Dawn* (*Poems and Impressions*) had received generally hostile reviews. Angus Óg ("Angus the Young"), who appears in *The Crock of Gold*, is the Celtic god of love and beauty, renowned for his magical powers. The Third Home Rule Bill was currently being debated in the British House of Commons. AE did not contribute any poems to the *Poetry Review*. The featured poet in the July 1912 *Poetry Review* was Emilia Stuart Lorimer. Lorimer's "The Wake" and "The Kelpie to the Drowned Baby" had been published in the *English Review* for January 1912.

The "Present-Day Criticism" column of *The New Age* for 20 June 1912 had been devoted to a rather strong attack on Stephens's poetry. The anonymous writer, either A.R. Orage or, more likely, "Beatrice Hastings", quoted extensively from Richard Aldington's prefatory note to Stephens's poems in the June 1912 *Poetry Review* and from a review of *The Hill of Vision* by the English critic John Middleton Murry (1889–1957) in the June 1912 *Rhythm.* Indeed, Murry's review began: "James Stephens is the greatest poet of our day."

Stephens had moved in late June from 91 Merrion Square, Dublin, to 20 Killeen Road, Rathmines, County Dublin. Rathmines was a suburb just to the south of Dublin.]

Dear Monro

Dont pay any attention to the expert critics – You can only have one critic & that is yourself & I expect you will be harsh enough – Your stuff is good & the few people (for they are very few) who like poetry will find you out – As to your "not having assimilated your material" – we all know the boys who say that sort of thing, the decent chaps – You have craft & ideas & you are not afraid to tackle a big job – The whole outfit is in that, provided the muse comes – Do you believe in the Muse[?] I do, sincerely. No poet can write unless he has been visited – Most of the stuff coming out daily or weekly has not been whispered by the goddess, so it is bad – Take a deity to yourself & worship him or her – My God is Angus Óg & he has treated me very well recently (not in verse) in prose that continually came very close to verse – Do you know that we are in the latter stages of the second Dark Ages – The artists & poets are hugely important folk just now, so keep at it – I would like to see any verse you care to send me – We have all suddenly gone barren over here in verse, not a poem in the world – Maybe, its Home Rule [–] There is an uncertainty in the atmosphere so that only prose is coming. I have just finished a novel to be published in October by Macmillan – I think you will like it – I was speaking to Russel, AE last night, he has just returned from vacation with 30 new pictures – You have not written to him yet about verse? – That woman poet in your present issue is good, very good. I saw two things of hers some months back in the English Review & I've been looking for more ever since –

Sincerely yours
JAMES STEPHENS

Who is the New Age man – He seems to be out after the lot of us – Murry of Rhythm gave him the handle of a big stick to beat me with; but Lord it doesnt matter a bit – What poem in "Before Dawn" do you like best?

Please note address –

To JAMES B. PINKER

Rathmines, Co. Dublin

[A/15] 13 July 1912

Dear Mr Pinker

Herewith is the completion of Messrs Macmillan's mss & a full copy for America –

You will see I have changed the title from – "*The Crock of Gold*" to – "*The Thin Woman's Husband*"[.] This is more in keeping with the fantastic character of the book –

Please acknowledge receipt & oblige.

Very truly yours
JAMES STEPHENS

To JAMES B. PINKER

Rathmines, Co. Dublin

[T/15] 18 July 1912

Dear Mr Pinker,

I am correcting the proofs of my book. As there are some changes being made in the mss I will send you a full set of the corrected proofs which you can forward to America – it will, I think, be better the publishers should work from these proofs than from the ms you have. I hope to be able to send you these shortly as the proofs are coming in very fast.

Yours faithfully,
JAMES STEPHENS

P.S. As to the little Christmas book of verse – it may be better not to do anything with this book until next year when I may replace it by a larger book – Have you done anything with them?

To JAMES B. PINKER

Rathmines, Co. Dublin
[A/15] 20 July 1912

Dear Mr Pinker

I have received your two letters –

I note your remarks as to the book of verse –

Messrs Macmillan also wrote me about the change of title – and I replied that "The Crock of Gold" might be used instead of "the thin W' Husband": so this matter is all right –

Very truly yours
JAMES STEPHENS

To JAMES B. PINKER

Rathmines, Co. Dublin
[T/15] 13 August 1912

[Macmillan agreed to this request.]

Dear Mr Pinker,

The page proofs of The Crock of Gold are nearing completion. The first time you are with Messrs Macmillan would you ask them not to put the salmon pink kind of cover on this book which they put on the Charwoman's Daughter. You will greatly oblige me by doing this as the cover is a very hideous one.

Sincerely yours.
JAMES STEPHENS

To JOHN DRINKWATER

Rathmines, Co. Dublin
[A/42] 20 September 1912

[In the September 1912 *Poetry Review*, Stephens had published a review of *Poems of Love and Earth* (1912) by the English writer John Drinkwater (1882–1937). Stephens stated that Drinkwater "has no centre from which he can sing with that calm assurance which is the voice of poetry, and so the whole mood of the poet is perplexed and the instability of inspiration which must follow such decentralization is over the entire book. Thus, a great part of the verse in this book must be judged, not as imaginative poetry, but as fanciful verse, often beautifully done."]

Dear Mr Drinkwater

It is very decent of you to write so kindly. I will take it that your honesty is equal to your forbearance and will, therefore, reply as honestly as I can, conceiving that you do not wish me to retract but to justify my opinions. (Good Lord! there's a prelude!) Monro of the Poetry Review sent me your book with an expression of his belief in its goodness and asked me to do a signed article. When I had read a couple of poems I knew that you were "all right", but it seemed to me that I had fallen upon a book in which your real powers were not being exhibited. That you have many and high powers is easily apparent, powers both of matter & of craft, but it seemed to me that in this book your fancy was being exercised at the expense of your imagination. The poets you mention have all written a mass of stuff which it would have been much better for them & for us had remained unwritten – Wordsworth, indeed, has sinned viciously against poetry. Shelly has left (beside gorgeous poetry) a mass of tenuous rubbish. Milton has left us plenty of supberb rhetoric, and the collected poems of all these men are cumbered with this uninspired stodge to such a degree that reading them is almost impossible saving in "Selections"

Poetry is a visitation, not a habit, and a poet ought not to seek to chain the Muse to his side[.] This is what is done when fanciful verse is written. The Muse should capture the poet not the poet capture the Muse. This last is too often done. Where writers measure their success not by their performance but by their output. They think they should live up to their reputation & that being a poet involves the production of tangible evidence at stated periods. Their are not many men capable of doing your work. It is a degradation to yourself to stoop to their work & in this book of yours I consider that you have so stooped. So do I, so do all of us, but you & I both cherish an ideal for which, even while we sin against it, we will clamour righteously & lovingly. Of course, there are no critics, or, at least, there is only one critic and that is a writers own self – You are your own touchstone & I am no more to you than a distant voice echoing certain interesting but entirely mistaken personal opinions. Different persons, different standards – You can only demand from me that I disagree appreciatively & I do that

Very truly yours
JAMES STEPHENS

To JAMES B. PINKER

[T/15]

Rathmines, Co. Dublin
25 September 1912

[Stephens was angered at the refusal of Small, Maynard & Co. to pay a £100 advance on the American edition of *The Crock of Gold.* After further difficulties, the edition was transferred to the Macmillan Company, New York, in November 1912. The "new book" was apparently either abandoned or transformed into some of the stories in *Here Are Ladies* (1913).]

Dear Mr Pinker.

I have received your letter.

The news is very unfortunate, as, in the expectation of the American advance, I have eaten all my Macmillan cake and shall find it difficult to get along until next January when Small, Maynard make their calculations. I suppose, as there is nothing else to be done, we must accept the latter's offer. Would Macmillan & Co of London deal in the American copyright – They might do it either on their own behalf or on behalf of their American Branch. In the meantime you have not, I suppose, yet heard from Small, Maynard in reply to your recent letter to them refusing to sign the agreement without an advance. It is a pity the time is so short.

Very truly yours,
JAMES STEPHENS

I have started my new book which will be on the style of the Charwoman's Daughter except that it treats of a young man instead of a girl. It promises to be good.

To [EDWARD MARSH]

[A/3]

Rathmines, Co Dublin
10 October 1912

[Sir Edward Marsh (1872–1953) was editor of the five volumes of *Georgian Poetry*, published from 1912 to 1922. Stephens's work was included in the first three volumes (1912, 1915, 1917). Marsh had written to ask for Stephens's approval to dedicate *Georgian Poetry: 1911–1912* to the English poet Robert Bridges (1844–1930). Marsh had described *The Charwoman's Daughter* as "a pure delight". The "new book" was *The Crock of Gold.*]

Dear Sir

Thanks for guinea. I do not know on what lines your Anthology will proceed, but I am sure it will be a very interesting selection. I look forward to having it. I think that Bridges, before all others, deserves your very graceful attention. By the bye, it is rather a pity that you are not including something of Mr Seumas O'Sullivans – he is a true poet. I am glad you liked the Charwoman's Daughter & hope you may get some pleasure from my new book

Very truly yours
JAMES STEPHENS

To KATHARINE TYNAN HINKSON

Rathmines, Co. Dublin
[A/36] 25 October 1912

[The Irish poet Katharine Tynan (1861–1931) published an article on "The Poetry of James Stephens" in the *Journal of English Studies* (London) for September 1912–January 1913. The article was quite flattering, placing Stephens alongside Yeats as the two major Anglo-Irish poets. Tynan had married the barrister Henry Albert Hinkson (1865–1919) in 1893; their daughter, Pamela Hinkson later became a novelist.]

Dear Mrs Hinkson.

Thanks for your letter & the copy of Studies which arrived this morning. I read your Article with very great pleasure. Its a great review and I am sure will do me a vast amount of good. Could you leave your invitation open for one further week – there is the remnant of a severe cold hanging about both of us & it would be a poor return for your kindness if we ravaged your household with our afflictions.

It is very interesting & queer about your daughters love of poetry, particularly of mine, many people have confessed to me that they find it difficult to understand – Her parentage, however, gives her an extra ability & maybe the Good gods have endowed herself. You must let me make Miss Pamela's acquaintence. Please remember me to your husband

Very truly yours
JAMES STEPHENS

To PAMELA HINKSON

Rathmines, Co Dublin
[A/3] 2 December 1912

[Katharine Tynan Hinkson had included "What Tomas an Buile Said in a Pub" in her article in the *Journal of English Studies.* There are only minor differences between the version below and the text in *Insurrections.*]

Dear Pamela

I should have written earlier, but, perhaps, I am still in time to wish you many happy returns and every other good thing that you may desire yourself. I could not find the original of the poem you wanted but I send you hereunder a copy & enclose the original of another thing thing which you may care tor.

Here are the verses–

– What Tomas an Buile said in a Pub:–
"I saw God. Do you doubt it?
Do you dare to doubt it?
I saw the Almighty Man, His hand
Was resting on a mountain, and
He looked upon the world & all about it;
I saw Him plainer than you see me now!
You must not doubt it –

He was not satisfied!
His look was all dissatisfied!
His beard swung on a wind far out of sight
Behind the worlds curve, and there was light
Most fearful from His forehead, and He sighed
"That star wert always wrong & from the start
I was dissatisfied."

He raised His hand!
I say he heaved a dreadful hand
Over the spinning earth! then I said "Stay,
You must not strike it, God, I'm in the way,
And I will never move from where I stand."
He said, "Dear child, I feared that you were dead".
– And stayed His hand."

I've written it from memory, but think it is all right. Remember me to your father & mother –

Very sincerely yours
JAMES STEPHENS

To THOMAS BODKIN

Rathmines, Co. Dublin
[A/3] 10 January 1913

[Thomas Bodkin (1887–1961), later Director of the National Gallery of Ireland (1927–35), was one of Stephens's closest friends during his early career. In 1913 Bodkin was a practising barrister. Stephens was apparently studying French in anticipation of his residence in Paris.

Henry William Massingham (1860–1924) was editor of *The Nation* (London) from 1907 to 1923. Stephens had published stories in *The Nation* for 7 December 1912 and 4 January 1913; after Massingham's offer, he published a story each month from February to October.]

Dear Bodkin

I find that my frenchman comes at 9 o'c tonight to give me a lecon & so I will not be able to get round to you. Could you name Tuesday or Wednesday next week. The pictures are splendid – I will bring them back next time. By the way Massingham of the Nation has asked me to let him have a story every month for a year at £4/4/ each – Wish I was going round but I have no time to put off the monsieur

Yours
JAMES STEPHENS

To [SEÁN MacGIOLLARNÁTH]

Dublin
[A/1] 21 January 1913

[The Gaelic writer Seán MacGiollarnáth (1880–1970) was currently editor of *An Claidheamh Soluis*. Stephens had been planning to act in *Mac na Mná Déirce*, a translation by MacGiollarnáth and the Gaelic writer Micheál MacRuaidhrí (1860–1936) of *The Shuiler's Child* by Seumas O'Kelly (1881–1918). Stephens had acted in the first production of *The Shuiler's Child* by the Theatre of Ireland in April 1909; *Mac na Mná Déirce* was produced at the Abbey on 2–3 May 1913].

A c[h]ara ["Dear Friend"]

I find to my great regret that I wont be able to take up the Shuler's rehersals. I have just got a commission to write a dozen short stories & upon my soul they'll take up every square inch of my mind & of my time. I return the ms. Forgive me & believe that I wouldnt back out only that I have to

Is Mise
["I am"]
JAMES STEPHENS

ms by separate post

To THE EDITOR OF THE *IRISH HOMESTEAD*

[Dublin]
22 February 1913

[The text is from the *Irish Homestead* for 22 February 1913. The letter is a response to a criticism of Irish writers by George Russell in "The Decadence of Popular Leaders", printed in the *Irish Homestead* for 15 February 1913.

The humorous allusion to Lord Verulam refers to the theory that Francis Bacon was the author of Shakespeare's plays. Rama, in Hindu mythology, is the name of three avatars of Vishnu; Arjuna is the main hero of the *Mahabharata.* In *The Marriage of Heaven and Hell* (1793), William Blake claimed that Milton's real sympathy was with Satan. The Irish writers mentioned are Thomas Osborne Davis (1814–45), one of the founders of *The Nation*; James Clarence Mangan (1803–49), best remembered for "Dark Rosaleen"; Samuel Ferguson (1810–86), author of several long poems based on Gaelic legends; William Allingham (1824–89), poet of Ballyshannon; Charles Gavan Duffy (1816–1903), famous patriot and the editor of *Irish Ballad Poetry* (1843); Thomas D'Arcy M'Gee (1825–68), poet and historian; John D'Alton (1792–1867), most important as an historian and genealogist of Dublin; Richard Dalton ("Shamrock") Williams (1822–62), a writer for *The Nation* best known for "The

Munster War-Song"; and Edward Walsh (1805–50), editor of *Irish Popular Songs* (1847).]

A POET IN DEFENCE OF HIS ORDER.

DEAR MR. EDITOR,–

I write as one who loves you. I do not rejoice over your lapses, and when your wayward and extravagant mind bolts from virtue as hard as it can pelt I only murmur, "These are his wild oats, it is right he should be reckless and spendthrift in dealing with them", and so I address you with a chastened and merely temporary severity.

The State of Denmark is a Cosmic Institution. There always is something crooked there, and this person and the other are perpetually seeking someone on whom they may fasten the blame for such crookedness. One time it is the King, another the Commons; the Lords are censured, the weather and the deity get a share of the blame and the thwacks. In Lord Verulam's tragedy the villainy was allocated between the king and the queen, but we know that the real culprit was the Ghost. That measly old stiff, instead of doing his purgatory like a man, was dandering around whispering pernicious gossip and setting people by the ears who were friendly enough. The Ghost also is an Institution, and in the last issue of your paper you held a high Ghost or Devil-Sniffing Festival and you sniffed out the unfortunate poets of Eirinn as the cause of all our woe. Have you no fear of the gods when you do this? After reading your article some agricultural gentleman might believe that it was the poets who created Cuchulain and Oscar and Diarmuid, Hector and Rama and Arjuna, and the rest of the notables. O Agricultural Gentleman! turn your wide, slow ear in my direction also for a little time. It was Finn and the Champions who inspired the poets to sing of them, it was not the poets who inspired Cuchulain and Diarmuid of the White Tooth to carve each others bones, to lop one another short from the thighs downwards, to slice each other from the shoulder blade sheer to the midriff. These happy and curious deeds were done before the poets sang of them at all, and not afterwards. The poet of those days was an historian, a teller of tales, and the censorship was rigid. He did not then and he does not now inspire a cent.

I think that editors have so much logic lying around loose that it bores them and they do not like to use it often. You, Mr. Editor, in the very maelstrom and fury of your sniffing, have halted for one calm second and penned these words: – "*Nobody could put one of our modern public men or so-called leaders into an epic or make them the subject of a genuine lyric.*" Dear Editor, I think that, like Milton, you are "of the Devil's party without knowing it". Or is it that you are unmasked. Are you a capitalist in mufti? Do you ask people to work for nothing? Are you an ancient Egyptian, built foursquare to the winds, with a false beard and no fear of plagues and asking people to make bricks without straw? Give us our overdue heroes and we will sing of them as lustily as the gods permit. The agricultural gentleman (to whom I forgot to say good-bye a moment ago) may get a wrong impression from your article. He may think that the poets of Eirinn have not done their duty and sung of murderers since the Abbey Theatre days when the mighty ones were sticky with anybody's gore. He may never have heard (or, if he has, you may mesmerise it from his remembrance) that Davis and Mangan, Ferguson and Allingham, Duffy and Magee, Dalton, Williams, and Walsh – their names are legion – sang badly and bloodily, every man jack of them bawling for blood like any bard without breeches. You ought to be bound over. Your article is an incitement to a breach of the peace. The first Intensive Cultivator we meet may call us destroyers of his country and kill us like the Playboy's Da with a loy. Don't make us responsible for more crimes than we have learned. We are not truly artistic yet. Do remember that every State of Denmark has its real right Ghost and so stick to your gombeen man and the President of the Department for we are guiltless in this matter. If I suppress my address it is because I am civilised and timid and modest and later than Abbey Theatre times and my blood is not worth any hero's half-holiday. – I am, more in sorrow than in anger, and yet in considerable personal trepidation, your friend,

JAMES ESSE.

To THE EDITOR OF THE *IRISH HOMESTEAD*

[Dublin]
1 March 1913

[The text is from the *Irish Homestead* for 1 March 1913. In "A Poet in Defence of His Class", George Russell had commented on Stephens's "A Poet in Defence of His Order": both pieces were published in the *Irish Homestead* for 22 February 1913. The following is Stephens's reaction to Russell's comments.]

THE HUMBLE PLEA OF THE POETS.

DEAR MR. EDITOR,–

You have thumped and belammed me. You have called me names, said I have no sense and likened me to a cinematograph. You have answered my popgun with a whole broadside of grape and canister, but I will drag my dreary bones from that carnage and have at you again, the way one of them there ancients of yours would have done.

I surrender you the priority of the egg or the bird. Whether the heroes inspired the bards or the bards the heroes is not pertinent to our case, but only whether the poets of to-day are guilty of malpractice towards Ireland. There are two sides to the moon, and the bards if they wish it might state a harsh case against the land of saints and scholars, the land of tin-trumpery of this and the other description, the land of incredible bunkums and blindnesses. Boston never claimed culture so vociferously and never had so little of it as we have, and the three millions odd of our free and fervent countrymen cannot muster more than a miserable hundred who will not sniff at the poet and all his work and bid him go bark at himself in some unsavoury solitude.

Indeed, there is no more woeful thing than patriotism, or, rather, the necessity for it – when the sick country creaks along like a more remorseless juggernaut, grunting "havoc!" as she goes, crushing her children to ruin, flattening every grace from life, shaking every decent ambition to the mud, confounding manliness and knavery to one horrid, conglomerate poverty, and breeding traitors and pedagogues and snobs and slaves so multitudinously that the good man and true must question does his eye indeed deceive him or does he hear aright.

Ireland has been stewing in that sink for how many years, how many centuries of years, and the poets were not absent at any time? The little poets, if you like, the good little poets saying the decent word if they could not say the noble one, keeping the slave from actually cherishing his fetters and the snob from quite kissing the king's toe. Ireland has been blessed in her poets. She has been blessed more than [any] other nation in the world, and (for economics are in the air) at no cost to herself. She has not put dripping on the bread of a single artist and, as far as I know, she never will. Saints and Scholars! She is the most comprehensive thug and murderer among the nations, infanticide is her choice pastime, and we who love her (as unaccountably we must love all bad things) should hit her big, fat farmery, peasantry, gombeenry head with a thick stick.

The royal succession has not failed. There are as good and as dutiful poets in Eirinn to-day as there ever were, but you would have them to sing dead ideals, to hark back from this era of nineteen hundred-and-ever-so-much to that year of dot-and-carry-one when the heroes ate raw enemies and drank the blood of whoever was handy. There is an especial providence which forbids yesterday to become to-morrow – it cheers us, we may be a rank and blotchy weed but we have grown out of and away from that most dismal swamp and we will not willingly go back to become "portions and parcels of the dreadful past".

"The poet," say you, "has no right to be anywhere save at the head of the human procession." Be comforted, for he is there all right, but you are looking at the wrong end for him. Humanity is marching gallantly forward with its tail well to the fore and its head tucked between its legs. In this age of every man for himself and the devil take the hindmost do you call the poet to lead in that van? Not him, he knows his job too closely. The poet is well to the rere keeping the devils off the hindmost. Rub your eyes again, my dear, and you will see him walking along with yourself, your right arms lovingly commingled and your left hands in each other's pockets like the decent gymnasts that your are.

Don't blame us for not being what we patently are not. Don't sniff at the duck's egg and say, "damn it all, this duck's egg is only the egg of a duck." When the phoenix hatches you will hear the rumour of that tremendous squawking, but, in the meantime, do not incite the ducks to abortion, let them comfort us with their own homely cackle and lay us their own eggs.

I will remove my hand for but one moment from your pocket while I subscribe myself most lovingly, – Your friend,

JAMES ESSE.

To JAMES B. PINKER

Rathmines, Co. Dublin

[T/15] 5 March 1913

[George Roberts was trying to obtain *Here Are Ladies* for Maunsel & Co., Dublin. "The story" apparently refers to a discarded manuscript. It does not seem that any of Stephens's works were translated into German until a 1936 edition of *Irish Fairy Tales* (1920).]

Dear Mr Pinker,

Thanks for your letter.

I am rather surprised that Messrs Maunsell & Co. have made so large an offer, but I am quite with you in preferring to remain with Messrs Macmillan & Co. I note the latter firm are prepared to advance £250 on account of the same royalties here and in America as they are paying on the Crock of Gold in England – Does this mean that they wish to take over the American rights as well as the English ones. We have already received on the Crock of Gold £200 on account of the English and American royalties, so that, in these circumstances, the £250 offered is not so considerable as at first seems – Maunsell & Co are not asking for the American rights. I would like your advice on these points. I take it that (supposing all is in order) Messrs Macmillan would be prepared to make the agreement and advance the amount agreed on at once?

As to the story – It will certainly be long enough to publish at 6/-, that is, it will be longer than the Crock of Gold. It is going forward rather slowly as I am writing a book of short stories at the same time and I am also taking time over the book as it is rather up to me to beat both the Charwoman's Daughter and the Crock of Gold. I hope to have it ready for their Autumn list.

Have you heard anything further as to the German translations?

Very truly yours,
JAMES STEPHENS

To JOHN QUINN

Dublin
[T/28] [13] March 1913

[John Quinn (1870–1924) was a New York lawyer and patron of the arts; he had a particular interest in Irish writers and acquired an important collection of manuscripts. Quinn had met George Russell in Ireland in 1902.]

Dear Sir,

I have your letter. Mr George Russell did speak to me about the ms of the Crock of Gold and, accordingly, I have today dispatched it under registered cover to you. I have marked on the outside of each of the note books the numbers 1 to 6 showing the order. This is the complete mss.

Thanks for the pleasant things you said about my work. I wonder whether the Irish Revival is, as you suggest, a matter of climate – that is a good beginning and a bad ending. If climate has anything to do with it why is not America producing better work? Why is England producing nothing, or very little, but vulgar stupidity. France and Germany are also being dexterously efficient but are not doing anything of importance. Barring Yeats I dont think there is a first class poet in the world – I dont think that climate has much to do with it. Ireland has lain fallow for so many hundreds of years now that, perhaps, even a little sowing will have to produce a notable crop. I often imagine that the artistic and literary soil of Europe wants a long rest. They are repeating themselves until all that they do is skilful rhetoric both of pen and brush. The wonder to me is not that Ireland has some kind of renascence but that America has not.

Very truly yours,
JAMES STEPHENS

To JAMES B. PINKER

Rathmines, Co Dublin
[T/15] 28 March 1913

[Pinker had proposed advance royalties of £150 each on the English and American editions of *Here Are Ladies*. Sir Frederick Macmillan (1851–1936) was Chairman of Macmillan & Co Ltd., London. When published in October 1913, *Here Are Ladies* contained several stories not listed here in the table of contents.]

Dear Mr Pinker,

Thanks for your letter.

The arrangement you have made with Sir Frederick Macmillan is quite satisfactory. I will sign the agreement as soon as you send it on.

As to the short stories – I am having these typed, and will send you the mss within a week. The book will be between 50,000 and 60,000 words in length, and can be published at 5/- or 6/- as may be thought advisable. I may say that I am very pleased with these short stories, which, in many ways, represent the best work I have yet done.

I have a commission with "The Nation" to supply them with one short story per month for a year. As some of the stories in this collection are required for the Nation I would be glad that Sir Frederick Macmillan would hold over publication until the autumn, say, August – Perhaps, if matters are satisfactory, you could arrange as to this. Will you require a second mss for America?

Hereunder I give a contents page for the book of short stories –

Very truly yours,
JAMES STEPHENS

——

I have thought of calling the book either "Triangles" or "Here are Ladies".

————

Three Heavy Husbands
1
2
3
Three Women Who Wept.
1
2
3
Three Angry People
1
2
3
Three Young Wives
1
2
3
Three Lovers Who Lost
1
2
3
Three Happy Places
1
2
3

There is a Tavern in the Town.
1
2
3
4
5
6
7
8
9
10
11
12

——

This last – There is a Tavern in the Town is a series of dialogues by the Old Philosopher of "The Crock of Gold"

To JAMES B. PINKER

Rathmines, Co. Dublin
[T/15] 6 April [1913]

[Stephens left Dublin for Paris on 6 May.]

Dear Mr Pinker,

Thanks for the agreements which I return herewith signed.

I will forward you a full copy of the short story mss tomorrow, and would like to hear what Messrs Macmillan & Co decide as early as is possible as Maunsell & Co are getting rather pressing on the subject.

I am going to France in a few weeks and will stay there for perhaps six months, so would wish this matter finished before I go.

Yours very truly,
JAMES STEPHENS

To JAMES B. PINKER

Rathmines, Co. Dublin
[T/15] 11 April 1913

[Pinker wrote on 10 April to ask if *Here Are Ladies* would be 60,000 words in length. Stephens's next novel was *The Demi-Gods*, but the reference here is apparently to an abandoned manuscript.]

Dear Mr Pinker,

Thanks for your letter with cheque.

As to the volume of short stories. Sir Frederick Macmillan is right as to the length of the mss submitted – There are about 50,000 words in it, but I can very easily make up the balance in a few weeks. I am finishing a few stories which will finish the book at a little over 60,000 words and this will be, I fancy, as much as is required.

I notice they will give the same royalty for this book as for the novel which I am writing and will advance £100 on account of royalties. I quite approve of this and will sign an agreement on these terms. Will you see about an American agreement and try for a similar advance from them.

As to the date of publication. My novel will not be ready for this year. It will be ready, however, for the spring catalogue, and, therefore, this volume of stories ought to be published later in the season: any time after August that Messrs Macmillan consider advisable; but not before August.

Would you care for me to send you a few short stories to dispose of? I do not know that there is as yet any particular market for my wares.

Very truly yours,
JAMES STEPHENS

To JAMES B. PINKER

Rathmines, Co. Dublin
[T/15] 16 April 1913

[Pinker wrote on 14 April with Macmillan's offer of a total advance royalty of £100 on *Here Are Ladies*.]

Dear Mr Pinker.

Thanks for your letter of 14th inst.

I note that the £100 is to be advanced on account of America as well as England. I wish Messrs Macmillan could see their way to making the advance something larger, say £150 – However, if there is any difficulty I do not press the point, but I recommend it for their consideration. I know, of course, that short stories have not the same welcome as novels: still, there is something to be said for the collection I am making. In the first place I think it is absolutely unlike any other collection of short stories in English. I am not saying it is the best but only that it is different, and from its very varied composition I am certain it will be, at the least, as successful as The Crock of Gold. I have written these studies with extraordinary care, polishing each again and again as if they had been poems instead of stories. Certainly as yet none of my books have been commercial successes but they have justified their publication; and yet about each in turn the same remark has been made that is now being made of the collection of short stories.

If you send on the agreements I would like to conclude the matter at once and I would like to thank you for all the trouble you are taking on my behalf.

Sincerely Yours.
JAMES STEPHENS

To JAMES B. PINKER

Rathmines, Co. Dublin

[A/15] 28 April 1913

[Although Stephens received a number of offers, *The Crock of Gold* was never dramatized.]

Dear Mr Pinker

Thanks for your letter & cheque received safely.

I would rather that Messrs Macmillan should wait for one month longer before they start printing. You know there is further material to be put into the mss & this is now almost ready – The name of the book will be:–

"*Here Are Ladies*"

I am leaving for Paris on Tuesday next 6th May and will send you my address as soon as I have one.

I enclose a letter received from some American person asking for permission to dramatise the Crock of Gold – I scarcely believe the book is capable of drama, but you may like to deal with it.

Very truly yours
JAMES STEPHENS

To JOHN QUINN

Paris

[A/28] 15 May 1913

Dear Sir,

You may remember asking for the mss of my novel The Crock of Gold. This note is to ask if you received it safely & to notify you of my change of address. I left Dublin a few weeks ago & intend to live in Paris for about a year.

Yours faithfully
JAMES STEPHENS

To THOMAS BODKIN

Paris

[A/3] 21 May 1913

[Until he found his permanent Paris residence at 11 Rue Campagne-Première, Stephens was staying in a small hotel; this letter was addressed in the care of the sculptor and portrait-medallist Theodore Spicer-Simson (1871–1959). Stephen MacKenna was currently planning a trip to Berlin. Bodkin's poems were eventually published by Maunsel in 1917 as *May It Please Your Lordships: Reproductions of Modern French Poems.*]

Dear Bodkin

Your "tracing" came all right. I am now beginning to feel more at home. The streets anyhow are mine, but the flats are not. We havent yet got a flat, but I am told that we can move into one on Monday next. It will be No. 11 Rue Campagne-Première. A very pretty four-roomed place on the first floor, infested now by Russians who swear they are doing their best to get out & have bound themselves before God & the concierge to quit on Monday morning. These concierges are strange people (I mean the system is strange, but I have quite forgotten how to write[)]. Meanwhile the beauty of this city grows more on me mixed with a certain gentle melancholy for Dublin. You know Dublin really has points, certain pleasant incompetences. The first shattering blow my preconceptions received was that of the polite french people. They are a mighty careful business-like, adequate people & they do not waste any more time in being polite than we do. Anyhow there is no more public politeness than there is in Dublin. No one has yet been rude to me or anything like that but somehow one had a tradition. Its shattered I'm glad to say – a race of polite people would be utterly horrible. I have not gone to any of the monuments or galleries & wont until you come across, which I pray may be soon. Meanwhile I have noted your programme of lectures as a way of learning French. It is admirable, but just now I am told the lectures are all over[.] School everywhere seems to close in June & wont reopen until September. There are sermons, however, & these I will listen to. We went last night by the Bould Raspail to the Place de l'Opera & watched the lights being turned up. The Place was really beautiful. Most of the time I was wondering why nobody was run over by a taxi, or a carriage but the people seem "native" to the noses of horses & the front wheels of motors. The finest view in (my) Paris, as yet, is at the end of the Rue S[o]ufflot just to the direct left of the Pantheon, a wide, severe place, the severity just toned down at the back by some broken towers or spires of a Church. Language deserts me utterly when face to face with the aboriginals but my resolve holds good that when I return to Ireland I will riot among your French books. I have been looking about to see could [I send] you any little nothing but there isnt a nothing worth sending here that I can discover. For so important & wealthy a city Paris is about as shoddy in her shops & as urgent in her prices as well could be. The girls in Dublin are much prettier than those & very often they are better dressed. The only thing that makes these French women & men really noteworthy is their attitude of independence & self-respect. I wonder is it sexual freedom which has made the women so self-possessed[.] You will be coming in August. That is still two months distant. Dont make other arrangements like a good man. I will be looking forward very much to seeing you & I have reserved many things which you can show me. Maybe the Clann Medicine ["the Medicine tribe"] will put poor Stephen right again – That decent man is having a particularly rotten time of it just now. Is he really going to Berlin & is he going to get better. If you go to Donnybrook on Saturday evening salute the pair of them in my name & wish them all the good things which I hereby seal to the three of you. About your poems – Have you done anything more with Maunsel? Have you translated any more of them? If you have I hope you will just type them out & drop them across to me to look at. I would be mightily delighted if you did so. Believe it that your verses are the best translations yet done & remain good original poetry to boot. I bet you a penny you havent read down to here. I will send you a P/O for stamps next week. I dont suppose you will have many more letters to forward except your own which I will look for.

Mise le meas mór
["I am with great esteem"]
JAMES STEPHENS

To STEPHEN MacKENNA

Paris

[A/19] [24–25 May 1913 & August 1930]

[MacKenna's projected trip to Berlin did not materialize. The combination of French and Gaelic in "chambre na leabhar" is perhaps an attempt to echo the Gaelic *seomra na leabhar*, "the room of the books". Mildred Aldrich (1853–1928) was an American writer living in Paris. Stephens's family consisted of his wife Cynthia

(1882–1960), formerly Millicent Josephine Kavanagh; his step-daughter Iris (1907); and his son James Naoise (1909–37).

William Gibson (1868–1942) became the 2nd Baron Ashbourne upon the death of his father, Edward Gibson (b. 1837), on 22 May 1913. As President of the Gaelic League of London, William Gibson argued for a revival of not only the Irish language but also the traditional Irish costume of saffron cap, cloak and kilt. MacKenna wrote of him to Stephens: "I curse his kilts & his bare knees & his ridiculous bottom, unseen but imagined, ruining the Gaelic cause." The Luxembourg Gardens were one of Stephens's favourite places in Paris; both the Gardens and the Panthéon were quite close to his flat. The English artist Aubrey Vincent Beardsley (1872–98) was best known for his illustrations to Oscar Wilde's *Salomé*. Bon Marché was a large department store in Paris.

The final paragraph of the letter itself was written on a page torn out of a book or magazine. MacKenna had given Stephens a letter of introduction to Martin Henry Donohue (1869–1927), the Paris correspondent for the London *Daily Chronicle*. Stephens was in Paris for almost three weeks before moving into his own flat.]

My dear Stephen

I was mighty glad to get your letter. I can see your empty spaces & I envy the walls. You will be getting well soon & you & I will be having a red time in the cities of the foes of France. I often play games with myself: particularly, I like to shut my eyes & walk through houses that I have been in – I have tramped through your halls and meads many times, always to the chambre na leabair [*leabhar*, "of the books"] & renewed my brains at your fountain. I will hit for Vienna or Berlin certain if you go there & will test the porridge for myself – Miss Aldridge, my wife & myself rolled forth a day ago & the lady stood us an absinthe in a cafè – She drank her drink & smoked her smoke like the fine man she is. Absinthe is the most drunken drink I have yet tasted. My left leg got quite intoxicated & would have misbehaved itself, but my right leg (a reliable shank,!) took care of us both & we bore obliquely but safely from motors & such – The busses here are incarnations of Satan [–] they want to run over one. Be damn to them!

I am sure the Gibson lord is a decent man, maybe his knees will live up to him after a time. The french nation is fond of our children & listens admiringly to their speech[.] "Ma mignonne" ["my darling"] s[ai]d a broad frenchwoman to Iris in the Gardens. Sonny regarded her & roared "Stop" in such a voice that the broad frenchwoman's husband became abashed. He hid his head with his hat & stole away trying to look like a real frenchman. We sat at a cafè two nights ago (Bd. St Michel a little to the left of the Pantheon) and we watched the motley throng go by. The men were nearly all English & the women deserved to be. Never have I conceived such fantastical figures. Vice! and not a rag of allurement on it, barring its hats. Such rouged, raddled, deplorable marionettes, smiling like hell. It would give you a pain in your inside & your outside just to look at them. Lust itself might blink at them & pass by. I fancy Beardsley got his faces on the Bd St Michel. We move on Monday to our own flat No 11 Rue Campagne–1ere & will be glad to get there. And this morning our little cat strolled out from a 5th floor window, scaled inaccessible & terrific pinnicled walls & disappeared. She is frantic for a mate[,] poor wee beast. We have warned the concierge, the police, the S-Simsons & the bon Marchè & hope to retrieve her, heavy with fruit –

I will start afresh (or rather have) in the French. I found a grammer here & am determined not to let go my holt until I can read the legends on the picture postcards in the Rue de Rivoli[.]

Forgive this sheet of paper – I have no other. I did not yet send your letter to Donohue, am waiting until I've an address of my own. Maybe he will tell me where one can get tobacco. I smoke Demi-Londres but am beginning to wish for a pipe. Remember me to your good lady – She has french, german, English & Irish now – Is mór é sin ["That's a great deal"]

do c[h]ara
["your friend"]
JAMES STEPHENS

[The following are Stephens's 1930 comments:]

This letter must have been written within a few days of my first arrival in Paris[.] The address given is that of the Spicer-Simsons. Theodore S.S. had promised that he would look out for an appartment for us: and, within I think a week or ten days he had found one, some few houses down from where he lived at 11 rue Campagne–Premiére. (We still, at this date, Augt 1930 are in possession of this flat)

To W. T. H. HOWE

[A/3]

Paris
31 May 1913

[W. T. H. Howe (1874–1939) was Manager of the Southern Division of the American Book Company; he was elected President of the Company in 1931. Especially after the death of John Quinn, Howe served as the equivalent of Stephens's American patron. Howe's suggestion for a book of fairy tales eventually resulted in *Irish Fairy Tales* (1920). The American poet Madison Julius Cawein (1865–1914) was known as "the Keats of Kentucky".]

Dear Mr Howe

Your letter has just been forwarded to me in Paris. I have taken a flat at this address and intend to remain here for one year, so that you can write safely to me now. Of course, I know you were not "hunting" for my copy of the Crock. It was only that I liked your letter & thought you would have trouble in getting the first edition you wanted. The American edition by the way is very poorly produced. Perhaps you will like "Mary Mary" [.] In some ways I think it superior to the Crock. & there are patches of good writing in it. Those two novels & the two books of verse are the only books I have published. I am bringing out a volume of short stories in September (to be called "Here are Ladies".) I fancy you will like some of these short stories. I think they include some of the best writing I have ever done. One can polish a short story just like a poem. Perhaps, as you suggest, the publishers on your side have not been too active in pushing my books. It cannot be helped. &, anyhow, I dont believe they would ever be very widely popular. Later, perhaps, I may make some money from them – Fame is a very pleasant diet but it is thin. I am extremely obliged to you for your kindness in making my books known to your friends. I am sure that when my royalties come in in January next a good part of my income will be traceable to your kindly efforts.

As to your suggestion for a book of Irish Fairy Tales – It interests me a good deal. I would, of course, have to entirely write them and am sure I would enjoy doing so. If you let me hear further on the matter & send me the specimen books you wrote of I will then give you a decided answer. I could send to Ireland for my books & work here in Paris.

By the way you said you had a book of Mr Caweins which you could let me have. If it is not troublesome I wish you would send it with your name inscribed.

I am having a very pleasant time in Paris[.] Plenty of sunshine &, after Ireland, one enjoys that

Sincerely yours
JAMES STEPHENS

To THOMAS BODKIN

Paris
[A/3] 9 June 1913

[Bodkin's translations of French poems were not published until 1917. The second postscript is written on the back of the envelope; the French should be *Je l'ai trouvée et les poèmes sont très bons*, "I have found it and the poems are very good".]

My dear Bodkin

I delayed writing to you because an unaccountable, an unforseen, an entirely abominable thing has happened. You know we have moved to our own flat & for a short time our affairs were in disorder. It was during that time your letter arrived & it got mislaid. I put it by with extraordinary precautions so that I might leisurely (that is when the children were in bed) enjoy your muse & I have not since been able to discover where the devil I put it. It will turn up, of course, & I hope it will turn up soon. I wont ask you to send me the same poems again (for I am quite certain to find them) but if you have others refresh me with them like a decent man. The time must be drawing near now for publishing. Would you think of sending me a duplicate copy of your entire ms to go over. It would give me great pleasure to read & I might be able to suggest commas & colons & such like small poetical change. Thanks for the list of good places you sent me. I will go & see them when you come over. The Dublin papers you sent were very interesting merci beaucoup. I am starting seriously now on a study of French & by the time you arrive mai foi [*mais ma foi*, "but my faith"]!

Your friend
JAMES STEPHENS

I do the book carts very often. Isnt there blood & thunker & bosoms & chemises on those carts! Remind Mr & Mrs Stephen MacKenna of our continued existence & do not forget it yourself.

I have just found your letter in a French grammer. J'ai le trouvè et les poemis sont très bon.

To STEPHEN MacKENNA

Paris

[A/19] 28 June 1913

[The following letter is a fragment. MacKenna was to go to London shortly for medical treatment. Stephens's reading in French consisted of the *Fables* of Jean de la Fontaine (1621–95) and *Lettres de mon Moulin* (1869) by Alphonse Daudet (1840–97). The story which Stephens wrote was "A Glass of Beer", included in *Here Are Ladies.*]

My dear Stephen

I shook hands with your letter.

I expect that, just at this time, Tir Lundan [for *Tír Lonndan*, "London Land"] is interesting at least, and I also expect that you dont care whether it is or not. It is well to be you & hitting the trail at your own sweet will & not caring where tomorrow is. There is gum on our feet & the Rue Campagne 1ère will probably stick to us until we jerk ourselves back to that suburb of Átha [for *Ath*] Cliath ["Dublin"]. Meantime we are quite at home. The conceirge who has a whiskey wart on her chin & a kind heart says "Ma petite, ma mignonne["] ["my little one, my darling"] as the youngsters go in & out. They accept French people, just as they do trees & rainy days, as things over which they have no control. I have started lessons & now, every morning at 9 o'c I turn into the Rue des Ecoles & have my hour of it – The good lady (one of a multitude) gives one terrific tasks to perform – Here is my stunt for tomorrow morning. The first four fables of La Fontaine (La Fontaine bores me to the very guts) [–] Ten pages of Lettres de Mon Moulin – To know one irregular verb straight through more tenses than you would believe in. To write from memory a story which she dictated about Napoleon's breakfast. There are still two further exercises but, thank God, I have forgotten what they are & so cannot do them. For this I have paid the folk one poem of four verses, to wit 25 francs, covering one hour every morning for one month. At the rate they are packing French into me per day I'll be swollen head & belly & belch french at a punch. I have written a short story, about 3,000 words, action Bd St Michel, time now, 10.30 p.m. [–] its real bon, my son. I will demand and flourish on your felicitations. When I write a quite bon thing it is my custom to go secretly apart & praise myself after the manner of my friends. I have

. . . .

To W. T. H. HOWE

Paris
[A/3] 2 July 1913

[The Blake quotation is one of the "Proverbs of Hell" from *The Marriage of Heaven and Hell.* Stephens did not publish any children's stories.]

Dear Mr Howe.

Thanks for your letters. I think the Christmas Card is delightful. It is rather ludicrous that publishers should employ illiterate agents to push their books. Perhaps they have a theory that things go by opposites & that the more ignorant the agent the wiser the book. You know even foolishness has its own philosophy. Do you remember Blakes dicta "If the fool would persist in his folly he'd become wise"[?] You are recommending my books so largely that in January next I will earmark 2/3rds of my royalties as received from you instead of from Macmillan. By the way. The Charwoman's Daughter & Mary Mary are the same book. The American publishers, for some extraordinary reason, decided to call the book "Mary Mary"[.] It is a title that gives me a pain when I recollect it; but they did produce the book nicely. (That is Small, Maynard & Co.) Macmillan of America produce their books horribly. I just hate to see their Crock of Gold. It looks like a Crock of Poverty rather than of Gold – However, and it is a great thing for an author, they are a straight firm –

Now as to your "children story" – I will send you a little story – it is not precisely on the lines you wish, but is very close to it, &, from it, you can judge whether my stuff would please the youngsters you have in mind – I do not wish to commence a book, get interested in it, & have to drop it because the business side could not be arranged, so if you let me know your firms suggestions on this side of the matter it would simplify matters. As to your little brochure for Christmas – I will be glad to do whatever I can to help you in this. I can send you some photographs of myself, of my flat in Paris & some Dublin scenes; my house in Dublin has changed hands & I have no photoes of it. Perhaps you would like a few little poems also to include. That reminds me, I have just written a lyric which satisfies me mightily, I enclose a copy as I fancy it will please you also. I am prepared to bet that my poems will be more appreciated ten years hence than my prose. At present they have got overlaid by the Charwoman & the Crock. There are real good things in Here Are Ladies, but it is unequal[.] I will be very anxious for your opinion on half a dozen of its contents

Mise le meas mór, do c[h] ara,
["I am very respectfully, your friend"]
JAMES STEPHENS

I open to say I have found a copy of the story I speak of herein and enclose it.

To JOHN QUINN

Paris
[T/28] 3 July 1913

[Stephens is acknowledging Quinn's payment for the manuscript of *The Crock of Gold*; Quinn had written to him that his manuscript would take its place among those by Morris, Swinburne, Hardy, Lady Gregory, Yeats, *et al.* Stephens had termed the current literature of England "vulgar stupidity" in his letter of 13 March 1913.]

Dear Mr Quinn,

Thanks very much for the cheque for £20.

I am sorry there is no typewritten revise or proof sheets of the Crock of Gold, I burnt them when the final proofs were corrected and returned to the printers.

I absolutely forget what it was I wrote to you on the first occasion, and you have replied to me in inverted commas! What the mischief did I say was "vulgarly stupid"? It certainly was not America. If anything I look at your writers over there with magnifying eyes. For example, I think probably more of Walt

Whitman than you do – I class him right up alongside of Shakespeare. Here is my list: Shakespeare, Wordsworth and Whitman, and, at their top notes, I dont know which of the three is the greater poet. Would it be possible to say that Wordsworth was the finest character, Whitman the finest human being, Shakespeare the finest poet. I dont know; but there are things in those three which I would chant against anything in the world's literature and back with your money (I haven't any myself) I would run Mark Twain to beat the Thackeray kind of people any day. IF I did say "vulgarly stupid" (and you aver it with those horrid little marks) then I protest that I didn't know what I was talking about, that I didn't mean it and that I beg the pardon of everybody concerned. But, what the deuce did I say?

That is a great collection of ms you recited, and mine has every reason to cock its tail and brag of its lodgings.

I have just reread your letter – its great, but its not a letter, its a scrap, what *are* you hitting me for?

Yours very truly,
JAMES STEPHENS

To ERNEST A. BOYD

[A/12] Paris
5 July 1913

[Later in 1913, the Irish critic Ernest Augustus Boyd (1887–1946) married Madeleine Reynier and went to Baltimore as a member of the British Consular Service. Stephens's poem in the July 1913 *Harper's Monthly Magazine* was "With the Daisies". "Mrs. H." refers to "Beatrice Hastings" of the *New Age* staff. The Irish poet and revolutionary Joseph Mary Plunkett (1887–1916) replaced Colum as editor of the *Irish Review* in July 1913. Boyd's article in the July 1913 *Irish Review* was "Dogmatism in Irish Life".]

My dear Boyd

I was real glad to hear from you & glad to know that America has opened hospitable doors. To me also these doors have just opened & in this months Harper's Magazine there is a little inconsiderable poem of mine, which they will probably give me a penny or two for. The whole business for myself & yourself is to get a beginning, a little hole & jump in & stay in. But your letter rather threatens a defection from pens in favour of Consulship[.] Thats no job for you, except as a temporary thing. I think you are really cut out for writing & will make your mark if you persevere. I'm glad you had the scrap with Mrs. H. One, of course, does rather see her as a bag filled with wind & vulgarity, but (& it is in her favour) she is well filled with these

Did she stand up anyway well to you. Is she as equal in the wordy as the inky scrap, and how did she take the whole thing. I havent, by the way, seen the New Age since I left Ireland, so dont know whether she has been hammering into me or not. Will she try to get back at you. She will be chagrined if you dont shortly publish somewhere a signed article. If she does go for you I would like to see it. Do you know if the New Age can be gotten anywhere in Paris? Houston is sitting opposite me in my little flat as I write, &, singularly, he has just asked me for your address. I dont know what infamy is meditated against you, but I do know that your address is included in his letter to Joseph M. Plunkett, the new Editor of The Irish Review. That paper reached me this morning with your name in the index. I promise myself a cigarette de Caporal & an interview with yourself within the next five minutes. Mdlle Reynier is I think coming to see us soon[.] I will be very glad to see her [–] she is a thoroughly nice girl. If you are able to run across for a while then my compliments & hurry up

Mise le meas mór
["I am with great esteem"]
JAMES STEPHENS

To THOMAS BODKIN

Paris
[A/3] 9 July 1913

[Theodore Spicer-Simson did not make a medal of AE until 1922. The "Art Journal" was the August 1912 number of *Camera Work* (New York), which contained reproductions of the work of Henri Matisse (1869–1954) and Pablo Picasso (1881–1973) and articles on the two artists by the American writer Gertrude Stein (1874–1946). The "Boulevard Story" was "Un Bock Brun", published in *The Nation* (London) for 26 July 1913 and included in *Here Are Ladies* as "A Glass of Beer". Bodkin was currently handling law cases in Leinster. "With shining morning face" is Jacques's description of the "whining schoolboy" in Shakespeare's *As You Like It* (II. vii. 146).

Stephens wrote "Gallic" because of Bodkin's opposition to the emphasis on the revival of the Irish language.]

My dear Bodkin,

Just a few lines to say we still exist. Dont be under the illusion that I do not enjoy my stay here. I do, mightily, & have now shaken down quite to the ordinary life & am quite as comfortable & as careless as in Dublin; but I do still think that our own people (& with them I include the English) are a better folk. I wish we could steal portions of this city & dump them solidly down in Dublin. Not their treasures by any means, only an odd, average boulevard or two, with an occasional "place" thrown in. By the way a medal of mine by an English man here has been sent to Ireland via Prof Houston. It has been forwarded for AE to look at (the Artist wants to entice AE over to sit for a medal.) Houston's instructions are to show the medal to Russell & afterwards to give it to you to bring over to Paris when you come. He has also the number of an Art Journal with Post Impressionist pictures & two articles explanatory by Gertrude Stein done as Post Impressionist *Literature*. Houston will give you this also. Will you keep it till I return to Dublin. It is très interessante. I met the lady a week or two ago & she asked me to her house. She has about 150 of the best pictures of Matisse, Picasso & the other men & to walk into her room where these hang is an experience. I will be able to take you there when you come over. If you desire it I can get you an introduction to Matisse. I liked much the little poem you sent & hope you have got a few more since. By the way again. I have finished a Boulevard Story which is I think very bon indeed. I sent it to the Nation yesterday & they may print it this Saturday or next unless they reject it – it is a trifle long for their usage – I can see you cavorting around Leinster, putting people "in" & taking people out with fine impartiality – I will just continue sending these Rires ["laughs"] &c till you come. It is easier to drop them on you than to retain or destroy them in a flat. I go to school every morning at 8.30 for an hour "with shining morning face" [–] I renew my youth. But my french is as coy as your Gallic. MacKenna wrote me very pleasantly. I hear he stays in London & that his wife hits Paris by her lone in about a week. My good wishes & my hand are your own property

JAMES STEPHENS

To EDWARD MARSH

Paris

[T/3] 14 July 1913

[Stephens is acknowledging payment for his poems in *Georgian Poetry: 1911–1912*, which had been dedicated to Robert Bridges. The other anthologies to which Stephens contributed at this time were *The Book of Irish Poetry*, ed. Alfred Perceval Graves (1914) and *The Dublin Book of Irish Verse: 1728–1909*, ed. John Cooke (1915). Marsh included two poems by the English poet Ralph Hodgson (1871–1962) in *Georgian Poetry: 1913–1915*.]

Dear Mr Marsh,

Thanks for your letter with cheque for £3.

I think your Anthology has rather made a record, first, in getting to a 6th edition, and, second, in paying its contributors – the latter does seem like a forecast of the overdue millenium.

Was Mr Bridges pleased with your compliment? There seems to be a number of anthologies in preparation just now; whether your magical 6th edition is responsible for them or not I dont know, but I am contributing to three and have refused to contribute to ten!

I will be very glad to make your acquaintence when I am next in London, if you continue in that mind.

Are you acquainted at all with the work of Ralph Hodgson? He is a mighty good poet: good, not great, but nobody else is great either and very few are good.

Your sincerely,
JAMES STEPHENS

To EDWARD MARSH

Paris

[A/3] 17 July 1913

[Bridges was appointed Poet Laureate on 16 July 1913. Hodgson's "To Deck a Woman" and "The Bull" were published in the *Saturday Review* for 3 September 1910 and 6 January 1912, respectively.]

Dear Mr Marsh

Thanks very much. I will be glad indeed to see the book you mention. I see by todays paper that Mr Bridges has been appointed

Laureat. There was no one better entitled to the post than he. However things go, & even if the word "great" is at issue between us, there is a very fine literary activity about. I do hold that there is no first class man either in prose or verse but particularly in prose – Hodgson's "Bull" has I think true imaginative observation & is a real piece of psychological delving. His "To Deck a Woman" also has both ecstacy & passion [–] Have you seen this latter. I must say that I dislike exceedingly most of the modern verse I have seen. Perhaps you will be in Paris before I am in London

Sincerely yours
JAMES STEPHENS

To W K. MAGEE

Paris
19 July 1913

[A/1]

[Magee's "The New Age" had been published in *The New Age* for 10 July 1913; the article argues for a "reappearance" in man's life of a "transcendental certainty". Magee's *Bards and Saints* (1906) was published as the fifth volume in the first series of the Tower Press Booklets (1906–8). Standish O'Grady (1846–1928) was an Irish historian and novelist whose works dealt with the heroic age of Ireland.

The quotation is from "The Triangle", published in *The Nation* (London) for 6 September 1913 and included in *Here Are Ladies.* The allusion to Francis Bacon is doubtless in reference to his *Essays.* AE had been editor of the *Irish Homestead* since 1905. The final story mentioned is "Un Bock Brun", published in *The Nation* (London) for 26 July 1913.]

My dear Magee,

Young Boyd, who has, I think, constituted himself your trumpeter, has sent me a copy of the New Age with an article of yours in it; and I am just scribbling this note to say how mightily it has pleased me. It is really a superb bit of writing, full of music. It continually swings & sings into passion and every blessed note of the orchestra is in it. Forgive me if I say that I had not quite realized before how completely you are equipped for prose. I always knew you were a fine writer, but now I know you are a great one. For the lords sake buckle into work and give us all the chance of being proud of you, not in a Tower Presslet but a fat volume which we can waggle in the face of the work of the Tyrant. Its fine to think that Russell & yourself & Standish O'Grady are all alive & that you can kick if you want to. AE's prose is magnificent, when he gives it the chance of being so, but he sort of opens the door & lets his prose loose; naturally it cavorts on orange peels & slips. He hasnt got time to be the great writer he ought to be –

I'm having an interesting miscellaneous sort of a time here. There are an extraordinary number of opportunities of smoking, drinking & getting syphilis and yet no one seems to smoke too much or drink too much or contract more syphilis than he can carry. It is all rather unpleasantly law-abiding. I havent seen one angry man or woman since I came except myself. There's something wrong with the French people. They are fat and smug & theyve too many women about them. I wouldnt swap one street of Dublin for all Paris, and the barbarians dont know how to talk anything but French. There is not much necessity, really, to travel. There are only buildings to look at & one can always imagine them better than they are, & the much vaunted postcards are only naked women – They have no idea of indecency at all. Legs & bosums. I am a much disappointed Irishman & am loosing my belief in vice – By the way I wrote a short story a week ago, the first four lines are nice – voila:

> "Nothing is true for ever; a man & a fact will become equally decripit & will tumble in the same ditch, for truth is as mortal as man, and both are outlived by the tortoise and the crow."

Let yourself & Bacon beat that, & then I'll have another shot at the pair of you.

If you see AE tell him that he has not sent me the Homestead. That he promised to send it & that he will not acquire merit unless he does the thing he says he'll do.

I think the Nation will have a story of mine this Saturday. Its rather good. I'm tired of Paris –

Yours sincerely
JAMES STEPHENS

To THOMAS BODKIN

Paris

[A/3] [late] July 1913

[The "Art Journal" was the August 1912 issue of *Camera Work.*]

My dear Bodkin

Thats good news. Be sure to let me know when you are coming. By what train and all that. I would like to meet you; and be sure to bring your ms of poems with you. Its too bad that Ireland is so crimeless. How are honest barristers to live if that damned virtue is triumphant? I have just gotten the Irish papers you sent me. Thanks – Mrs MacKenna is here just now. Her news of Stephen is not too encouraging. He stays in London. I did not think any compulsion could have detained him there. The Art Journal which Houston was to give you, you can keep for yourself. It has, at least, the merit of being quaint. The medal has to come back here to Spicer Simson.

A bientôt
JAMES STEPHENS

To GEORGE W. RUSSELL

Paris

[A/17] 28 July 1913

[Russell had been on the staff of the Irish Agricultural Organisation Society since 1897. On 20 March 1913 the British government awarded the I.A.O.S. £2,000 for the furtherance of agricultural co-operation in Ireland. Although there were some conditions imposed, the grant ended a year-long controversy with the Department of Agriculture. Sir Edward Carson (1854–1935) was the leader of the movement to exclude Ulster from any Home Rule for Ireland, organizing in 1912 the Ulster Volunteer Force to that end. The American publisher was W. T. H. Howe. The editor of the *Saturday Review* from 1898 to August 1913 was Harold Hodge (1862–1937). Rathgar was the suburb of Dublin in which AE lived.

The first postscript explains the missing section of the letter. Magee's "The New Age" was published in *The New Age* for 10 July 1913. Russell's poem in the July 1913 *Irish Review* was "The City". In the second postscript, written on the margin of the first page, the references are to the August 1912 *Camera Work* and the medal of Stephens by Spicer-Simson.]

Dear AE

I also have a cosmopolitan soul & so find no good in Travelling. I have discovered that there is nothing to be found in foreign parts but drink & syphilis in astonishing variety. Behold me entirely cured of the itch for travel and looking earnestly forward to the time when I will go back to the Kingdom of Dublin. You promised to send me some numbers of the Homestead but they didnt come. I gather from your terrible caligraphy that the I.A.O.S has got its grant, free from all restrictions! I would shout with you but, I suppose, its too long after the fair. A young Frenchman here has asked me for an introduction to you & I dispatched him & it before your letter arrived. He has learned Gaelic. God knows why! & he has some kind of mercantile-alliance-between-France-&-Ireland-plan which he wishes to speak to you about. Now that I have warned you, you can manage it so that he wont be able to get in a single word on his own subject. Is there anything I can do for the Homestead. Isnt there another little row we could get up on some subject. I dont care what its about so long as I can talk wisdom to you & listen to you barging back. For instance we might convulse the North. I attacking Carson & you defending him in Ballad. I am sure there are a lot of bad things to be said about Carson. You could write them to me & I would return them with an added virulence. I'm not doing anything in particular, just marching about the streets looking at the people – they swarm! Every possible kind of person, and yet, after a few weeks, they all look absolutely alike. I am suffering, not so much from indigestion of speech as from the desire to hear somebody saying something. I have fallen among Americans but, although they make a continuous noise with their mouths, they do not speak – They all tell anecdotes. I have spent interminable evenings listening to little stories about railway trains

. . . .

conclusion that I'm rather a fraud & I'm not going to bother any more about it. An American publisher man has asked me to do him a book of Irish Fairy Stories. Three American Theatre-men have written to know would I dramatise or let them dramatise the Crock of Gold (The gods have surely made these men mad!) & the Editor of the Saturday Review enquires will I write articles for his paper. I'm not going to do any of these things. I find I have just enough money (with the Nation Stories) to last me until January next when my book royalties will pour tempestuously in & pay my fare back to Rathgar – So, & therefore, I'm not going to work except at my own stuff if the gods are propituous. Forgive me, but there is a spate of chatter coming from the end of my pen. I could write on to you until tomorrow, but you would hardly thank me if I did & I dont want to frighten you from writing to me again

Yours
JAMES STEPHENS

Just as I was putting up your letter, a gentle gale arose & wrapped itself about two sheets of your letter & leaped with them out of the window (and I hadent even time to copyright them)[.] So you a[re] spared a sure 200 to 400 words of reading. I can see you putting a blessing on that wind; but I'll shut the window next time & then, have at you. I was only talking in those pages about Magees recent article in the New Age & asking if you had any new poems & that if you would send them to me I would duly render them back again. I saw your poem in the Irish Review. Do you remember reading or, rather, chanting it in MacKenna's house.

Did you read the Post Impressionist Articles I sent by Houston & did he show you the medal?

To THEODORE SPICER-SIMSON

Paris
[A/30] August 1913

[Mildred Aldrich had accompanied the Spicer-Simsons on a seaside vacation. Although Spicer-Simson had married Margaret Schmidt, also an artist, in 1896, "Mrs. Schmidt" was apparently a friend of the Spicer-Simons, not a relative.]

Dear Spicer · Simson.

I was glad to hear from you & to know that you are all going on well. Miss Aldrich got back here & has been taunting our hot misery with stories of your bare legs – I think she is indiscreet. We know exactly what the ladies wore (or, perhaps, didnt wear) & were invited to guess how they looked. I am gallant and endowed them all with Supernal attractions. But it is hot here, & the brisk foreigner is overrunning the land. Isn't it queer how, when one squats down in a place for a year, one dislikes & dispises all others who want to do the same.

Mildred A has given me a little room at the top of her place and I like it well. Not a soul round. Quiet as a sunny tomb. Myself, a water bottle and a cigarette! Behold me well content; & I have got nicely into work.

Mrs MacKenna still inhabits your appertment, with her companion – They are very well behaved indeed. The younger lady likes going to mass. It is a pardonable dissipation.

You havent looked at that "arty" Article of yours yet? You'd be an ass if you did. Isnt there sea & land & legs & (does there be bosums at a seaside or are they prohibited?) casinoes & sand & shells. You stride lengthily in sandals! Micky said so. Myself I like the feel of sand between my toes. Dry sand is roughly nice to sit on, but it does be full of small quick bugs, all running like blazes to nowhere in particular. Dont like bugs – should be abolished.

The medal didnt turn up yet, but I'm not shouting[.] Everything comes at last except this, & this & that. There are cigarettes; we blow smoke at that & this & this & grow philosophic & bald & virtuous –

Please make two kowtows on my behalf to your wife & give the girls each a kiss. I know they'd hate to have it from me but it will give you an extra chance. I am Mrs Schmidts servant &

Yours very truly
JAMES STEPHENS

To EDWARD MARSH

Paris
[A/3] 30 September [1913]

[Marsh was planning a trip to Paris with his friend James Strachey Barnes (1890–1955). The book by the English poet James Elroy Flecker (1884–1915) was *The Golden Journey to Samarkand* (1913).]

Dear Mr Marsh

Thanks for letting me know you will be in Paris. Could you come to see me here on the 2nd Oct^{r} (You mention that as a possible date.) If Mr Barnes has nothing better to do perhaps he would come with you. I feel equal to boring any number of people. I will be in any time after 8 o clock in the evening. If this does not suit you send another card. That book of Fleckers was very interesting

le meas mór
[“very truly yours”]
JAMES STEPHENS

To THE EDITOR OF THE *IRISH HOMESTEAD*

[Paris]
4 October 1913

[The text is from the *Irish Homestead* for 4 October 1913. The allusion to the previous controversy between Stephens and AE is to the exchange in the *Irish Homestead* for 22 February and 1 March 1913.

“The Song of the Shift” is apparently a reference to the disturbances at the opening night of Synge’s *The Playboy of the Western World* at the Abbey Theatre on 26 January 1907. The disturbance became loudest at Christy’s Act III statement that “It’s Pegeen I’m seeking only, and what’d I care if you brought me a drift of chosen females, standing in their shifts itself, maybe, from this place to the Eastern World” (W. G. Fay, the actor playing Christy, substituted “Mayo girls” for “chosen females”).

James Larkin (1876–1947) was the main organizer of a General Strike in Dublin in August 1913. Larkin was tried by the British for sedition and briefly jailed. The strike collapsed early in 1914.]

THE SIROCCO!

MY DEAR MR. EDITOR,–

I write to you in tribulation of spirit, making public confession of ancient waywardness and ignorance. I dump my apologies on your slippers. I hand up my half of a brick and my three feet of gas-pipe, and, however, you wave me off, I enrol myself your volunteer.

Some time ago when you were ravaging for the blood of Irish poets, I stood between them and your teeth: I ventured my tiny buckler between them and your terrific mace. I bore the shock and have licked my wounds in silence. But now I withdraw my dinted shield and beg you to slaughter the petty crew as horridly as you can.

It is a commonplace that in every country the literary men, even if they do not always take the side of the under-dog, are sufficiently agile in mind to say something on one side or the other, and it is to the poets and writers these populations look for interpretation and heartening. But just as no civic duty has ever been imposed on our citizens so no intellectual obligation has been felt by our writers (these he-widows who are divorced from their surroundings). I have been watching the Irish newspapers lately, searching in them for letters or reports of speeches made by these poets (I must not say men, for one should be biologically exact). I have been looking for rhapsodies from these folk of inspired but private moments, threats even, shrieks, some of these wild, foolish things which in times like these are wiser than wisdom. I have not found any! Not a poet of them all! Not a proser of them all has anything in his mouth but his tongue, which is as dumb as his teeth and nearly as false. An indigestiony lot! Not a word from one of them. Poets, say you! Kill them for me, I beg you. I expect you will discover them squatting in their decent retirements forging The Song Of The Shift and being still mistaken for men. (There is no biological exactitude in Ireland.)

But I have found what is their malady and it is from the same sickness our public and private life is suffering. They are antiquarians! They sit in their decent retirements cutting lies into verse lengths. Lies which are so musty that one wonders how they can exist any longer even as lies. Certainly they are national lies. Every futile negative which man can conceive has been elaborated and patched and painted and hooped and furbellowed into virtues. There is rhapsodical rubbish about our chastity which has produced lunatics; our religiosity which has made of our people slaves and illiterates; our wit, when we know ourselves in secret as the stupidest collection of vertebrates in the universe; our art which would be sniffed at in disdain by the average Bushman; our hospitality which insists that the other man shall pay a drink for the drink we pretended to give him; our noble peasants who are known blacklegs and scabs in every industry; and our bravery! The things that have been bawled and bawled about our bravery! We do not get hot with shame – we have no capacity for that decent vice; but ten thousand of us bolt squealing like rabbits from eighteen wooden cudgels, and five hundred of us go to hospital with cracked skulls and come out again mild as soapy cherubs, beautiful as Sunday-school pictures of happy resignation. Of course, we do not wear our haloes in the street because that would not be truly modest, only for that the nations should see them. In athletics it is well known (among ourselves) that we lead this world and the next; that is why the Irish contingent of athletes at Rome, when they were hooted by a mob of one atheist and a nursemaid, marched prudently to the Vatican in cabs, leaving the Belgian and French contingents to continue their journey on foot. The Irish poets sing these heroics very properly, for their own verses have neither bones nor brains in them. They are just aggregations of vanity and wind without a decent idea or a spark of courage among them. Let them belch to one another in their shy retirements; or let them go to Jericho carrying with them all their baggage of extinct wolf-hounds and spidery round-towers, and their shadowy or shady women and their purity and hospitality, and bunkum and bunkum.

As to our Members of Parliament! We will hold the rest of our hair on with one hand and point with the other to them and to our gifted people saying: These things were chosen by those things. There they are, and the devil wouldn't be bothered with them, but they are what we deserve and we will be proud of them if they cost us our eye-teeth.

At the least, Ulster is promising something. I hope they do march along, that they do mash the heads off the noblest peasantry in the world. They have seventy thousand men who say they want to be moving, but Tipperary and Connemara and Dublin, and the County of Mayo! They are just hogs and dogs and slaves and knaves, poets and fools, every croaking bat of them.

Larkin, also! The entire Press of Ireland has been shouting knave at him so loudly that I divine there must be good in the man. He says, anyhow, that he is discontented, but the poets don't. They sit in their shady retirements, saying: How quite un-nice all this is, and how very unladylike our working men are.

As to our women! Let them be sterilised quickly, for the mothers of Erinn have brought forth rats. – I am, dear Mr. Editor, yours obediently,

JAMES ESSE.

To STEPHEN MacKENNA

Paris

[A/19] [6 October 1913]

[The "three act play" apparently refers to an unpublished work. The Nationalist leader Arthur Griffith (1872–1922) edited *Sinn Fêin,* which had opposed the conditions attached to the gift of an important collection of paintings by Sir Hugh Lane (1874–1915), later Director of the National Gallery of Ireland. MacKenna published a letter defending Lane's bequest in *Sinn Féin* for 27 September 1913.

Hodgson's "The Song of Honour", dedicated to Stephens, was published in the *Saturday Review* for 11 October 1913. Stephens's reply, eventually entitled "A Tune on a Reed", was not accepted by the *Saturday Review*; it was printed in *The Sphere* for 27 December 1913. "Ben Bulban" is an anglicisation of *Beann Gulbain* ("Gulban's Peak"), a mountain near Sligo. The possible variants for *beann* in Irish are *binn, beinn*, or *béinn*; "benn" is a good anglicisation since it retains the double *n* of *beann.* Unfortunately, "bean", which Stephens uses in a letter to Bodkin on 29 October 1913, means "woman" in Irish.

The letter to the *Irish Homestead* was published in the issue for 4 October 1913. AE's volume was *Collected Poems* (1913).]

Dear Stephen

I am glad to see ye have gotten at last to some kind of anchorage. Me! I have written a three act play since ye went away & a poem. Its about the last I want you to give me an information. By the way I saw your letter in Sinn Fein & I wrung my hands for Griffith. The devil's in him, Poor devil & poor him – Here is the pedigree of my poem. Ralph Hodgson has just sent me the proof of a poem which he is dedicating to me in, I think, this weeks Saturday Review. One sings back, of course, &

> Ere the day had dawned I had
> Writ a poem twice as bad –
> And it is dispatched unto
> That same Saturday Review –

Well! he has sung about a hill & I have parried him with a mountain. I want to call my poem Ben Bulban (Sacred Mountain of Irel[d] & all the rest of it) – But, & heres the rub, the dogs will likely read Ben as being short for Benjamin Bulban – Can one say The Ben of Bulban, or Ben*n* Bb[n] [–] Do drop me a card with authorities on it before the Sats send me proofs – tomorrow if you can. I bless you & I commend me to your wife.

JAMES STEPHENS

Do you notice that your address rhymes

39 Kensington Square
London W –
Angleterre

The Capucine and the Little Miller are waggling their hands in yeer direction as near as they can get it. Dublin seems to be in a real hell of a stew. I wrote a letter to The Irish Homestead which AE may have printed in this current issue[.] Did you see AE's collected book of verse. Its mighty! Its most remarkably good! Its the biggest thing!

To THOMAS BODKIN

Paris
[A/3] 7 October 1913

[Stephens had published four poems in *Harper's Monthly Magazine* between May and October 1913. "To hit your da with a loy" is a reference to one of the main actions in Synge's *The Playboy of the Western World.* The room in the Rue Boissonade was provided Stephens as a place of work in by Mildred Aldrich.]

My dear Bodkin

I was real glad to hear from you, and I hope it wont be so long until you write again (that is how I traverse your accusation.) The fact is, as you surmised, & as I warned you, that my bark has drifted into the shallows & I was piled high & dry on those rocks. I am going to be towed off them either this week or next for Harpers have written that they have laden a vessel with specie to the value of £8 & that the wind is fair & the sailors in spirit – A tot of rum all round bos'un & pipe a chanty – So far – Let me have your poems as quickly as you can & believe that I will be interested in them twice, once as a brother in the craft, & once as your friend. I will return them within three days. You mention (inter alia, for your letter was well packed) AE's book. He has sent it to me. I have read it four times and will reread it 24 times – I am amazed at the greatness of this man. It is the most superb book of verse published in these times. It is my intimate conviction that AE is a greater poet than Yeats. There are things in this book, many things, of the most wonderful beauty & ecstasy. It is I think a book unique in the English language. Ireland has reason to be proud of her sons today, but particularly to be proud of AE. I bow me down & wallow before him. Get you that book even if you have to hit your da with a loy for the money. I am writing in my little room in the Rue Boissonade & the book is at home. I would have liked to name some of the poems to read first. I beg you to read them aloud to yourself & tell me what you think of them. I am so glad that you are going more to see him. Believe that he is of all men living the best & kindest, the more you see of him the more you will like him, & I am quite sure that the closer he gets to you the closer he will like you. If you disagree in this & that what does it matter. By the way. I have just written a three act play which I expect will never see a stage, but I would like your opinion on it. I will, if you dont mind send it to you when I get it typed. Ralph Hodgson (of whom I told you) sent me the proof of a poem which he is dedicating to me in the Saturday Review, to appear sometime. One replies, of course, to the courtesy, & in two nights I had made my reply[.] I sent it to the Sat. Rev. people, but the dogs returned it. They wouldnt even take my stuff as a gift. I send you the verses to read. You will notice that I slipped in a little poem which you once liked. Dublin is in the throes! I am real glad you are with the working people. Every generous mind should be. By the way I sent a letter to the Homestead (Signed "James Esse") [–] I wonder have you seen it & could you send me a copy. AE does be always forgetting me. Here are Ladies ought to be published any day.

Your friend
JAMES STEPHENS

To EDWARD MARSH

Paris
[A/3] 7 October 1913

[Stephens sent Marsh a copy of Hodgson's "The Song of Honour". The poem by the English poet Wilfrid Wilson Gibson (1878–1962) in the October 1913 *English Review* was "Solway Ford".]

Dear Mr Marsh

I enclose a poem of Hodgsons which you might like to read. His address is – 3 Paulton Square, Chelsea, S.W. If you care to make his acquaintence you will find him a mighty decent chap. I am sorry your stay in Paris was so short but perhaps I will have an opportunity of seeing you again sometime, somewhere. There is a poem of Gibsons in the current English Review which is very well done.

Sincerely yours
JAMES STEPHENS

To EDWARD MARSH

Paris
[A/3] 14 October 1913

[As printed in the *Saturday Review* for 11 October 1913, Hodgson's "The Song of Honour" began: "I love a hill for in its hands – /If it's a friendly hill – /I can get back to magic lands/Of boyhood when I will." Hodgson later removed the first four stanzas from the poem and published them as "I Love a Hill".]

My dear man

Would you have me look a gift poem in the mouth? You talk to Hodgson about it; you will find that he is easy to talk to. Personally I am not troubled at all by the first verse. The "unfriendly hands" imply the malign as well as the beneficent powers – Mystically, a hill equally with a man can be inimical. Anyhow! As you say these are nothings, the thing is that you liked the stuff & you liked the Bull. I wish you could see his other long poem "To Deck a Woman"[.] I dislike that title; but the poem is astonishing in spite of many inequalities. At times, & through long stretches, the verse is of the most amazing technical excellence, full of passionate lyricism, an extraordinary emotional & impulsive rapture. The Bull I regard as one of the most valuable pieces of imaginative psychology that I have ever read. Hodgson is a better poet, in his sphere, than any of the others. It is still a matter for speculation how wide his realm is & out of what depth & variety of life he writes. I have nothing to guide me in this, & it may be that he is as limited as Francis Thompson (I am not making a comparison) but he is great inside of his present limitations. Whether he is set in life, or whether he can grow in life is the question. I enclose, as you suggest, a mss poem. It is one I wrote two nights ago (I have written ten since you left) & I think it is pleasant. I told you I had written a reply to Hodgsons poem. I sent it to the Sat. Review, but they sent it back. My heavy curve on them

le meas mór
["very truly yours"]
JAMES STEPHENS

To THOMAS BODKIN

14 October 1913
[A/3] Paris

[This letter, a detailed discussion of manuscript versions of some of the poems later included in Bodkin's *May It Please Your Lordships: Reproductions of Modern French Poems* (1917), has required special editorial treatment. As written, the letter has no clear paragraph breaks and is inconsistent in the handling of quotations. For convenience, I have arbitrarily divided the letter into paragraphs and have centred (without quotation marks) all lengthy quotations. The paragraphs in the rest of this headnote follow the paragraphs of the letter.

The first poems mentioned are Henri de Régnier's "The Vase" and Paul Fort's "Meudon" and "That Girl Is Dead".

In Charles-Adolphe Cantacuzène's "Tormentum", "sweetly descried" was eliminated but "warm" retained in the published version. "The Cavern" is by Charles Fuster. The remainder of the paragraph discusses Francis Jammes's "It Will Snow", given here in full:

I recollect last year: 't will snow in a few days.
I recollect my griefs last year beside the blaze.
If asked: What troubles you? I could but say:
nothing, nothing at all: yet go away.

I meditated much last year in my own room,
while out-of-doors the snow fell heavy though the gloom.
It came to naught: and I remember how
I smoked a briar, amber-tipped, as now.

Day in, day out, my chest of oak smells rare.
But I was dull, indeed, for things stood as they were
and did not change a bit. It is a pose
to grow so weary of the things one knows.

Why do we think and talk? Is it not very strange?
Look how our tears, those kisses that we interchange,
though dumb, are understood: and friendly feet
sound sweeter far than words, however sweet.

They have baptised the stars, and have not taken heed,
when dealing out their names, that stars have no such need.
The figures that foreshow, through some far night,
the comet's path, can never force its flight.

And now, where are my griefs, my old griefs of last year?
I scarcely can recall. If one should enter here
within my room and ask: What troubles you?
I'd answer: nothing, leave me quiet: do!

The opening lines of "Ultima" by Émile Despax are: "It rains. I dream: and think I see in the wide square,/Shining afar beneath a tree,/A bust. . . ." "When Coming Back" and "The Only Song" are by Charles Vildrac. "Sad, sad my heart did grow" and "In this unending/Weary land" are the opening lines of two poems by Paul Verlaine, both called "A Little Forgotten Air".

The fourth paragraph discusses "We Are the Wayward" by Henry Spiess, given here in full:

We are the wayward gone astray,
　　in toleration smiled upon,
who, far from off the beaten way,
　　serenely dreaming, wander on.

We are the vague and errant kind,
　　romantic-minded men and light,
for whom the lake, the shade, the wind
　　make melodies at fall of night.

At times, untimely, we are glad
　　at times, unseasonably, grieve;
and ditties mad or dirges sad
　　we, wending by the wayside, weave.

Folk find our fancies singular,
    our fads and freaks ridiculous.
we are the wayward strayed afar,
    and nothing can be made of us.

The second Spiess poem discussed is "I Did Not Seek You", the final two stanzas of which follow:

The lusts of my unbridled strength, arrayed,
    with all the fevered fury of my thought,
storming upon your soul made you afraid.
    I did not seek you, though I hold you caught!

What e'er the morrow bring, what e'er it do
    with us who watching in the darkness wait,
it matters not, alas! But this is true:
    a shadow lies for ever on our fate.

The sixth paragraph deals with Spiess's "A Gay Sonnet" ("My soul is a garden clear"), the second and third stanzas of which follow:

Mirror thine eyes therein,
Thine eyes that deeper glow;
And let its water flow
Upon thy pallid skin.

All the fair sky above,
The azure thou dost love,
With festal chiming rings.

In the published version of Jean Richepin's "The Sunken Path", the opening stanza read as follows:

Beside a sunken path where no tree grows,
A wide, ripe cornfield drowses in the glare;
On the dividing bank a hedgerow goes
Like a green ribbon binding golden hair.

The eighth paragraph mentions "Forgotten Poets" by Ernest Raynaud and "The Rebel" by Charles Baudelaire. *May It Please Your Lordships* contained two odes by Jules Romains ("I leave my house" and "A light is searching me out"). The second and third stanzas of André-Ferdinand Hérold's "The Bitter Flute of Autumn" were as below:

> The flowers slowly wither.
> The birds fly to the plains
> Where, haply, young April
> Hymns her rich strains.
>
> And my soul, pale traveller,
> In avenues alone,
> Sad and chill searches for
> Songs that are flown.

The final paragraph mentions the second line of Spiess's "I Did Not Seek You". The published version retained "me from afar off spied".

It might be added that in *May It Please Your Lordships*, Bodkin acknowledged the assistance of not only Stephens but also AE and George Moore.]

Dear Bodkin

I hope I did not keep your poems too long[.] Herewith I return them. I have read them to some folk here, among others a few English speaking Frenchmen, & they, as well as I, were very pleased. I think some of the poems are astonishing pieces of translation, notably de Regnier's "The Vase"[.] The verse in this is excellent. For so long a poem you have wonderfully controlled it. I wish you could have taken one day off over here so that we might read the poems over a few times together, not that I would have suggested any alterations, but for the mere pleasure of it. The two poems of Paul Fort could not be bettered. They also read more like originals than translations.

"Tormentum" doesnt please me so well. I can see that, if you must show the metric system of the original, it is the devil to translate; but "sweetly descried" in the first stanza and "warm" in the second knock me badly. How you could remedy these I could not suggest, but I think, that it is up to you. "The Cavern" I like also. I think the last verse is wonderfully done[.] "It will Snow" [–] I think the two "or's" could be left out in the 2nd last verse – The line could run without any break "Whether the mighty stars names or numbers need"[.] In the first verse "*Will you leave me bide*" fraps me as too Irish idiomatic. I would suggest a change to something like

> If asked: what *troubles* you? I could but say,
> Ah nothing, nothing; will you go away –

"*Yet* I *was* dull" in the 3rd verse [–] I would change *yet* to *But*

> *But* I was dull *that* things were as they stood [–]

There is a second *because* in the next line. I would even change it to something like this

> But I was dull that things were as they stood
> And *did not* change – *You know* it is a pose.

In the next verse I would say "Is it not strange" leaving out "very" or like this

> Why should we think & talk? It is so strange
> *The* tears, the kisses that we interchange
> *Tho* dumb, *are* understood [–]

The last verse I would leave out the first word "And" & begin

> *Even* now *the* griefs – or –
> And now the griefs that troubled me last year
> Are half forgotten. If one entered here
> *To* ask my trouble I could only say
> Tis nothing – nothing – only go away.

"Ultima" [–] Can there be ["]A *Shining* tree["]? "When coming back" is excellent – I do not believe ["]The Only Song" could be bettered. It is however a singularly rambling, centripedal-footed affair, but that has nothing to do with you[.] "So sad my heart" is very good. The 2nd last verse is wonderful. "In this unending weary land" is fine also –

"We are the wayward ones" &c" [–] Could it begin

We are the wayward ones who stray
Whom toleration smiles upon
Serenely, from the beaten way,
With our dreams we wander on –
At times untimely we glad
At times un grieve
Singing the happy songs or sad?

I cant fit a last line to this verse & in the last verse the case made for these *changeful* strollers is thrown up by the statement that they never change. Now is it you or Spiess who is responsible. I'm afraid that this poem as it stands is too clumsy for printing. I cant better it I confess. Maybe you could hatch it a little more. It is still in embryo.

In Spiess again No II you have done this one very good. The only remark I would make is that the last line of the 2nd last verse bothers me a little. Would it be any good to say

I did not catch you altho' you are caught –

In the last verse – the 2nd line is a little awkward, could it go thus –

To us who in the darkness sit & wait – or –
" " " " " " have to wait.

I think the "*with*" of that line should be "*To*" [–] Thus –

whate'er it do
To us who &c,

& the last line

Whate'er the morning brings, whate'er it do
To us, who watch the darkness round us flow
It matters not alas!, this thing is true
One shadow goes with us where'er we go [–]

This *in the 2nd line* is still awkward – It is only tentative, as are all my suggestions. It is merely that I am interested as a fellow worker & am giving my interest utterence.

In the "My Soul is a garden clear" [–] I think the line "azure as thou dost love" does not emerge quickly as sense. I would suggest

All the fair sky above
(The blue that you always love) or

The sky like a pealing bell,
The blue that you love so well,
With festive chiming rings.

In the 2nd verse – And let *its* waters flow, instead of "the"

You did not include the Richepin poem in your french enclosure – so dont think I lost it – In this poem I think the first two verses are bad; the other five are so well done that these two should be lived with for a longer time – I am sure you could ring several changes on it – Here is an attempt.

A long low path, without a single tree
Runs through the cornfield drowsing in the glare,
A hedge between is twisting timidly
Like a green ribbon amid golden hair [–]

The second verse would put me in a lunatic asylum if I had to do it –

Are you sure that Raynants "Forgotten Poets" is worth translating. You have done it very well, but it seems to me no more than a fancy & flimsy enough at that? The Rebel is all right. So is the Ode of Jules Romains – I like the Bitter Flute of Atm but, as you would say in painting, the tone values are not fully observed, the word weight is different in the 2nd verse from the first – Could you try something like

The flowers slowly wither
The birds fly to the plain
Where young April as richly (or, "perhaps")
Is singing again –

Next verse, *And* my soul – I w[oul]d try *But* my soul for the sake of the antithesis. If it could be done I would revise this verse also. As a trial [–]

And my soul, pale traveller,
In avenues wan
Searches sadly & coldly for
Songs that are gone

And now I have to ask your pardon. It is very likely that none of my remarks are pertinent. They are no more than curious observations such as I might make up in your little room & which we could talk over & dismiss with a laugh; so dont go giving them any extra weight than they are meant to bear. In spite of all these notes your collection is excellent. It is easily better than any of the translations by other folk which you sent me – Oh! In one of the verse there is a line ["]Me from afar off spied.["] Instead of afar off could you not say Me from a distance spied. I may have mentioned this before. I'm an interminable devil God help me. Many thanks for the five – my ship has just come in so I will send back the £5 which at least you want as much as I. You were very decent & thoughtful. I may claim it another time.

Yours
JAMES STEPHENS

Dont tear up your French mss. Sometime you can send it to me, when I can read the poems with your translations & so learn a little more french!

To GEORGE W. RUSSELL

15 October 1913
[A/17] Paris

[Stephens is commenting on AE's *Collected Poems*. The last line of "Parting" is "Because her ["the Mother's heart"] ways are infinite". "Indian Song" and "Children of Lir" are found on pages 157 and 160–1 of AE's volume. The Irish writer Susan Langstaff Mitchell (1866–1926) was an editorial assistant to AE on the *Irish Homestead.* AE had married Violet North in 1898.]

Dear AE,

First to thank you for sending me your book. Then to wonder if you quite realise what a monument you have raised. A monument with a good deal of the Sphinx in it. As yet I have only reached page 115 "A Summer Night"[.] My practice is to read with a pencil and I mark each poem I like, or the parts of a poem. I have marked almost every page & the entire of most of the poems – Honestly I am filled with admiration and wonder at your book. I always knew you for a fine poet, but you are one of those whom we take for granted and read with one eye shut & the other only half open, but these hundred odd pages I have chanted out aloud to myself with pure delight &, for the first time, with real comprehension. You are not only a fine poet, dear man, you are a great poet. One of the greatest that is or has been, & this book will be giving nourishment & wonder hundreds of years hence. I declare to you that I am astonished at the beauty & depth of your songs. Again & again I have said – These are the subjects for poetry – You know how poetry has carried with it an implication of fozzle, graceful fozzle. You are the finest, cleanest singer in English. I can see you smiling kindly & saying this fellow is talking wild, but I'm not. It has always seemed to me that even the best English poets had only secondhand brains. Wordsworth in about a dozen songs is intelligent in the sense I mean – Who else? Beautiful, graceful, dancing [–] all of that[.] But the usage of poetry has never seemed to me to be adequate to its own loftiness. If I were to start naming your songs I would never be done & yet I will suggest a few – Some of these I am going to learn by heart – they will help me perhaps to forget some other toploffical rubbish – The Hermit is marked the whole length[.] I love the Great Breath. Dusk is delicious & wonderful. Dawn & Echoes I have marked for rereading. Frolic – The Place of Rest – I have underlined "The Dawn of Darkness["] in two places. Waiting [&] The Symbol are marked[.] The second verse of "Pity" delighted me as verse [–] The City also. Dana is marked down its full length & is interlined – So the Earth Breath, I have read this poem a dozen times to folk here. It is queer that I had not known Sacrifice was [a] hymn. Almost better than anything else I love The Voice of the Waters – It is a wonderfully beautiful poem. I read & reread it & like it better every time. Krishna also is lined & interlined. Parting I have marked but pardon me, I dont like the last line – it is too easy & makes the poem epigrammatic. The Hour of the King & Heroes are lined all down – the second last verse of Man & Angel made me jump – A Vision of Beauty! I dont know anything so rapturous, so much of ecstacy in later day verse – The Free I have drawn *two* lines down it & one line down Comfort. So Skipping page from page I hastily note the look of the book. Carrowmore is delicious. The entire of the Summer Night is marked. Indian Song & Children of Lir are marked in full & between these poem after poem has lines & passages of sheer delight which I have noted. There is a strange sadness in your songs my dear man. I did not think your poems could have been so sad in spite of their ecstacy. I will love this book –

Yours
JAMES STEPHENS

I will write to Susan Mitchell tomorrow. Commend me to your wife. I wish I could drop in on ye both on Sunday evening –

To THOMAS BODKIN

Paris
[A/3] 29 October 1913

["Bean Bulbain" was later re-titled "A Tune on a Reed". The quotation is from "Hesperus", included in *Songs from the Clay*. The play is the unpublished work mentioned in a letter to Bodkin on 7 October 1913. For his leadership of the General Strike in Dublin, James Larkin was convicted on a count of sedition and sentenced to seven months on 27 October 1913. The presiding judge was Dodgson Madden (1840–1928), Judge of the High Court of Justice, Ireland, from 1892 to 1919 and also Vice-Chancellor of Dublin University from 1895 to 1919. *Toiler: A Monthly Review of International Syndicalism* was published in Kansas City, Missouri, from 1913 to 1915.]

My dear Bodkin

Thanks for your letter – As to the £5 I will take your advice & hold it for another month at least. You have taken my remarks on your poems in the very nicest spirit. The fact is, that I am almost as anxious as you are that they should be thoroughly good. They are that; all that is wanted is a little brooding over them. Will you, when you have considered my notes, send them to me again in their ultimate form so that if there are any "and's or buts", or such like poetical insecta to be slaughtered we can go into consulation on the matter

I have practically rewritten the poem Bean Bulbain (which I sent you) and think it is all right now. I have also written about a dozen others & some of these are good. I have enough stuff now to make a very pretty book. I can tell you that I sit on these poems like the most motherly of hens. Practically all day I am singing them over & over. The mss is only out of my hand to be in my pocket. A regular tornado of poetry has overtaken me – Praise to the Gods! and I do not believe I have touched the mother lode yet (I like mixing my metaphors, that is why I do it)[.] Really I have the feeling that there is a thundering poem thundering to get out of me. I am seeking diligently for the door to let it out. Do you remember the verses on Evening in which there occurs the lines

> The hushed & reverent sky
> Her diadem of stars has lifted high.

That poem, after a very sickly, almost rickety childhood has stumbled at last to something like a real maturity. I have medicined & surgeoned it so carefully that it is now, I think, an adequate poem – The poem which is pushing for existence should be called, I imagine, "A Song of the Earth". I have received intimations of it already. Pray heaven it survives the birth pangs. As to the play – I dont think I will bother to type it. Just now it really seems to be no good at all. A Strindbergian cleverality & nothing more – Certainly it is not, & will never be marketable. The Subject is unpleasant & the treatment is no more than So So. I hope you succeeded in getting off your two striker men in despite of that learned but unjust Judge. I have just seen that he has sentenced Larkin to 7 months imprisonment – That sticks deeply in my gizzard. I think (on the charge) that it is flagrant, base injustice. It howls in my ears for vengeance. I am distant from all the facts & have every opportunity to make an ass of myself. Tell me your opinion on the matter. MacKenna sent me a sheet called "The Toiler". It is the comicalist of papers, but the trail of the Capitalist is over it all. Everything, however, in these latter times, seems to me to be good for Ireland. There is a physical, there will be a mental stir, and next year we start from scratch. The pot must be kept boiling or the soup will not be good. Voila! We live in good times

Your friend
JAMES STEPHENS

To THOMAS BODKIN

Paris
[A/3] [*ca.* 10] November 1913

[For her birthday on 16 November, Stephens was planning to give Mildred Aldrich either *Cuchulain of Muirthemne* (1902) or *Gods and Fighting Men* (1904), both by Lady Gregory. Yeats had written on 18 October 1913 to tell Stephens that *The Crock of Gold* had been awarded the Polignac Prize; the award was presented in London on 28 November 1913. Stephens's next book of poems was *Songs from the Clay* (1915); the "big poem" was the "Song of the Earth" mentioned in a letter to Bodkin on 29 October 1913. Sarah Henrietta Purser (1848–1943) was an Irish portrait painter. "Le Printemps" (1873) of Jean François Millet (1814–75) is in the Louvre.]

Dear Bodkin

I want you to do me a favour: that is to send me, as early as you can manage it, a copy of either "Gods & Fighting Men" or "Cuchulain" (Lady Gregory) whichever is easiest to get. Miss Aldrich, whom you met, intends to enjoy a birthday next week & I want to give her something. I have just had a piece of news which will please you. Yeats wrote me that the Polignac prize of £100 is to be given to me at the end of this month for the Crock of Gold. The notification is not official & I have been asked to keep the matter secret, so dont like a dear man say anything about it. I will be able to repay you the fiver & for this book in about a fortnight. When you write be sure to let me know how the translations fare & whether you have added anything to them. My next book of verse shows promise already of being a good one, but that big poem I wrote you of died at birth.

Yours
JAMES STEPHENS

Thanks for the papers which arrived this morning. I went to the

Louvre yesterday with Miss Purser & had a perfectly beautiful time. We talked a good deal of you. I still adore Le Printemps of Millet –

To CLEMENT SHORTER

Paris

[A/3] 14 November 1913

[Clement Shorter (1857–1926) founded *The Sphere* (London) in 1900 and edited it until his death. Shorter had offered £10 10s. for a short story and £2 2s. for a poem; Stephens published poems and articles in *The Sphere* but not short stories. The notice which Stephens mentions was published in the *Literary World* (London) for 6 November 1913. *Here Are Ladies* was reviewed in the issue for 4 December 1913, Shorter's *George Borrow and His Circle* (1913) in the issue for 1 January 1914.]

Dear Mr Shorter

Thanks very much for your letter. I will certainly let you have the next short story I write at the price you name – I would not care to accept £2/2/ for a poem.

I recollect very well meeting you in Mr Roberts house. Indeed, I was invited especially to meet you, but George Russell monopolized your conversation so entirely that the rest of us got a poor "show". I saw a preliminery notice in the Literary World today wherein they threaten to review your book & mine in their next issue.

Yours very truly
JAMES STEPHENS

To STEPHEN MacKENNA

Paris

[A/19] 14 November 1913 [& August 1930]

[This letter is a fragment and has the last sentence and a half cancelled. It is likely that in 1930 Stephens decided to remove his remarks about the rise of the Irish language.

"Very lengthy time" and "veer and break and yaw" occur at the end of Part II of "A Tune on a Reed", as printed in *The Sphere* for 27 December 1913. "No one sings as well as me" was not included in the published text. In *Songs from the Clay*, stanzas 2 to 5 of "A Tune on a Reed" were printed as a separate poem entitled "A

Reply"; Stephens is thinking in 1930 of that latter text. He quotes the opening line and slightly misquotes most of the second stanza of the first section. "And tell it to some other mother/Than the one that walloped me" is from "The Nodding Stars", published in the *Saturday Review* for 17 January 1914 and included in *Songs from the Clay.* Hodgson's "Song of Honour" was published not in the *Spectator* but in the *Saturday Review* for 11 October 1913.

William Martin Murphy (1844–1919), Chairman of the Dublin United Tramways Company, was the leader of the opposition to the General Strike organized by James Larkin in August 1913. In 1905 Murphy had founded the *Irish Independent* to combat the influence of the *Freeman's Journal*, which was controlled by the Nationalists. However, the kind of "clerical remarks" alluded to in the 1930 comments may be illustrated by the report in the *Freeman's Journal* for 10 November 1913 of a sermon by the Rev. J. C. O'Flynn: "The country is up in arms against the means and leaders of the workers. Many a tale of sadness I could tell as the result of strikes in this very city of ours. They introduce the blackleg foreigner, they increase the poor, fill full the jails, workhouses, and asylums, dishearten the good, and completely paralyse the National cause. . . . Shake off the Sassenach [for *Sasanach*, "Englishman"]! First enlist the sympathy of the priest." In "Come off That Fence!", published in the *Irish Worker* (edited by Larkin) for 13 December 1913, Stephens wrote that "In Ireland today the church is a lie. The attitude of the clergy throughout this dispute has been cynical and disgusting to the last degree. . . . If they do not come off the fence and do their duty the clergy must be added to the number of those you have to fight."

Here Are Ladies had been published in October 1913. The passage from Shelley's "Ode to the West Wind" is correctly "O, Wind,/If Winter comes, can Spring be far behind?"]

Dear Stephen

I would have written to you sooner, but that I was in the extreme centre of an article for the Irish Worker & a cold in the head. & other horrid but necessary or unavoidable things. All your remarks about my verses are true, Still I could make a case for those seeming lapses. "Very lengthy time", "Veer and yaw" [–] Those, if you heave your mind back, occurred in the 2nd stanza of the poem beginning:

"You have sent your verse to me"

The opening you see is conversational, even casual, & the entire three verses of that stanza carry the same tone. In no other verse of the poem afterwards, which is the poem proper, is there any carelessness of language until the end where the language again becomes casual. I wonder will you have noticed this. In the end I quite agree that the line – "No one sings so well as me" is indecent; but my idea was to mitigate the egotism of the childish statement by simple, childish bad grammar. But you are certainly right & I will, with just a trifle of regret, change the thing. I can do it very easily, but I can no longer hide behind that tree when you remind me that Yeats is still alive.

As to my book "Here Are Ladies" [–] I took it up yesterday & gallopped through a bit of it – upon my soul, its quite good! I can hold up my head again. I have been sneaking round in the furtivest manner feeling that the passing stranger might sneer at me "Are you the abortion that wrote the abortion". I had a most exhausting hunt all yesterday & today through my published & unpublished poems for a line which I could not find. Bodkin quoted it to me in a letter the other day. It is

"O Wind!
When winter comes can spring be far behind"?

I simply could not find that line anywhere among my stuff, but tonight while peeping through Shelley, I found that it is the last line of his Ode to the West Wind. I could have sworn I wrote it! But wasnt it tactless & unkind of Bodkin to throw another poet into my teeth? He'll never make a painter. Russell has just written me affirming that he is indeed surrounded by disasters and alarums. [The rest of the letter proper is cancelled.] It seems to me that out of the whole tangle of Irish affairs one definite good will result: that is, the cause of the Irish language will be pushed forward with an emphasis such as it has never known before. I prophesy that, before one year is gone, every village & hamlet in Ireland will be the centre of an Irish speaking propaganda & this quite apart from

. . . .

[The following are Stephens's 1930 comments:]

The article for the Irish worker had afterwards an history. It was entitled "Get off that Fence", and was addressed to the Irish clergy. At this time an agitation still referred to as the "Great Strike["], under James Larkin, was paralysing Dublin. Feeling in the city, and, by extension, in the whole country was extraordinarily high. The animation on both sides was actually murderous and some clerical remarks quoted in the Freemans Journal, the journal of Mr Murphy against whom the strike was directed[,] goody-goody, temporazing ineptitudes (such as harassed clergymen in difficult times must perhaps use) annoyed me. My article was an ill-timed invitation to the Irish clergy to "get off that fence", and it created a stir. Some good clergymen, apparently as young as I was, were as annoyed with my article as I was with what I considered the Church's backing and filling. I was surprised in a weeks time to find that I was dubbed "Anti-Christ" in some Irish papers, and was even more surprised, a few years later, to find that the reason giving for the murder of a man on the steps of the Pro-Cathedral (Dublin's principal Catholic house of worship) was that he was "known" to be the author of this article, which was nevertheless signed by me.

The poem referred to beginning

"You have sent your verse to me"

is not as good as I could have wished it to me, nor as good as the circumstances that fathered it should have warranted. Ralph Hodgson had written his famous Song of Honour. He had printed it in the Spectator, and forwarded me a copy. On opening the paper I was surprised to find that the poem was dedicated to me. I was even alarmed, for it then seemed to me that so notable a dedication demanded a reply in kind. To reply in kind when so wonderful a poem as the Song of Honour is in question is not easy. Of course I knew that it could not be done; but since the great compliment was public I thought that my acknowledgment of it must be public too, and, worse, must be immediate. By immediate I mean should be in time for the next issue of the Spectator. Such coquetteries are of course very natural in a young writer: and I can recall the tensing of the spirit, and the (as it were) inflating of one's self with life that such an effort demanded. I had not written any verse for a considerable time: indeed I had arranged with myself that perhaps I should not write any more. Not really in the sense that I should be unable so much as in the sense that I did not then & might not thereafter want to. The poem began (I quote from memory:

Verse has fled from me so long
I can scarce begin to sing:
I who had a hoard of song
Now can scarce find anything
Worth the singing

The note to MacKenna is on some criticism he made of this poem, and I think properly explains a usage that I have often made of careless and, at times, ungrammatical phrases. So, in an earlier poem, I used the phrase

And tell it to some other mother
Than the one that walloped me.

The word "walloped" was not to the liking of several good critics; but I needed just that word to relieve, humoursly, an egoism which the fantastic poem gave an impression of, and which egoism would be intolerable (as all egoism is) without some such humourous or brisk or human handling. I dont quite think that Milton, by this, or some other means, should have apologised for daring to write the Paradise lost; but he could have done so, and have harmed not even himself, born of woman, fated to die, and doomed to know more of theology than of religion, and of the earthly than of the heavenly estate. It is not easy, especially for a poet, to be modest, but it should be more difficult to be as immodest as many poets have contrived to be.

To THOMAS BODKIN

Paris

[A/3] 15 November 1913

[The article was "Come off That Fence!" The "new long novel" became *The Demi-Gods* (1914), which was dedicated to Bodkin.]

Dear Bodkin

That was a fine letter – I dont care how long you make them. The longer the better for me – I plump entirely for Larkin. I wish you would see him (I never have) not in his public & audacious moments. Then he has to be a demagogue. Russell sees a good deal of him and Houston. Ask Houston when he & Russell & Larkin will be meeting together at Houstons house & observe Larkin there for me. I would like to have your closer opinion of him. I have just sent an Article to the Irish Worker. It is entirely Anti-Cleric. You will have to pardon a great deal in your friend, but, & particularly in these days, one has got to be intellectually honest. I am enclosing a little batch of poems [–] Many of them are not in their final state. Perhaps you will like some of them. Run them back as early as you can, as I am still brooding very contentedly on them. Now as to your own poems. I want to suggest that, say, every four days you should send me two of them (I want to see them again, but it is difficult to look at them minutely when they are in bulk[)]. If you will send me them I will return each couple, within three days of their receipt, with my further notes. I want them to be as good as poems can possibly be before they are published & they are now so good that it is not worth while delaying publication much longer. You are very good about my [Here Are] Ladies. I will start a new long novel almost immediately

Always your friend
JAMES STEPHENS

To THE EDITOR OF *THE NEW AGE*

[Paris]
20 November 1913

[The text is from *The New Age* for 20 November 1913. Stephens is criticizing "Arjuna-Kartavirya" by "Beatrice Hastings" (E. A. H. Thomson), printed in *The New Age* for 13 November 1913. Felicia Dorothea Hemans (1793–1835) was an English poet. The English writer Joseph Hilaire Pierre Belloc (1870–1953) had been publishing a series of articles in *The New Age* on the "National Guild System". "R.H.C." was a set of initials used by A. R. Orage. Holbrook Jackson (1874–1948) was an English critic. Stephens doubtless never had met the American painter James McNeill Whistler (1834–1903). "A.E.R." was A. E. Randall, who wrote the "Views and Reviews" column in *The New Age* and also dramatic criticism under the pseudonym "John Francis Hope".]

ENTER MR. JAMES STEPHENS

Sir,–

As one who (but for his fear of cliché) might have signed himself "Constant Reader", I feel obliged to protest against the inclusion of Mrs. Beatrice Hastings' verses in THE NEW AGE. I have to ask you if the verses entitled "Arjuna-Kartavirya", and which you purport to be a rendering from the Mahàbhàrata, printed in your last issue, are not the worst verses which have ever appeared in any journal. THE NEW AGE has frequently published good verse – I will assert that against any man – and the fact that the good verse was invariably printed within quotation marks does not matter in the least, but no reputation for badness quite justifies this amazing debility. As one who has some small practice in the art of poetry, and who has been enthusiastically praised by THE NEW AGE (Please do not put a footnote to this), I would point out that long poems should never appear in four-line stanzas – this form makes them appear even skimpier than they really are; length without breadth is a crime against harmony. Philosophical poems should never appear in this form. (Please do not quote me the exceptions to this rule. I know them.)

In vindication of my plea that this is the worst poem ever written, I implore you to insert the following verses taken from it. Let nobody say I made them up myself, they are the truly original inspiration of Mrs. Hastings:

> Give me in war a thousand arms,
> Among my troops high deeds to do.

I almost wrote, high doods to dee, I am sure it ought to be that way –

> But when I rest 'mid homely charms,
> Grant me, O sage, my usual two.

Here is another verse which I wish someone would set to music –

> Here me, O invisible seer,
> Counter thy thesis of some old Purana!
> Thou sayest – the Brahman rules the Kshatriya:
> I say – the Kshatriya rules the Bràhmana.

The following is a highly superior verse truly –

> What kind of earthly thing is a Bràhmana –
> This highly superior ornament?
> Doth he resemble the wind-god, Pavana?
> Or is he like Water, Sun, Fire, or the Firmament?

It would be a pity to let these verses go without giving your readers an opportunity of reading them a second time. (Did I say that the word "cliché" is not appearing as frequently in THE NEW AGE as heretofore – I meant to.) It might be interesting if Mrs. Hastings' poem were criticized by printing it side by side with examples from the poetry of Shakespeare and Mrs. Hemans. You have precedent for this course. (I notice, with regret, that the words "split-infinitive" have not appeared in THE NEW AGE for some weeks past. I put it to you, as an editor, that serial matter should not be discontinued without warning to your readers.) I do not say that all Mrs. Hastings' work is equally bad. The high level of the ridiculous to which she has attained in this poem could not be sustained by any but a comic genius, and I will admit that many of her poems have been quite chic. By the way, in "Military Notes" of the same issue, "Romney" begins with this line – "The British Army is officered by the British upper classes." The dear man is encyclopedic: information such as this should be watered a little before being tapped. Mr. Belloc opens his sixth article thus – "So far I have explored (at great tedium to the reader and not a little to myself)." Surely he went down the Well and found Truth there. Do ask him not to write anything more about guilds. Why fatigue himself and us at the one moment? The opening lines of "R.H.C.'s" "Readers and Writers" are surely models of ineptitude.

"Mr. Holbrook Jackson is right to resent the description of his book." Loud cheers from Mr. Holbrook Jackson.

"Melancholy in Mr. Kennedy's opinion."

"Having been myself a student of Pater." Hush!

"The little dispute between Reuter's and the Press." Mamma's boy will be dood.

"On the subject of Mr. Rabindranath Tagore." This is known as the ex-cathedra turn – it is so impressive.

"Apropos of my recent note on Shakespeare's 'Othello', I learn via a German magazine." What! what! what! as my old friend Whistler used to say.

"Such a deal of 'brilliance' is common in these days." I call that envy, and envy is a sin.

"A new volume in the World's Classics."

"Was it right, I have been asked."

"Another objection has been raised to these Notes!" Blasphemy.

"I will add to this the remark made of Stendhal." Without money and without price.

"A story of Wagner has just appeared in the 'Journal de Bruxelles'."

But this man is a very hot-bed of culture: you could grow mushrooms on him. I suggest you could fill your "Current Cant" page with greater ease from "R.H.C.'s" opening paragraphs than by the extended and troublesome method you now use.

I hold strongly that the person who bowdlerises a Sacred Book should be strangled and stuffed and stuck in a wax-works.

I had intended to say something about "A.E.R." It was very unpleasant, but I have forgotten it.

JAMES STEPHENS.

To THE EDITOR OF *THE NEW AGE*

[Paris]
27 November 1913

[The text is from *The New Age* for 27 November 1913. "Beatrice Hastings" (E. A. H. Thomson) had commented on "Enter Mr. James Stephens" directly below its printing in *The New Age* for 20 November 1913. Part of her reply ran as follows: "Mr. Stephens was clearly born to be ridiculous. Another man, to whom buffoonery was not native, might have been shocked into respectable self-criticism after such a public guy as was made of Mr. Stephens when 'Rhythm' strung all the names of the major poets to make a garland for his feet."

"R.H.C." (A. R. Orage) also commented on Stephens's letter in his "Readers and Writers" column in *The New Age* for 20 November 1913: "If Mr. Stephens was not being run for a lion of English literature I would have nothing to say against him – I do not make war on accepted rabbits. . . . Mr. James Stephens has a philosophy.

And what do you think it is? Let Mr. Stephens reply: 'This is what I think that a man should obey the law with his body and always disobey it with his mind.' Concerning this I might say a great deal and nothing complimentary. I will content myself with Nietzsche's observation that it is an admirable doctrine for a hopeless slave. . . . What exactly Blake meant by his myths I do not care rationally in the very least." The passage which Orage cites is a slight misquotation from *The Crock of Gold.*]

RE-ENTER MR. JAMES STEPHENS

Sir,–

It is so pleasant to be able to pour my varied woes into your sympathetic ear.

I do not mind when Mrs. Hastings calls me a ridiculous, a buffoonery, a guy, a skittish and an aesthetically disreputable – it is the penalty of greatness; but I protest when she charges me with wearing garlands on my feet. This is a cruel, a malicious invention, for everybody knows I wear them on my tall hat.

But I have been grievously disappointed by Mrs. Hastings' reply to my last letter: she must be off her feed. She seeks to justify her villainous poem by stating that it is just as bad in the original, and that she only slung it into four-line stanzas because it takes that form in the Sanskrit, or is it Italian? (Ask "R.H.C." what is the Mahábhárata's native tongue. He reads all languages with his eyes shut, and he talks them all with his mouth shut. God bless him before he bursts of culture, but not after!) How am I to expect that Mrs. Hastings will respect my genius when she will not respect that of the English language? and, although the very basis of trades unionism is to stick by one's class, she is not content to be criticised comparatively with Mrs. Hemans! I mourn for a bright spirit gone under.

"R.H.C." rose gallantly, if obliquely, to my letter. He said I was – an accepted rabbit running for a lion – and he properly refused to give battle to such a portent. I am sure he found the words "accepted rabbit" in foreign tongues; he is such an original researcher! Later, in a frenzy of culture, he quoted that Nietzsche had said I was a hopeless slave. Bad, bad man! Nietzsche never spoke of me except in terms of affection. Alas! "R.H.C." is a "quoter", and this is a malady from which one never recovers. He is of those who run about the world with another man's verb in his mouth. He says he "doesn't care in the very least what Blake meant by his myths". He is able to read Blake with his mind shut. Prodigious Man! Do give him my love, and ask him is he able to write all the languages of Europe and Asia with his hands tied behind his back?

JAMES STEPHENS.

To HAROLD MONRO

Paris
9 December 1913

[A/36]

[Monro, now editor of *Poetry and Drama*, had rejected "Beann Bulbain" ("A Tune on a Reed").]

Dear Monro

You have certainly succeeded in astonishing me. You must not take it that I agree in your judgment, for I consider Beann Bulbain one of the best poems I have ever written.

Yours very truly
JAMES STEPHENS

To THOMAS BODKIN

Paris
9 December 1913

[A/3]

[Stephens had gone to London to receive the Polignac Prize. "Miss Kirwin" (unidentified) was apparently a friend of MacKenna, who lived in Donnybrook; Sophie Solomons was a sister of Estella Solomons; Joseph Maunsell Hone (1882–1959) was an Irish literary historian.

"Whereas" is the prefatory poem in Bodkin's *May it Please Your Lordships*. The published text read as follows:

A Wanderer was set upon a road,
A long, grey road and dusty; yet he went
Forward along that road and was content.

For, as he strode unswerving on his way,
On either side him lay
Green fields and song
Helping his heart along.

So, I upon the high way of the Law
Have walked a little way with ease,
Aided thereto by these,
That are the songs I heard, the fields I saw.

Bodkin published an unsigned review of *Here Are Ladies* in the *Irish Times* for 21 November 1913; he wrote that "Nothing of all the items that comprise this book is makeshift or unworthy". The American publisher was W. T. H. Howe. As is Kilmashogue, Tibradden is a mountain to the south of Dublin.]

My dear Bodkin

Your letter was awaiting me when I got back from London crowned with a cheque for £100. Herewith I enclose you with my thanks a note for £5 and a P/O for 7/- for the book you so kindly sent me. Tomorrow I will run you along a few french papers as usual. I saw MacKenna in London, but the poor man seems much worse than when he was in Paris. His head, I fear, will never let his body get well. He is too sensitively imaginative and even if there were no horrors to be seen anywhere he would create them for himself & hatch them into monsters. I rather despair of him. There were some other Irish folk with him – Miss Kirwin of Donnybrook, Sophie Solomons, Mr & Mrs Joe Hone & George Roberts. I expect there is, besides these, a solid battalion of others whom the Lord spared me but will not relieve MacKenna of – He will hold the Board you know when visitors are present & he is not fit to do it[.] For at least 6 months Stephen should hold converse with the West Wind and a dog but not with mortal men & women –

Now about your verses – The three stanzas called Whereas are really good. They will make a beautiful prelude to your collection & they add the needed personal touch which shows what manner of man has made the collection. The poem is quite equal to any in your list & is superior to a good many of them. If I had been writing it I might have written the last verse differently – something like this –

So I, upon the highway of the law,
Have walked a while in ease
Aided by these
The songs I heard, the fields I saw

Of course your "ease" was "comparative" but verse admits only of superlatives

In the 2nd verse I think I would say

> Green fields and song
> Helping his heart along

[this paragraph up to here is cancelled with a single line] but your own words are excellent –

If it could be managed I would like the last line of the 1st verse changed to – perhaps:

> Travelled that road in peace & found it *good*?

Between "feet" and "sweet" there is a gulf fixed which can not be bridged, even by a poet. But you can change it in many ways without loosing a scrap of your intention. You can give it the antique austere air

> . . . . Nathless he
> Travelled that road in all security

Or if, as a citizen of the 20th Centuary, you hate antiquity & will be modern tho' the gods weep

> . . yet he went
> Along that road in peace & good content –

No! I fear I am inflexibly antique tonight. Think over it & let me hear, for I have come indoors without my brains.

Your review in the I. Times was excellent. No better has appeared that I have seen.

> (Travelled that road without perplexity)

In the 2nd verse I would say

> On either side *there* lay

A man, a publishing man has written me from America to know can I do him an Irish hero book & a book of Irish fairies written so simply that they can be read at free lunch counters. He has been writing to me for some months now and he assures me of both fame & fortune if I do the deed. Do you know anything about Irish fairies or do you know of any dusty volume which has collected them. The same man wants me to send him some photographs to ornament a "brochure" which he is to publish at Christmas. In this brochure he has compressed me into tabloids to be taken immediately after eating. Would it be possible to get a few picture post cards, one say of Stephens Green, Grafton Street & Phoenix Park re Charwoman's Daughter and one or two of Tirbradden or Kilmasheogue for the Crock of Gold. If you could send me these I would be mightily obliged & will direct him to send you his "brochure" whatever the devil that is & however you may be loath to accept it. AE & Magee have both written to me, & Miss Purser sent me a most delightful epistle which I dare not answer until I find my brains again. Is there a chance of your rushing to Paris at Xmas? Believe that I would welcome it. Write as soon as you can & as long a letter as you can manage.

Is mise
["I remain"]
JAMES STEPHENS

Miserably I put this letter by & then could not find it again. I turned the place up side down & le voila. I'm maybe in time to wish you a happy Christmas[.] Herewith is a cheque with many thanks – Write me as soon as you can & send more poems along.

To CLEMENT SHORTER

Paris
[A/3] [9–10] December 1913

[Stephens submitted "A Tune on a Reed" for publication in *The Sphere.* Stephens did not publish any prose in *The Sphere* until an article on Charlotte Brontë in the issue for 22 April 1916.]

Dear Mr Shorter
I enclose a poem which is, I think, the best I have written for a

long time. I will be very glad to know if you can use it. Shortly I hope to be able to let you have some prose matter

Sincerely yours
JAMES STEPHENS

To CLEMENT SHORTER

Paris
[A/3] 12 December 1913

[On 11 December 1913, Shorter accepted "A Tune on a Reed" for *The Sphere.* He wrote to Stephens that he would "pay 5 guineas as it is so long".]

Dear Mr Shorter.

Thanks for your letter –

Herewith I return the corrected proof of my poem.

You will see that it is dedicated to Mr Ralph Hodgson, &, unfortunately, I sent him the original ms some little time ago.

In future I will take care to keep these mss for you.

I fear I will not be back in Dublin until the spring. Perhaps I will be able to see you then. Or, maybe, you will think of paying a visit to Paris!

I am, dear Mr Shorter:

Yours very truly
JAMES STEPHENS

To EDWARD MARSH

Paris
[A/3] 12 December 1913

[Caxton Hall in London was the site of the award ceremony for the Polignac Prize. "A Tune on a Reed" was published in *The Sphere* for 27 December 1913. Wilfrid Wilson Gibson was married in Dublin in December 1913. In *Georgian Poetry: 1913–1915*, Marsh included Hodgson's "The Bull" and "The Song of Honour" but not "To Deck a Woman".]

My dear Marsh

That's good news. I will be very glad to see you and Barnes again and will keep any appointment you care to make. I did not know you were in the Caxton Hall. That was a horrid ordeal, and if Yeats had not written to me I would not have gone near the place for a thousand pounds, let alone £100. Yeats did not know my address, and, at the time, I could not remember yours or I would have looked you up.

By the way, isnt Harold Monro a friend of yours? My heavy curse on him. He has just returned me the best poem I've ever written with the statement that it isnt up to his standard. Clement Shorter has accepted it, however, for the Sphere, & he will give me real gold for it. Do keep an eye on next week's Sphere & tell me do you agree with Monro's judgment. If you dont I beg you to murder the man for me and you can keep all the profits from his carcass for yourself –

You liked my [Here Are] Ladies! I wrote every line of it with care, my next book will be better. I am sorry about the poem I sent you – tear it up & I'll give you another when you come over

I am interested about Gibson and wonder do I know the lady. He's a good chap & I hope he'll get a good wife. My own remembrance is that there's a terrible lot of little devils over there. If livliness is a virtue they are not up to the chin in it –

You've read Hodgson's "To Deck a Woman" – Your remarks are quite true; as a whole it is not nearly as good as the Bull or Song of Honour, but in some parts it soars & flashes far beyond the best of either of these poems. I sometimes am afflicted with the idea that poetry is all damn rot (except when its been written by me) [–] look at Monro! Imagine that chap turning me down and I hitting him with masterpieces. Do kill him. Kill him bloodily & painfully (Barnes will help you) [–] Do agonizing things to him: Read him his own poetry as long as you can stand it & then choke him with his own book. Make him eat his words while Barnes holds him

Yours sincerely
JAMES STEPHENS

To ERNEST A. BOYD

Paris

[A/12] 12 December 1913

[Boyd had published articles on Bernard Shaw in the August 1913 *Forum* and on W. K. Magee in the November 1913 *North American Review.* Boyd's apparent hopes for a position with the Irish

Agricultural Organisation Society were not fulfilled. In the November 1913 *Irish Review*, Seumas O'Sullivan printed two poems from "The Praise of Angus". Stephens began to publish in *Sinn Féin* on 26 April 1907.]

Dear Boyd

Thanks for writing.

I am real glad you are getting into the American papers. I am sure you will make good there without any great labour. I did not know that R.H.C. was Orage, but I do know that I could lick the whole New Age Staff too easily to bother any more with them. I hope the I.A.O.S man will hop out of that job & leave the place free for you. There's going to be good times over there next year and I go back in the Spring. Have you seen AE's collected book of verse (Macmillan 6/-) [–] Its mighty. He is a great poet, perhaps the greatest living today, and he's a great man to boot. You should have that book. I saw the O'Sullivan poems in the I. Review – frankly I thought they were no good – its only playing at poetry but he is always skilful and pleasant – Here Are Ladies isnt any good either. Magee is a fine chap. He has just written me sounding his trumpets in praise of Here Are Ladies. I infer from that, that he is not well & I pray for his recovery.

As to your questions – What Irish writer influenced me most? None of 'em singly but I did soak myself to the scalp & beyond in the older Irish writers. The newer school Russell, Yeats, Colum, O Grady &c were entirely unknown to me when I began to write[.]

Part of your question runs thus – "Had *you* any definite influence on *you* when *you* started to write?" Young man! You've been hitting cocktails –

My first published efforts? – For nearly 2 years everything I wrote, poems, essays, stories, were printed in Sinn Fein. These would have been in 1909. So I am only 4 years at the trade, say 5 not more.

I am in great haste or I would send you a better letter, but I wont write to you unless you write to me!

le meas mór
["Very truly yours"]
JAMES STEPHENS

To HENRY McBRIDE

Paris
[A/42] 21 December 1913

[Henry McBride (1867–1962) was an American art critic, currently associated with the *New York Sun*. The "dedication" apparently refers to an inscription, most likely in a copy of *Five New Poems* (1913). "Mick" is Mildred Aldrich. "Cornillac" is probably an error for the French artist Pierre-Emile Cornillier (1862–?).]

My dear Henry

That dedication was affectionate & consolatory. Anyhow, you have no right to look a gift dedication in the mouth. Your hope that my book wont be successful is a villanous hope. I hope your hope will get knocked out. If I'm not successful I'll borrow money off you & get a living that way. Man jewel! I've had rottener times than you've ever dreamt of in nightmares. Did you see I got the Polignac Prize for the Crock of Gold. They gave me £100. Now gnash your teeth. If you dont unhope that hope I'll ask Mick to put arsenic in your tea & tea in your cocktails.

Mick introduced me to a hell of a decent chap. His name is Cornillac, I think, but you pronounce it Peter. He paints & has a nice American wife. I'm sure you know him. His paintings interested me & his dinner was a masterpiece. Really he is an excellent *artist* with a mind that is open to other than the soft murmur of the dealers. Every artist, as you know, tries to paint God no matter what else he is painting at the time, and that is what I always look for in a picture. Damn those realists as they call themselves – there's no reality but God in Art anyhow but most painters never heard of him. I was at the Salon D'Automn the other day. A barbarous lot! Miles & miles of rubbish. You did not think too badly of my "Ladies"[–] The book has some qualities here & there but I do not believe that this particular class of work is my metier. I have written some good poems since you left [–] When do you come back? All good greetings. I will turn the next cocktail I get upwards in your honour

Is mise le meas mór
["I am very truly yours"]
JAMES STEPHENS

To PADRAIC COLUM

[A/3] Paris
26 December 1913

[Colum sent Stephens a copy of his edition of *Broad-Sheet Ballads* (1913). Colum had married the critic Mary Catherine Maguire (1887–1957) in 1912.]

Dear Colum

It was good of you to send me your book of ballads. I have already sung & read joints of it to folk here from An T'Oilean Ur [for *An t-Oilań Ór*, "The Fresh Island", i.e. America.] I hope you are full of work: Me! The thought of it gives me fits & I look at a pen as other people look at a bomb. For my sins tho' I've got to start a book soon. Dam! No sooner is one finished than another has to be commenced. Are there any poems in your neighb'hood. I got a dozen or so in this foreign land & am as astonished as if I'd had twins all by myself. Tell your wife I hope she's in the best of form & that I am wishing herself & yourself the best of new years

Is mise
do c[h]ara
["I am/your friend"]
JAMES STEPHENS

To THOMAS BODKIN

[A/3] Paris
26 December 1913

[Edmund Swayne was the lawyer for whom Bodkin worked. *Songs from the Clay* was not published until March 1915; Bodkin's *May It Please Your Lordships* did not appear until 1917. The other books mentioned are *Broad-Sheet Ballads* by Padraic Colum and *Lyrical Poems* (1913) by Thomas MacDonagh.]

My dear Bodkin

Heres to wish you the best of new years & all Swain'es business. As soon as you've a chance write again & send along some verses. I arranged with Sir Fredk Macmillan at lunch the other day to bring out a new volume of verse in the Spring[.] Much of this you've seen but some will be new &, perhaps, between now & then the gods will permit me a few more poems. I got a copy of Colums ballads (from himself) and I see that MacDonagh has just brought out his book. Have you made any arrangements about yours. What about the Springtime when my book is due. I'll be in Dublin then and we can faire les noces [for *faire la noce*, "go on the spree"] or whatever should be faired. My french is hastening slowly but your bookcases will not vanish. You are seeing AE. Its good for the two of you. I will convert you to his poetry someday. I mark this on your brief that he's the biggest poetical thing that has happened in English for years & years & years. So! Remember me kindly to your father & mother

Your friend
JAMES STEPHENS

To W. T. H. HOWE

[A/3] Paris
30 December 1913

[Stephens did not go to Ireland on his trip to receive the Polignac Prize.]

Dear Mr Howe

I have unfortunately only got your letter. I have been away from Paris for some time in London & Ireland and have only returned. You may have seen in some paper that the Royal Academy of Literature have presented me with the Polignac Prize for the Crock of Gold – The reception of this brought me to England & it was a good while before I could get away again. So the photographs for your Xmas brochure would, at this date be of little use to you. In order, however, that you may know what I look like (sometimes) I enclose the photo of a medal which T. Spicer-Simson made of me in Paris. Some folk say it is a trifle "heavy" for me. Still it is better than a mere photograph. You were very kind to send me the engraving – It is very beautiful & I will keep it among the little collection I am making. By all means send along any books of mine you want signed. I will be here for some months longer & you need not fear they will go astray. As to the Fairy & Hero books – If you are still of the same mind I will prepare & send you the first chapter of each of these. I begin to fancy that I would enjoy writing them. Paris is snowed &

frosted & fogged all over, noses are red & lips blue and everyone looks like a pessimist –

Sincerely yours
JAMES STEPHENS

I am preparing a book of verse for the Spring publishing season. I think you will like some of the stuff –

To THOMAS BODKIN

Paris
[A/3] 30 December 1913

[The French reads: "Miller, you are sleeping,/Your windmill, your windmill/Goes too fast/Miller, you are sleeping/Your windmill, your windmill/Goes too strongly."]

Dear Bodkin

You were good to send these presents to the kids. It is the first letter Iris has received & she insists on keeping it in her own possession. She reads it aloud every few minutes generally in French, & your words sound strangely like

Meunier, tu dors,
Ton moulin, ton moulin
Va trop vite
Meunier, tu dors
Ton moulin, ton moulin
Va trop fort.

The toys were not pulverised, & the little lady appeared as fresh & happy as on the day you canned her & the ball has its own native hop –

As to the photographs I wrote about – Dont bother any more about them. The man from way yonder wont be able to hit another Xmas until we do, so he wont be in any hurry. If, however, you can discover any thing in the nature of a fairy storehouse I'll be glad if you'll buy it for me & I'll run you the necessary stamps by return. You know my royalties are due next month. If you come over I'll stand you a bottle of Champagne. I am digging away at my poems so as to be ready for the Spring publishing season. Get yours ready at the same time & we'll swap reviews.

Toujours, my dear man,

Your friend
JAMES STEPHENS

Is it possible for you to run across for two days or twenty two?

To STEPHEN MacKENNA

Paris
[A/19] 12 January 1914 [& August 1930]

[Lascelles Abercrombie's *Emblems of Love* was published in 1912. The Goncourt Prize was awarded on 3 December 1913 to *Le Peuple de la Mer* (1913) by "Marc Elder", the pseudonym of Marcel Tendron (1884–1933). *Sans Famille* by Henri Hector Malot (1830–1907) was published in 1879. Stephens is thinking of the French idiom *il fait du bien*, "it will do you good". The article in the January 1914 *Poetry Review* was "AE and James Stephens" by J. Wall. Stephens's article was "An Essay in Cubes", published in the *English Review* for April 1914. The "series of stories or sketches" was apparently never completed. The "french painter" was Claude Monet (1840–1926), who in 1890 began to do a series of treatments of the same scene; in May 1891 he exhibited fifteen paintings of haystacks (done in different seasons of the year). The description of the "Apache" is probably intended to be *coupe avec son couteau chaque nuit*, "cuts every night with his knife". Maud Gonne (1865–1953) was a leading Irish Nationalist, as well as the long-time beloved of W. B. Yeats.

The Polignac Prize for 1912 was awarded to the English poet John Masefield (1878–1967) for *The Everlasting Mercy* (1911); in 1914 it was awarded to Ralph Hodgson for "The Bull" and "The Song of Honour".]

My dear Stephen

I will concede Abercromie's greatness to you for 2 reasons. The first is that you couldnt praise bad work without spraining yourself; the other is, that I have read next-door-to-nothing of your decent man. Emblems of Love I have never seen but when I get it I will read him with your admonitions in my mind. The book I sent you I did not read either. You will have noticed that it is written in the French lingo; a tongue to which I am superior by birth. The reason I sent it is, that it gained the Goncourt Prize within 2 weeks of my getting the Polignac. & I fancied it might serve to bury one of your London hours. It has been very variously reviewed over here. I am reading, by the way, a French book which is giving me great delight. Its an old book "Sans Famille" by Hector Malot. A rambling narrative where the scene & action change as quickly & variously as a cinematographe. I really believe it would do you good (I wonder is "*do* you good", french? (faire). If you say the word I will launch the first volume you towards. Its as easy reading as a french cigarette is easy smoking & as pleasant. I will stand for this book altho' I dont for the one I sent you. I did not see the Poetry Review you speak of & I would like to know how they deal with AE & this deponent. I am writing Articles. I sat up last night until 6 o'clock & finished a 4,000 word affair on the psychology of novelists [&] the mediocrity of the classical novelists (English) & the base of criticism. At the least, it is readable & has some sentences. I am now meditating a series of stories or sketches on what seems to me a rather novel plan. The idea is to tell the same event four or five times. In each story different personalities would be subjected to the exactly-same disaster. (If disaster it will be) & I wish to discover what variety I could put into such a subject. You recollect the french painter who painted a (the same) haystack 12 times allowing between his works just sufficient time for the light to change. I have arranged with my publisher to bring out a new book of verse this spring or summer. I may call it Songs of the Earth or Songs from the Clay. Things move here as little as they can. The winter (I am told) is more severe than is usual, snow on the roof, ice on the ground – the shoulders which one was used to admire respectfully are veiled, I might say, bogged in layers of coats or furs, noses are red or sparkling, each with its pendant. The Cafès are deserted outside & are uncomely within. The Apache coups his couteau chaque nuit & the young homme of fifteen years revolverises his amant ["lover"] as regularly as tho he were driven by machinery – Those poor trees along the boulevards would make you weep – the cats are all in doors & the leg of no actress has been discovered for a month. One of my two canaries sings with untimely sweetness & the other thinks he is either showing off or has a religious mania. God be with you for he has departed from Paris. Mes salutations to your wife & my love to ye both – Md[m] Gonne has a monkey & a parrot, one has bitten my ear & the other ordured my shoulder. One submits but fiercely –

JAMES STEPHENS

[The following are Stephens's 1930 comments:]

The Polignac Prize mentioned was given me that year for The Crock of Gold. Masefield got it the year before me, and Hodgson got it the year after[.] The prize was of £100, and I was very glad to get it, for, on the day before I was notified of the prize, I had made the discovery that my total wealth in visable and moveable goods was, item, one wife, two babies, two cats and fifteen shillings. I was not acquainted with the mode of distributing a literary or other prize, and was vexed and nonplussed when a letter from Yeats instructed me that I should go to London about a week from that date and there receive from some official hand, the prize money. I was vexed because I knew I should have to borrow the money for two fares to London, and nonplussed because I was not skilled in the art of borrowing; and did not know from whom of my few acquaintences money was borrowable. Everybody whom I knew could, and occasionally did, stand one a cup of coffee: I could myself: but I could not feel certain that anyone could stand me two fares to London with something extra and over for food on the way and a nights lodging into the bargain. I have never entered into London without a certain sense of adventure and romance rising within me. Of all cities it is a satisfactory city. The very names of the streets seem more satisfactory than do those of other cities

To EDWARD MARSH

Paris

[A/3] 20 January 1914

[Stephens is thanking Marsh for another royalty payment on *Georgian Poetry: 1911–1912*. Meudon and its forest are close to Paris. In *Songs from the Clay* (not published until 1915), Stephens divided the original "A Tune on a Reed" into three distinct poems: stanza 1 became "The Rivals"; stanzas 2 to 6 became "A Reply"; stanzas 7 and 8 – the section mentioned here – became "A Tune on a Reed". Stanza 9 was not republished. *The Adventures of Seumas Beg/The Rocky Road to Dublin* was published as a separate volume in 1915.]

My dear Marsh

Thanks for the £4 – That is a miracle of a book! I am sorry I was out when you & Barnes called, but that day I was away on the heights of Meudon. I was a petrified man & the frost of Meudon is still in my bones.

About my book – I hope to send you the mss in a few days. I have just given it to the typist. & I will get it back tomorrow or the next day. I have cut a lot of stuff out of it & have put in a lot since you were here. For the last 2 weeks I have bathed in verse, twelve poems in two days is my average. I get my harvest, & then for months together I am a dumb bird – If you will suggest what poems you consider should be left out of this collection & what poems you think are faulty you will do me a real service. Also will you advise me as to my Hodgson poem? Is it too long? & should I retrench from it the tail piece beginning

"I have a little piece of straw"?

In the arrangement of a book of verse I am rather an ass. I have put these in some kind of order. When you are putting a book together do you work on any plan or do you pray to God & then go forward? The section of verses called "The Adventures of Seumas Beg" you need not bother very much about. I think I will not include them in this book, bulk in poetry is the devil, & without them there is quite enough matter for a readable volume. Remember me to Barnes & Hodgson when you see them. I wonder will you like my ms.

Sincerely yours
JAMES STEPHENS

To EDWARD MARSH

Paris

[A/3] 23 January 1914

[Stephens was sending the manuscript of *Songs from the Clay* to Marsh. If Stephens had any particular poem of Blake in mind, it was probably "Infant Sorrow" from *Songs of Innocence and Experience* (1794).]

My dear Marsh

Herewith are the poems, if they are poems. I am sitting like Blake's infant in a dark cloud & the verses no longer seem to be any good. I am not sending you the Seumas Beg verse, as (unless the publishers fight for more) I think the book will be quite big enough with this crowd.

le meas mór
do c[h]ara
["very truly yours, your friend"]
JAMES STEPHENS

To SIR FREDERICK MACMILLAN
(Macmillan & Company, London)

Paris
[A/23] 28 January 1914

[The book alluded to is *A Necessity of Life and Other Stories* (1913) by Betty Van Der Goes. When eventually published in March 1915, *Songs from the Clay* was 106 pages long.]

Dear Sir Frederick Macmillan,

Thanks for your letter. I am glad you had a pleasant time in Rome. I delayed writing you until you had returned. So that I might thank you for Mrs Van der Goes' delightful book. It is really excellent writing & I am sure if she cares to continue her literary work she will do considerable things –

As to my poems – The terms you mention will suit me very well. I have now put the ms in order & can send it to you this week. My only trouble is a title, but I can find one while the proofs are going through. So far as I can see the book will have about 90 pages. I could make it larger but I would not like to do so[.] I can guarantee these 90 pages to be entirely my best work. They are in a mood quite different from my other published poems – Have you any feeling as to a bigger book? or do you think this amount will suit?

As to the advance royalty – I would prefer to receive this on the signing of the Agreement if this is convenient. My wife joins in sending our compliments to yourself & Lady Macmillan.

Yours very sincerely
JAMES STEPHENS

To EDWARD MARSH & RALPH HODGSON

Paris
[A/3] [early] February 1914

[Marsh and Hodgson had sent Stephens a joint letter criticizing the manuscript of *Songs from the Clay.*]

My dear Marsh & Hodgson

That was the devil of a letter. Behold me ever since squatting with my chin on my knees in a cold silence, my hair plastering down & my eyes fixed. It was a good letter but I disagree with some of your accursed little crosses. (I will never like the Christian emblem again) & here's my trouble, that, even before your letter arrived I had already signed my agreement to publish the poems & there's no getting out of it. Its up to me now to transmogrify that book within three more days, for even now the proofs are due. But all the same I vow to astonish you with the book when it does appear. I will retrench certain of these poems, the Blakeish ones and I'm going to write a big, georgeous gigantic, magnificent & truly inspired poem this almighty present minute. I will surround myself with lightning & fury. I will call on the gods and the devils, but that collection is going to have a big poem in it for which these other bubbles will be a pretty background. If I fail then I intend to allow the two of you to eat each others hats. Now (as the Americans say) watch me smoke!

Mise le meas mór
["I am very truly yours"]
JAMES STEPHENS

To THOMAS BODKIN

Paris
[A/3] 7 February 1914

[The Montparnasse district of Paris, in which both Stephens's flat and the *Closerie des Lilas* café were located, was the centre of artistic activity in Paris from about 1910 to 1930. The French poet Paul

Fort (1872–1960), who in 1912 had been elected "Prince des poètes" by over four hundred of his contemporaries, was editor of *Vers et Prose* from 1905 to 1914. Fort used to preside over a gathering of writers and artists in the *Closerie des Lilas* every Tuesday. The literary movement of *Futurisme*, begun by the Italian poet F. P. Marinetti (1878–1944), flourished from about 1909 to 1912.]

My dear Bodkin

Thanks for your letter. Did I really neglect to write thanking you for the Yeats book & the photoes. Je suis bête ["I am stupid"]. I was down by the bookstalls on the river yesterday searching for likely pictures. They are selling piles at 3 Sous each, but there were so many cock-roches & winged dragons crawling in the barrows that I had to leave them their peace & their pictures. I went to the Salon d'Hiver also on opening day. There was nothing to be seen but the toilettes of lady visitors. Not one person looked at pictures. It was a very real winter here, Snow, hail, sleet & skating on the big basin in the Luxeumbourg Gardens. but Spring is here now, mild as she can be & smiling in sunshine. In another few days I expect the green will be –

> Peeking through
> The rusty shroud of hedge & tree

I have completed an Agreement with Macmillan for the new book of verse & am sending him the mss this week (tomorrow) [–] It is only a book of bubbles, but there is some irridescence in the bubbles et Je suis assez content ["and I am content enough"]. Its a little book in every way, no masterpiece sort of thing. I expect it will be broken on the wheel for being what it is instead of what it isn't. It is the critics complaint that he hasnt got what he hasnt got. I sent a long article to the English Review called "An Essay in Cubes" [–] If they print it, it will make you smile. Glad you see AE so often – I have just sent him a small verse epistle. I am writing this in the Closerie des Lilas at 10 min. to 7 o'c, soir ["in the evening"], Paul Fort is sitting at the table beside me. He lookes at me now & again with an extremely Montparnassian air which I have just returned by a Futurist glance. The Gods be with you

Your friend
JAMES STEPHENS

To SIR FREDERICK MACMILLAN
(Macmillan & Company, London)

Paris
[T/23] 16 February 1914

[Macmillan granted this request, and the book was not published for over a year.]

Dear Sir Frederick Macmillan,

I write to ask if it would be possible to delay the publication of my poems "Songs from the Clay" for a little time. I sent them to A.E. and he is strongly of opinion that it would be unwise to publish them until certain other poems had been added so as to give a greater variety to the collection, and, as a matter of fact, I am now engaged in writing these additional poems. I am quite sure that with a little delay I can make the book, not alone much bigger, but very much better. I wish this first book of verse which I am publishing with you to be as good as ever I can make it, and I can promise that it will be good. If you can agree to this delay you will very much oblige me.

As to the advance royalty – I can return this to you to be held until I send you the completed ms.

Please pardon me for the trouble I am giving in this matter.

Very truly yours,
JAMES STEPHENS

To GEORGE W. RUSSELL

Paris
[A/17] 19 February 1914

[AE had sent Stephens a rather critical letter about the manuscript of *Songs from the Clay*. "It is a happy thing, I say/To be alive on such a day" is from "April Showers", included in *The Adventures of Seumas Beg*. Stephens's poem "Deirdre" was published in the April 1914 *Irish Review* and in *Songs from the Clay*; AE's play *Deirdre* was first performed on 2 April 1902. *Songs from the Clay* contains a number of poems about evening, but they do not form a "series". AE's book was *Collected Poems*; Stephens's article was "An Essay in Cubes".

One of AE's objections to the manuscript of *Songs from the Clay* was the over-use of the word "little".]

Dear AE

Thanks for your letter – It was really good & kind of you to write it. I have just written to Macmillans asking will they put off the date of publication to next autumn[.] I expect they will do it & then you & I can go over the things together. If not I'll have to try [to] hammer the stuff together. I am adding matter to it every day & since I sent you the ms it has become very much more varied. At least a dozen of the things you have read I am cutting out of the collection. By the way the line you quote –

> It is a happy *day* I say
> To be alive on such a day

was a typists error – It is a happy *thing* I say &c is the correct, but that poemette disappears. I have just finished my Deirdre – Be at peace; she is only nine verses long, but she is as beautiful as the Stars of Morning[.] The bosh about the muse (in the detached series of poems I sent you) has also been suppressed & there remains a series of night pictures which are slowly shaping into decency. You know you are responsible for these poems (as you have been for almost everything I have done) [–] I read & reread with extraordinary elation your collected book & after each reading I perspire poetics. You have a most peculiar effect on me both in person & in your verse – You make me jump. By the way also. I wrote a article of yours & sent it to the English Review. It will make you smile when you see with what grace I have robbed you; but we all do that in Ireland & you are very wealthy. I am real sorry that troubles have come your way & I wish that I could shake your hand

Yours
JAMES STEPHENS

P.S. The English Review will probably decline to receive my stolen goods – Remember me to your wife & to the boys.

I have suppressed the word "little" [–] Do you know I never noticed it. I wonder have I other mannerisms but I'm quite cured of that one.

To THOMAS BODKIN

Paris
[A/3] 22 February 1914

[Bodkin's *May It Please Your Lordships* was not published by Maunsel & Company, Dublin, until 3 September 1917. Anatole France (1844–1924) was a French novelist and critic.]

My dear Bodkin

Thanks for your letter & the letters. I am afraid that, as regards the verses which I sent to AE, he was quite right in thumping me well. He did thump me, by the way, four pages of solid whacks was what he wrote me on those miserable poems. Since then I have transfigured them. I had a regular fury of verse & the book is no longer anything like what he saw. I do not think he would dislike it now & I think you also will be pleased at least with parts of it. The fault as AE pointed out was a lack of variety but thats not its fault now. Meanwhile I have postponed the publication for a few more months & its very likely we will be able to go over the verses together in Dublin before it is printed. I am sending you a little Anthology which (because it interested me) I thought would do the same for you. I expect you already have it. Do your verses march? Have you added to them? & is Maunsel agreeable to publish? By the way the french language is beginning to capitulate to me. Not in speech, for I never talk to anyone but I read now with some ease & every week sees me better at that art. Anatole France is almost as easy reading as English. I have been doing very little but verse lately. I did write a long article which I called "An Essay in Cubes" & sent it to the English Review. They will probably reject it, but if they dont you may find it amuzing. You & Russell are getting along well – that is good news for me. I will send a few of my lastest verses to you next week for your opinion & let you send me some of yours

Your friend
JAMES STEPHENS

I am calling my book "Songs from The Clay" –

To JOSEPH MARY PLUNKETT

Paris
[A/26] March 1914

[Plunkett's poem in the March 1914 *Irish Review* was "The Dark Way". The only book Plunkett published before his death in 1916 was *The Circle and the Sword* (1911). Stephens had four poems in the April 1914 *Irish Review.*]

My dear Plunkett

Your poem in the I. Rev. is very beautiful. I think it is the best thing of yours I have seen yet. As mere verse it is magnificent. Have you thought of bringing out a second book yet? There ought to be things in it when it comes. It has struck me that you might like to use some of my stuff in the Rev. If so I send you a little batch. Return them to me, like a decent man, if they dont please you. All good wishes to you.

Yours
JAMES STEPHENS

4 poems

To STEPHEN MacKENNA

Paris
[A/19] 20 March 1914 [& August 1930]

[MacKenna, who had formerly been employed by the *Freeman's Journal*, did not publish any of his short stories. Stephen McKenna (1888–1967) was an English novelist. I have not traced a note in *The Smart Set* on *The Crock of Gold.* "Rury" was MacKenna's dog. Honoré de Balzac (1799–1850) was a French novelist.]

My dear Stephen

Thats good news. If them scientific men set you up again I'll forgive science all its lunacy. (Do you remember how you and I quarrelled about science on Saturday night in Donnybrook of the Fields and the wide spaces?) As to the Journal [–] I'll run it along to you as usual. Its no trouble. It costs un sou and I read it myself before you get it. The grippe has just unloosed me and to day, for the first time I walked abroad[.] Its Mi-Carême [*mi-Carême*, "mid-

Lent"] & the queens are being feted. They have been pelted with confetti, rain and hail stones big as a church-steeple and bigger, as you would say. Do you recollect the gooseberries of Donnybrook each big as a Cathedral bell and I suppose one might say they tasted like the music of the Spheres. As to your stories – I would strongly advise you not to try selling even one, as yet, but write like the devil, pile them up beside you and dont begin to unload until you have a cartful. Il fauts [*Il faut*, "it is necessary"] altogether that when you begin to sell you should be able to follow up & up & up. I am sure you'll do good stories[.] You've got the writing in you & that's all a story is, or rather thats what makes a story good. You've got a sense of logic & thats what tells a story. You could amuse yourself by slinging a few of the Journal murders (or the Saxon murders for that) into story form. Or here is a thing you might like to do, for you've a curious mind – take any one of these bare-boned dramas of the newspaper, then take the names of the original actors out & insert in their stead the names of inoffensive people whom you know well, stick them pitilessly into the drama & develope a tale along their psychology. Do you remember in the Freeman you used to keep the barnacles off your mind by saying "Tonight I will write philosophy [&] tomorrow night I'll write humerously & the night after my Article will porte ["wear"] the light sarcastic or the cosmopolitanish touch perhaps." You can play with stories in the same way[.] There is a Stephen MacKenna already storying – What are you going to do about a pen-name? or will you try to injunct the other one. I didnt see the Smart Set note on my Crock but if you could tear the bit out & send it to me I'd be glad to see it. There will be an Article by me in next months English review but the pen has gone against me for some time or, perhaps, its more that I dont want to write. There are no green things in my mind yet; myself & the trees in the boulevard are howling for spring

Beannacht Dia [*Dé*] ort
["God's blessing on you"]
JAMES STEPHENS

[The following are Stephens's 1930 comments:]

Something had in these days gone wrong with poor Stephen's head; and the doctors had been busily at him. They came to medicate but remained to chatter as doctors will. And he, (when he was afoot, all of whose motions made him look like a man with the "head-staggers" like poor Rury whose head-staggers were frequent,) he would chatter like an inspired jackdaw, for he was courteous, & a great believer in the idea that cultivated society is more held together by conversation than by anything else whatever. The fruitfullest act that a man can do is to marry a question to an answer. That this marriage is often infertile does not much matter. Conversation does not lie in such answering, but in an expatiation upon the field, and in a delighted cavorting in that endless meadow.

The "Journal", referred to is "Le Journal", a French daily, which MacKenna approved of. He held that the daily conte ["story"] in this paper was the finest piece of continuous short-story writing that could be found anywhere, and that the psychological curiosity which underlay all of these stories was invaluable to the writer & student. Personally I agreed with him in theory (as I almost always did) but a half dozen of these tales sufficed me. The world of the French short-story writer was too-too-populous with French females for my taste; & these females were all too-continuously preoccupied with the same husband-cheating, lover-cheating, cheating-cheating, to be artistically interesting. First of all the nations the French writers were busily engaged in turning the sex-fact and function into a physical and intellectual play-ground. It was at once a game and a puzzle, and it was so played and pored on. Exit matters that were good and precious! Enter another matter, whatever it be, that is to be good and precious. A loyalty of some type it must be, for only loyalties are humanly admirable and sanctified. The Germans were then busy learning to love the State. Perhaps we shall find that only the Hive is large enough to be loved, and dear enough to be loyal to. As to Stiofán's stories [–] if he were to say that the least said the better, I should agree with him. He made an exhaustive study of the art of short-story writing. I remember sending him Le Journal for that purpose, and all the short tales of Balzac and others, and it is still a mystery to me that one who could write so well, and talk so marvellously well, should be so utterly inapt in the art of "creative" writing.

Certain men, like MacKenna and George Russell or Willy Yeats, have their true being and true residence in the world of ideas. They move there with an altogether astounding competence and freedom, and they are as singularly unable and frustrate when they adventure in the common ways and modes. If we have power here we pay for it there or somewhere, and even when we are superhuman tis at a corresponding cost somehow & somewhere.

To STEPHEN MacKENNA

Paris

[A/19] 7 April 1914

[Arthur Lynch (1861–1934), journalist, writer and civil engineer, was elected a Member of Parliament for Galway in 1901. On 10 February 1914 he wrote to ask Stephens: "Of all Shelley's poems which would you consider – to cite a single passage – the most (1) characteristic passage; (2) the passage which best exhibits his elusive, haunting, fascinating musical quality?" The novel dedicated to him which Stephens saw was a new edition of *Le Briseur de Fers* (1908) by Georges d'Esparbes (1863–1944). Jean Humbert (1755–1823) was the commander of the French forces which landed in Ireland in 1798. The "Journal" is *Le Journal.*]

A c[h]ara Stiophan ["Dear Stephen"]

It was good of you to write me. I knew my Cube article would please you, at any rate, in parts, &, as you know, I would prefer a few lines of applause from yourself to columns in newspapers. I called it an Essay in Cubes because, like the Cubist pictures, its eye is sometimes on its knee & its ear on its shoulder. God watches over the unity of most things & that there is a unity in the Article is more due to him than to me. But it skips & dives & drops & between one sentence & the next there is often a chasm, to be bridged, surely, but not by the average reader.

So much for it. The vice of nearly all the modern storytellers, can be put in one sentence; it is, that, while they know how to tell a story they do not know how to write it. Did I tell you before that I met Lynch over here some time ago, he writes me from the House of Commons about Shelley & Whitman & such like – He is a curious man. I saw today a french novel just published dedicated to him in high terms. It is about Humbert & the French landing in Ireland & is, I should say, rather sentimental. I have become interested in mathematics & the Franco Prssn War. Do you remember any good book, novel or memoir on the latter subject? As to the books & the Journal, they go to you after I have read them myself & are, so, neither a loss nor an expense to me. I read like fury but without any direction[.] French literature is as yet a jungle to me but I'll get the points of the compass shortly. The best of good luck to you & nos hommages à votre femme

Yours
JAMES STEPHENS

To THOMAS BODKIN

Paris
[A/3] 8 April 1914

[Stephens did not return to Dublin until 30 July 1914. On 17 March 1914 the wife of Joseph Caillaux, the French Minister of Finance, shot Gaston Calmette, the Director of *Le Figaro*. *Le Figaro* had been accusing Caillaux of corruption in office. The much-publicized trial ended in an acquittal on 28 July 1914. The new book by James Starkey was *An Epilogue to the Praise of Angus and Other Poems* (1914). Stephens had four poems in the April 1914 *Irish Review*; Plunkett's poem was "The Dark Way".]

My dear Bodkin

Heres ages since we heard from each other. I am posting up my flat to let so that we may get to Ireland in June when I hope to bavard avec ["chat with"] you until the Small hours. Theres nothing doing here barring the trial of Madame Callieux in which I am not wildly interested, but Spring is waving her green banners all along the boulevards & (when it isnt raining, as it is at this minute) the sun would roast your bones. I see by an advt that Starkie has published a new book of verse. I wish you would tell me what you think of it. (Dont send it to me as I'll be going to Dublin so soon) but just mention whether he is worth while. MacKenna writes me frequently from his retirement & seems to be getting better[.] He is taking to story writing & I am very curious to see how he will emerge. I sent some verses to the Irish Review, which they may print & which may please you. By the by, there was a poem of Plunketts in last issue which I thought remarkably good. Have you written more. I am reading french now with great facility, but I do not talk at all, being a very wise man. The Sack of your bibliotheque is at hand. I wish, before I go back, that you & I could have one more run round together.

Tout mes hommages à votre père et à votre mère; et pour vous-mème

Je suis votre ami, n'est pas
JAMES STEPHENS

I write you from the Cafè at the end of the Place St Michel. The rain has stopped, the Sun is here & the bookstalls are ten paces away – allons!

To THOMAS BODKIN

Paris
[A/3] 10 April 1914

["An Essay in Cubes" contains two references to the French painter Hilaire-Germain-Edgar Degas (1834–1917): "the abominations painted by Degas" and "Degas's soldiers". In this postcard Stephens corrects the reference to the Spanish artist Francisco José Goya y Lucientes (1746–1828); the particular allusion is probably to the series of etchings *Los Desastres de la Guerra* (1810–14).]

The Degas in my Essay ought naturally to be Goya. I've a memory that I'd change with anyone. That was a fine letter of yours.

JS

To THOMAS BODKIN

Paris
[A/3] 28 April 1914

[The National Volunteers were organized in November 1913 to counteract the influence of the Ulster Volunteers. The "coup of Ulster" was the landing of guns and ammunition for the Ulster Volunteers at Larne on 24 April 1914. The new novel was *The Demi-Gods.*]

Dear Bodkin

I wrote a letter to you (2 hours ago) in the Cafe de la Paix & I lost the letter. Some kind person may! put 25 centimes on it & send it to you but I doubt that[.] I am writing you now from the Cafe

Rotondo [for *Café de la Rotonde*] opposite the Galleries Lafayette. The letter was to beg you send me, if you can find time, an Irish Blackthorne Walkingstick. I yearn for one. A short stick that does not bend when you lean on it. If you can find such that fits your heighth get them to cut off 2½ inches to fit my lowth & send me along the bill & make me your eternal debtor which I already am. I will discharge you the bill by return of post. Also write me a letter saying how you are & what you think of things. I would like your opinion on the Ulster Volunteers & what you think about the National Volunteers – That coup of Ulster a few days ago gave me great joy. Have you written any poems & if so can you send me copies. My new novel has started, painfully, & when I get back (1st week in June) it will be sufficiently advanced to talk over with you. Mes hommages à vous et à votre pére et votre mére. The stick I would like not to have a handle but a nice grippable knob with a decent swivel at the bottom. My blessing on you[.] I want that stick bad, because I cant have an Irish terrier

Your friend
JAMES STEPHENS

To THOMAS BODKIN

Paris
[A/3] May 1914

[Stephens is thanking Bodkin for the walking-stick requested in his letter of 28 April 1914. The combination of French and Anglo-Irish would correctly be *une très dure canne begorrah*, "a very hard walking-stick, by God".]

My dear Bodkin

What a stick! Its surely the champion of the world. Its the ideal, & I have marched before it today like a sapling trotting by an oak, I being the sapling. The Boulevard St Michel admired me discreetly but passionately. Three juene gens [for *jeunes gens*, "young men"] came along swinging canes which were jewelled all down the front, but when they saw my stick they hid their canes & were abashed. I honestly cant tell you how pleased I am at your present, for I take it as a present, & it engraved & all in massy silver & with a ferrule on it that would split a hill if it hit it. Myself & it have sworn brotherhood, it snuggles into my hand as if that was its home planned by the gods. Its, in fact, the stick. One of these days, when I can think of something I'll make you a present –

We leave Paris on the 22nd June & hit Dublin Tuesday the 23rd [–] I am asking AE to mention this at his Sunday conference, so that anyone who knows of 3 rooms in Rathgar direction, with a stove, at £30 a year for say 3 months can take that place for us. I am looking forward very much to seeing you again. The new story by the way, is marching, marching & I'm in glee, but I'm gleefuller about the stick. The douane ["customs-house"] man tried to pull its head off to see was there a sword inside it & he told me it was un très dur canne begor – By the way – before I leave France, is there any kind of book or picture thing you would be hankering for.

bien a vous
JAMES STEPHENS

To THOMAS BODKIN

Paris
[A/3] [*ca.* 19] June 1914

Dear Bodkin –

Thanks for your letter – You may have noticed by the dropping of your papers for some time back that I had again struck the rocks. However I will again float off them in about a week for my new novel was finished the day before yesterday &, so, all is well. We had on that account to put off our visit to Ireland for another month & so on the 23rd July we set sail to Dublin & yourself. We must stay here for those few weeks to enable some cheques which are due to come in – If you could get us three rooms somewhere, anywhere between Rathmines & Upper Mount Street you would do us a real favour. I will have money in a week as I'll get the advance royalties on my new novel "The Demigods" & I can then send you on one two or three months rent in advance to make matters easy. 3 rooms so, with a gas stove in one & a rent of about £2.10/- a month. Do you think this could be managed. I think you will like my book. I hope you will. Myself I think it is better than "The Crock of Gold"[.] But, of course, one is still rather close to it. Hastily.

Your friend
JAMES STEPHENS

Any kind of rooms

To STEPHEN MacKENNA

Paris

[A/19] 20 June 1914 [& August 1930]

[The sentence which Stephens "concocted" is a slightly misquoted appraisal of bad novelists in "An Essay in Cubes". AE's "Krishna" is included in his *Collected Poems.* Stephens spent about seven weeks in writing *The Demi-Gods.*]

Dear Stephen

I emerge from silence with a book finished, typed, dispatched & today with the weighty advance gold clinking in my pouch! I was buried in that book up to three days ago. It is to be called The Demi-Gods. At this moment I think it is good, but what I will think when I see it printed is another thing. Anyhow you'll be able to tell me is it good or bad or middling when I send a copy to yourself & your wife

It is real good of you to send me the papers & its true that I look forward to them. Like yourself I dont read these articles [–] I skim & slide & get the impression of an enormous competency that is yet no good. These people dont know how to write & you discovered it long ago – Do you recollect a phrase I once concocted. "They think that an adequate statement of any fact or event is all that is required in the way of Art"[.] In the way of facts the average well-read person can't be told anything new & for events they are only newspapery. I believe you have the knowledge & the gift of writing & if you care to dive for them you will bring black & white pearls & chunks of red coral & the gleaming skeletons of Great Whales out of the waters. Thats my thought – You have been & are increasingly writing-conscious. & that means you can do the job if you'll handle the tools. By the way there is a poem of AE's called *Krishna* which is worth reading aloud & at the full range of your grave voice. I would like to hear you do it & then I'd do it myself at you & then the two of us could intone it together while your wife hung chords & floating glories of sound about our happy voices.

Hommages a the pair of you de the pair of us

JAMES STEPHENS

[The following are Stephens's 1930 comments:]

I think that The Demi-Gods was written in one month. I wrote it mainly in the big cafe at the end of the Boulevard Montparnasse, opposite Lavenue's: and I finished it about eleven o'clock one night in the Closerie des Lilas. I can still remember the sense of relief that flooded me as I came to the end of that book, and how, out of extraordinary little money, I presented myself with an extra and additional drink to the cup of coffee that had been cold an hour at least before that moment. I was very tired for I had written practically all day for every day of that month; and had thereafter sat up every night in bed for hours, rereading, polishing, and perfecting all that I had conceived and penned during the day. So this night also, being prepared for bed and with a cigarette already lit, I leaned from the bed to the chair upon which my coat hung, and felt in the pocket for my manuscript-book. When a calamity knocks at the door of my mind it is instantly recognized & admitted, & as shortly banished. When my hand met nothing where a ms should be I knew in one swoop of knowledge that the book was gone, or lost or stolen[.] I thought rapidly 'I have left it on a table of that crowded Café: or I have dropped it in the street coming home: or it was picked out of my pocket in a City, and in a quarter which, in those days at least, was not pick-pocketish.['] In the quiet of my bed I caught the glooming of a vast, dull, mournfulness that was beginning to close upon me, and dissipated it, as I could then, contenting my wraith of woe with the reflection that on the morrow, if the ms were indeed well and truly lost, I and misery's self could collaborate and contrive us a round and complete mourning: I went to sleep, just blinking that away. How obedient then misery was, that later will stir how reluctantly from our incantations. On the morrow, when the quickly dispatched French breakfast of one cup of coffee and one stick of bread had been got through in the one minute that is sufficient for it, I went again to the Cloiserie[.] I had provided myself with a spare ms book, the duplicate in appearance of the one I had lost. This I showed to the waiter who had served my table on the previous night, and explained to him my loss. Ah, the good smile that overspread the face of that good, pre-war waiter. He went behind the caisse ["cash-register"], and returned with my ms book in his hand. As in the old times there were giants in the earth in these days; so, and almost as unbelievably there was gold in the earth in the pre war days; and a piece of that gold, twenty-five pre war francs of it, the last of its clan I hooked from my pocket and offered happily to my good waiter. He rejected it. A smile of rich happiness was on his face, and with pride and humility he explained – "I, too, am a writer, sir: ["] quoth he. I was happy. I had my ms safely in my pocket, and which I needed almost as badly, I had my last and only twenty-five francs in my pocket. That was a good day.

To THE EDITOR OF THE *IRISH HOMESTEAD*

[Paris]
27 June 1914

[The text is from the *Irish Homestead* for 27 June 1914. Stephens is responding to a letter in the *Irish Homestead* for 20 June 1914 asking for a newspaper written in a simple style for "the man on the bog". The author of that letter used the pseudonym *Garruidhe*, a variant spelling of *Garraidhe*, meaning "garth", "garden" or "cabbage-patch". The Anglo-Irish interjection "musha" derives from *maiseadh*, "if it be so".]

THE MAN ON THE BOG

Dear Sir,–

As a "man on the bog", or a bog-trotter, I entirely object to Garruidhe making so free with my name. He may be a "little garden" or a "little green field" (very green) or any other branch of agriculture he likes, but I do not see that that gives him any authority to legislate for me, and tell me what sort of reading I am best able to enjoy. Have I ever complained of the HOMESTEAD, or said in an unappreciative sense that it was over my head? When I am out beyond on the bog the high heaven is over my head and I do not feel it is a bit too good for me, nor do I want to change it for the circus-tent Garruidhe wants to tether me into.

In spite of Garruidhe there may be a few co-operators in Ireland who enjoy what the HOMESTEAD gives them week by week, and see more chance for the future of their country in the co-operative countryside it preaches than in any amount of "pithy pars", boiled-down news, snippet nothings that Garruidhe would give them. They can get more of that stuff than they want in the local sheet. Musha, Garruidhe, did you never get beyond the infant-school form yourself, that you want to keep us all there tied to your pinafore?

The kind of paper you are asking for won't ever come our way, please goodness. With all its contributors and all their salaries each copy would take sixpence to produce, and you would have to pay us a penny with every copy to make us read it.

The "Man on the Bog", indeed. I am sick and tired of hearing how things are to be evened down to him. More big thoughts come into his head out there than you in your tied-in garden could guess at. – Yours faithfully,

SHEMUS BEG.

To THOMAS BODKIN

[A/3]

Paris
11 July 1914

Dear Bodkin

You are sure the best of men. We were unable to leave on 23rd of last month for we had no money, but the book is now finished & the English royalties are clinking in my pouch. We are really only waiting in order to give the American advance royalties a chance of reaching us.

As to the rooms – I do feel a beast to be giving you all this trouble, but if you can manage *any* three rooms, & practically anywhere within reach of yourself, you will save us an infinity of worry & add to the many debts of kindness which I already owe you. I can now send you a cheque any day for rent in advance on hearing from you.

That girl of fifteen Case in which you are briefed must be rather distasteful to you. I wonder would we look on it in the same way[.] I am so apt to look on things as stories that in some ways I lose all touch with reality. This is the reason why the thought of a literary gent is more picturesque than profound – How would you formulate the mental disabilities of a lawyer?

I am tremendously relieved that the book is off my hands & I am mightily curious to know what you will think of it. Textually I fancy it is an improvement on my other books, but imaginatively & thoughtfully it is all to question. The proofs are coming in & I am still too close to the job to be able to see it.

By the way I have to ask your pardon for a liberty. We ordered three folding chairs at the Bon Marché to be sent to Ireland &,

villanously, we gave your address for storage. Naturally we wont send anything more, & perhaps you could apologise for us to your mother. It was too late to withdraw when the idea struck us that we might be overdrawing our credit with you. They are quite small things & maybe they won't be too much in the way

Yeats was over here a few weeks ago – he dined a couple of times with us & I find that he more than improves on acquaintence. He was really modest & he listened with quietude to a few of my poems & spoke of them afterwards as though he had been interested. Perhaps he was'nt, yet it was tres gentille of him n'est pas?

This year of France has made me singularly detached as regards Ireland. I love it & all the rest, & still, after yourself & Russell there is nobody in Ireland whom I have the slightest wish to see – That strikes me as queer, for one ought to have more than two friends in ones very own country & yet there's the fact. I tried to read Shakespeare yesterday & found again that I couldnt. I wonder whats wrong with me on his behalf. Dont tell your father or he'll throw out my folding chairs. Mes hommages to him & to your mother & for yourself here's my hand & seal

JAMES STEPHENS

To THOMAS BODKIN

Rathmines, Co. Dublin

[A/3] [2 August 1914]

[After a short stay at 12 Leinster Road, Stephens moved to 2 Leinster Square, Rathmines, County Dublin. Joyce's book was *Dubliners*, published in June 1914.]

Dear Bodkin

I find, sorrowfully, that I will not be able to get up with you for that trip. My wife is not in the best of health &, until we get a bonne ["maid"], I must help to keep the children in humour. However we will meet again. I have dipped into Joyce's book[.] It is interesting, but unpleasant & must be counted among his many wild oats, that mans crop seems interminable. I wonder what he would do now if he were to write, having got rid of these illnesses he might do good work for he knows how to write, or he may be one of those whose youth is his sole energy & who grow old & barren in a flash. Hommages à votre père et à votre mère & all good things to yourself.

JAMES STEPHENS

To EDWARD MARSH

Rathmines, Co. Dublin

[A/3] 11 August 1914

[Marsh's book was *Georgian Poetry: 1913–1915* (1915), which included five poems by Stephens. "As Evening Falls", the poem quoted here, appeared in *Songs from the Clay* with only minor differences in puctuation and a change of "his nest" to "its nest".]

Dear Marsh,

I have just managed to get settled at last. I thought I was coming across to a big row here, but, alas, I have left the lovliest row behind me in France and there is nothing here but sunshine & peace. I think Dublin is the lovliest city in the world – After Paris & particularly under this sunlight it seems to me entrancing. Those big cities have something of the proprieterial & official & servile-statish about them & in spite of their orderliness & convenience they leave me with an added admiration for my own little place that has grown through all the centuries as irregularly & yet as harmoniously as a tree.

But heres stuff to be writing you, & you, perhaps, too busy to read as much as a newspaper! I really took the pen in hand to ask were your plans for the new book disarrayed by the war & would I hold my manuscripts back or send them on to you? I dont know whether this war would interfere with you very much. I expect it would. For my own part I have just completed the page proofs of my new novel – The Demi-Gods – but whether the publishers will publish it now or hold it over I dont know. Meanwhile you must be rather in the centre of things & full of interests & excitements & urgencies. When you can get a quiet couple of minutes drop me a postcard saying "send" or "dont send" & I will unbale or keep buried my mss. By the greatest of luck they got out of Paris – a week later than myself – Here is a pretty little verse I got –

At eve the horse is freed of plough or wain
And all things turn from labour unto rest;
The scattered sheep are gathering home again,
And every bird is winging to his nest,
And every beast goes to his den once more
By hedge or hill – Each mother is aware
That little feet
Have paused in field or street,
And she will hear a knocking at the door,
And open it, and see her children there.

Yours
JAMES STEPHENS

To HENRY McBRIDE

Rathmines, Co. Dublin
[A/42] 27 August 1914

[*The Demi-Gods* was published in England on 14 October and in America on 30 October 1914.]

My dear Henry

I am the proprietor of a past that could not stir the heart of the great American Nation. It is tame, it is hygenic, let us hasten to forget it. Unlike Jesus Christ I was born with the aid of a father as well as a mother. I will stir these ashes no more or I may discover other lapses from the tradition of true greatness. By the way Spicer Simson has gorgeous portraits of his medal of myself – Wont one of those suit you. I havent got any portraits & I hate sitting for them. Forgive me, but I've never been interviewed & I havent the least idea of what to write you – My first book Insurrections was published in 1909 & from that my career has been one of unbroken spirited successes culminating in my tragedy of Hamlet. By the way I just got a royalty a/c from the States for years sale of the Crock of Gold & Hill of Vision & I still owe them money after 2 years. We are all at peace over here, a repulsive peace. I wish I was back in Paris. We read every day in 10 editions the news of the week before last. I wish the war would get on & get ended or that our people here would work up a row all for our little selves. My book "The Demi-Gods" is to be published in October. AE has read the proofs for me & he says its the best I've ever done

A vous
JAMES STEPHENS

To HARRIET MONROE

Rathmines, Co. Dublin
[A/11] 5 September 1914

[Harriet Monroe (1860–1936), the editor of *Poetry: A Magazine of Verse*, had written on 5 January 1914 to ask Stephens for some poems, four of which appeared in the August 1914 issue.]

Dear Miss Monroe

Thanks for your letter. I note that you have £11 for me. In the circumstances, will you please keep the money until times become more peaceful. As you see I have left Paris for a while but I will return there as soon as I can, & will write you. We also are at war in Ireland but are not yet certain against whom we are to fight. We are ranged, at the one moment, against Germany & England & Ulster & while we are all laughing at our problem there is an undercurrent of real uneasiness amongst us. Meantime, practically all Ireland is under arms & we drill & hold our whist – We are marvellously silent, but we all realize that when a sufficient number of guns have been gathered together in any place they are likely to go off by themselves.

My new novel is to be published in England & America in October. I think you will like it, principally, I confess, because I like it myself. An address, by the way, which will always find me is care of Messrs Macmillan & Co. St Martin's Street London.

Very truly yours
JAMES STEPHENS

To CYNTHIA STEPHENS

Virginia, Co. Cavan
[A/1] 11 September 1914

[On 10–12 September 1914, Stephens, Bodkin and AE went on a vacation to Virginia, County Cavan. The "big lake" is Lough Ramor. AE's main purpose on the trip was to paint.]

My dear girl

I found last night that no post leaves this place until 2 o'clock today so I could not send you a card. We had a 6 mile drive from the station through the dark last night but there was a moon you would have liked & as we went along I was often thinking of our little expeditions years ago when we went moon-hunting. Do you remember those good nights. Do you recollect the night when we stalked the moon round Merrion Square & some women yelled at us thinking we were bold, bad people, which we surely were. This is a very pretty place. I was surprised to learn that we are now in Ulster & that Ulster is quite good-looking. There is a big lake just outside the back window. It is five miles long & fairly broad & damned rough looking at the moment for theres rain & wind & other unpleasantnesses at the moment & its rather cold. AE & I & the hotel keeper (a very intelligent man) have marched out skirting the lake into the woods which run all round it. You would like them also [–] also they are wet woods & we have now just come in for lunch. Russell is going to bring his canvasses out after feeding & he hopes to imprison some of their beauties. Maybe when we get back you'll be able to see the pictures & thus know what kind of world we are tramping about. Tell Seumas & Iris that their daddy sends a kiss to each of them & to yourself I send a thousand. All the same I would rather give them to you than send them.

JAMES STEPHENS

To STEPHEN MacKENNA

Paris

[A/12] 1 November 1914

[Stephens had just returned from Dublin to Paris. Stephens kept one of MacKenna's kittens and named it Noirro; the other was given to Maud Gonne and became the Minnaloushe of Yeats's "The Cat and the Moon". Robert Lynd (1878–1949), who was born in Galway, was on the staff on the *Daily News and Leader* (London). Stephens published four reviews in that newspaper: of *Connaught to Chicago* (1914) by "George A. Birmingham" (J. O. Hannay), in the issue for 13 November 1914; of a 1914 edition of *The Kasîdah of Hâjî Abdû el Yezdi* (1880) by Sir Richard Francis Burton (1821–90), in the issue for 29 December 1914; of *Welsh Poems and Ballads* (1915) by

George Henry Borrow (1803–81), in the issue for 17 March 1915; and of *Fifty-one Tales* (1915) by Lord Dunsany, in the issue for 5 May 1915.]

My dear Stephen

A note to acknowledge your letter & to say how sorry I was not to have seen yourself & herself. Lord! Paris is the triste ["sorrowful"] city. The streets that were once murderous in their traffic are now so deserted that children can roll their hoops in the middle of the roads. Women are everywhere & they all porte [*portent*, "wear"] black draperies & they are all subdued. Sometimes a child laughs in the street & the folk look at it astonished, & one has the feeling that it ought to be reprimanded. We came over in a boat crowded with French & Belgian refugees returning to their regiments & they were all sick as at the word of command. I wish this damned war would cease or that I was taking a hand in it, & I wish that our own country was more settled. It was about that I would have welcomed a chat with you. Ireland is in a real bad state. There is no leader, &, as yet, no national policy (How could there be)[.] Meanwhile they drill, but who they will fight against no man knows. The "intellectuals", now as always, range themselves against the nation, preaching their accursed pacifications & their belief in Englands virtue. Maybe England will be true to her word this time, but if Germany is beaten (& I believe & half hope that she will be) there will be no longer any reason for England to keep her promise. We have our history & our remembrances of her treaties. But I believe in Ireland & in her star, & that she will lift out of this turmoil like a star lifting out of the waves. The more I think of ourselves & our history (for our history seems to me more glorious than that of any other nation in the world) the more I believe that Ireland is a land of destiny where the gods are brooding their great events & that Ireland will be the beloved of the world in a way that no other nation ever has been. For such a birth there must be a long gestation & a hard travail, but we will wave yet in the winds of the world & all the people will call us blessed – So!

Meanwhile, your cat has kittens, God bless her, & she had them with the assurance & ease of a great cat. I attended her all the time (they were born in Dublin & are Gaelic cats)[.] I was amazed at the rapture of the poor beast. Her eyes were starting out of her head with that agony and she (who never purrs) purred a loud triumph against her pain. She has two black kittens, but of a blackness without alloy, & she adores them.

I expect by this time you will have received a copy of my new book. Robert Lynd of the Daily News & Leader has given me some reviewing to do & I'm glad to get it. He is a nice chap & has a bit of the Gaelic. All good wishes to ye both from us twain & the greetings of our cat & kittens to her gendre ["son-in-law"] "The Pounder"

JAMES STEPHENS

To STEPHEN MacKENNA

Paris

[A/32] 11 November 1914 [& August 1930]

[The first book mentioned is *The Demi-Gods*, in which Art is one of the central characters. The book of verse was *Songs from the Clay.* "A Prelude and a Song", "The Lonely God" and "Eve" were included in *The Hill of Vision.* Clamart is a few miles from Paris; Tuam is in County Galway. Seumas Óg ("James the Young") was Stephens's son. The "tinker drunk" may refer to "What Tomas an Buile Said in a Pub", included in *Insurrections.*]

Dear Stephen

Thanks for your letter. One good thing does come from it, that, on the whole, you are getting better. & there is nothing in the world will give myself greater pleasure than to hear you are quite well & ready to tramp the roads of the world the way you did when you were all in it – Your remarks about my book were very kindly & they were all correct. It is not as good as The Crock, but then I had the subject there & I hadn't here. The remark, you quoted, by Art was a real bad remark. He must have said it when he wasnt thinking. I wish I hadnt got to write books whose stupid characters estrange me from my friends & make them hate me. Lord! Paris is a dull city – My book of verse is now ready for the press. I am sending off the last proofs. I am not sure you will care for it much – There are nice things in it, but there is no Prelude & Song, nor Lonely God, nor Eve. Man its no good – Its been raining here all night & all day with special intervals for hail stones, each, as you said of the blackberries in Clamart, as big as a Cathedral bell. The women are all dressed like widows & they all look like widows, & a mile away two million men are trying to gut each other – If you could eat them there'd be some sense in it – There is nothing in this war but dirt & stupidity & the infernal activity of hordes of insects & its raining all night & all day with special intervals for hailstones each as (See Clamart)[.] My reviews for Lynd wont be worth reading – He seems to be sending me books at the longest intervals & none of them are worth reading, let alone reviewing. He should pay me a lot for this, but I bet he wont & it raining beside that with hailstones (see 1st page)[.] You dont know what a Café looks like now – I am not well acquainted with Lynd. I met him twice & he seemed a very decent kind of chap. His accent is from Cuchulain's country but maybe his hearts in the highlands. If I were to open the window here & let out a yawn I would put the whole world asleep – I'm half a mind to do it too – The Closerie des Lilas looks like the room where the Tuam Board of Guardians do be meeting on Wednesdays & Fridays & they talking about the crops. I'll have to do something to keep myself awake here in the middle of the day. I'll beat Seumas Og when he comes in. I'll tie a can to the cats tail. I'll give the two kittens fish bones to eat. I'll put pepper in the birds cage & I'll throw the ordure tub into the conceirge's window. Its hailing now, & every stone is as big as a Cathedral Bell

JS

[The following are Stephens's 1930 comments:]

I dont recollect that "book of verse" I referred to in this letter, but when I write that in it there is "no Prelude and Song, no Lonely God" I think that I am not writing from myself, but answering, or writing on, some remark MacKenna made in a previous letter. At the height of my youth and imbecility I was not really enamoured of these two poems. I still think that in the Lonely God there are some good verses, and that the subject (as a mere painting or landscape, or canvas[)] was vast enough to satisfy the craving for "vastness" which then (& now) was an ever-present desire with me. I recollect that AE, in criticising this poem complained that he preferred my tinker drunk to my God sober. In truth while I had a continuous feeling of and for God, I had another as continuous feeling of and for woman: and (the whole ill is here) I mixed these unmixables. The God of that poem is too anthropomorphic even for poetry. But in those days I did not expect nor suspect an Absolute, & was willing to credit deity with my own desires, and very generously to confer these on Him. Well, I suppose I am the only poet that ever married God the Father. It was well meant

To HAROLD MONRO

Paris
[A/10] 1 December 1914

[The "matter" was Monro's rejection in December 1913 of "A Tune on a Reed" for *Poetry and Drama*. Stephens split the poem into three separate works in *Songs from the Clay*. *Poetry and Drama* ceased publication with the issue for December 1914.]

Dear Monro,

I am an ass. There was so little to forgive in that matter that I have taken your advice & chopped three quarters of the poem off itself. I was waiting for my mss to arrive from Ireland before writing you, but I expect it is much too late now to send anything for your Dec. issue. The proofs of my new book of verse are finished, but I expect it will not be published until January. Are you working yourself & have you had good harvesting?

Yours
JAMES STEPHENS

To THOMAS BODKIN

Paris
[A/3] 13 December 1914

[The description of the Paris houses would correctly be *fermé à cause de la guerre, maisons séquestrées & maisons.* "closed because of the war, houses isolated & houses". Stephens sent Bodkin copies of *La Robe rogue* (1900) by Eugène Brieux (1858–1932) and *Le Rire, journal humoristique* (Paris). Balzac's *La Cousine Bette* was published in 1846. *The Demi-Gods* was dedicated to Bodkin, "The Lonely God" to MacKenna.]

My dear Tom

Thanks for your budget. & for the papers. Dublin is dull you say. It cannot be one half as dull as Paris. It is true that folk are beginning to come back here, but in every rue there are houses after houses fermé a cause de guerre, maisons sequestré & maisons gone bang for lack of trade. These streets that used to be so murderous are not so any longer. Children may play in the middle of the Avenue de l'Opera. I used to cross that street with my heart in my mouth & my eyes skewways. The Luxemburg Jardin would make you weep. The Cafés are like tombs. Beside that the newspapers are censored with a rigour far beyond that in Ireland. The cinemas even are censored – There are no war pictures shown there. The voice of the American lady which rang of yore from every grove is heard no more in the land and chez nous ["at home"] we have the whooping-cough, on which a malison. I sent you the proofs of Songs From the Clay – Maybe they'll reach you. I also sent a Brieux play – all about the villainy of barrister people & I am now forwarding two copies of Le Rire – They are the first I have seen in Paris, & as you will notice, they are assez bête ["rather stupid"]. I am reading Balzac. Lord! he is tremendous. La Cousine Bette is the book I'm on now. Will you write me & say which are his best books, that is which of them pleased you most. My publishers have been sending me press notices of The Demi-Gods. They are not entheusiastic, but, with yourself, I believe in that book. The tepidity of those reviews sent me to reread the book & it is, I'll swear, a good one & almost worthy of having your name on its preface page – One gets terrified about dedications. Whenever I think of poor Stephen MacKenna I blush to think that I saddled my friend with that idiotic Lonely God. There are folk who laud that poem to my teeth. I put my trust in God that you & I will not be ashamed together (in 6 months) of our connection with The Demi-Gods. I have begun a new book six times & dashed these beginnings into a thousand fragments – its an accursed m[´]etier ["career"] the storytelling. Songs From the Clay has been postponed to the Spring. I will search tomorrow for some Fragson or other 2 sous songs & will wrap them to you. When you have an evening and nothing to do write to me & tell me all about yourself & all about la patrie ["the homeland"][.] My compliments to your father & mother & when you meet AE embrassez-le bien pour

Votre ami
JAMES STEPHENS

To SIR FREDERICK MACMILLAN
(Macmillan & Company, London)

Paris
[T/23] 16 December 1914

[In reply to this letter, Macmillan declined to raise the price of *The Charwoman's Daughter* but offered to increase Stephens's royalty from 10% to 25%. The 1917 reissue of the novel was priced at 4s. 6d.]

Dear Sir Frederick Macmillan,

I have your letter and the "copy" for The Adventures of Seumas Beg. When you require this ms. I shall return it.

I note you have postponed the publication of Songs From the Clay until March 12th 1915.

As to Mr Brett's remarks re the Demi-Gods – I believe myself that his confidence will be justified. At the first, and perhaps for a couple of years, my work will be a little difficult to handle and the critics may be puzzled, as he suggests. My work is in several respects different from current American fiction but the critics will discover a standard of some kind whereby to measure it. I continually receive letters from American writers and others congratulating me very warmly on my books – These ideas will become more audible as time goes on.

As to an agreement for another novel – I shall be very glad to enter into one with your firm. The only suggestion I make is that the American royalties should begin with 15 per cent and 20 per cent after 5,000 have been sold.

There is another matter as to which I should be glad of your advice – I believe that in a very short time my books will begin to move more freely. I also believe that the most popular of them will ultimately be The Charwoman's Daughter. I have not yet written anything better than this book; I do not think I ever will? However, that is all for the future to show. I think that the format of the book is wrong, it looks too skimpy, and that the price (3/6) is a mistake also. I think that this price is always a mistake. Bookbuyers often consider that a second-hand price means second-hand matter. In America this is sold at 5/-, and by the use of a somewhat larger type, etc, the volume is quite large enough for that price. I consider it would be quite worth while to reissue this book (there are 270 pages in the American issue) and list it at 5/-. If this suggestion meets your approval I will be glad to revise the book for such re-issue and make it as perfect as I can. I believe The Charwoman's Daughter will be the most successful of my books and that is why I make this suggestion.

Having made the suggestion, however, I will be quite willingly governed by your experience, but I beg you will consider the point. The 3/6 price not alone depreciates the profits of both publisher and author it also, by implication, depreciates the literature on which it is marked.

Yours very truly,
JAMES STEPHENS

To ALICE STOPFORD GREEN

Paris
[A/26] 28 December 1914

[Alice Stopford Green (1847–1929) was an important Irish historian. Among her works were *The Making of Ireland and Its Undoing* (1908), *Irish Nationality* (1911) and *The Old Irish World* (1912). *La Comédie Humaine* was the generic title which Balzac gave to a seventeen-volume collection of his fiction, published from 1842 to 1848. In this letter Stephens is echoing the advice given to him by W. K. Magee in a letter of 2 August 1913: "Your subject is not really Paris but that manifestation of the Supreme Brahma known as Dublin, and you must come back and write many more chapters of its comédie humaine."]

Dear Mrs Green,

I know you are tremendously busy, and I am really loath to trouble you, but you are the only person I know of capable of giving special advice. – Following this woeful prelude here are the facts – I have been suddenly attacked with terrible & weighty ambitions. I want to write a book, or, better, a series of books, which will be as Irish as the novels of Balsac are French – that is I want to slice off a period of our countries history & explore that period with the particularity of an ant in his den. From the Viceroy to the peasant on the one hand & from the Nationalist Catholic gombeen-man to the spoiled-priest & the organgeman-athiest (if such monsters there be) on the other hand. I find I have only been playing at literature up to this, and I believe, egotist that I am, not alone that I can build big & deep stories, but that I can hit our country such thumps on the head as will awaken her from the artificial torpor that she is in. In short I want to write La Comedie Humaine of Ireland. Every writer should have some kind of literary ambition big enough to explain his failure if he is too little for the job. That may be my fate but I want to put it to the test, and I implore you to help me. You are a millionaire of the knowledges I lack & I crave alms of your wisdom. I am a moder[n], not only in time but in spirit, & I want to know the section of Irish life that will best illuminate the good times that are coming & I want to know how best I should study that period. What books of yours, for instance, should I read? What other books would you advise me to read? What study local (for I will return to Ireland for the writing – I will study here in detachment) archaeological, historical, social? I am a villian, dear lady, to be bothering you this way, but I believe, there is nobody but myself to do the work, & nobody but you who can help me – Every good wish to you for the New Year.

Sincerely yours
JAMES STEPHENS

To ERNEST A. BOYD

Paris
[A/12] 7 January 1915

[The article on American literature was apparently not published in *Life*.]

Dear Boyd

I was glad to hear from you & to know that yourself & your lady are in form. What a woeful country you portray the Mighty States as being. & yet a few days ago I picked up an American paper in the Ave. de l'Opera & it opened a world to me that I thought had ceased to exist. If you [read] a French paper now you wouldnt know what it was. War news on the first page, the denial of the same on the second page, the 3rd & 4th pages the deads & woundeds & they are the sole *facts* one can learn about the war. Rumour of course is talking in the Cafés with her thousand tongues & a lie on the tip of each of them. Faith! its dull & every woman is a widow or swings those ensigns[.] The American paper gave me my bearings again – There it was full to the twentieth page with bulgaries, rapes, divorces, bludgeonings, police-corruption, boxing, & whatnot – Civilization at last, said I with a gasp, & I hugged the rag to my chest. This world has so accomodated itself to war that one can not imagine another method of life. We have all settled down to it & we look back to seven months ago with a kind of wonder that such modes were, but we dont look forward at all. "It will end sometime" they say, & that 'sometime' has about it all the implications of eternity. Let it be. I was sick of it ten years ago, before it started & the schoolboy barbarism of it all make me sicker.

You liked my Demi-Gods! I have not seen any American references to it & dont know whether it is like to please the land of your adoption. Now I am ruminating on a bigger theme. I dedicate myself to write le Comedie Humaine of Ireland taking some thirty years of its history, morals, socialogy, religion, economics & write it north to south & east to west & in & out & round. Will I be able to do it? Here's my difficulty that I have tons of wisdom & no knowledge, but knowledge is sold in every shop & I'll buy it. If I can digest all these informations I feel I am strong enough to do the job, & if I fall why I'll fall with a certain emphasis. Meanwhile, some years of study & then I'll start tunnelling my mountains & then I'll swing Ireland out of her dungeons & ditches & perch her astride one of the horns of the moon. Does your wife dislike the States also? I sent by the way an Article to Life on American literature. They may accept it (they asked me for it so probably they dont want it) but if its printed you may find it interesting.

All good wishes to ye both
JAMES STEPHENS

To AN ANONYMOUS CORRESPONDENT

Paris
[A/14] 10 January 1915

[Stephens's contribution to the series of "Flying Fame Chapbooks" published by Lovat Fraser (1871–1926) was *Five New Poems* (1913), which contained "The River", "The Cow", "Spring", "The Lake" and "Evening". All of the chapbooks by Hodgson mentioned were published in 1913.]

Dear Sir

In reply to your letter of the 15th Dec The Chap Book you mention is published by Mr Lovat Fraser, 45 Roland Gardens,

London S.W. My verses in this chapbook are not very good, but, if you are interested in poetry, I would suggest you should get the poems by Ralph Hodgson (in the same series & for which he has just been awarded the Polignac Prize) [–] His booklets are entitled "Eve" ["]The Bull" & "The Song of Honour" [–] They are priced at 6d each –

Very truly yours
JAMES STEPHENS

To HENRY McBRIDE

Paris
[A/42] 1 March 1915

[I have not traced McBride's article on *The Demi-Gods.* The "Paris 1915" stories were not published. I have not identified Dr. Whitney. The book of poems was *Songs from the Clay.*]

My dear Henry,

I did not know you were still at "The Sun". In every blessed letter you have written me you took such care to leave an address out–! Ah me! You'r the best of men, but America is a wide address even for Cleopatra or the Moon or Mrs Thaw. I got your Article on the Demi-Gods all right, & was real pleased to read it. I came back to Paris after a months vacation in Dublin & have had a copy of the Demi-Gods packed for you & waiting until I could discover an address to send it – but now I expect it would be like making a man a present of a bucket of coal in midsummer. We are worrying along here – They have shut off the absinthe (my heavy curse on them) & nothing is active but boredom. I hate this war & I hate everyone that's in it & I hate everything about it. So out of that hate I am beginning a series of Articles on "*Paris 1915*" which I am trying to make interesting in spite of the war. Mick Aldrich descended twice from her chateau, but I was out each time. Dr Whitney is here & talks friendship & cocktails & Madame Gonne has come back from nursing the wounded. Lord, if you were to look at the Champs Elysées now you wouldn't see it. & the Ave de l'Opera is anyone's Avenue that wants it. My ends are all loose. I've got the gigs & my book of poems is coming out next week chez Macmillan's – Come over to Paris for Gods sake & hold my hand while I get drunk. I am, I always was, I ever will be

JAMES STEPHENS

To THOMAS BODKIN

Paris

[A/3] [1 March] 1915

[The Balzac novels which Stephens mentions are *La Cousine Bette* (1847), *Le Père Goriot* (1835), the posthumous *Un ménage de garçon* (1913) and *Les Illusions perdues* (1837). "The time is out of joint; O cursed spite,/That ever I was born to set it right" is from *Hamlet*, I. iv. 188–9.]

My dear Tom.

I was glad to get your letter & to hear your news. I dont think I have spoken to a living soul (until Sunday last) since I left Ireland. & I envy you much your opportunities of dropping in on AE for, as that remark implies, I am more in need of being talked at than of emptying my own sack (No, I'm not). My throat has gone rusty & my brains do not function any more (Its not true)[.] As to the said Balsac & your remarks thereon [–] I have now read seven or eight of his books & he still fevers me. Its true enough about the turgidity & the rest, but after the turgidity there is the big man & the big job done bigly. I have read The Cousine Bette & Goriot & Un Mènage de Garçon & les Illusions Perdues & some others. I think the Menage du Garçon has interested me more passionately than any book I have read for years. It is always difficult to begin any Balsac book but that book is worth even your attempting. But pleasure in reading is not the only reason why I am chez Balsac ["in the house of Balzac"]. I am studying his method of dealing with large masses of people & events in order that I also, even I, may attempt something before I die. I want, putting the thing in an indecent nakedness, to write Le Comedie Humaine of Ireland. What a story there is to tell there. None of our men seem aware of the passionate, varied story that Ireland is & has been, but "is" for me who am modern & interested almost entirely in the things that I touch & feel. My plan is to take a slice of Irish time, say the twenty years culminating in this day & the tomorrows during which I will be writing & explore these, with the particularity of a grub working through an apple, until I have attained to a consciousness of Ireland in all its dimensions, & which consciousness I can impress, not alone into my books, but into our people – Behold a job! AE says that before Ireland can achieve a social system it must become somehow conscious; this will never be done for us by the politicians, or even the traders; the cooperative society itself will not do it, but I think I can do it – Behold a think! I think that in ten years Ireland, with the material we have now, can be made the literary capital of the world, & I want to be there swinging a mace as big as a weaver's beam, & whacking into shape & out of shape everything thar I come across. We lack a mirror, a synthesis, we cannot see ourselves & so we cannot see any thing but angles & distortions & nonsense. Am I big enough for the job? Can I make them read me if only from intellectual snobishness? It is a question! for before I can capture Ireland I must conquer the world – and I lack, I lack, I am a chasm of ignorance & radiating from me are subterranean caves filled equally with ignorance; but ignorance is only emptiness & a hole can always be filled. I have to fill these pits with economics, & history & social knowledge, & knowledge of our bureaucrats, traders, farmers, thieves, prostitutes, what not & after it, discover or invent a national psychology. Oh Lord! "Oh cursed Spite – " Oh I hate study. Meanwhile, perhaps I cannot do the job; the certainty is, that I can try – You asked me for a letter with some egotism in it – This is the letter, and I am

As Always
JAMES STEPHENS

Wish I could talk to AE about it. I could not write before for I was not able to raise the postage this last month – I am all right now for the royalties have just arrived & I smoke again –

To THE EDITOR OF *THE NEW AGE*

[Paris]
18 March 1915

[The text is from *The New Age* for 18 March 1915. The letter is Stephens's response to "Affirmations VII: The Non-existence of Ireland" by Ezra Pound (1885–1972), published in *The New Age* for 25 February 1915. Pound had written that "Even James Stephens, whom one would think, in all conscience, a mild enough writer, has chosen a life in Paris." Pound "can find no proof of continued Irish existence": "When Ireland turned against Synge's genius it (Ireland) ceased, quite simply, to exist."]

AFFIRMATIONS.

Sir,–

I write to you in sorrow, for I prefer always that my mind should dwell on pleasant things. Mr. Pound is not pleasant. And he has mentioned my name in THE NEW AGE. I am ashamed. I frankly confess it. I apologise to everybody and beg them to believe that I did not ask him to do it, for I have never met him. There are so many things I wish he would do: I wish he would not mention my name; I wish he would not write quite so mistakenly about Synge; I wish he would not write quite so mistakenly about Mr. Lawrence; I wish he would not write quite so mistakenly about Mr. Joyce; I wish he could believe that we knew all about Mr. Joyce's work long before he did, and that we still prefer Mr. Joyce's verse to his prose; I wish he would not repeat a conversation of Mr. Yeats and call it an "imaginary portrait" of Sir Hugh Lane; I wish he would not say that I ran away from Ireland; I wish he would run back to America; I wish he had never run away from that great country; I wish he would bury himself and stay buried. Judge, dear sir, of my outraged modesty when I, usually so original, find myself wishing what everybody wishes – that one touch of Nature. . . . I have written Mr. Pound's name. I am going to fumigate my pen –

'Tis God can do all things he will, and will all things He do;
He can make an ape, an ox, a fox, or a lively kangaroo,
For God who made all things has made the world and
made it round,
And He made policemen's feet to beat in the verse of Ezra
Pound.

JAMES STEPHENS.

To THOMAS BODKIN

Paris
[A/3] 27 March 1915

[Stephens's response to Pound's article was published in *The New Age* for 18 March 1915. Bodkin did write to the French novelist and poet Henri de Régnier (1864–1936) about "The Vase" and published his reply in *May It Please Your Lordships.* "Burnand" is an error for Burton. Although Stephens contributed a flattering "Centenary Appreciation of the Author of 'Jane Eyre' " to *The Sphere* for 22 April 1916, he apparently did not publish in the *Daily News and Leader* a review of *Brontë Poems: Selections from the Poetry of Charlotte, Emily, Anne and Branwell Brontë*, ed. Arthur C. Benson (1915). Stephens's "The Old Woman's Money" appeared in the *Century Magazine* for May 1915. "The Cherry Tree" was included in *The Adventures of Seumas Beg.* AE's remark was made in a letter in March 1915. The Irish poet Francis Ledwidge (1891–1917) did not publish any poems in the *Spectator* at this time; Stephens may be thinking of "The Burial of Love", printed in the *Saturday Review* for 6 March 1915. "And have some peace" is from "Peace in War Time", published in *Collier's Magazine* for 11 December 1915.]

My dear Tom.

That was a tremendous letter of yours & the ["brief paper" cancelled] (I'm forgetting my training) the Case-paper nearly made me homesick. I would almost like to go back to the 10 to 6 hours & make out case to Counsel & Interrogatories on Title Pleadings. Did you see the article of Ezra Pounds to which my letter referred? To think of a dog like that attacking Ireland. He is chasing notioriety with a hatchet, & if he doesnt mind he'll find it. When I read over the letter I had written to the New Age I got sorry for him & modified it to the kindly note you read. By the way, a young French friend of mine assures me that Henri de Regnier reads English with ease & I have been thinking he might be pleased if you sent him a copy of your translation of his poem "The Vase" is I think its name. It would be pleasant to hear from him on the subject. My recollection of your translation is of a remarkable, original poem in the English. Have you translated any thing more since that epock? Long ago is'nt it: that is, "before the war"[.] I wish you could come over here for a week – I would prefer a month, but I dont tempt the Gods, so, for a week & wander with me. The Spring is commencing & all along the boulevards the trees are poking up green knobs & are beginning to stir themselves & talk to one another. As you wish to know where my stuff appears – I do very little at any time, but the Daily News sends me a book every month to review & gives me two guineas for it – not even a junior counsel's fee – You would sneer at that yourself. The books they send me are always rubbish. The Kasidah of Burnand. Geo. Berminghams Connaught to Chicago & Borrows Poems. Unreadable tosh, & now I have received the Brontê poems! I'd sooner read an Abstract of Title. I'd sooner read an advertisement about soap. I'd sooner read all Homer in a crib. I'll swot the stuffing out of them Brontes; blast them [–] why couldnt they stick to their own lasts & leave poetry alone? An Article of mine will appear in the Century Magazine, either this current issue or the next one – Its not much good & I have completed 9 or 10 articles of a series entitled "Paris 1915". It is a series of little pictures, imaginings, thoughts, nonsense, anything, & while there are sentences here & there which gave me pleasure I am not to be taken as saying that these are the best articles ever written. I enclose you a small poem "The Cherry Tree" [–] I like it, but I really think my poetry days are finished. I have been dissipating it in novels & as AE wrote me "you cannot eat your poetic cake in prose & have it afterwards in verse" & thats true. Damn it thats true. Me voila; c'est fini ["Here I am; it is finished"] & as the Americans say "Prose for mine" from this time forth, praise the Lord, but dammit. As to the Balsac scheme – I am quite ready to disavow that too-heroic advertisement, but I'll try it first. Show "The Cherry Tree" to AE & tell him that I'll out-write him one of these days. You dont agree with me but I would barter all my verse for one or two of his poems. No I wouldnt but I'd swap poetry with him & wink at the devil. No I wouldnt do that either but I'd like to have his brain in my pocket. He is a great man & there he is boiling away like billy-oh, as you would say, & all as if he wasnt 47 years of age & never would be. Bless him & long may he wave. Did you see some verse of Ledwidge's in recent Spectators? – They are delicious. They leave me in the straw. He is some poet that chap & he'll be some more as soon as he is taken off the bottle & can digest plain food for himself. He is young yet & is honourably vomiting his ancestors. I wish I was'nt in France. I wish I was in Dublin. I wish I was in Kilcool[e], or Kilcock, or Kilfenora or Killygar. My humble respects to your mother & my upstanding, man of the world, same-job regards to your father, & to yourself behold my hand & seal

JAMES STEPHENS

P/S The scrap of verse you mentioned "And have some peace" is mine own workmanship. On Russell's advice I did not publish it in Songs From the Clay. He thought it would be better as the end poem of a collected edition one million years hence. I have just torn up a thousand poems, no one will ever know how badly I can write when I bend my brows to it.

JS

To STEPHEN MacKENNA

Paris

[A/19] 30 March 1915 [& August 1930]

Dear Stephen

It was a sad letter you wrote me & it was full of the gaiety I love. Dont make any mistake about the evenings in Donnybrook. They were real & the talk was good, & the master of the house was full of wisdom & cheeriness & courage, & the bean a tige [*bean an tighe*, "the mistress of the house"] shed music around her & around us. By the Gods I've had no talking since I didnt see you, & I wont have any until I see you again, & if the Lord is good he'll give you back the health & the little income will bob up from a queer place. Dear man hold a good hold on the health so that people who love you will be able to think about you with laughter & good hearts. Both you & herself are having a bad time & its lasting too long. I wish I could get good news from you, & hear that you were making plans, for I'm certain sure that when you are well you will be able to do anything you please. The big work under cover of the little work. Theres stuff in you, & I am anxious to see it so that I can say "Theres another Irishman" to the people, & so that we can fight about it between ourselves. I wish I was in Donnybrook walking round the garden with yourself & herself & going into the big room for the music & marching into the bookroom for the talk. There is no barm brack in Paris like the barm brack of Donnybrook – There are no trees on these boulevards like the one at the corner of your road. The bonnes ["maids"] are gentil [*gentilles*, "nice"] here but they are not as decent as Maire (or was she Nora) was. The dogs here dont have the welcome on their tails that Rury had & one cant view the sea from these roofs nor a field full of lambs from the 2nd top window. Wouldnt ye have a better chance over here than in Lundan [*Lonndan*, "London"]? The Spring commences & in a month the Luxembourg gardens will be habitable & sunny. Tell your lady I was asking for her.

do c[h]ara
["your friend"]
JAMES STEPHENS

[The following are Stephens's 1930 comments:]

Rereading ones own old letters is rather a curious thing. First, on writing them one was certainly sure that one would never see them again. That being comfortably read, they would (or might) be dutifully replied to, & would then light the pipe of the excellent reader. Not that Stephen MacKenna smoked a pipe. He had yearnings that way, but the cigarette came more easily to his fingers and held more easily to his lips. Held indeed! Stuck is the word. He used [to] roll his own cigarettes: badly too: lumpily and jaggedly and raggidly: & then, having put it in (or on) his lips he left it there, & talked wildly and entheusiastically upon it. He had the cigarette stuck to his under-lip, & it dangled therefrom as he talked & was drawn again to the perpendicular when courtesy warned him that he ought to listen as well as speak. I have presented him with a dozen pipes, and a tobacco-pouch went with each pipe: and each presentation was received with a statement that nothing whatever but this was needed to round and complete happiness, and circumvent misery: and the pipe was smoked thereupon with delight, but on the next day the ill-shaped, bulgy, tattered cigarette was again a dangling upon his chin. Alas! he was at this date having a bad time, and it had lasted, and was to last yet, for a long time.

To WARREN BARTON BLAKE

Paris
[A/3] 8 April 1915

[Warren Barton Blake (1883–1918) was on the staff of *Collier's: The National Weekly*. Stephens published four poems in *Collier's* between May and December 1915.]

Dear Mr Blake

I was glad to hear from you & particularly glad to know that you preferred my Demi-Gods to the Crock of Gold. We are in a minority of three. AE and you & myself are agreed on this point, but the vast majority of reviewers think otherwise & will continue to do so for some time. The Demi-Gods is certainly much better written & organized than the other, & there are passages in it which give me great personal pleasure. As to work for Colliers – I am afraid that at the moment I have nothing in prose which would be, in your phrase, "available" [–] I am engaged on a series of little studies of French life which I am calling "Paris 1915" & I fancy you will like them, should you ever see them. So the only matter I can let you have is some of my recent poems. If you do not like any run them back to me as quickly as you can. I would be glad to hear what you think of "Songs From The Clay"

Sincerely yours
JAMES STEPHENS

By the way you will notice that I am not in Ireland. I left Dublin for Paris a few weeks after you departed & have been here ever since. Its a Sad place, but the spring is coming –

Enclosed 6 poems

To JOHN OTWAY PERCY BLAND

Paris
[A/37] May 1915

[J. O. P. Bland (1863–1945), who was born in County Antrim, was a writer on Far Eastern affairs. On 26 April 1915, Bland sent Stephens a copy of AE's "The Spiritual Conflict: A Coming Recoil", printed in *The Times* (London) for 14 April 1915.]

Dear Mr Bland,

Your "dool" has reached me safely & I send her back to you with an olive branch in her throttle. I got the article all right & it was *the* article. You were real kind to have sent it & I was a yellow dog not to have acknowledged receipt. I see you are in the County Antrim. God be with the County Antrim & with yourself – I wish I was there or anywhere but in Paris which, having bored my body to death, begins to bore my soul to the devil. The sunlight has begun here & it is hatching widows out of every street, but you were here only a few weeks ago, & besides that you do descriptive articles yourself. I'm always shy of writing to a writer. He knows how the thing is done, & every second line I hear him saying "Va! petit ["Go! little one"], I said that yesterday!" But you are going to see AE. I envy you, & would sacrifice any mans leg to have half an hour with you both & me with my ears flapping as I gathered in the good talk & thought of the articles I would make of it all – I've coined pieces of eight out of AE many a time, & if the Lord will preserve both our healths I'll continue to feed my family on his spare verbs. Get him to show you his pictures, & get him to say a poem to you, one of his own, for he has the queerest way of saying verse that ever you did hear, & tell me honestly did he make you go asleep or did he set your spine creaking? I wish I was there. I do so.

Yours
JAMES STEPHENS

To WARREN BARTON BLAKE

Paris
[A/3] 20 May 1915

[Stephens did publish in the *Century Illustrated Magazine* but not in *Lippincott's Monthly Magazine.* His poem in *Collier's* for 22 May 1915 was "Charity". Blake's numerous articles were on varied topics, ranging from "Eating in Paris" to "John Synge and his Plays". Colum had emigrated to America earlier in 1915. Stephens may have come across the Biblical allusion to the "strong bulls of Bashan" in "September" (l. 124) of Spenser's *The Shepheards Calender.*]

Dear Mr Blake

It was very good of you to write me giving information about "Lippincotts" & the "Centnary". I note you will send me on the May "Collier" with my poem in it. I hope there is something of yours in it also. I remember that just before my leaving Ireland you sent me a few cuttings from your own articles. I wish you could continue that admirable practice, for I am greatly interested in the writing & opinions of men I have met, so when you have written something you like if you could get someone to snip it out & stick it in an envelope with my address I would feel that "the wrinkled sea" was not really so much of a barrier as it looks. So Colum is lecturing in the interests of the German-Americans! He is consistent, for he was doing that before he left Ireland. I remember a comical battle one evening in AE's studio between Colum & Lord Dunsany on this subject Dunsany being about ten times as ferocious on the English side as Colum was on the other & Dunsany is the proprietor of a voice three times louder than that of any bull of Bashan. It was I who kept the peace on that occasion for I peppered Dunsany with small jokes & kept his eloquence from full flood, otherwise he would have become excited & batted us all into English regiments with his umbrella. It was a joyous evening, but Colum is not a match for Dunsany

As to the war – I dont know what I think about it. I dont think I am able to think about it. Do I want England to win? I want France to win. On the subject of England I am all at sea. When I think of England I think, by extension, of Ireland, & of seven miserable centuries during which England has dragooned us & sacked our cities & violated our women & performed every bestiality that her statecraft or her trade-craft could devise & execute. The fact that the world is sick of the Irish question does not make it any the less real. We are sick of it too, by God we have been sick of it all those long seven hundred years and like dogs we have had to eat our own vomit many times. I say I dont know what to think about England in this crisis. I have been told that when this war is over England promises herself to regulate her account with Ireland once more, &, over there, she will be able to do things that even the Germans cannot do in Belgium. We know England. We know what she has done to us so often, & we know that she is very capable of doing that all over again con amore, & redoing it after that. I've no brick to swing at Colum, and I've no laurel wreaths for anyone else either – sticking bayonets into each others bellies for the love of God & for the sake of freedom & for the furthurence of Civilization!! Va petit ["Go little"] bamboozlers – I wish I could take out papers of naturalization as a dog or a hedgehog or a cat, and I wish I could give all them armies one vast wallop with the heel of my fist.

Sincerely yours
JAMES STEPHENS

To W. T. H. HOWE

Paris
[A/3] 20 May 1915

[The correct titles for two of the poems from *Songs from the Clay* are "The Rivals" and "A Song for Lovers". *The New Word: An Open Letter Addressed to the Swedish Academy in Stockholm, on the Meaning of the Word Idealist* by Allen Upward (1863–1926) was published in 1907.]

Dear Mr Howe

I was very glad to hear from you again. I did get your little figurine last Christmas, and am very much obliged to you for sending it. My wife instantly made sacrifice to it by burning insense – bois de mariage ["wood of marriage"], and reciting more or less appropriate praise & welcome. Meantime & ever since he has from my mantle-shelf presided over our hearth & I doubt not he has preserved us not only from robbers but also from incendiary bombs & the typhus which these eventuful days must be manufacturing. It is a great pleasure to know that you like my Songs From the Clay. Naturally it is not as "big" a book as the Hill of Vision. It represents a different set of moods and ideas & technique, but I think that, slight as the songs are, they have been generally successful. I am very pleased myself with many of these songs, such as Your Rivals. The Messenger. The Song For Lovers, the Nodding Stars, the Centaurs, The Snare & others. On the whole, altho' one is never satisfied, I am not dissatisfied. As to your enquiry as to how America is treating my work. I am afraid that America has not yet put any butter on my bread, but, as you say, that will come. The chief thing at present is not to make a fortune but to get the work done, & by not remarking it the lean years will slip insensibly into the fat ones. I place that matter in the charge of your little god & beg him to fatten those years for me and preserve me mine appetite. As to the war – I hate it & despise it, and would like mightily to be in it, for, on this side of the world, this vast feeling of suicide is extending its sway & it becomes increasing difficult for any man to preserve his detachment. Europe is beginning to see red & these rabies are contagious. I look for worse weather. When the war is over I look for a peace a thousand times worse than the war.

Yours sincerely
JAMES STEPHENS

Did you ever come across a book called "The New Word" (I think) by Allan Upward? – it is a singular & very beautiful book –

To THOMAS BODKIN

Paris
[A/3] [16] June 1915

[This letter refers to Stephens's application for a position at the National Gallery of Ireland. The "other thing" was the Directorship, which was to become vacant in 1916. The French should be *Voilà un prospect, et me voilà content. . . . Je vous écrirari plus longuement un autre jour, maintenant je cherche la poste. Amitiés respectueuses à votre famille et à vous-même* – "There is a prospect, and behold me content. . . . I will write longer on another day, now I am looking for the post. Respectful regards to your family and to yourself."]

My dear Tom,

Many thanks for your letter (I was afraid you were never going to write again) & for the enclosures. If that Clerkship can be gotten for me I'll take it & be glad, for at this moment affairs are going, for me, in miserly fashion. No one will buy my stuff. The war has flooded over & drowned me. The articles on Paris about which I wrote you are not appearing in the Century so you need not subscribe to it, nor are they appearing anywhere else, & the months of this year still to come loom before this deponent with a bleak gaunt & hungry appearance. Nor is there any new book in process. I can't write here & have almost Forgotten that I ever could write. If the job doesnt come off dont let this wail distress you in the smallest, for, as you know, I made friends with poverty long ago & am acquaint[ed] with her ways. So much for that & be damned to it. I hope you will get the other thing. First because it would be to your liking, second because you would be the exact right man in that gallery, third because if I get this & you get that why we can pull on the same oar, the while I steal from you informations & knowledges of which I am empty to say nothing of neutral conversations[.] Voila un prospect, et me voila content. I enclose an application. Je vous écrirai plus longuement un autre jour, maintenant Je cherche la poste[.] Amitiés respectueus à votre famille et à vous-même

JAMES STEPHENS

To WARREN BARTON BLAKE

Paris

[A/3] 8 July 1915

[A meeting of about forty prominent Socialists was held in London on 14 February 1915; the attendance of some members of the French government became a point of controversy. Joseph Jacques Césaire Joffre (1852–1931) was Commander of the Allied Armies in France; Ferdinand Foch (1851–1929) was Commander-in-Chief of the Allied Armies on the Western Front; Victor Louis Lucien d'Urbal (1858–1943) was a French general; Alexandre Millerand (1859–1943), Minister of War from 26 August 1914 to 29 October

1915, was a strong supporter of Joffre. Stephens's "The Proud Mountains" was published in *Collier's* for 14 August 1915. The book was *The Adventures of Seumas Beg.*]

Dear Mr Blake

Thanks for your letter & for all the news you have therein. I have met a good many of your countrymen in Paris & they are disquieted as to what your people are going to do in the war. For my part I hope they continue to do as they have started – that is, attend to their own affairs & let Europe go hang – Its not their scrap. The French regard the entry of Italy on the scene as a real joke & both France Germany & England will smile broadly if America gets hooked in by the leg. Nothing goes here but rumours & they are mostly lies, but I find a growing dissatisfaction (not a disloyalty or dislike) on the English account. The opinion is that England is not holding up her end. I dont know whether she is or not, for in this war one does not know anything. From subterranean politics there pokes now & again a reptilian head. for politicians simply can't quit their job, which is disturbance of the public peace. Twice already the government here has only just failed to tumble. Once was only a week ago, the other time was just after the Socialist Congress in London. A battle is being waged with the intention of deposing General Joffre & putting either Foch or D'Urbal in his place & beads are being pulled on Millerand the War Minister. I think that in simple despair the present ministry & Commander in Chief may order an earlier offensive than is in their opinion advisable.

I return you "The Proud Mountains" & a few other of my recent poems to look at. As I am going to print these in a book (in I should say September) I hope you will use whatever you can early. & as I am thinking of going back to Ireland I hope your people will send me whatever cheque is coming as early as possible –

Sincerely yours
JAMES STEPHENS

To THOMAS BODKIN

Paris

[A/3] 9 July 1915

[Stephens was elected to a position in the National Gallery of Ireland at a meeting of the Governors on 8 July 1915. William Frederick

Bailey (1857–1917) was one of the Governors. The "place" in the postscript is Virginia, County Cavan.]

My dear Tom,

Thats great news. Me voila content. and it certainly was a wise idea of yours. I have just gotten letters from AE and Bailey giving the tale. I hope to the Lord you will get the other job when it falls in. I wish you had it now. AE mentioned it in his letter, as being practically certain that next year you would be there waving the sceptre & the orb. I will carry a banner at that festival, & we will go in joyous procession "about the temples of the young compassionate gods". Meanwhile let you engrave on your bedpost & on the lintel of your porte ["door"]

"Do this god and there shall be
Myrtles offered up to thee."

As to your kind enquiry about money – If you have any loose pieces wearing holes in your breeks I'll be glad to have them. About a week after I get to Dublin I'll be able to repay you, for I am arranging with Macmillan to bring out "The Adventures of Seumas Beg" & when the ms is completed & the agreement signed I will touch an advance royalty of (let us pray) monumental proportions. Are there any things over here you have an envy for, books or illustrations or soups or whatsoever other vanities. You & MacKenna have seen each other. Have you noticed that Stephen has an extraordinary pleasant giggle. May he get well & may you never get ill.

Toujours ton ami
JAMES STEPHENS

I see you write from the place where you & AE & myself holidayed. Did the patron give you honey? I would give two lyrics & a shilling for some of that miel ["honey"].

To THOMAS BODKIN

Paris
[A/3] 15 July 1915

[The Director of the National Gallery of Ireland was Walter G. Strickland (1850–1928), who had been appointed temporarily to fill the vacancy caused by the death of Sir Hugh Lane aboard the *Lusitania* on 7 May 1915. John Pentland Mahaffy (1839–1919), Provost of Trinity College and a member of the Board of Guardians and Governors of the Gallery, had been opposed to Stephens's appointment. The letter which Stephens enclosed was addressed to the Governors and read "I regret that circumstances oblige me to withdraw my application for the position of Clerk to the National Gallery"; Bodkin did not forward it. "To be with you among the daubs" refers to Bodkin's hope to become Director when Strickland resigned in 1916; he was not, however, elected.]

A c[h] ara T[h] omá[i] s ["Dear Thomas"]

Here's a pretty mess,
Here's a how de doo!

You've got to advise me, and by your advice I will go. Examinons le position. A director implacably hostile to me, & having under his thumb thirteen subordinates each of whom, by nod & beck & wreathed smile, can be enlisted in the same hostility. Mais quelle boite [*boîte*, i.e. "but what a box I'm in"] ! and at one remove, but within coup de téléphone ["telephone call"] guardians holding protéges in leash & all eager to get a bite at my flying heels. I am solemn enough, God wots it well, & on occasion I can bear me with the gravity of a mummy, but no solemnity will cover me from the thirteen subordinates (unlucky number, be dam but!) or from the implacable director who will smile & be a villain still (Coke 3 cap 6) [–] Do you see me drawing my meegre screw at the end of one lunar month? My vision is obscured[.]

But here is the graveman – if it spells itself thus – Your position! If I go in will those other baulked senators nourish hatred against you, & pickle your rod, & proclaim bans & excommunications against you. They may. If they are Mahaffyish they will, & next year will be more important than this one is. When I wrote the application I wanted the job; myself & Destitution were bowing to each other; but, since then, things have changed. In a week I will get a decent advance royalty for my (now completed) manuscript & the tides will go with me again. So I enclose you a billet ["letter"] which (would I be able to hold the job a month?) I think you had better forward to the Gods. To be with you among the daubs would be all right, but one would have to wait a year for that & even £3 per week would not be value for the Implacable Director & his thirteen

Mamelukes. By the way, & as you will see from above, I wont be wanting any money. Toujours all my best thanks to you on that count for you are always & for ever the decentest of men. My respects to your Father & Mother for yourself behold my hand

JAMES STEPHENS

To THOMAS BODKIN

Paris
[A/3] 16 July 1915

[In *The Adventures of Seumas Beg/The Rocky Road to Dublin*, Stephens included poems associated with all the Dublin places named here. "King Billy" refers to a statue of William III (1650–1702), conqueror of the Catholic forces in the Battle of the Boyne (1690). James Larkin's meetings during the 1913 General Strike were held in Liberty Hall on Beresford Place. Mahaffy, angered by Stephens's appointment, published the following letter in the *Irish Times* for 9 July 1915: "As I have been for some years intimately connected with the Board of Guardians and Governors of the National Gallery of Ireland, having acted as its Chairman, I think it right to say that, after what was done there at the last meeting (July 8th), and still more how it was done, I will have nothing further to do with the Board." As reported in the *Freeman's Journal* for 10 July 1915, ". . . there were nearly 150 applicants for the position, including a considerable number of ladies with University honours and other literary qualifications. Dr. Mahaffy supported one of the lady candidates, who was defeated on a vote."]

My dear Tom

Our letters have crossed. I have just received your registered letter with £15 in it for which I thank you heartily. I think I will keep this money and shortly will send you a cheque for it. Today I sent off my ms to Messrs Macmillan, & during the course of next week, not later, certainly, than the week after, I will get an agreement from them with a cheque for advance royalties. The fact that I can pay you back so quickly does not render me less grateful, but it makes me content knowing that you have none too many monies in your own breeches pockets. May they be filled, & overflow to your boots & grow up steadily to your neck, Amen. Ainsi soit-il, and so-be-it.

I want your advice by swift return. With The Adventures of

Seumas Beg I am also issuing a collection of Dublin sketches under the title of "The Rocky Road to Dublin"[.] My memory fails me a little far from my native land. I have remembered for instance that one walks in Grafton Street at four o'clock & have harvested that fact. I have remembered that flower-pots & patriotic verse fell from the windows of York Street, that one sees the moon well from Rathmines Bridge & the coloured clouds from O'Connell Bridge, that at Dunphies Corner you can get funerally tipsy & that King Billy rides in College Green & Larkin rides in Beresford Place. If you can recollect any small street facts & refresh my memories with your recollects I'll be your servant. Some of the things I have done in this series will amuse you. I look forward to going through the proofs with you if the job comes off. I have not yet heard from Strickland or from any responsible person that I have been elected, and until I hear officially, of course, I can not take my job. I would have liked to see Prof. Mahaffy's letter. That resigning of his Governorship & writing to the papers is a curious, childish petulancy for a learned & reverend gentleman. qu'il soit damnee ["that he be damned"] & the back of my hand to him. However, what you advise me to do that will I do. My respects & compliments to your clann.

JAMES STEPHENS

To GEORGE W. RUSSELL

Paris

[A/17] 19 July 1915

[The Provost of Trinty College was Mahaffy. The figures are inaccurate in general and are weighted in favour of the Allies. The actual ratio of killed to wounded for the entire war was approximately 1 to 2.5.]

Dear AE.

I see the Provost of Trinity has been trying to put me out of my job. I am still officially in the dark as to whether I am appointed or not. Mr Strickland has not yet written me. I have just been given some figures relating to the European losses in the war up to May 31. They have been made in the French War Office, and, I think, may be relied on. By the way they must not be made public, as the government here have decided not to print the figures, fearing something in the nature of public panic should the figures get into the papers. The Servian losses do not appear to be known & the list is to be further swollen by the Italian casualties. It is possible that the English & French losses have been softened down & that the German & Austrian losses have been heightened somewhat.

	Killed	*Wounded*	*Prisoners*	*Total*
France	460,000	660,000	180,000	1,300,000
England	181,000	200,000	90,000	471,000
Belgium	49,000	49,000	15,000	113,000
Russia	1,250,000	1,680,000	850,000	3,780,000
Germany	1,630,000	1,880,000	490,000	4,000,000
Austria	1,610,000	1,865,000	910,000	4,385,000
Turkey	110,000	144,000	95,000	349,000
	5,290,000	6,478,000	2,630,000	14,398,000

There must be a large number of Irishmen in the second list, but what a bill for Europe & it may be only the commencement[.] The proportion of killed to wounded is extraordinary & goes entirely against expert calculation.

JS

1915 – 1924

I have been reading Stephens and like him. He is a very good writer, but will he ever be able to find a subject? It does not much matter if one writes well.

George Moore to John Eglinton, 6 January 1914
(*Letters of George Moore*, ed. John Eglinton)

Stephens's activities at the National Gallery of Ireland left him with sufficient time for creative activity. Soon after his return to Dublin, he published *The Adventures of Seumas Beg/The Rocky Road to Dublin*; however, this volume (written in Paris) is not representative of Stephens's primary aim during the second part of his career. As early as December of 1914 Stephens had decided that his aim as a writer would be to produce a huge work which would embody and define the national consciousness of Ireland. His first thought was to write a Balzacian survey of contemporary or near-contemporary Irish life – what he called "La Comédie Humaine of Ireland." This project apparently did not proceed beyond the planning stage.

In any event, Stephens's next works were *The Insurrection in Dublin* and *Green Branches*, both written in direct response to the 1916 Easter Rebellion. Stephens seems to have then decided that his aim of producing a peculiarly Irish work could best be fulfilled by delving into the past. This process began with *Reincarnations*, published in April 1918, a volume of re-workings of poems by several Gaelic poets. In his next three works he went even further into the past: *Irish Fairy Tales* (October 1920) is based in the main on the Fenian Cycle of Irish mythology, *Deirdre* (September 1923) and *In the Land of Youth* (October 1924) draw upon the Ulster Cycle. Stephens's plan to make *Deirdre* and *In the Land of Youth* part of a five-volume cycle did not come to fruition. While at work on these Irish materials, Stephens also found the time to write *Hunger* (1918), a short story dealing with a major motif of his fiction, *Arthur Griffith: Journalist and Statesman* (1922), a tribute to one of his old friends, and *Little Things* (1924), a privately printed volume of poems which show his growing interest in Eastern philosophy.

Late in 1924 Stephens decided to resign from his position in the National Gallery and move to London. It is not entirely clear why he gave up what was in effect a semi-sinecure: the reasons may include the urging of his wife, his own failing health, and the financial attractions of lecture tours in America. At any rate, in January 1925 he left Ireland, thereafter to return only on an occasional visit; at the same time he abandoned his aim of producing an Irish work of epic proportions.

To THOMAS BODKIN

Dublin
[A/3] 20 August 1915

[Stephens had returned to Dublin on 29 July 1915 and was now living at 42 Fitzwilliam Place.]

My dear Tom,

I enclose cheque for £15, and I give you ten thousand thanks for the loan. It was a real help in getting us back from France; that blessed little trip, with the furnishing here, has let me in for, up to the present, certainly £70. I sent you yesterday the proofs of Seumas Beg and I'll be looking forward to your notes – if you have time to do any. The Job is going along peacefully so far. I have not yet set foot in the Gallery, or seen one of our pictures; and I am waiting with interest to see will permission ever be accorded me to step out of the Clerks office, Maybe it wont. Over all these things, & many more, we will converse when you get back from the somewhere you are cachéd [*caché*, "hidden"]

Yours
JAMES STEPHENS

To EDWARD MARSH

Dublin
[A/3] 25 August 1915

[This letter (like many others of this period) is written on National Gallery stationery. The "last book" was *Songs from the Clay*. Marsh included five poems by Stephens and three by Ledwidge in *Georgian Poetry: 1913–1915*.]

My dear Marsh

As you will see by the address I have not only left Paris, but I've actually got a job – Your letter of the 16th has been chasing me [–] Your remarks about my last book are just – It is not nearly as good as the Hill of Vision, but there are good things in it, & its temper is quite different from the other book. On the whole I think I like it – As to the poems you mention for your Anthology – certainly you can have them, but drop a letter also to Messrs Macmillan on the subject.

Hastily yours
JAMES STEPHENS

When you get further on with your arrangements I would like to know who else you are going to include. You might write Lord Dunsany to send you some of Ledwidge's things to look at. I think some of his verse is wonderful.

To DENIS ROLLESTON GWYNN

Dublin
[A/26] 2 October 1915

[Denis Rolleston Gwynn (1893–1971) was the editor of *New Ireland.* Stephens published both poetry and prose in *New Ireland* from 1915 to 1917, beginning with "The Fur Coat" in the issue for 2 October 1915. Crawford Neil's "James Stephens: An Impression", a rather unsympathetic assessment, was published in *New Ireland* for 14 August 1915.]

Dear Mr Gwynn.

I have received your letter of the 27th [–] I am quite willing to do some articles for New Ireland without payment. Thanks for sending Crawford Neil's article. I enclose herewith another poem which you may care to use.

Yours sincerely
JAMES STEPHENS

To EDWARD MARSH

Dublin
[A/3] 5 October 1915

[A. R. Orage's *National Guilds: An Inquiry into the Wage System and the Way Out* was published in 1914.]

My dear Marsh.

I was sure you would find something to like in Ledwidge's verse. Your remarks about him are very just, but he is yet only a beginner and must digest his ancestors before we know what he really is like. Meanwhile he has a true singing faculty, and his promise is, I think, greater than that of any young poet now writing. I do not believe, however, that he will ratify this promise by any almighty performance. I dont believe that his thought will equal his faculty for utterence, or his sense of beauty, and I am inclined to think that when he has published another book of verse he will have delivered (should one say "reaped") the entire of his harvest, and will issue only stubble thereafter. A man is a mind & so is a poet & they are man and poet only to the extent of that. This is the croaking of a crow & I hope the future will deny it. I do not know Ledwidge at all well. I met him twice & then only for a few minutes. He is what we call here "a lump of a lad" & he was panoplied in all the protective devices, or disguises, which a country man puts on when he meets men of the town [–] Country people & children are all playacters. Dunsany, by the way, has gone to the war also. May the lord send all good men home, and may the lord defend that any more good men go out there.

Have you ever read Orage's "National Guilds" or do you ever look at his paper "The New Age"[?] I think Orage has in many ways the most interesting mind in England. In some ways he approximates to our AE & it is curious to see how closely these two minds meet & yet how profoundly they differ. One could write a tome on the psychology of these two men & when it was finished I fancy the story of England & Ireland would be written also. They have both had the same philosophic training & they are both doing the same thing, even they are greatly in sympathy, and yet the seas wash between these two men as certainly as they roll between their respective countries. God help us all & me with geography to contend with, as well as grammar. Sometime, when you've nothing better to do, write me your intentions as regards the Anthology, who is to go in & what verse of who. I have an idea as regards a future Anthology which, perhaps, when you are through with your present labours, you may be interested in. I meant to write you a note but it has lazily blown itself into a letter, and I beg your pardon for it.

Yours sincerely
JAMES STEPHENS

To THE EDITOR OF *THE NEW AGE*

[Dublin]
7 October 1915

[The text is from *The New Age* for 7 October 1915. The letter is Stephens's response to "The End of 'Romanticism' " by Ramiro de Maeztu (1875–1936), published in *The New Age* for 30 September 1915.

"A forked radish" is Falstaff's description of Justice Shallow in *Henry IV, Part Two*, III. ii. 285. The allusion to Wordsworth is a parody of a stanza from "The Tables Turned": "One impulse from a vernal wood/May teach you more of man,/Of moral evil and of good,/Than all the sages can." Beginning in March 1915, de Maeztu had contributed a series of articles to *The New Age* on the ideological basis of Guild Socialism.]

THE END OF "ROMANTICISM."

Sir,–

I wish some wise person would tell your readers whether the last article by Mr. De Maeztu is or is not nonsense. Possibly the time has come for the re-valuation of the values, and in such a stocktaking many errors will creep into our new dictionary, but your contributor's overhauling of the term "Romantic" comes as a surprise. For the condition and thought which he discovers under this term we already have an adequate name. It is Sentimentality, and if it pleases him to treat what is noble as base and what is decent as sham our dictionary is going to have a fine start. Mr. De Maeztu appears to think that man should not talk much about man, but only about the machinery whereby man expresses himself. He would imply that man has not accumulated any knowledge about himself, and cannot, therefore, talk a little in advance of the clock. We may say that a child will be a man without being stoned for soothsaying, for we know pretty fully the progression of our kind from birth to burial. We should also escape a violent death if we hold that man will surpass the "forked radish", which was the last definition of men by a man, for, leaving aside all esoteric speculations, there is a certain continuity in the historical and biological story of our race and of our fellow-creatures, and this record is open to both logic and imagination to work upon. Logic and imagination are as true human functions as are breathing and digestion; they have work to do and the ability to do it, and as with breathing and digestion, the one is very little good without the other, so it is with logic and imagination, remove the one and the other is the lamest and wobbliest of lame ducks, without a single egg in its head, the place where eggs ought to grow; but Mr. De Maeztu will take a hatchet to me of these twin functions. He says in effect, that Romance begins by making you proud and ends by leaving you foolish. It does not. He says: "For what can men do if filled with pride but exterminate one another?" and he leaves me with the assured conviction that he does not in the least know what he is writing about. He says (and it is so easy to say) that "the spring of every action is discontent". A hungry man is not discontented; he is hungry, and he knows beyond all argument exactly what will mitigate his woes; for the seed of every action is knowledge and the desire which comes after, and which knowledge alone can breed. He says: "What is bad in Romanticism" (I hate these "isms" that do not get plastered on to honest words) "is that it explains our discontent by saying that our position is not as high as we deserve." Never in the history of the earth has that been said until it was said last week in THE NEW AGE by Mr. De Maeztu. He has discovered that faith without works is dead, let him discover that work without faith is damned; and he says we must look for man among things – the beetle and the bat, and the ten-legged bug. Worsworth, of course, said it, too:

"One influence from Wall Street will teach you more of man."

Every good Romantic should shake a savage fist at Mr. De Maeztu, and bid him get off that word, and begin his dictionary at the letter A with the word Guilds – as is proper.

JAMES STEPHENS.

To EDWARD MARSH

Dublin

[A/3] 14 October 1915

[*Georgian Poetry: 1913–1915* included *King Lear's Wife* by the English poet and dramatist Gordon Bottomley (1874–1948); there was no note to the play in the published volume. The poets who had died before the book was published were Rupert Brooke

(1887–1915) and James Elroy Flecker. Only one of the poems in *The Adventures of Seumas Beg* was in print when *Insurrections* was published in May 1909; by 1912, though, over one-third of the poems in the volume had been published.]

My dear Marsh.

Thanks for that so-unexpected pound. The list you give of contents &c looks good. & the note you append to Bottomley's "*King Lear's Wife*" makes one curious. Two of your poor men are dead. May the grass lie lightly on them. I am glad you are including Hodgsons *Bull* & *Song of Honour*. The Song of Honour is one of the most sustained & beautiful things I know & the Bull is a really remarkable piece of psychology and insight. I love that Bull. I think if Hodgson can stick it he will produce a book at least which Englishmen may be proud of & which Irishmen may envy them. My book of (theyve been called so in the preliminary puff) childrens verses – they are not verses for children – is to be published on the 19th of this month, &, with its appearance, I rather think my poetry shop will close. They were nearly all written ages ago – at the same time as my *Insurrections*, & altho' there's not much in them still there is something, and they make a decent "good-bye" to the craft, unless this war sets us all into a second childhood when it is finished. Second childhood does rather sound like senile decay, but that is the opposite of what I meant.

Yours very sincerely
JAMES STEPHENS

To W. K. MAGEE

Dublin

[A/1] 29 October 1915

[Magee was currently on the staff of the National Library of Ireland.]

My dear Magee.

Is it possible for one to borrow books from your library for home reading. There are several subjects I want to study, but as the books are £100 each I cant buy them, & as I have to be in my own office during the day I cannot go to the Library to read. The fact is also that I cant read in a Library. Could you tell me if there is any machinery whereby one could borrow books from your place. I hope I have the chance of meeting you soon –

Yours
JAMES STEPHENS

To THOMAS BODKIN

Dublin
[A/3] 10 December 1915

[Crawford Neil had reviewed *The Adventures of Seumas Beg* in *New Ireland* for 4 December 1915, in an article entitled "Little Jimmie (alias Seumas Beg)". Neil had written that "We must not be taken as wholly depreciating this book; we are angry with a poet for dissimulating his gifts in the interest of a clever disquietude of thought and expression." Bodkin had defended Stephens in a letter published in *New Ireland* for 11 December 1915. The "last time" was Neil's article in *New Ireland* for 14 August 1915.]

My dear Tom.

I have just seen "New Ireland" & must thank you for your letter – If that doesnt make the beggar wild – as the saying goes – It was decent of you to write & you have thoroughly welted & walloped the lad. I did not see the review for I guard myself carefully against reading anything by Neil, since the last time. I get criticisms from all parts & in all tones, but his depress me –

Mise
["I am"]
JAMES STEPHENS

To [STEPHEN MacKENNA]

Dublin
[A/19] "Early in the year 1916"

[Apparently Stephens had misplaced an inscribed copy of one of AE's books. The journal mentioned is the *Mercure de France*. *La Culture des idées* by the French critic and novelist Remy de Gourmont (1858–1915) was published in 1901.]

My dear man.

You have given me such a crescendo of reasons for believing that you have not got the dog that now even if the dog barked at me from your mantlepiece, & I on a visit there, I would not believe it was there at all. I bet that ① the first time I put my hand into a corner of my own room there he'll be, or ② Bodkin will confess, or ③ AE, knowing he was short of a copy to give you, will be unable to continue his practices or will be unable to rub out the inscription well enough to put your inscription in. I'm sure it's on my mantlepiece, and one of these days I'll look there. I'd have looked before only that I hate putting matters to the test. It does not seem fair to ones friends to make up ones mind that they have not as much as nailed one miserable book off one. I am real sorry you had to walk home the other night & I can't remember whether it was raining or snowing at the *time* or if the *times* were – singular! plural! queer! [–] good – The *times* passed, (for me) so pleasantly & you were in such form of joke & anecdote & happy phrase that I didnt look at a watch, didnt remember to look at it & I'm afraid might have deliberatily remembered to forget to look at or think of the time. Thus we treat our friends, we make them lose or aid & abet them to lose the last Tram, & then we publicly accuse them of stealing our yellowest dog, Être homme, quel metier [´] ["To be a man, what a profession"]! if there should be another l and an e in quel I'll not be taken be surprise. The Mercure came up just as you went down – Its not an exciting number & I'll send it to you tomorrow. You made a remark about Remy de Gurments "Culture des Idées", said, I think, that it was not his best. Would you tell me what you think is his best. Mes compliments á Madame

JS

To STEPHEN MacKENNA

Dublin

[A/19] 8 January 191[6]

[The article on the poetry of Paul-Louis-Charles-Marie Claudel (1868–1955) was "La Bonhomie de Claudel" by Fernand Divoire, published in the *Mercure de France* for 1 January 1916. The "extracts" are from Claudel's *Corona benignitatis anni Dei*.]

Dear Stephen.

Here is the "Mercure".

I wish you would look at the article on "Paul Claudel" & tell me am I an ass for admiring him so much. The extracts given from his poem do appear to me full of savour & humour, but in french poetry I am a babe and still say "goo-goo" & "wumps"[.] I'm writing. I have just re read "Seumas Beg" & now range myself on your side. Confusion to those who say it is a bad book. That is confusion to all the world barring our two selves & the self of Tom Bodkin, to whom, & to you, laurels. My compliments & a genefluxion toward your wife. I wish I could see you some time when that crowd would be absent. In Donnybrook of blessed memory the grease of the world did not coagulate as it does in Fitzwilliam Place. What a monde ["world"]! but it is that you have the gift for a salon & I am a bird of the wrong feather. I have heard no talk since I came back to Ireland and man does not live by bread alone. I think Claudel is mighty & full of health but please God I have not used up all my bétises [*bêtises*, "trifles"] yet.

le meas mór
["very truly yours"]
JAMES STEPHENS

To W. T. H. HOWE

Dublin
[A/3] 12 January 1916

[Most of the work of the American artist Edward Timothy Hurley (1869–1950) was set in or near Cincinnati. Neither the "story" nor the "book" can be conclusively identified.]

Dear Mr Howe.

You have a gift for Christmas cards. There is no one sends such nice ones, nor such pleasant letters. I have just received the Cawein book & will read it with pleasure. A thought that came to me while turning over American poetry & chatter about American poets is that while your poetry is not as yet particularly good your poets are remarkably decent human beings. The converse obtains on this side of the world. Our poets are to a great extent competent in their art, but as human beings they are disreputable. I am rather surprised that you were able to get a first edition of Insurrections – it is, I am told, very scarce, & people offer more money for a copy than I got out of all the four editions in 24 years. You will see from the address at the top of this letter that I am back in Ireland. I have been clouted back by the war. It began to be difficult to live by literature, so I accepted a job in our Gallery until after the war. We say "after the war" in these countries, & until that prophetic dawn nothing can be done by anyone. Under the intense, superficial activity of the war it seems to me there is a profound langour – In England, that is, not certainly in France where the entire nation is strung & keyed & eager, & in it up to their ears[.] A nation like an individual can lose energy. I think England has lost, not strength, but a certain quickness of grip [–] that thing which boxers lose after a few years of success. All these things are on the knees of the Gods & I am well prepared to leave them there. The etchings of your friend Mr Hurley are delightful – they are full of charm &, in his woodland scenes, full of that sense of mystery without which all art is no more than artistic exercises – I have often wondered what sort of a world Cincinnati is – It sounds mighty foreign to me for I dont even know where it is on the map. Do you have a pleasant climate there? Are there fruit trees bordering the roads, and do the raspberries grow there as big as cathedral bells or do the rains perpetually soak you & the winds skin you & is there nothing to drink there but water & nothing to eat but acorns and oats. All good wishes to you. I started a new story last week – & I ought not to be writing to you at all for every letter written is so much energy lost to the book

Yours sincerely
JAMES STEPHENS

To W. T. H. HOWE

Dublin
[A/3] [late] January 1916

[Stephens sent Howe a copy of Francis Ledwidge's *Songs of the Fields* (1916). Stephens's work had not been discussed in the *Atlantic Monthly* since a brief, favourable review of *The Crock of Gold* in November 1913.]

Dear Mr Howe

Just a line to say that I am sending you along a copy of a book by which I set much store. It is a first book & the writer is a young Irishman who has gone to the wars. I think it is the most *original* first book that ever was, packed with errors, & poetical & philosophical tags – and poetry. You mentioned in your last letter that something has been written about my books in the Atlantic Monthly – The A. Monthly cannot be got over here these woeful times & if you have a copy by you I would be glad to see it – I wonder will you like Ledwidge's book

Yours
JAMES STEPHENS

To WARREN BARTON BLAKE

Dublin
[A/3] 22 February 1916

[Frederick Palmer (1873–1958) was an American war correspondent who published regularly in *Collier's*. The French writer Romain Rolland (1868–1944) had published in 1915 *Au-dessus de la mêlée*, a pamphlet appealing to the intellectuals in all countries to agitate for peace. The translation of *Mille Nuits et une nuit* by Dr. Joseph-Charles-Victor Mardrus (1868-1949) was published in sixteen volumes from 1898 to 1904. Claudel's *Corona benignitatis anni Dei* was published in 1914.]

Dear Mr Blake.

The sole fault in your letter is that it was not long enough. I will be glad to see the Colliers when they arrive – I have already seen some of Palmers articles & found them very good indeed. Your letter interested me a great deal from the number of questions it aroused, and left me fâché ["vexed"] because you did not attempt to answer any of them. Every question, of course, supplies its own answer, but not immediately – it has to be grown up to, as a boy has to grow up to his whiskers. An answer is the fruit of a question, and until the plant is ripe there is no fruit and no answer. Our plants are not ripe yet but they are getting towards it, and already eager minds may set out on prophetic adventures. You will find that the majority of these soothsayers are forecasting what they wish to happen – nor is this in the least unphilosophic, it is the normal course, for the "wish" becomes in time a "will", and the will becomes inevitably a deed. The job of a prophet is to formulate a desire, & if this desire is in line with the desires of man it must come true no matter what powers or vested interests are opposed to it or threatened by it.

So I will prophesy for you a new social order, & I name you that with the certainty of one who already sees his dream taking on flesh. What kind will it be? That I do not know nor does anyone else. All I will promise is a baby, & I cant even tell you its sex. Certainly the world is shouting just now with a masculine bellow, and it does seem that the child is being born of the father instead of the mother; but for me I redoubt exceedingly the female gender and the neutre that she keeps up her sleeve. All this is bosh, of course, barring that you and I are of the age that will enable us (if we live twenty years longer) to overlook two worlds which will have no further correspondence except that of memory. I am not a pessimist. I am the very pole of that, as I fancy you are; therefore if I proceed to forecast immediate woes you will understand that I shadow them forth as immediacies and not at all as ultimates. Before you can make anything you must have *raw* material, before you can create anything you must have *chaos*. That chaos is due for after the war. Europe is going, for some years, to be exceeding poor. The standard of living will inevitably fall all over this part of the world, and with the standard of living there will go tumbling and sliding almost everything that was contemporary to it. There are already disintegrating powers at work, and these come not from below but from above. Education in England has already been threatened in the House of Lords. Female labour has thronged into the markets, child labour has been sanctioned, individual liberty has gone with a run and the purchasing power of a soverign is no more than ten shillings & will be less. Meanwhile (in England alone) after the war there will be demobilised, as combattants & munition &c suppliers, over seven millions of men, and all over Europe the same thing but on a larger scale will occur. The social order we have will be unable to withstand this, these impacts. Trades-unionism will crumple up and go smash, so I think a little later will Capitalism, as it is now known. The first thing after the war will be an immense European emigration, and the set of that exodus will inevitably be towards America. Canada Australia & Africa will absorb some of the crowd, but America will get the bulk, & Europe will almost smother her in paupers. You cant escape; humanity and water & economics all seek their level, & America will get her full share of the world distress. I dont believe that in the long run America will make enough out of this war to buy herself a cocktail. I'll shut up on that side for fear if I get really going I will never stop. A word more as to your mention of the "East" [–] If the standard of living in Asia should rise on account of the falling standard of living in Europe then we will undoubtedly witness a great Oriental renaissance. The Eastern lethargy of which we hear so much will disappear with a change of food & the railroads & aeroplanes will see to it that the change does come. The world is about to organise itself as a world & the Oriental will be there and powerful & mighty fresh

As to Romain Rolland – He is a fine man, but to the French people, who are living in anguish and giving their labour and their blood with both hands, it may easily seem that his intellectual detachment savours too much of neutrality to be applauded. The issue is terribly real for France. Understand that if they had been beaten this time it meant the partition of France as it did some time ago of Persia and of Poland. When all Frenchmen are in the ditch no frenchman has a right to be on the fence. No frenchman or German or Englishman has any right to intellectual detachment in public. His nation claims his body & his soul, & he should not withstand the collectivity of his race. Call it "mob" if you please. but that mob cherished him and shaped him, & out of it he drew the entire of his physical & mental sustenance. If he can do nothing more for his country he can at least hold his tongue for her. Solomon says, there is a time for heaving rocks & there is a time for throwing kisses. Rolland's clocks are out of gear, & if matter in the wrong place is dirt idealism in the wrong time is dirtier.

Certainly let the Idealist think ahead for us as is his duty, and project for us the City of God full of fruit trees and sunshine and with love laughing in the streets; but let him not burn down the granaries that we must eat out of, or kill off the cows that will give immediate milk to our babies. I have a certain claim to detachment, as a member of a country that has been overun by war ten thousand times, my country is scarred & unseemly with war, & my people have been booted into starvation & slavery through eight unending centuries; but this damned thing weighs on me like a physical pain – what must it be to those frenchmen, and with what stupefaction must they read Romain Rollands intellectualities & detachments and artistic idealities. To them with their sons dead, their brothers dead, their fathers dead, living in a maimed & mangled one-eyed, no-eyed, legless, crutched & bandaged world Rolland must appear as a kind of blasphemy & the worst kind of that maybe. It is so easy to be gracious & detached & forgiving but the others have their bellies blown out, and lie there in the rain thinking it over, & with nothing to keep them warm but love for their country & their kind. In the country that is *beginning to win* there let the Idealist talk, otherwise his place is with the guns & he must throw his life on the table as his fellows have done – Thats rather heroic, I fear, and I apologise to you for it, for I am not a bit heroic, my nearest approach to the masculine spirit being that I've got a bad temper, & I would part with it for a sou. If you are looking for something to read in French I can give you a title to begin with – Les Mille Nuits et Une Nuit par le dr J C. Mardrus. As I think the Bible is the finest book in English, so I believe that this is the best book in french. Indeed, it is wonderful, richly and amply written, and, especially in these days, of a marvellous refreshment. Get Volume two, and bless me afterwards. Paul Claudel has just published a poetry book Corona Benignitatis Anni Dei which is something more than remarkable. Very religious, too religous indeed; for he rather wallows on his back with his legs cocked up in religion, but it is a remarkable book. I'll send you a photo when I get one. I wonder will you read this letter as far as this word! I dont blame you if you fail, but indeed its your own fault, & it was your own epistle set me off. I have lots more to say, but in pity I will close up. Take your revenge by sending me a letter twice as long –

Yours sincerely
JAMES STEPHENS

To EDWARD MARSH

Dublin
[A/3] 4 March 1916

[Stephens is acknowledging payment for his contribution to *Georgian Poetry: 1913–1915.* Ledwidge was not killed until 31 July 1917. Robert Bridges's *The Spirit of Man: An Anthology in English and French from the Philosophers and Poets Made by the Poet Laureate in 1915* was published in 1916.]

My dear Marsh.

Many thanks for the cheque. I doubt if your second book will break records like the first – the times are out of joint – I have not heard a word from Ledwidge. We got a rumour some months ago that he had been killed, but, thank heavens, a second rumour said that he was all right. I am reading Bridges Anthology. I wonder do you like it as much as I do – Have you any further literary plans? It would be a tonic to hear of such a thing these mad days – For myself the war has shut me up and I have forgotten how to write

Yours
JAMES STEPHENS

To [STEPHEN MacKENNA]

Dublin
[A/19] 9 March 1916

[The salutation is perhaps intended to be *A chara Oireasach*, "O Learned Friend". "Clann Sassanach" [*Sasanach*], rather strained Irish, is probably intended humorously as a pseudo-Gaelic tribal-territory name: "[land of] the English Children", i.e. England. The Irish after "Seumas" would correctly be *Bárd agus r'i i nÉirinn*, "[A] bard and [a] king in Ireland".

In "A Centenary Appreciation of the Author of 'Jane Eyre' ", Stephens concluded with *Beannacht Dé len a hanam* [better as *lena hanam* or *lena h-anam*], "God's blessing [be] with her soul".]

A cara Oiris

I am doing an article for Clement Shorter on Charlotte Bronte (Centenary). She was an Irish woman, perhaps once removed, but Irish, and, when she reads my oration in the Shades with Ossian or Finn himself at her elbow, I would like that they should meet a scrap of the Irish to remind them and her of their politics[.] I used to know the consecrated formula, but teanga na n'Gall [*nGall*, "the language of the Foreigners"] has hunted it from my cells – Can you give it to me, just the good little, Irish, "God rest her soul" that will finish the work when the work is finished – In Clann Sassanach they do not have the true type on their heathen lino machines; so, perhaps, the simplified spelling would be simple enough for their Roman needs. I am a bother to you, but, however dark the deed may appear to themselves, it is a patriotic one.

le meas mór, mise
["very truly yours, I am"]
SEUMAS.
Bard agus righ in Eirinn

To WARREN BARTON BLAKE

Dublin
[A/3] 19 April 1916

[Stephens is thinking in particular of Frederick Palmer's "Is Germany Winning", published in *Collier's* for 22 January 1916. Palmer wrote that "Germany is in the position of a man who strikes for want of air, for want of room. Next summer . . . the walls will begin to fall in on the Germans." Herbert Henry Asquith (1852–1928) was Prime Minister of England. The German Chancellor at this time was Theobald von Bethmann-Hollweg (1856–1921), who was trying to end the war by conciliation.]

Dear Mr Blake.

I read your letter with great interest. I am not inclined, however, to place much importance on the factors you enumerated as being signs that peace, if it is not in the bay, is in the offing. They are mere rumour and newspaper guesses. All the belligerant nations would I am sure welcome peace, but excepting Germany, none of them can propose it. Recollect that (despite Mr Palmers articles) Germany so far holds the trumps. It is true she has lost the entire of her export trade. She must put up with that. It is true she has lost the entire of her colonies. She is at this moment stronger for that loss as her singleness of objective is strengthened, & she has in exchange the entire of Belgium, that part of France from which 70 per cent of french wealth comes, the entire of Poland and its productivities (as those of Belgium), the entire of Serbia & Montenegro & a large part of Russia[.] These places are today organised & worked in German interests, and they are more than an offset to her colonial & export losses, or at least they must mitigate those losses too seriously for a blockade policy to be really effective. Mr Palmer may write these things "down" as much & as cleverly as he pleases – they are the facts, and an endeavor to arrive at some intelligent appreciation of the war situation & of peace must give them full consideration. It is for these reasons that the other bellegirant nations cannot even think of discussing peace. Before they can open the most tentative negotiations they must have obtained a success somewhere – and, as you see, it is from Germany that the peace rumour comes. People infer from this a laxity in the German morale. The contrary is true – they talk of peace because they can *afford* to do so, and the others are silent because they cannot afford to reply. If the Germans can hold what they have they win the war. If they cannot they lose it. The problem is entirely a military one & will be resolved in battle. When you wish to judge of the facts that are behind the scenes examine curiously the utterences of the various combatant prime ministers. Not the Cabinet utterence, but the prime ministers utterence. Examine what was said early in the war & compare it with what is said now. The difference, or discrepancy, will mark the state of that national morale. You will find that Mr Asquith, after two years of fighting & thinking about it, has modified his demands. He does not now claim the total destruction of "Prussian Militarism" but that international complications must in future be settled by other than bloody methods. The German Chancellors late speech contains, with an intimation that they are prepared to consider the question of peace, an insulting and provocative expression towards Russia. His tone is more assured than it was two years ago, and you will find that each combatant increases or modifies their national demand strictly in accordance with their estimate of the chances for or against them. Germany, at this moment (& even if she never wins another rood of land) can afford to want peace, the other countries cannot afford to accept peace. When you begin to see "peace talk" in the Daily Mail & the London Times, then you may believe that there is something in it, but at present it is the eagles take the air and not the doves.

In discussing a question such as this one must strive for a neutral mentality, otherwise one can only prophesy one's private wishes or ones private prejudices. All good luck be with you

Sincerely yours
JAMES STEPHENS

To THE EDITOR OF *THE NEW AGE* &
GEORGE BERNARD SHAW

[Dublin]
[22 April] 1916

[The text is from *The New Age* for 4 May 1916. Stephens discusses writing this letter – on the Saturday before the Easter Rebellion – in *The Insurrection in Dublin* (1916), pp. 2–3.

Stephens is responding to George Bernard Shaw's "Irish Nonsense about Ireland", published in the *New York Times* for 9 April 1916 and reprinted in the *Irish Times* for 22 April 1916. Writing about the First World War, Shaw stated that "the war is a convincing demonstration of the futility of the notion that the Irish and English peoples are natural enemies. They are, on the contrary, natural allies." Thus, "this war is just as much Ireland's business as England's or France's". Shaw's earlier advice to the English people was contained in "Common Sense about the War", published in the *New Statesman* for 14 November 1914.]

To MR. SHAW.

Sir,–

I enclose a letter addressed to Mr. Bernard Shaw which I should be glad if you could publish. The reason I desire to publish it in England rather than in Ireland is that the Press in this country is entirely commercial, and would possibly refuse it, and that Irish people do not even know of the existence of Mr. Shaw, and would not be interested in his opinions.

J.S.

To Mr. Bernard Shaw, apropos of his article, "Irish Nonsense about Ireland", which the "Irish Times" reproduced from the "New York Times".

It is so easy for you, it is even so profitable for you, to be wise and to counsel the people of Ireland as to how they should bear themselves these thorny days. Earlier in the war you advised the English people on the same subject, and it is possible that the Turks and Bulgarians are awaiting the overdue pronunciamentos which you may be now writing.

It is easy for you to do these things, for in doing them you do not incur any danger, nor do you run counter to any opinion strong enough to hurt you. You never do. No military escort will thump your door and accompany you to the quays for deportation. This has happened lately in Ireland. No policeman will tap your shoulder, preliminary to a term in prison on account of your injudicious opinions; for your opinions, when they are wild, are carefully wild, and under the energetic language they will be found to be the prescribed opinions. You flout authority by obeying it, and, even if an Englishman should be impatient, not at the things you say but at the way you say them, he can always shrug you away as a rather clever and well-recommended foreigner. The English fleet will protect you from German enemies, but I do not think you have any. Remembering your writings, it seemed to me that you had covered yourself there also.

Indeed, you are quite safe, and as long as your advice is marketable you can continue to reissue it. It is a pity, however, that a certain intimate feeling–shall I say a home feeling?–does not prevent you writing about your own country. You have made your peace with England (let us call them, for the joke, the hated Saxon.) Your home is there, your fame, your bank. Even–and I say it with neither malice nor regret–your heart is there, for where the treasure is there will the heart be also. But the fact that you have negotiated with England does not entitle you to speak for your nation, not even in these days when the Gombeen Man straddles the world. Ireland has not made peace with England. It is true she is committing racial and economic suicide for her "dear enemy", but she is too small, too poor, too inconsiderable in every dimension to make either war or peace, or to make anything but a pitiable clamour and, perhaps, like an angry kitten, scratch a little. It, of course, serves kittens right when they are chastised with a club as big as an oak tree. Is it not better to say that England has not made her peace with Ireland, although, long enough, Ireland has been howling and begging and scratching for that peace?

If England had been your country, and if you had said of her, and in that tone, the things you have said (in America) about your own country, it would not have been safe for you in England. But it is only your own country that you so write about, and are witty about, and superior and finely careless about, and you are quite safe in doing it. Did you not know it?

You did not send your national counsel directly to Ireland. You sent it to Ireland via America–the Trade Route.

We can all on occasion advise each other, and I will advise you to make a compact with yourself, and save your soul, by resolving, that if you can say nothing good of your country you will not say anything evil of her. It is not a too heroic resolve, and with your intellectual activity it will not be expensive. Every Irishman feels bitterly at times that there is nothing he can do for his land, but, at the least, he can hold his tongue for her, and he can refuse to make any profit out of her national bewilderment.

To all literary men words at last cease to be speech and become merchandise. This is beyound assistance, and need not be deplored, but every literary man might take a vow of silence on some subject; and I suggest that Ireland is a subject on which you should never again either write or speak, and if you can cease to think of her that will be so much gained also.

JAMES STEPHENS.

To THE EDITOR OF *THE NEW AGE*
& GEORGE BERNARD SHAW

[Dublin]
18 May 1916

[The text is from *The New Age* for 18 May 1916. Stephens discusses this apology–accepted by Shaw in *The New Age* for 25 May 1916–in *The Insurrection in Dublin*, pp. xiii–xiv.

The letter is Stephens's apology for his attack on Shaw in *The New Age* for 4 May 1916. Shaw's comments on the Easter Rebellion were contained in "Neglected Morals of the Irish Rising", *New Statesman*, 6 May 1916, and in "The Easter Week Executions", *Daily News* (London), 10 May 1916. In the latter article, for example, Shaw had stated that "the shot Irishmen will now take their place beside Emmet and the Manchester martyrs in Ireland, and beside the heroes of Poland and Serbia in Europe; and nothing in heaven or on earth can prevent it".]

AN APOLOGY TO MR. SHAW.

Sir,–

On the subject of my letter headed "To Mr. Shaw", which appeared in your issue of May 4, I trust you will print the following.

J.S.

TO MR. SHAW.

Sir,–

I humbly and earnestly apologise to you for everything contained in my letter to THE NEW AGE. It was written at a time of national unrest, and contains an utter and gross misconception of your character. Your public utterance on the Irish insurrection has given the lie to everything I said in that letter, and I beg you to believe that I am deeply sorry for having written it.

–Your obedient servant,

JAMES STEPHENS.

To THEODORE SCOTT DABO

Dublin

[A/36] 23 May 1916

[Theodore Scott Dabo (1877–1928) was an American artist. The three-act play was the unpublished *The Demi-Gods*. Stephens did not reach an agreement with Dabo for either work.]

Dear Mr Dabo

Your letter of the 5th May reached me this morning, & I at once cabled to your "Lend Representative" [–] Your suggestion to dramatize the Crock of Gold is the fourth I have received from America[.] I did not reply to any of the others as I did not consider that this book would bear dramatization. I have also been approached several times by Cinematograph people, but we have yet, over here, a slight dislike to this mode of reproduction. Your letter, however, shows so much faith in the project that I am quite willing to consider it with you, & during the time of such consideration, I promise not to discuss the matter with any other party. Further than this I would not care to go in the matter of giving you dramatic rights.

Should we come to an arrangement I think it would be desirable that a complete copy of the dramatic version should be sent to me, as I would like the atmosphere of the book to be in the play. Further, the words used in the dramatic version should in every possible case be those I have used in the book. Further, a proper agreement shall be prepared between us, and a sum of money shall be paid to me on the signing of such agreement, and an undertaking given that the play shall be produced within a specified time.

As I understand it, you are seeking for no more than the dramatic rights of this book in the United States of America. All the rights of reproduction &c are, and will remain, my property.

Yours very sincerely
JAMES STEPHENS

P/S
I am, by the way, working on a three-act play, &, perhaps, if we agree to do business that business might be extended.

JS

To THOMAS BODKIN

Dublin
[A/3] 10 July 1916

[Massingham was editor of *The Nation* (London), for which Constantine Peter Curran (1883–1972) was currently the Irish correspondent. Stephens's "Spring in Ireland, 1916" was printed in *The Nation* for 6 July 1916. As published in *Green Branches* (1916), the poem lacks a dedication.

The poem discussed in the postscripts is "Autumn 1915", also included in *Green Branches.* Line 7 of the published text reads "As long boughs swing"; the second line of the second stanza retains a period.]

Dear Tom.

I am recovering from a severe, red madness. Massingham asked me, via Con Curran, to let him *read* my poem, and, with the idea in mind that you wot of, I sent it to Curran. I heard nothing more until I saw to my amazement the poem in print. Got no proof, got no nothings, except the errors in the printing. And they struck out my dedication! & no word said. That milk is spilt however. I only read to the end of the second verse, & therein I read no more. I will send you tomorrow, for advice & the assistance that never yet failed to be coming & be first rate, the new version of that "Autumn 1915" poem. I have added two verses to it. Good luck to you.

Mise
["I am"]
JAMES STEPHENS

I find I've been able to get it ready so I post it along. I begin to be satisfied with this poem

By the way, as to your query on "As the long boughs swing" [-] You are quite right that to leave out "*the*" would give a fine long sound to the line, but the preceeding & succeeding sounds are quick & thin & so I retain the "*the*"[.] Also with regard to verse 2, 2nd line, I have put in a full stop to meet your query.

JS

To THOMAS BODKIN

Dublin

[A/3] 23 July 1916

[This anthology was never prepared. In *The Spirit of Man*, Bridges placed his selections under headings such as "Ideal Love", "Sin", and so on. Bodkin's *May It Please Your Lordships* was not published for another year.]

My Dear Tom.

What do you think of yourself & myself working on the Irish Anthology that AE suggested? It is a matter on which I had often thought, & I think it would be worth doing. There is not an Irish Anthology that is worth a curse. The disembowelling method of Bridges commends itself to me. I would have no long poems & no war poems. And what do you think of bringing out your french translations at once, but at immediate once. It will do Maunsel's good to have such magnificent poetry & such a wonderful piece of scholarship on their list.

Mise
["I am"]
JAMES STEPHENS

To WARREN BARTON BLAKE

Dublin

[A/3] 24 July 1916

[Stephens's "Leaders of the Irish Rebellion" was published in *The New Republic* for 1 July 1916 and his "Spring in Ireland, 1916" in *The Nation* (London) for 6 July 1916.]

Dear Mr Blake.

Many thanks for your letter & the Republic draft—You were very kind in getting the Article printed for me. I had a poem printed in the English "Nation" a few weeks ago, &, if that paper gets to your shores, you might have a look at the poem. Barring the misprints (& they are lamentable & many) I think it is a good poem, or, at least, that it is as good as I am capable of. Things are very curious, & gunpowdery, & suppressed, & half-cock over here. All good wishes to you

JAMES STEPHENS

To PHILIP D. SHERMAN

[A/7]

Dublin
7 August 1916

[Philip D. Sherman (1881–1957) was an Associate Professor of English at Oberlin College in Ohio. Charles James Lever (1806–72) and Samuel Lover (1797–1868) were Irish novelists. Jack Butler Yeats (1871–1957) was best known as a painter.]

Dear Mr Sherman.

I have your letter of July 14th. The Crock of Gold was published simultaneously in England and America in 1912, by the Macmillan Co. of both these countries. The American edition is the better printed; the English the better produced. I do not believe you could get a first edition easily of the English edition, the 8th edition has now been printed. As to your other question – It would require a book to answer it. Irish literature in the English tongue is yet in its infancy – a lusty infancy, but still–! Only sixty years ago the vast bulk of our population (about nine millions) spoke habitually in the Gaelic, and altho' the Gaelic has been broken as a medium of exchange a great number of our people who speak only English still think in the Gaelic mode. A great number of our Anglo-Irish writers, Lever & Lover & all of that ilk, wrote English with great cleverness, but no great prose or poetry (or scarcely any) was produced in English by Irishmen. Our race had not thoroughly learned the language, or had not thoroughly learned to adapt the Irish mode to the English tongue – We have now learned it; &, outside of their real literary merit, it is for this that Yeats & Russell, Synge & Lady Gregory are remarkable – They have succeeded in freshening both the English tongue & the Irish thought. With Yeats & Russell (AE) & Standish O'Grady Anglo-Irish literature re-commences. Are the types drawn by Synge & myself true Irish types? you ask. Yes, they are true as types; but they are not *the* type. Every country is too complex to be summed up in any man's formula. In literature as in every other affair a man answers at last only for himself. Every character that he draws is a facet of himself. Synge's types are at last a synthesis of Synge, & Synge is an Irishman. My types are true to me, and I am an Irishman. I represent something that is true of my country; my types or "creations" represent something that is true of me. If you look at the illustrations of Irish life by Jack Yeats (Willy

Yeats' brother) you will see that he reproduces in line and colour the very men whom Synge reproduced in word & thought. We can all have an idea of a typical Englishman or Frenchman, for the literatures of these races have been engaged so long & so profoundly on their psychology that at last the type has emerged, not as a man, but as an understanding, a notion. In Ireland *the* type is there all right, but the destruction of the Irish language, Irish culture & tradition, the Irish "mode" in fact, has hidden or veiled the type; so that we Irish writers must go searching for it again, & we will find it all right. These preliminary essays of the writers you have mentioned, and among whom you are pleased to include myself, are as yet no more than examinations made by the way–They are the beginning of our stock-taking. This is I believe true, that we are a good race; but our national evolution has been hindered, our traditional culture subjected to every kind of interference, so that it is a marvel it exists at all, and we have almost entirely lost the Gaelic language which is our national storehouse, & into which the Irish psychology had been precipitated. England is so strong in men, & money & culture, & yet Ireland has withstood the terrific pressure of this threefold power. That is an amazing feat, & the country which, having been impoverished in men and money & culture, could yet withstand the energetic trinity has something in it worth discovering. Has American literature been working long enough to evolve a national type, or national types. I dont believe it has. Something that is true of New York has arrived, but do you know anything that is true of America.

Yours faithfully
JAMES STEPHENS

To WARREN BARTON BLAKE

Dublin
[A/3] 25 August 1916

[Blake sent Stephens a copy of "The Spirit of Japanese Poetry" by Arthur Leslie Salmon, published in *The Dial* for 15 July 1916. Salmon stated that "the distinctive spirit of the older day [Japanese poetry] is brevity".]

Dear Mr Blake.

I have just received your note on my return from Connemara, so I suppose its too late to write to you in Paris. I hope you had as good a time there as I had away in the west, where nothing stirs excepts bees & dragonflies and interminable waters. It is a land of lakes & mountains, & I doubt if there is anything quite so beautiful in the world – Hills & waters & bogs & a quietude so complete that almost the song of a bird would startle you. I dont suppose you found Paris very different from the city you knew before the war – The difference has still to come when peace gets a change to riot & ravage

I read with pleasure the article on Japanese poetry which you sent me. Such a compression is not suited to our tongues or ideas. But there is no doubt we others are much too wordy. It is due largely to the newspapers which insist that an article shall fill a column. Most things worth saying can be well said in three or four hundred words; but they have to be elaborated to 1,500 words & the devil's to pay in prolixity & boredom. Many of our books (for this reason) could be boiled down into pamphlets and nothing lost except adjectives, but telegraphic poetry is nearly as bad. We live here still on the edges of gulfs and precipices, & no man knows what complexion tomorrow will wear – We sit on the knees of the Gods and play with our toes –

Yours always
JAMES STEPHENS

To EDWARD E. LYSAGHT

Dublin
[A/26] 25 September 1916

[Edward E. Lysaght (1889–) sent Stephens a copy of his *Sir Horace Plunkett and His Place in the Irish Nation* (1916). Sir Horace Curzon Plunkett (1854–1932) was the leader of the agricultural co-operation movement in Ireland, having founded the Irish Agricultural Organisation Society in 1894.]

My dear Lysaght.

It was very kind of you to send me your book. I delayed in writing as I wished to read you first & I am now in the centre of the book. I know from it a good deal about Cooper[n] that I did not know before, & a good deal about yourself. It is a very fine thing for our country that books like this should be written, & I hope you will write many of them. We ought all to be thinking about every plane &

surface & depth of Ireland, so as to have some real knowledge of her rather than the sentimental or the patriotic guessing which has served us up to the present. There are, by the by, more than one hundred thousand things I would like to talk to you about on the subject of writing. As regards Cooperation you have me skinned; but on the art & craft of writing we must have a chat one of these days, & you can pay for the drinks. Are you back yet from Alba? &, if you are, had you adventures there? & what do you think about the war?

Mise, le meas
["I am, yours truly"]
JAMES STEPHENS

To JOHN QUINN

Dublin
[A/28] 28 September 1916

[Quinn had been working to secure clemency for Sir Roger Casement (1884–1916), who had been convicted of treason for attempting to secure German aid for Ireland. Casement was hanged on 3 August 1916. The article referred to was "Roger Casement, Martyr: Some Notes for a Chapter of History by a Friend Whose Guest He Was When the War Broke out", *New York Times*, 13 August 1916, V, 1–4.]

My dear Mr Quinn,

I cannot tell you how much I was pleased with your article in the New York Times, only now come to my knowledge. It is a most eloquent, brave and moving piece of writing, & with that it is as finely "of a piece", as anything I have read these days. Indeed I think it the best piece of writing & feeling which this lamentable war has brought forth, & our poor friend is justified anyhow in some part of the earth. Here everything is wrong, & set hard for worse; but I know we can stand whatever comes, for we always have stood it. All good luck be with you.

Yours sincerely
JAMES STEPHENS

Portrait by William Rothenstein, 1922 (privately owned) ; reproduced in Rothenstein's *Twenty-Four Portraits, Second Series* (1923). Inscribed "For Mrs Stephens (wd it were more worthy of her & of him) W Rothenstein Feb/29"

Stephens in youth

Portrait-medallion by Theodore Spicer-Simson, June 1913
Reproduced in Spicer-Simson's *Men of Letters of the British Isles* (1924)

James

Cynthia

James Naiose

Iris

The Stephens family, ca. 1919

Stephens at the National Gallery of Ireland, 1923

Portrait of Stephens by George W. Russell, *ca*. 1910 (privately owned)

The *Aonach Tailteann* festival in Dublin, August 1924. Standing: G. K. Chesterton, Stephens, Lennox Robinson. Seated: W. B. Yeats, Sir Compton MacKenzie, Augustus John, Sir Edward Lutyens. "Gogarty and Yeats are in their glory, & Yeats has bought a tall hat."

Stephens and Joyce in Paris, probably 1934

Stephens at the B.B.C., 1937 or later

Stephens at Freelands, W. T. H. Howe's Kentucky estate, 1925-1935

National Gallery of Ireland,
Merrion Square,
Dublin.

29th May 1923

My dear little Iris:
Thanks for your nice letter & for the photo of Douglas. Yes, I read "Ivanhoe" – three times, I think; and, in those days, I thought it lovely. Somehow, I never cared a very great deal about Scott, but I did like Ivanhoe, & for long after reading it I longed to be a Crusader, and to perform deeds of chivalry, & rescue lovely damsels from other fellows. But, on the whole, I think I prefer these days to the days of yore; & I prefer Iris to any Rowena (or whatever her name was) of them all. I read Adam Bede, too. George Elliott, the author, was you know a woman – in those days I was a small boy in knickers, and, like your friend, I also thought her very nice: But, really, she was much too wise for me, and if I had told the truth, which I never did in those days, I would have admitted that I thought her very dull – In fact I only really enjoyed real bad books – Deadwood Dick, and Montezuma the Merciless and Alligator Ike, or the Terror of the Plains. (please spell that word for me) I loved bluggy stories, where someone was always shooting someone else, & people were being slung down precipices, & searching for buried treasure, and all that kind of thing, which I suppose you will think of as rot. However there is no doubt that Adam Bede is a very good book, & George Elliott's masterpiece – other books I could not read at all. We have had the beastliest weather here for months: raining, sleety, east-windy weather, and we are looking forward to our vacation in Paris in September. Mammy will go before me to get you, I suppose at the beginning of August, & will bring Noiro with her. He asked me this morning to send you his love. He asked me this morning to let him into your room, I did so, & he took a long smell at one of your boots, & then he asked me to send you his love & a long purr – I can't enclose them, but I send them. He is really the nicest thing that ever was except you, & you are the nicest thing that ever was except me. I think the girl whose portrait you sent this morning is a good sort, & am glad you are friends with her. You can give her half of Noiro's love, & some of his purr. Please remember me to Miss Smith & Miss Slater, & give my kind regards to the 3 Squirrels & the Kingfisher. Here is Noiro's love & this is his purr . . . . . .

[illegible]

I have to make a speech tonight at Trinity College. Hate making speeches. Pray for me.

Letter to Iris Stephens on 29 May 1923

To LEWIS CHASE

[T/20] Dublin
10 January 1917

[In 1916–17, Lewis Chase (1873–1937) was an Instructor and Lecturer on Contemporary Poetry at the University of Wisconsin. Chase wrote to Stephens (as well as many other poets) to gather material for his lectures.

The solicitor's office was that of T.T. Mecredy in Dublin. The passage in *The Demi-Gods* which Stephens mentions is in Chapter VI. The "National paper" was *Sinn Féin*. "The Rebellion in Dublin" is an error for *The Insurrection in Dublin*. The article in the *English Review* was "An Essay in Cubes".]

Dear Sir,

I have just received your letter of 16th December, and I have dispatched to you four of my books, the others are, for the time being, out of print. They, can, however, if they are necessary for your purpose, be got in America. As for the other material to which you refer, reviews & so forth, I have not got any by me, and cannot, therefore, assist you in this instance. The books which I have sent, i.e. The Hill of Vision. The Charwoman's Daughter (published in America under the title "Mary Mary") The Crock of Gold, the Demi-Gods do represent pretty fairly my particular abilities and disabilities (putting the latter word in for form's sake, for I don't plead guilty of disabilities.) Of these books The Demi-Gods is, in my opinion, the *best written*: that is, it is the most skilful in the handling of words and phrases, also I think in the presentation of events. The Crock of Gold is the most curious, but the Charwoman's Daughter is, of this I am certain, the best, in the true sense of that word, and leaving literary technique aside for the moment. You might look at "Here are Ladies", a collection of very short studies which illustrate another and different kind of writing by me. Of my poetry, I consider the best I have yet done is contained in the Hill of Vision and in some places from my first book "Insurrections" published in America by the Macmillan firm. The books which I have not sent you, and which are all to be got from Macmillan, are: – Insurrections, my first book, 8 years ago. – I wrote it after reading for the first time Browning. At that particular period, and for a few years afterwards, I was seized with an amazing poetical impulse, so that, in one night alone, I have written as many as fifteen poems at a sitting, and on many other occasions I have managed to write down six and seven poems in one night. I always wrote at night, partly because of the stillness and sense of darkness and remoteness which comes with the dark, and partly, indeed largely, because I was at that time employed in a Solicitor's office until six o'clock at night, and would then have to bring home further work which had to be completed before morning. – This almost every night; so I seldom got to sleep before three o'clock in the morning and seldom do to this day. I had a method in those days for preserving poems which came to me while I was employed at full pressure in the Solicitor's office. I could not allow my head to go playing about with a poem while my employer or a superior stood at my elbow dictating stuff to me at about a hundred words a minute and which I hammered from his lips direct into a typewriting machine. – I knew I had a poem, not because an idea was in my head, there never was, but because I had a feeling there, which I never found to be a false intimation; and my task was while doing the unending work of the office, and it was unending, to keep hot for five or six hours that feeling, so that some part of my mind was occupied sitting on that (what shall I call it) warmth, intimation, radiance – like a hen sitting on an egg, while the other and normal parts of my head were listening to the voice of the dictator, watching the keyboard, and spelling out the rotund legal utterance. I don't know whether that retiring into a special part of oneself is common or not, but it was, or became, so easy to me that I could at home, copy from a legal document, whistle a tune, and think about something else, all at the same moment. Am I inflicting on you terrific balderdash? I mentioned that the impulse to write came to me after reading Browning, and I am sure that in Insurrections a certain amount of the Browning method will be discovered, but a great deal is my own – I did not get what Tomas Said in a Pub from him, nor Chill of the Eve, nor the Tale of Mad Brigid, nor Hate and some others, and those which I did get are not among the best things in the book, which does contain poems that I shall never beat. I hope you will read Insurrections, and, particularly, the poems I have mentioned. I suppose every writer has some kind of general aim, perhaps it is no more than an idea, of what he is really at himself; for every man is so sunk in his environment that it is with difficulty he can disassociate himself from it, or see his own acts apart from the general stream of life around him. One seldom knows what one is truly at, for somewhere else your work is hingeing on to a larger issue and becoming instantly modified and amplified and digested and (apparently) lost. But so far as I am concerned I believe there are certain qualities in my work which are my own and, if there is any value in me, it is in these qualities. Most writers (it is nothing against them) seem to make all their contacts through persons, or life. I think I portray *living*, or the sense of being alive, or the sense of receptiveness better than most others can do. In my books (prose) I try to capture for my readers, and hand it to them hot, the feeling of the wind, of the sun, of spaces, of things which can be touched and digested by man, rather than of things which he is capable of doing, such as, say, the murder and adultery and trade trickery, which many others (and legitimately) write about. They give the idea of action, I try to give the idea of being, or I think I do. The parts of my books which I read with pleasure, and upon which I have expended all the writing and art and craft that is in me, are precisely those parts which other people treat with something of disdain: i.e. the hinging-on parts. The scrap of writing which lies between two pieces of action, the beginnings of chapters where one is only preparing for the story, the ends of chapters where one is wiping up the mess which the action has made, into these I put all the energy I have got, much more than in the *important* places. Read, for example, in the Demi-gods the description (I haven't got the book and cannot give you the page) quite early in the book of the awakening of the little encampment the morning after the arrival of the Demi-gods – it begins with the awakening of the ass and continues to a description of the dawn, and altho' there is no action, there is what I call "life", or "living", and this is the best example I can suggest from memory of the quality which I think of (when I do think of it which is seldom) as my quality. You know you asked me to prattle, and here I am prattling. If you think I am talking nonsense you invited it. It is in response to a feeling of "life" my best writing comes, and even with thinking I use somewhat the same method, seeking to take it into me like sunlight or eyesight or smell, and then to hand it out to the reader hot or visible or savoury. So much for that. What else were you asking me. Reviews: I have sometimes been well reviewed in the sense that large and flattering comparisons have been made between my work and the work of dead giants. I have not been well reviewed in the sense of true comprehension, and it has not been seen that under the apparent ease (and that is a word used in the reviews) of the narrative there has been an infinite, patient, curious care to do the work well. I wrote prose as I write verse. That is, I scan and pore over every line of it, and I do that an hundred times before the "easy" phrase has been evolved. I will say no more on this personal aspect lest you should conclude I was the most egotistic of writers instead of one deeply interested in the art and craft of letters – the blatancy is not personal but crafty. I wrote first in a National paper here for some years, it is in that kind of school most of us have appeared. Papers, that is, which never pay their contributors (they couldn't) and which are read by a curious mingling of intelligentsia and patriots who may be barmen or shopmen or coalheavers. Yeats did the same and Russell, Colum and O'Sullivan and all the rest of us. My first book was Insurrections then followed: The Charwoman's Daughter, The Crock of Gold, The Hill of Vision, Here Are Ladies, Songs from the Clay, The Demi-gods, The Adventures of Seumas Beg (little poems) The Rebellion in Dublin and Green Branches. I have written practically nothing as journalism and very little of my work (saving for the National paper aforesaid) has appeared in newspapers or magazines. As to my life – It is to a greater extent than appears distilled into my books, (?) not in the way of direct narrative, but in revolts, and angers and enthusiasms and vain imaginings. I am Mary in the Charwoman's Daughter, and I am her mother and the Policeman [–] I am the Philosopher in the Crock of Gold, and I am the children, the leprecauns and the goat: so, in the Demi-gods, I am the gods, and Patsy MacCann and Eileen Ni Cooley, and whoever else goes through those pages. So in the rest of my books, and I could give a reason, if I was drove to it, or bribed to it, for such and such a sunset, or fight, or feasting, or whatnot. There are two approaches to the same kind of knowledge: one is to study other people, the other is to study yourself: the result is inevitably the same thing – consciousness. My approach to humanity or life is through myself, and I try to cultivate the blessed cosmos inside my own head. My way, too, is the shortest way, for the data is easily arrived at and can be sifted, while in the other, one must set out on perpetual, weary adventures and with no counter on which to ring one's facts. I have never written a story that I heard, and hope I never will. Always the tale has been my own adventure or my own imagining, which is the same thing. Just as you cannot digest another man's meat, so you cannot digest another man's story without indigestion in the second chapter. What more is there to say now the wind has got into my sails? A criticism which is beginning to be levelled at me, discharged indeed, is that I am of the band who despise thought. I, who hardly ever make a phrase without hooking a definition to its tail. If that gadfly buzzes in your neighborhood please swat it for me. What else? That I am unkind and harsh and volatile. I am none of those – There is the volatility of a bee bustling from the lily to the poppy, but merely attending to its business all the while. And if I vol it is because I am at work. As to my people. I am reduced to claiming the entire Irish nation for ancestry, my own parents died when I was about six years of age, and I have not met one of my own clann since that time. I went to work about sixteen, and was discharged from, and discharged myself from innumberable situations. I would sooner be a corpse than a clerk, and I have been a hungry man many, many times. Some people think hunger and hardship is necessary to art. It is not. All that comes from hunger and the lower hardships is dullness, and I wish the good people who would forcibly starve young talent could be forcibly starved themselves. Of education I got the ordinary stuffing provided by most schools twenty years ago. I learned geography and grammar and the bible [–] things like that, and forgot them a great deal easier than I learned them. That quickness in forgetting is a kind of activity also, I suppose. I was active that way in my early days. The dislike I got of teachers has lasted to this day, coupled with a dislike for clergymen and policemen and politicians. As to my contemporaries. I think Russell and Yeats are the best things in English poetry. I think Hodgson is, or may be, the best Englishman in English poetry. I think the art of writing prose has been lost to English people, but not to Irish ones. At their best, Russell and Yeats, Lord Dunsany, Standish O'Grady are wonderful prose artists. What more? I have been in Paris for three years before the war and one year after the war. I think their literature is (in its latest phase & time) rubbish. Paul Claudel has done good things, but for the rest of them there is nothing to be said. I wrote an article about two years ago for the English Review in which I set out my ideas of criticism. I remember I set out therein all I had to say on that subject. And I remember that our mutual friend (horrible phrase) Stephen MacKenna, in his pleasant way told me, that all England would be talking of it in a week, and the rest of Europe in a month. He assisted me to believe that it would even come to the cognizence (sic) of the gods, but so far as I am aware no one either in heaven or earth has ever read that article – It wasn't bad. Now I have typed enough. I am not able to write or think decently on a typing machine, so I'll stop. I hope you may get some where among the words something of use to you. Needless to say I do not wish you to publish this stuff – it is merely that you asked me to chatter to *you* and I have done so.

All good-luck-be with the lectures.

Sincerely yours
JAMES STEPHENS

To JOHN QUINN

Dublin
[T/28] 20 January 1917

["Spring 1917" is an error for "Spring 1916", the second part of *Green Branches. Green Branches* had been published in limited editions of 500 copies each by Maunsel (Dublin & London) and Macmillan (New York). Stephens did not make his first trip to America until after Quinn's death.]

Dear Mr Quinn,

Many thanks for your letter which I delayed replying to as I could not put my hand on the ms of "Green Branches" which you asked for. I now enclose the ms of the Spring 1917. As to what I should ask for it – I really dont know and will leave the matter to your own knowledge of ms value.

I am sorry you mislaid the copy of Green Branches. Over here it is difficult to get as the entire edition was sold before the date of publication, and the book is now listed at £2: 2: 0. However if you write me that you would care to go to that price I will try to get one for you.

A good number of American producers are writing to me lately about plays, and I am thinking of trying my luck in that art: also I have been written to about a series of lectures for America, so there is a chance that one of these days (after the war bien entendu) I may have the chance of shaking your hand.

Yours very truly,
JAMES STEPHENS

To JOHN DRINKWATER

Dublin
[A/42] 18 April 1917

[Stephens had been in Enniskerry to recover from pneumonia. Drinkwater had sent him a copy of *Olton Pools* (1916). "Anthony C." is "Anthony Crundle".]

My dear Drinkwater

I have returned from Enniskerry. I read your book last night, and like it indeed. In particular I was pleased with – Birthright, Nineteen-Fifteen. Holiness. The City. Old Oliver, & Anthony C. The Derbyshire Song, & the final Petition. On a first reading I liked these the best, but a first reading, or a first anything, is not final, and it is possible that when I go over the verses again I may find the others are just as good (the poems are indeed good) & that some of them may be better than any of those I have mentioned.

Alas for that world of gentleness & humour of which you write. It is distant these times. But it was always distant. I believe that everything the best mind of humanity really wishes for, & formulates the wish, must come to pass. So I look on certain abstract words such as "love" "honour", "spirit" as prophetic words, having no concrete existence now, but to be forged in the future by the desire which has sounded them. Poems, too, are to me prophesies, & there will be a gay old world sometime. I'm getting didactic, so I'll stop with my best good wishes to you.

Sincerely
JAMES STEPHENS

To SEÁN MacGIOLLARNÁTH

Dublin
[A/1] 20 April 1917

[Edmund Curtis (1881–1943) was Professor of Modern History at Trinity College. An edition of *The Ancient Irish Epic Tale Táin Bó Cuálgne* was published in 1914 by Joseph Dunn (1872–1951), a professor at the Catholic University of America. This letter was mailed six days after it was written to the office of *An Claidheamh Soluis.*]

My dear Seaghan

It was very thoughtful & kind of you to send me the portmanteau full of eggs, expecially in these days when the most one sees of an egg is a cock sparrow, & it cleaving the airy blue. I "batter" them in the way you described, & I am cheefully working my way through them. You say "maybe I dont care a traneen for eggs" but there is no man in Ancient Eire has a greater personal regard & respect for an egg than this man. By the way Curtis (the Trinity man) (Perhaps I should put it – the only man in Trinity) – put me on to a new edition of the Táin Bó by an American Professor name of Dunn – its a great book. Will you present my best thanks & compliments to your sister & wont you drop in here again Sunday.

Mise
["I am"]
JAMES STEPHENS

P/S I find I can't post this – I've forgotten your new address –

To W. T. H. HOWE

Dublin & Cincinnati
[A/3] 24 April 1917 & 14 August 1929

[Stephens has answered a letter from James Burton Pond (1889–1961), head of the Pond Lecture Bureau in New York, on 20 November 1916, saying that he "might possibly be open" to a lecture tour in 1918.

Joyce's *Chamber Music* was published in 1907, *Dubliners* in 1914 and *A Portrait of the Artist as a Young Man* in 1916. Joyce left Dublin in 1904, ending up at Pola, Austria; he returned to Ireland twice in 1909 and once in 1912. Stephens added the postscript during one of his visits with Howe.]

Dear Mr Howe.

Your letter has just arrived. Mr Gibson is quite wrong & I am not going to America. Mr Pond, a lecture agent, had written to me on the subject & that is all happened. I would just hate to live on board a train – that is how a lecture tour represents itself to me. When I go across, which I may do sometime, I would prefer to have a free leg & shake it in whatever direction I pleased without regard to time-tables or the whistle of the guard. The Irish Review should be rather scarce now, particularly the 1st year volume. I think it is full of good things, & congratulate you on your purchase.

You ask about James Joyce – He is an Irishman, of course. He has written three books. The first, about 12 or 15 years ago, a tiny collection of lyrics entitled "Chamber Music.["] Very pleasant little songs. Then, about six years ago, a rather disconnected, unpleasant prose work called "Dubliners" [–] It is anything but representative of Dublin, & just now "The Life of the Artist". Parts of this latter book were in ms ten years ago and were read over here. I think that, in the handling of words, he is a clever, competent writer, but he is by no means a great writer. He lacks material, & those two prose books, written so long ago, are about himself, his youthful memories at school, & his youthful escapades in sensuality. I do not think his books, well done as they are, were worth doing, & I think it was a mistake in technique to dwell so persistently on the gross side of life (I beg pardon of life) his life I should say; for the reader is tempted to skip the book & just nose out the scandalous scraps. About eight years ago he went off to Austria as a language teacher, & saving twice I think he has not come back. He is a disappointed, envious man, in my judgement and a succée [*succès*] de scandale is all he can hope for. There are comical tales of him here, for he had the vanity of a peacock & the cheek of a devil, & thats a foundation for legend to work on. But his two books are exceedingly & unnecessarily unpleasant, & they are thin into the bargain. I fear I am writing harshly of him & I think life or fate or chance may have dealt harshly enough with him, but these are my impressions & are worth no more than any other man's

Yours
JAMES STEPHENS

P.S. Reading this letter years afterwards – I unthink all these unthought thinks. Joyce has done great work, & has written beautiful prose. Time will judge him, & me, & us; & we, none of us, need to greatly mind it.

Aug. 14. 1929
at Cincinatti.

To JOHN DRINKWATER

Dublin

[A/42] 24 April 1917

[Drinkwater sent Stephens a copy of his *X=0/A Night of the Trojan War* (1917), which had been performed at the Birmingham Repertory Theatre on 4 April 1917.]

My dear Drinkwater,

Thanks for the little play. It is true drama, most tragic and beautiful & moving. It makes war seem such calamitous nonsense, & during the reading one thinks that war is such. Human evolution is, I suppose, always in advance of social evolution, but the latter has its own equally organic existence & modes & phases, & will we or nil we it follows the laws of its own being to its own destination – Write another little play now, a companion to this one, showing not Trojans & Greeks, but social forces struggling together in order that they may come to unity, and disposing carelessly of the only thing that is disposable – life. Although it wrings our hearts it is yet accidental & superficial that the life which goes out is young & comely. It is the sad duty of every man, & particularly of every artist, to sacrifice that which is dearer for that which is better, & the job is to show was the harvest worth the ploughing, & not that here was nipped in the bud high hopes & generosities & faithfulnesses. So far as Death goes you & I will go. That Trojan, that Greek will not plumb death any deeper than I will, &, on the whole, I think we can afford to be as careless of death as we were careless of birth – Write the companion play and reveal the coral island to the insect that built it, for our minds must rest on something stable or go to pieces themselves. This also is a serious letter, but not five minutes ago I was reading your play, and the impression of it is still with me as something poignant & desolating, and (or we may despair at once & become stoics) partial. I believe in reincarnation. Your play does not – Do you?

Very sincerely yours
JAMES STEPHENS

To GEORGE MOORE

Dublin
[T/1] 15 May 1917

[The texts of the four letters from Stephens to George Moore in 1917 are taken from unsigned carbon copies; the location of the originals is not known to me. The letters relate to Stephens's part in the writing of Moore's *A Story-Teller's Holiday* (1918). Moore reviewed this incident in a letter to Stephens on 16 March 1923: "I wrote some three stories (or was it four?) in the language of the people of Ireland as well as I could, having picked up a little of the jargon during my stay in Dublin; but feeling that my vocabulary was inadequate I asked you to heighten the colour. I thought you would limit yourself to three or four corrections on a page, but you did more, and you did it so well that I hadn't the heart to undo what you had done, and so I kept all your corrections; had I not done so, I should have for ever regretted it and looked upon myself as an iconoclast."

Alec Trusselby is one of the two main characters in *A Story-Teller's Holiday*, the other being Moore himself. Moore seems to have adopted Stephens's first suggestion: the story of Liadin and Curithir, which begins in Chapter XVIII, is preceded by a short introductory chapter containing the following statement: "The names [Liadin and Curithir] seemed to kindle a new personality in him [Trusselby]." Moore did not adopt the other two suggestions of Stephens: during the telling of the tale, Trusselby makes continuous asides to "your honour"; and there is no break between the second and third tests.]

Dear Mr Moore,

I am today returning you, by separate registered post, the part of the ms which you sent me.

While reading the ms there were a few things which I noted, and, with your permission, I will mention them:

At the point (page 116) where Trussaby commences the story of Liadain and Curithir, there occurs, I think, a break in the *tone*. Up to this Trussaby has been a rather casual person talking on casual things. At this point and abruptly he becomes fluent, connected and poetical. In a story a break in tone must be preceeded by a break in narrative, and that break can prepare for the change by explaining it. This need not take more than a half a dozen lines, for the story is really told by a listener, an observer and not by Trussaby. The observer might, to preserve the unities, make an observation, to the effect, say, that in entering into a story Trussaby was entering into his kingdom: that here he was no more a countryman but an artist conscious of a beautiful thing and intent on keeping it beautiful, and that consequently, and almost visibly, his mind, and certainly his vocabulary purged itself of the trivial and everyday, and his tone and phrase rose to the height of his matter – Something of that kind might be interpellated for two reasons: first, to justify the break, and second to dismiss the observer who henceforth is in the way.

These remarks are necessary because, from this point the whole idiomatic scheme must swing from where it started and base itself on an absolutely new convention. No literary form is more sensitive than idiom, and I find that if Trussaby carries the phrasing he commenced with into the narration of the Liahan and Curithir tale the effect (unless prepared for as suggested) the effect will be to vulgarise the entire succeeding tale. The slight machinery suggested will be sufficient to swing the tone, the idiom and the tale into the new direction; without such a device the idiom by mere logic, which after all is mere continuity, by mere momentum must become vulgar.

Another matter – After a lengthened story telling in which the "observer" is completely forgotten, Trussaby by a few explanatory asides brings him in again. I would suggest that these asides should be struck out, and that the observer should be absolutely eliminated from the narrative until the time comes, at the very end when he may come in again. The story does in the most admirable way transport one under the larches, under the centuries indeed, and I think the observer is de trop ["superfluous"] and ought not to be remembered by the reader at all.

One more matter – I would tentatively suggest that the action towards the end of the story tends to become too hasty and that the last episode climbs uncomfortably on the back of the previous episodes. I fancy a short break might occur immediately before the lying-together-test in order that this latter might be sharply differentiated from the previous tests. Trussaby himself might here, and legitimately, become the observer: he might speculate as to how the hermit balanced the possibilities: he might even speculate as to what the little altar-boy thought, or something else, but the action ought to be slowed down before the last episode commences.

These, however, are all matters for yourself, and like the scraps of idiom which I have sprinkled here and there they are put forward as possibly having an element of interest. I am the dog and you have tied the story on the dog who applauds with interjections.

Yours very sincerely,
[JAMES STEPHENS]

To GEORGE MOORE

Dublin
[T/1] 16 May 1917

[This letter is about Stephens's work on Moore's *A Story-Teller's Holiday*.]

Dear Mr Moore,

When your letter of the 14 inst came to hand today I had already written to you that my work on the ms was finished, and in the covering letter I included a few suggestions which came into my head while I was reading the story.

I have unfortunately posted this letter, and perhaps gone beyond your wishes.

I do not look on this matter at all as one to which the word "collaborate" could possibly apply. My attitude was, is, that we are two writers (you a great writer, and I a doer of my best) who are discussing a certain piece of literature from a stated angle, and the fact that my remarks come in ink instead of conversation does not alter the other fact that these remarks are tentative, diffident, conversational.

I fear, in view of your latest instruction, that I may have interested myself too much in the story – it did interest me – and have sown more of the idiom than you may care to harvest. But it was done with the idea that you would accept or reject it as largely or as slenderly as you pleased.

Now that I know the very small assistance you require I shall be able to follow your wishes more particularly in the succeeding ms.

I have not kept any notes of the idiom supplied, and it is understood that this is a matter which interests no one but ourselves.

Yours very truly,
[JAMES STEPHENS]

To GEORGE MOORE

Dublin

[T/1] [*ca.* 21 May 1917]

[The story of the nuns of Crith Gaille immediately follows that of Liadin and Curithir in Moore's *A Story-Teller's Holiday*.]

Dear Mr Moore,

Your letter of yesterday gave me the very greatest pleasure.

As to the question of postulating a new eloquence in Trusselby – My idea was really that a slight pause might be made at the point indicated: a halt of three lines to indicate the breath taken before commencing a journey, for here your story really commences, and the fact I think might be slightly underlined. I, in the same case, would have commenced a new chapter: but on this as on all matters in writing you know far more than I do.

I look forward to seeing "The Nuns of Crith Gaille[")] and to talking these pleasant matters over with you.

Yours very truly,
[JAMES STEPHENS]

To AN ANONYMOUS CORRESPONDENT

Dublin

[T/32] 25 May 1917

["Ouida" was the pseudonym of Marie Louise de la Ramée (1839–1908), an English novelist. The correct quotation from Exodus 39:26 is: "A bell and a pomegranate, a bell and a pomegranate, round about the hem of the robe to minister in." *Bells and Pomegranates* was the title that Browning used for eight pamphlets published between 1841 and 1846. Stephens's position on the parallels between Nietzsche and Blake follows that of W. B. Yeats. Henri-Louis Bergson (1859–1941) was French philosopher.]

Dear Madam,

Your letter dated 23rd April has just come to my hand.

Your question is one which is difficult to answer, more particularly when one has not thought much along the line opened by your question – to what extent do I consider myself the spiritual child of Blake?

Here, shortly, is the road by which I went into verse. During the entire of my boyhood I had read, I might say day and night, with a voracity which could not be appeased, and I read everything: Dickens and the Bible: the classics and Mrs Radcliffe: Meredith and Ouida: with that all I could attain to of popular, that is watered down and peptonised philosophy and science. I may say I did read everything at that time – except poetry. I did not read any verse. I thought it great rubbish, and, with some exceptions, I think so still. The reason at that time for my neglect of verse was, that for a young person poetry is exceeding difficult to read, and also that the recurring rhythm and balance of verse tends to put a boy to sleep. Anything which puts a boy to sleep is very rightly distrusted by him. Further, in a medium where the idea is expressed, not by intellectual postulates but by an emotional appeal, a boy does not know what the devil the thing is about. When you have found a child who reads verses and advertises that the verse is understood, you have then found a prodigy: it is a thousand to one you have also found an aimable young liar and poseur: it may be different with girls: but with boys that is the law and the prophets. You may have remarked that the scientists are always talking about the poets: they have a very uneasy feeling about the latter tribe, and justify themselves to themselves by murmuring into their rigid pages: "we also have read them, the poets, and maybe, and possibly, and very likely, and we dont know but . . ." and I also said: "possibly, and why not, and let us give the fellows a chance"

I said, at the beginning of the 3rd paragraph to this letter, that I would explain to you *shortly* the matter in hand: but, having commenced a third paragraph who can foresee to what fell lengths it will carry him. I fear, Dear Madam, that I must continue to explain to you shortly but at great length the subject raised by your letter.

I then thought that I also would give the poets a chance, and finding that Browning was the King of the Castle at the moment I bought his wares. I was surprised when I read him, and was very proud to find that I knew what he was talking or singing about. The poetry I had read in the school books were either too lucid or not lucid enough, but I did not know what they were about, and I suppose I will never get the kinks out of my system which Shelly tied there with 'The Cloud".

But, I said, for after reading Browning my mind was whirling with rhyme and rhythm and all the flood and balance of his songs,

But, I said, I can do this myself, and thereupon I sat me down, and before you could wink twice I had made a poem which was easily better than the very best thing the poor Browning had ever done – I was quite satisfied about that. After that I read Tennyson, but he moved me on no more than the War Horse is moved who hears the tinkling of a tin kettle when his ear is turned for the roll and thunder of the drums. Almost he drove me back to the reading of peptonised science.

Then I came on Blake. Here certainly the history should be continued by a long line of astericks with a good looking note of exclamation standing to attention between each little star – You remember in the Bible: "a bell and a pomegranite, a bell and a pomegranite all around the Priests vestment" [–] So it should be: an asterick and a note of exclamation, an asterick and a note of exclamation to the blessed end of the chapter –

The first night that I read Blake I wrote fifteen poems. and I kept on like that for a year. It was as though I had found a father and a mother and a fortune. A phrase from him could set me drunk, and if I did not always understand what he was saying, understand that is in terms of logic, I knew what he was saying by the sense he awakened in me, by the emotion which was like a bridge thrown between the dead man and the living one. In good truth we understand far more than we can ever talk about or give an intellectual shape to. Long afterwards I discovered that all Nietsche has said was implicit in Blake and seemed as native to me as my bones: so afterwards when I heard about Bergson (I have never read the decent man) it seemed to me that if he had known how Blake forestalled him the Frenchman would have given up philosophy and gone into the grocery business.

I dont read Blake now: I dont need to. Just as you get used to your husband so you get used to any man, and the fact of accepting a thing implies the other fact that you are going to forget it. Poetry is one of the interests of life, but there are a thousand others, and we cannot delay long with anything.

Yours very sincerely,
JAMES STEPHENS

To SEÁN MacGIOLLARNÁTH

Dublin
[A/1] 1 June 1917

[Although it cannot be determined what sentence MacGiollarnáth quoted from Tolstoy, a good possibility is "Life without vanity is almost impossible", found in Chapter 23 of *The Kreutzer Sonata.*]

My dear Seán.

Your letter interested me. In the sentence that you quote from Tolstoi I dont think the great old man put all the truth. I think there are (3) species of egotism as there are (3) kinds of ecstasy. Mere physical well being mounts the blood, & from it there results an egotism which is the most brutal thing the world knows. You must know lots of men who because they feel healthy think they must be wise: indeed they feel wise. And all that jostling & elbowing & tread on my coatism is an egotism rooted in animal spirits & the mere flowing of blood. There is then the intellectual egotism which emerges always in snobbishness & vulgarity. It, I expect, you know only too well. It is the least harmless but the most unpleasant of all. Afterwards only do we come to the matter which underlies Tolstoie's phrase. It is, of course, in its readiest definition, vanity, & it is reprehensible chiefly because it has reason on its side. That is, you can defend it by saying or proving that the vain man has a right to be vain. The case against it is; here is a man who has gone so far, but he has not gone far enough; & vanity or egotism implies the limitation conveyed in that phrase. It implies that the egotist is educated but not well educated; that he has knowledge without culture. He has separated, or segregated, himself forcibly not from men, but from man, & he sins thereby against the social spirit which is man. This is also the famous sin against the Holy Ghost, which again is man. We are getting metaphysical, you & I, god help us. Au voir

Mise
["I am"]
JAMES STEPHENS

To SIR FREDERICK MACMILLAN
(Macmillan & Company, London)

Dublin
[T/23] 20 June 1917

[The other American was Scott Dabo. The "book of prose", probably a collection of short stories, was not published; Stephens's next book of verse was *Reincarnations* (1918).]

Dear Sir Frederick Macmillan,

On the 24th May 1916 you very kindly wrote to me suggesting that I should prepare the scenario of a play with the idea of having it produced in America by Mr. John D. Williams. I replied that at the moment I was in communication with another American who had made an appointment to come to Ireland to see me on the same subject. Owing, I suppose, to the increasing war dangers by sea this gentleman has not been able to come over, and I do not consider I need hold my play over any longer for his consideration.

I have completed a play in three acts on the motive of "The Demi-Gods" and with that title, Might I send the play to you.

Yours very truly,
JAMES STEPHENS

By the way I may have a book of prose & another of verse finished in a few weeks: but these will I suppose stand over until peace comes.

To EDWARD MARSH

Dublin
[A/3] 26 June 1917

[Stephens is thanking Marsh for another payment for his contribution to *Georgian Poetry: 1913–1915*. Both Stephens and Hodgson were included in Marsh's next volume, *Georgian Poetry: 1916–1917*.]

My dear Marsh,

Many thanks for cheque, & more for letter. Its a wonderful book. I had not been flourishing since the war began until the 1st of this month when I began to flourish like a whole nursery of green bay trees. On the 1st June I began to write at the rate of one short story per day & 3 poems per night. One night I wrote nine poems. If I keep on I will get back to my old form of 15 poems between dark & dawn. But the war is there, & it will close down on me in a few days. I am glad about Hodgson – he deserves all the success he can get. What new Anthology are you meditating. How about a Georgian Prose Anthology!

Yours
JAMES STEPHENS

To OLIVER ST. JOHN GOGARTY

Dublin
[A/43] 7 July 1917

[Oliver St. John Gogarty (1878–1957) was an Irish writer and physician. Yeats's play was *The Dreaming of the Bones* (1919).]

Dear Gogarty.

Here is a copy of the verses you asked for. The play Yeats read us last night is marvellous. I can't help thinking it is a pity he should put so much artifice between the play & the audience. The drum, that is, & the unwinding cloth, & the little journeys round the stage. The play is so beautiful that these first aids to the feeble are not needed – When a convention is native & belongs to a country it is understood & takes its proper subordinate position; but in these cases it can easily be the play which is subordinate. Of course this play is such that it requires to be elongated from the world of the audience. Maybe he is right. It was good last night in your house, but it always is.

Mise
["I am"]
JAMES STEPHENS

To GEORGE MOORE

Dublin
[T/1] 18 July 1917

[The story of Adam and Lilith is the fifth tale in Moore's *A Story-Teller's Holiday*; it is told by Moore in a contest with Trusselby. Moore's remark that he began the story "without leaving him [Trusselby] time for reflection out of which might spring thoughts of his parish priest, who had never heard of Lilith'' appears to be indebted to Stephens's suggestion.]

Dear Mr Moore,

I was hoping to hear from you again. You write the kindest and pleasantest of letters.

It is unfortunate that you must recommence the Garden of Eden story, but you are right in thinking that this tale, following as a tailpiece to the ms which I saw, must not be impersonal. It will inevitably be a story-telling contest between yourself and Trussleby. As I remember that admirable Trussleby he will surely consider that no person, saving your presence, can tell a story as well as he can, and I fear he will listen to you with condescension. He is very well-mannered of course. However, the extraordinary elongation in time and event of the Garden story will help to overawe him, and the curious, abstract, sexless sexuality of Lilith will afflict him with the idea that there are some things which he does not know. He will not even be able to cite the opinion of the Parish Priest, for, as far as Trussleby knows, the P.P. never heard of Lilith or he would have surely mentioned her from the pulpit – We are warned against our grandmothers, and against our neighbour's wife, against our own bondmaid, against Magdalenes and Scarlet Women and the daughters of Baal, and Trusselby knows the case against all these female tormentors, but no authority ever cautioned him against Lilith.

These thoughts may exercise poor Trussleby, and the fact that you are possessed of occult knowledge will disturb his artistic complacancy and help him to believe that your story is better than his.

From my own point of view, the story, as you outlined it to me, should be delightful, will of course be delightful, you being the story-teller. Indeed you conjured up for me a rare and thrilling atmosphere and a sense of beauty and moral freedom.

I think that in this story the sexual atmosphere should only be indicated and should not be emphasised even slightly. I think the action should take place (for you must provide an extra-normal atmosphere for the extra-normal events) the story should be told as if the people concerned in it were all asleep (the sleep-world belongs to Lilith) [–] It should be a mindful but bodiless tale, and I do not know how you will, begging your pardon, castrate the body from the mind in order that the tale should be purely psychic. I dont know that there is in any language a story in which the action takes place on a plane so far removed from the physical as this story of yours. There is a wonderful tale in it, and you are a courageous man.

Very sincerely yours,
[JAMES STEPHENS]

To JOHN QUINN

Dublin
[A/28] 30 July 1917

[Quinn had sent Stephens a copy of *'Noh' or Accomplishment: A Study of the Classical Stage of Japan* (1916) by Ernest Fenollosa (1853–1908) and Ezra Pound. Yeats's play was *The Dreaming of the Bones*, which is rather closely modelled on the Noh play *Nishikigi.* At the time of this letter Quinn was quite interested in the work of Joyce, and doubtless some remark of his prompted the postscript.]

Dear Mr Quinn.

Many thanks for the book "Noh" [–] I have begun to read it, & find it full of interest. Yeats was reading me a new play the other day & I find he has adopted much of the Japenese convention. Have your written anything new yourself. I am always glad to see your writing, & I hope you will remember to have a copy of whatever paper you publish in sent to me. I have been working like ten devils for the last couple of weeks, & have garnered in that time 14 stories & 25 poems, which is no bad harvest.

Yours
JAMES STEPHENS

P/S I dont like Joyces work. but he can write.

To EDWARD MARSH

Dublin
[A/3] 6 August 1917

[The five poems of Stephens which Marsh included in *Georgian Poetry: 1916–1917* were all taken from *The Adventures of Seumas Beg.* The book by Robert Malise Bowyer Nichols (1893–1944) was *Ardours and Endurances* (1917).]

My dear Marsh,

I delayed sending you the few specimens of my latest crop, but here are four. I am content with them. I have not seen the Robert Nichols book yet! but I have been writing so furiously the last month that I have not seen anything.

I wonder will your new Georgian book be as good as the older ones. What do you think?

Yours
JAMES STEPHENS

To JOHN QUINN

[T/28]

Dublin
8 August 1917

[The £10 was in payment for the manuscript of "Spring 1916". The four poems had recently been published in *New Ireland* and were later included in *Reincarnations*. Three of them are based on the work of the Gaelic poet Anthony Raftery (1784–1835); Stephens's source was *Songs Ascribed to Raftery* (1903), edited and translated by the Irish critic and historian Douglas Hyde (1860–1949). The poems which Stephens drew on were "Mary Hynes, or The Posy Bright" (from which he took more than "one line"), "Nancy Walsh" and "Peggy Mitchell". "The Coolin" is based on "The Cooleen, or Coolun", which Stephens read in Hyde's *Love Songs of Connacht* (1893); Hyde does not ascribe the anonymous poem to Raftery.

The "Party" was the Irish Parliamentary Party, led by John E. Redmond (1851–1918). The Irish Home Rule Convention had first met on 27 July 1917 in the Regent House, Trinity College. Stephens's optimism about the Convention was not fulfilled.]

My dear Quinn,

Your letter of July 18th has just reached me, that is, it takes 21 days now for a letter to come from the States to the Isle of Destiny.

I received the Order for ten pounds all right, and was mighty glad at the time to get it. I wrote you acknowledging its receipt, but the letter seems to have gone on the seachrán [i.e. "gone astray"]. I was quite satisfied with the amount. If I can come across the rest of the ms of that poem I will forward it to you. Manuscripts drop off me as leaves drop off a tree, and I never do know where the Dickens they get to.

I have just recovered from an almighty fit of writing. In twelve days I wrote twelve short stories and twenty five poems, and that was some going. It was a good harvest, but just now I am leaning against a rail with a straw in my mouth and feeling very contented with myself. By George, I mean, by Saint Patrick, its a great thing to be able to do work, and to have done it. I praise the gods, and entreat from them another twelve days and a similar load to stagger under.

Here, by the way, is one of the blessed little poems I wrote. I nailed one line from the Irish of Raftery, and round that line I blew a bubble of English verse, as follows:–

Mary Hynes.

She is the sky of the sun
She is the dart
Of love,
She is the love of my heart,
She is a rune,
She is above
The women of the race of Eve
As the sun is above the moon.

Lovely and airy the view from the hill
That looks down Ballylea,
But no good sight is good until
By great good luck you see,
The Blossom of the Branches walking
towards you
Airily.

I say that's a poem to lift a man's heart. Alone I did it, barring for the noble assistance of the gods. I got another one, which I will quote for you for the sheer pleasure of quoting it. It also I pinched from Raftery, that is, I hooked one line out of the decent man's Irish, and I played on that line the way Pan plays on his pipes, only better. I call this poem "The Coolin" and here it is:–

Come with me, under my coat,
And we will drink our fill
Of the milk of the white goat,
Or wine if it be thy will:
And we will talk until
Talk is a trouble too
Out on the side of the hill,
And nothing is left to do
But an eye to look into an eye,
And a hand in a hand to slip,
And a sigh to answer a sigh,
And a lip to find out a lip:
What if the night be black,
Or the air on the mountain chill,
Where the goat lies down in her track,
And all but the fern is still!
Stay with me, under my coat,
And we will drink our fill
Of the milk of the white goat,
Out on the side of the hill.

Can you beat it! Then there is a poem small as a pebble and complete as the universe, called Nancy Walsh. Let me introduce you to the nice girl

I, without bite or sup
If thou were fated for me,
I would up
And would go after thee
Through mountains.

A thousand thanks from me
To God have gone,
Because I have not lost my senses to thee,
Tho! it was hardly I escaped from thee,
O ringletted one!

and here is Peggy Mitchell, my blessing on her:–

As lily grows up easily,
In gentle, modest dignity
To sweet perfection;
So grew she,
As easily.

Or as the rose
That takes no care,
Will open out on sunny air
Bloom after bloom,
Fair after fair,
Sweet after sweet,
Just so did she,
As carelessly.

She is our torment without end,
She is our enemy and friend,
Our joy and woe;
And she will send
Madness or glee
To you and me,
And endlessly.

I got the "Noh" book all right, and wrote to you the day it arrived. I am reading it with a kind of complicated pleasure, One has to blow away the dust of many ages in order to arrive at the sense of these plays, but I understand it fairly well. One who has read the Upanishads if he is not exactly at home in these pages he is only next-door.

The present Irish situation will naturally seem confused at the distance. The fact is, however, that the Irish situation is rapidly clarifying itself, and we are a good deal nearer to a united country than we have been in the whole of the later period. For the Party it is, of course, a land-slide; it is so for more than the Party, for the Unionists even will come sliding down the slippery slope and be clasped to our bosoms in what will be a death-grip for them. The word bosum reminds me of my, our (we are a communal people) latest joke. You know Seumas O'Sullivans work? Someone said, If

Seumas does not stop drinking he'll come to Abraham's bosum, and the rejoinder was, he'll never get further than Abraham's booze. A small joke, I dont know why I told it, but in talk a thing has an air which it loses when a pen is stuck through it.

It has been said, against the Convention (which is holding its second meeting today) that it has no mandate from the country. That is not the fact. It has, unexpressed indeed, but very definitely, a mandate. When one gathers together a number of facts there gathers around them an air, an atmosphere, a kind of psychological fringe, and the man who can interpret this brings home the bacon. Around the grouped facts of our Convention there is such a fringe. The country has declared for and against Partition, it has declared for and against a Republic, it has declared for and against the old Home Rule Bill which is on the Statute Book: it has mentioned, without much emphasis, it is true, but without any antagonism, the idea of Colonial Self-Government. All the other ideas have been advanced and have been attacked. Colonial Home Rule has been advanced, and has not been attacked by anyone. That is the psychological fact which surrounds the other facts, and the absolute mandate of the country to the men gathered in the Regent House (that last infirmary for noble minds) is, Let ye talk about Colonial Home Rule, and if ye dont talk about that then shut your gobs and go home – Gob, by the bye, means in the Irish the beak of a bird.

Well, I dont suppose you'll have read as far as this, and I would not have made the letter so long but that I am very busy and consequently have plenty of time. Have you noticed that when you are really busy you can find plenty of time for everything.

Yours very sincerely,
JAMES STEPHENS

To LEWIS CHASE

Dublin
[T/20] 3 September 1917

[Although Stephens retained "The Lonely God" in the revised third edition of *The Hill of Vision* (1922), he eliminated it from *Collected Poems* (1926). Only four of the eleven sections of "A Prelude and a Song" were printed (as separate poems) in *Collected Poems*. "The Goat Paths" was included in *Songs from the Clay*. Francis Ledwidge had recently been killed in the First World War. "The Shell", "The

Tale of Mad Brigid" and "Fossils" are from *Insurrections*; "In the Cool of the Evening" is from *The Hill of Vision.*]

Dear Mr Chase,

Many thanks for your very pleasant letter, which reached me today. As to the questions you ask me, first:–

I do not care any longer for the poem entitled "The Lonely God". At the time I wrote it (I remember I wrote it in two sittings) I did think that I had managed a very considerable poem, but with age comes wisdom, and I regard that so-antropomorphic conception of Deity with a wry mind. The verse is, I think, good, and there are passages in the poem which I can repeat to myself with a good deal of pleasure.

At that time, to this day, for that matter, my mind was peculiarly concerned with the idea of God and my imagination was continually exercising on that theme. There is a poem in my "Hill of Vision" called "The Breath of Life" which I like in this regard, but I have rather sowed gods with both hands in that book. I am still inclined to think that the poem in that book entitled "A Prelude and a Song" is my best poem. I wrote it, or it wrote itself, in three days, and although I would now if I got the chance prune it a good deal yet it has merits and tons of them.

As to your query regarding "The Goat-Paths["] – I do not now recollect from what particular impulse of adventure it had birth, but I do remember that in the verse-form I tried to reproduce the goat-paths that twist and return, and go on and go back, and lead to shy, sunny recesses and spurs of rock, and are always discreet and secret and delicious. Here, by the way, is a goat-path poem which I have just written. I nailed one line from an old Irish poem called "The Coolin" but the poem is my own:–

Come with me, under my coat,
And we will drink our fill
Of the milk of the white goat,
Or wine, if it be thy will;
And we will talk until
Talk is a trouble too
Out on the side of the hill,
And nothing is left to do

But an eye to look into an eye,
And a hand in a hand to slip,
And a sigh to answer a sigh,
And a lip to find out a lip:
What if the night be black,
Or the air on the mountain chill
Where the goat lies down in her track
And all but the fern is [s] till;
Stay with me under my coat
And we will drink our fill
Of the milk of the white goat
Out on the side of the hill.

I like that poem, and think in its way it is quite as good as the other goat-path poem which you tell me Ledwidge liked, poor Ledwidge, beannacht De le'n a h-ainm [*beannacht Dé lena anam*, "God's blessing [be] with his soul"].

I notice you pick "The Shell" out with a query as to its genesis. Indeed I cannot tell you how it came or why, only that when it did arrive it came well. I am thoroughly content with that poem, but am yet more contented with another of a like structure, two of them rather, one called "The Tale of Mad Brigid", of which I shall never tire while the gods remain good to me, and the other entitled "Foss[ils]" [–] There is a poem of mine called "In the Cool of the Evening" with which I am very pleased. As you are interested in the speaking of verse it may be worth mentioning that this poem is peculiar in its sound value. It must be said in a whisper, and the effect of it is not got unless it is whispered, the last four words being said very loud. Then I wrote a poem called "The Voice of God" printed in ["] Songs from the Clay" – this poem ought to be shouted through a megaphone, that is, the last two verses of it should be shouted. I would want three more lungs to deal adequately with the volume of sound which I have imprisoned in that poem. Here, by the way, is a scrap which I have written lately. I had a great burst of prose and verse, so that in twelve days I wrote twelve short stories and more than twenty poems. I felt for a while that my old form was coming back, but I do think this is pretty:–

Mary Hynes.

She is the sky of the sun,
She is the dart
Of love,
She is the love of my heart,
She is a rune,
She is above
The women of the race of Eve
As the sun is above the moon.

Lovely and airy the view from the hill
That looks down Ballylea,
But no good sight is good until
By great good luck you see
The Blossom of the Branches walking towards you
Airily.

I cannot say just at the moment what poems of mine were influenced by Browning and Blake, for I have none of my own books and the tides in my pocket have ebbed so low on account of this war that I cannot buy them. I dont particularly want to buy them either. Some time, when I see some of my books, I will give my memory a rub on the hone and look into the matter with the poems before me.

Poetry is the top game of all, and I thank the gods that I got the chance of writing it. I dont believe there is any other excitement so keen as it, and it doesnt hurt any body in the world.

Yours sincerely,
JAMES STEPHENS

To JOHN QUINN

Dublin

[T/28] 16 October 1917

[The £4 was in payment for the manuscript of "Autumn 1915", the opening section of *Green Branches.* Quinn's speech on Lafayette Day, 6 September 1917, was in favour of Allied patriotism and Irish nationalism; his "Jacob Epstein, Sculptor" was published in *Vanity Fair* for October 1917; his letter to the *New York Times* for 6 September 1917 was an attack on the continued commercial ties between Germany and the United States. The "convention pamphlet" was George W. Russell, Sir Horace Plunkett and John Quinn, *The Irish Home-Rule Convention* (1917).

Russell had gained membership on both the Grand Committee and the Committee of Nine of the Irish Home Rule Convention. The members of the Sinn Féin Party had refused to participate in the Convention. In *Reincarnations*, Stephens included nine poems based on the work of the Gaelic poet Daíthí Ó Bruadair (1625–1702); *The Poems of O'Bruadair*, edited and translated by John C. MacErlean, was published in three parts from 1910 to 1917.]

My dear Quinn,

Many thanks for your letter of September 11th and for the £4.

The other matters, your speech at the Lafayette Monument, your letter to the New York Times about bankers, and your note about Epstein's sculpture have not come to me, nor did Russell's convention pamphlet with your introduction.

Our convention is still sitting, but by now it has really begun to work, and in about a month from this we will be able to say with some certainty if the various parties in it will coalesce, and whether there is an irreducible party among them. So far no man stands out in its deliberations as being first-class except Russell, and he is splended. He has had to wait a long time for something to come along which would stretch him out to the full, and he is proving himself the man we always said he was. His is the dominating figure, and I hope he will keep notes of the speeches he makes there. He is, with reservations, hopeful of the outcome of this business, but no man in Ireland would risk a dollar, nor a sou for that matter, on the outcome of the convention. There is an air of extraordinary distrust abroad, and an air of quite extraordinary tenseness and expectancy through the whole country. Sinn Fein – we no longer know what Sinn Fein stands for, because that very tiny party has received so sudden and overwhelming an avalanche of recruits that the original party is lost beyond hope, and the new party or political formula has not yet emerged. After this great war Ireland like the rest of the world will be different, but in Ireland the difference is already apparent. We are not the folk we were in August 1914. We are harder, more careless and very ready to live or die as opportunity serves or demands.

Send me a letter saying how you judge things politically and socially for America, for after the war. Will your people, do you think, be stretched to their full capacity? do you apprehend for America anything like the social change which one inevitably prophesies for the European countries? or do you think that America would be only a bit richer in money and geographical ideas than before the war. For myself (this is supposing the war ends before America has weighed all in) for myself I do not believe she can escape the terrific repercussion political, social, economic, ethical of Europe. We will certainly live for ten or fifteen years in a curious mental environment when the war is ended. I would like your ideas on these matters.

I am working away at verse, and have done some more very pleasant stuff. There is an Irish poet named David O'Bruaidir who lived in the time of Cromwell. His verse has only this year become accessible and he is one of the most interesting, tormented, angry and eloquent bards I have met with – a very considerable man. I will send you a few translations I have made from him very soon, when they are licked into better shape. Did you ever read a book by an American author, Hermann Melville, called Moby Dick – thats a book!

With kind regards to yourself,

Sincerely yours,
JAMES STEPHENS

To LEWIS CHASE

Dublin
[T/20] 29 October 1917

[Stephens refers to lines 13–14 of "The Cooleen, or Coolun" in Douglas Hyde's *Love Songs of Connacht:* "Let us roam, O my darling, afar through the mountains,/Drink milk of the white goat, wine and bulcaun in fountains." The correct spelling of Hyde's pseudonym is *An Craoibhín Aoibhinn.* The book by Ralph Hodgson was *Poems* (1917). W. B. Yeats married Georgie Hyde-Lees (1892–1968) in London on 20 October 1917. Yeats's "Easter 1916" had been published in a limited edition of twenty-five copies late in 1916; Stephens's poem on the Easter Rebellion was "Spring 1916". *Hero Lays* by the Irish poet Alice Milligan (1866–953) was published in 1908; of the various poems by Milligan on the Rebellion, Stephens may be thinking of "Glasnevin", published in

New Ireland for 21 July. *The Vengeance of Fionn*, the first book by the Irish poet Austin Clarke (1896–), was published in 1917.

Both of the poems had been published in *New Ireland* for 27 October 1917 and were later included in *Reincarnations*; the title "Righteous Anger" was changed to "A Glass of Beer" in the *Collected Poems*. The first poem is based on "The Poet on His Death-Bed Writing to His Friend" of the Gaelic poet Aodhagán Ó Rathaille (1670–1726); Stephens found a translation in *The Poems of Egan O'Rahilly* (1900), edited by Patrick S. Dineen. "Righteous Anger" is a close translation of O'Bruadair's "Once an Insolent, Vindictive", which Stephens found in Part II of *The Poems of O'Bruadair* (1913).]

Dear Mr Chase,

Your letter of the 4th instant received today. I know I am quite safe in your hands, and, therefore, beg you to do exactly whatever you want to do: carte blanche as far as that is concerned.

You ask about "The Coolin" what lines I nailed from it – they are

> Come under my coat . . . and we will
> drink the white goat's milk.

That is all. The original poem is in Irish, and can be found in "The Love Songs of Connaught" by Douglas Hyde. This is a book which I recommend especially to your notice. I am sure you can get it in America, but if not I might be able to discover you a copy. It has the Irish on one side of the page and a literal prose and verse of Douglas Hyde (or as he is called here An Creeven Eeveen, thats a phonetic rendering and means The Delightful Little Branch) where was I? his English prose and verse is delightful, the work of a true literary artist and fine poet. I am still hammering away at these, I dont know what to call them for I cannot call them translations, adaptations from the Irish. There is a man named O'Bruadair who lived and sang and was very hungry and exceedingly thirsty in the time of Cromwell, Crumwell as we call him and with whose name we inevitably link the worst of our curses. But O'Bruadair is georgeous, a very learned man and a very poor one, a man who was devout and thirsty in equal and terrific extreme. I have never met such an avalanche of eloquence, poetry and rage under the one skin. Perhaps later on I may be able to let you have some specimens of him translated into me. This machine is not doing its duty by me to day, it is continually pushing a letter under my finger for which I have no use, this public scolding may shame it into virtue and dicipline. I wonder are you acquainted with the work in verse of my friend Ralph Hodgson. He has just published, with Macmillan, a small book of poems. I think he is the best poet Young England has produced in these days. Unfortunately, and this is the case with practically every good man who is working at the present time, his lode is thin, and one must not expect from him that amplitude of matter and treatment which is the unfailing mark of a really great man. Among our Irishmen the same holds true, and while many do exceeding gracious or curious work they dont do much work; you may put Ledwidge into the same catagory; men with a small mine, quickly worked out and who must live by turning their clothes inside out and outside in until the stuff will bear turning no longer and they perish of inanition. Seumas O'Sullivan is another of those and James Joyce: I dont bracket these two together for any special reason for O'Sullivan is far better than Joyce, but they are both bankrupt. In English verse I really dont know of anybody who is specially worth watching. There are men of one poem and two poems, but the man of half a dozen poems is not to be found in any country in Europe. Yeats by the way has just got married and everyone is wondering why. The fact that she is a nice girl or even that she is the nicest of girls does not explain it, for he has wandered in and out of nice and nicest girls this quarter of a century and brought their gossamers to naught. But I know why he married and will, in the friendliest way, let you into the secret. Yeats wants to do everything that is in the tradition and is prepared at a moments notice to be a martyr to art. The chiefs of the craft have all written an Epithalamium (the Lord guide me in my spelling and keep this typewriting machine in his own care) [–] Yeats must do as has been done, and he is unable to enter into the miseries of his friends sufficiently deeply to do an epithalamium for them: therefore, he seeks the immediate personal contact, and if, at his age, there is an epithalamium in reach he will hook it down and print it in his next volume. The poor man will then wonder why the girl doesnt go home. He has written, by the way, a very beautiful poem on our little insurrection, it is better than anyone's except mine. Alice Milligan has also done some nice verse on the same subject. Did you ever see her book, published some five years ago, Hero Lays – There is fine stuff in that. A.E. says that a new man named Clarke has poetry in him, but A.E. and I do not agree about this.

We may find a poet again ten or twelve years after the war is over. I dont think any fine verse or art will come directly out of this gigantic row. A victorious nation makes poetry, but the victory must have been rather easily gotten, and the nations are putting their last ounce into this fight, even the victorious nation in this war will be a beaten nation, licking its wounds and with no time for art.

Well, I've written a lot and said very little, for your sake I'll stop.

Mise,
["I am"]
JAMES STEPHENS

I enclose 2 poems (translations) under my nom de plume of James *Esse*

Egan O'Rahilly.
Here in a distant place I hold my tongue.
I am O'Rahilly.
When I was young,
Who now am young no more,
I did not eat things picked up from the shore.

The periwinkle, and the tough dog-fish
At even-time have got into my dish!
The great, where are they now! the great had said
– This is not seemly, bring to him instead
That which serves his hand serves our dignity,
And that was done.

I am O'Rahilly!
Here in a distant place I hold my tongue.
Who once said all his say, when he was young!

Righteous Anger
The lanky hank of a she in the inn over there
Nearly killed me for asking the loan of a glass of beer:
May the devil grip the whey-faced slut by the hair,
And beat bad manners out of her skin for a year.

That parboiled imp, with the hardest jaw you will see
On virtue's path, and a voice that would rasp the dead.
Came roaring and raging the minute she looked at me,
And threw me out of the house on the back of my head.

If I asked her master he'd give me a cask a day,
But she, with the beer at hand, not a gill would arrange!
May she marry a ghost and bear him a kitten, and may
The high king of glory permit her to get the mange.

James Esse

To MILDRED ALDRICH

Dublin
[A/12] 13 November 1917

[Joseph Hone had married an American, Vera Brewster, in 1911.]

My dear Mildred.

Your letter of the 7th crawled in to me today having lost a good deal of strength, for the ink had faded, & it had the look of a letter that had gone through many hardships and was in a rapid consumption to boot. Until, that is, I read it, when I found that its heart was as big as a bulls and twice as sound. Mick dear I dont care how fat you get for you slip into my heart like a sylph – Now! Seumas the lesser & Iris were asking about you yesterday & had rather the idea that armies were camping on your chest, & that you were furrowed in trenches & littered with ruined churches, & the bones of the enemy. It is amusing what you tell about the American boys – 30 years was rather a lot to give that lad, & he full of fun! We had rather a similar experience here. We had sailors of yours in the South, & the County Cork declared war against them by return of post unless they took the pledge. The belief grows here that all the rigours of peace will be upon us shortly. Do you find people talking much about it over there – Russia. Italy! But for France the world may be proud. Indeed she, England for that matter, have done wonders. I saw MacKenna a day or two ago. He is as eloquent as ever and twice as stately, but he is not well, & one despairs that he ever will be. The Hones came to see us also & Mrs Hone & I chattered about you. I think she would like to go back to America. AE has become a great man. He is a member of the Convention & he has an ace in every sleeve. Do you ever hear from Mrs Schmidt. I suppose she is still in America with the girls. If you should see the Cornilliers remember me to them. There is a great slu[i]ce of orderly uproariousness here, & a great tension, & a great sense of waiting, & lowering brows, & no fear. Ireland stands away from this war stiff as an iron bar. But yet there are few homes here which do not mourn a dead man or a crippled one[.] Write again as soon as you can. Love to you from the lot of us & in special from

SEUMAS.

To CHARLOTTE F. SHAW

Dublin

[A/6] 18 December 1917

[Charlotte F. Shaw (1857–1943) was the wife of George Bernard Shaw. Stephens had sent her some of the poems to be published in *Reincarnations.* The stories were probably those published in various periodicals in 1918–20.]

My dear Mrs. Shaw.

Many thanks for returning the verses. No: you are not right in chiding me, tho' so gently, for playing in the midst of universal misery. The war had its effect, & still has, on me: so that for nearly three years I could not write a word, & after, when I tried again, I had to tear up almost everything I wrote. These verses, & some short stories which I wrote this year represent in reality an effort of my will to escape, not to play, but to be master of my brains. In the verses, I think, I have succeeded, although you would scarcely discover from them what a labour they really were: if that fact was apparent of course the work would be faulty or bad. In the case of the stories, however, I have not succeeded in escaping the war. They are not bad stories, but they do not represent me as I was known to myself a month before the war. Temperamentally they are not mine, & whatever quarry I dug them out of – I had to dig for them – some other poor author may be wailing for a dozen meanly-tragic tales which belonged to him, but are written by me. My compliments to you both & my best wishes for the coming year.

Yours faithfully
JAMES STEPHENS

To SIR FREDERICK MACMILLAN
(Macmillan & Company, London)

Dublin
[T/23] 31 December 1917

[Stephens corrected "400 years" to "300 years" in his "Note" to *Reincarnations.*

Dear Sir Frederick Macmillan,

I write to tell you that I have now found a name for the book the ms of which I sent you some time ago: the name will be – *Reincarnations.*

Although these poems are all taken from the Irish of from 100 to 400 years ago, I do not put them forward as translations, for, in many places, I have taken no more than a phrase from the original poem, and around this phrase I have, as it were, blown a bubble of verse. My effort in each case has been, not to produce the translation of an old poem but to give a new poem, and I am inclined to think that this book is as good as anything I have done in verse. That, however, is for others to decide. Since sending the ms to you I have done four other short poems which are much too good to leave out of this collection, and I will send these on immediately.

Yours very truly,
JAMES STEPHENS

To JOHN QUINN

Dublin
[A/28] 21 February 1918

[Quinn sent Stephens a copy of *Ezra Pound: His Metric and Poetry* (1917); he doubtless told him that the anonymous author was T. S. Eliot. Stephens's book was *Reincarnations.*]

My dear Quinn.

Many thanks for the book on Pound's metrics &c. I would many times prefer to see something of your own. But it was nice of you to think of me.

Yours very truly
JAMES STEPHENS

I will send you a book shortly. I have just finished the proofs.

To W. T. H. HOWE

Dublin
[A/3] 5 March 1918

[The second book by Francis Ledwidge was *Songs of Peace* (1917); the posthumous *Last Songs* (1918) had not been published yet. The English writer Paul Creswick (1866–1947) dedicated *Our Little Kingdom* to Howe.]

My dear Mr Howe.

Your letter of 3rd Febry come to me today, & I was glad to see your hand again. Alas! poor Ledwidge was killed a year ago in Flanders; that blackbird will sing no more. Did I only send you his first book. I will let you have his second and last. It too is very unformed, but it is a[s] fresh as dew on grass. My new book is not out yet, but it may be any time this month, & I will then send you a copy. Creswick wrote to me the day before yesterday sending the novel he dedicated to you – I have as yet read only some dozen pages; & find myself already in contact with one of the tenderest minds in contemporary literature. Beyond that I cannot say until I have read the book. Thanks for the postcards. You surely do have more ice in your neighbourhood than we can imagine here in nightmares, & those unfortunate strainers seemed hardly used. I think the war is in its last phase, which may the gods grant. All good luck to you.

Yours very truly
JAMES STEPHENS

To JAMES B. PINKER

Dublin
[T/15] 29 June 1918

[As published in *The Novel Magazine* for December 1918, "The Birthday Party" had two sections: "The Letter" and "Blind Rage."]

Dear Mr Pinker,

Many thanks for your letter of 27th inst.

I have no objection to the opening chapter of "The Birthday Party" being omitted if the editor you speak of wishes to use the story without it.

Yours very truly,
JAMES STEPHENS

To SIR FREDERICK MACMILLAN
(Macmillan & Company, London)

[Achill Island, County Mayo]
[A/23] 10 August 1918

[Stephens was on holiday for the month of August. Macmillan had declined to publish the play *The Demi-Gods*. *Irish Fairy Tales* was published in 1920.]

Dear Sir Frederick Macmillan.

Your letter of the 7th inst has been forwarded to me here, where I am taking my first holiday since the war started, & where I shall remain until the end of this month. I have also received the ms of the Demi-Gods; but the bad news in the first part of your letter is amply compensated for by the pleasant suggestion in its latter part. I shall do the Fairy Tale book you suggest with the greatest pleasure, & will start it immediately on my return to Dublin. I have been working indeed on Irish Folklore, custom, history & fairy stuff so that your proposition comes to me on the top of the tide, and I think I can promise you a good book, and will try to let you have the copy before the end of this year. The terms you mention are most satisfactory, but your terms always are.

Yours very truly
JAMES STEPHENS

To [SEÁN MacGIOLLARNÁTH]

Dublin
[A/1] 14 October 1918

[MacGiollarnáth had recently moved to Galway, where he would soon take up practice as a solicitor. MacGiollarnáth must have been associated with the Candles Press, which had published Stephens's *Hunger* earlier in 1918. Apparently Stephens had submitted the play *The Demi-Gods* for publication. Marie MacKenna did not die until 4 July 1923.]

A C[h]ara ["Dear Friend"]

I was glad to hear from you & sorry to know you are now living in Galway, for I shall not be able to see you easily, and although you were always scarce you become with this unprocurable. About the papers which you took away for Candles – I agree with your members that it will not make a book which will make any money, and possibly it will not make even your expenses; so I would counsel you that the matter be declared "off" and the script sent back to me. That is my very sober & friendly opinion. The stuff will be interesting some years hence; but at present, & for years to come, it would not have a market, so let them run me back the copy & we will shake hands all round. It is very sad about Mrs Stephen MacKenna. The poor lady is making a marvellous fight for life; but I fear, and am told, there is no possible chance of her recovery. May the Augers be confounded, & she recover. As to Stephen, he bears his trials like the hero he is; but he is having the very worst of a bad time, poor lad! he is admirable in every circumstance. Good luck to you, & my compliments to your people whether they be with you or not

Mise
["I am"]
JAMES STEPHENS

To JAMES B. PINKER

Dublin
[T/15] 6 November 1918

[Earlier in 1918 Stephens had sent the following stories to Pinker: on 30 September "Mongan's Frenzy", included in *Irish Fairy Tales*; on 11 October "The Adventures of Nera", probably worked into *In the Land of Youth* (1924); on 19 October "The Vision of Angus Og", perhaps worked into *In the Land of Youth*; and on 29 October "The Beech Wood", published as "In the Beechwood" in the *London Mercury* for November 1920 and *The Dial* for December 1920 and incorporated into *In the Land of Youth*.]

Dear Mr Pinker,

Many thanks for your letter of yesterday.

At present, I am afraid, I am too deeply committed to the stories I am engaged on to venture on any others, and I do not see any immediate prospect of my writing the type of story for which you have been asked.

In the matter of the tales which I have lately been sending you, however, they are easily the best things I have ever written, and the treatment, in each case, is so modern that modernity itself is put out of date by it. Forgive me if I brag a little. I have fallen on real treasure-trove, from the story-teller's point of view; and I doubt if stories equal to those I have lately sent you are being offered anywhere to editors. If, however, there is no market for them neither you nor I can help that. Again, pardon me for bragging.

Yours faithfully,
JAMES STEPHENS

To RICHARD IRVINE BEST

Dublin
[A/26] 26 February 1919

[The Irish scholar Richard Irvine Best (1872–1959) was currently Assistant Director of the National Library of Ireland. Stephens was enclosing payment for the eight published volumes of *Ériu: The Journal of the School of Irish Learning, Dublin*, with which Best was associated. Stephens had apparently borrowed Best's copy of *Silva Gadelica* (1892), an edition and translation of old Irish tales by Standish Hayes O'Grady (1832–1915). In *Irish Fairy Tales* Stephens drew upon O'Grady's "The Little Brawl at Almhain" and "The Wooing of Becfola".]

My dear Best,

I enclose, for fear I should forget it, a cheque for £4 for the Eriu series. If there is more to pay you can let me know on Tuesday. By the way, I never will be able to thank you enough for all the help you have given me, help I could not have got from anyone else; & that says nothing of your courtesy & sympathy & encouragement. I give you the branch & no better man will hold it in Erie [*Éire*, "Ireland"]. I have come across a magnificent story in your Silva Gaedelica. "The Little Brawl at Allen". What a story that is. What a pair of demi-gods Finn and Goll are! I am going to tell that tale. I think when we have finished this "fairy book" we will have deserved well of Ireland.

Mise, do c[h]ara go deo.
["I am, your friend forever"]
JAMES STEPHENS

To HERBERT EDWARD PALMER

Dublin
[A/36] 9 April 1919

[The English poet Herbert Edward Palmer (1880-1961) sent Stephens a copy of *Two Fishers and Other Poems* (1918). The current Director of the National Gallery was Captain Robert Langton Douglas (1864–1951).]

Dear Mr Palmer.

Your letter, dated 9th March, with your book "Two Fishers" has only reached me. It seems to have got mixed up with the Directors papers, and I have only discovered it. I like your poems very much indeed. You have an ease, naturaleness and freshness in the ballad form which anyone might envy. I think they are all good, but in especial I like "Altenahr", "The Soldiers" ["] Griefswald" "The Pupil" "Chess" "Snow" [–] But if I continue I will admit that I do like them all. You have written one poem which I had intended to write myself [–] "The Bushrangers". You saw ten of them, I saw three, and I followed them for ten minutes marvelling at the magnificent goodness – badness – what? of those three. They were like Doom. They were kindly, cultivated killers, who would capture you & treat you like a brother &, when the time came, would kill you as carelessly as if you were a flea. They dont belong to our time, but are survivals from the days of yore & the mighty unfit. I think you got your lot remarkably well. I think Blake has been a good friend to you. "Nature in War Time" "Sacrifice" "Prophesy" remind one (no more than that) of the great master. But your book is one of the very few which I have lately read that gives the impression of having been honestly seen, thought on, and recorded. Do not pay attention to reviewers, even when they praise you. Not once in two years will you meet a review that will bear the examination which your verse can bear, for it is well-felt, & that (forgive me the cliché) is the root of the matter.

Yours very truly
JAMES STEPHENS

To SIEGFRIED SASSOON

Dublin
[A/16] 22 May 1919

[The English poet Siegfried Sassoon (1886-1967) was collecting manuscripts to prepare a "Poets' Tribute to Thomas Hardy". Stephens contributed four poems to the volume: "The Tinker's Brat", "The Voice of God", "The Rivals" and "Mary Hynes".]

Dear Mr Sassoon.

As to the tribute to Thomas Hardy. I will certainly fill up the sheet if you send it to me.

May I take this opportunity of saying how much I admired a good deal of your own work.

JAMES STEPHENS

To MILDRED ALDRICH

Dublin
[T/12] 10 September 1919

[AE's poem was "Michael", printed as a pamphlet in December 1919 and also included in the *Irish Statesman* for 20 December 1919. Apollyon appears in Revelations 9:11, as the angel of the bottomless pit. On 10 September 1919 the British government had suppressed the Dáil Eireann, the parliament established by members of Sinn Féin in January 1919; the British also moved to stengthen the Royal Irish Constabulary by bringing in the "Black and Tans" and the "Auxiliaries".]

My dear Mildred,

I was as glad to see your hand as if I had got a lyric. But, God help us all, lyrics are scarce these days. A.E. has just been presented with one and we are all excited over here, it is like the birth of a new baby, only more so – Our little Insurrection has in it marvellously fertile seeds, and it is on it or from it that A.E. has got a baby to his old age – Its great stuff. I am rather alarmed at the things you dont say in your letter. You were never a complaining lady, but I wish you would complain now and let me know whether you are only poorly or if you are really suffering. No news has trickled to me from any of the people I knew in Paris of long ago. Not even Dr or Mrs Whitney have sent me a line. I am very anxious to get back for a visit if not for good, but prices stand like Appollyn in the path. We will send you that photo of the children. Seumas went to a boy's school for the first time today. He is very excited and reports that he beat two boys, and is trying to camouflage the fact that three other boys beat him. He seems to have decided to consider the beatings he receives as jokes but that the beatings he gives are the true work of the world. He is the dearest little fellow, but flighty as a bird and as liable to be swept off his feet by chance as a straw is. He has all the signs of a sense of humour so I forsee much perplexity in store for me, a vista of explanations to outraged citizens. Iris now weighs a ton. I dont believe it is all flesh: her mind has a gravity such as you, poor Mildred, will never understand. She can listen to a joke with the unmoved tranquility of a Sphinx, and sets instantly to and at her food no matter who else laughs. She is as safe as houses. But she is growing very pretty. She got a boil on her nose last week. She has a boil on her leg this week, but otherwise she is delightful to look at. She runs with precision but no speed, and although she may pant she arrives always in good humour. This morning Dublin was "proclaimed" as a military area, a disreputable area, and a hot-bed of the divil knows what-not. All the people who are not shot will be put in gaol and the rest are to be hanged. God look light on the lot of us all for the universe is becoming a stench instead of a habitation. Write on receipt of this, like a dear, and tell me some more about yourself.

All our good wishes and our love to you.

JAMES STEPHENS

To JOHN QUINN

Dublin

[A/28] 29 September 1919

[Stephens had been on holiday for most of July and the first part of August 1919.]

My dear Mr Quinn,

I got your letter telling me you were going on vacation while I was on vacation. If you had as good a time in the Adirondacks as I had in the County Wexford (the Yalla-Belly County) then you must have had a good time indeed. For one month the sun shone day and night in the County Wexford, & I'll bet it did not do that in the Adirondacks (What is an Adirondack anyhow?) You hinted, or threatned, that you were going to shoot bears and bisons, & that by these massacres you would recover the health you were lacking; but in the County Wexford you dont have to kill anything to get healthy – You love god & the neighbour, & you get all the health you can stick by sheer, downright, unremitting peace. If you shot more than ten bears & have the eleventh skin & dont want it you can send it to me, & I'll mail you all the skins of all the creatures I didnt shoot in the County Wexford. Everything in Ireland dies of old age except policemen. They have an anxious, heated existence, & they are being served out with bombs so as to make other lives as hazardy as their own. A policeman without a bomb was not liked in Ireland: a policeman with a bomb will be less liked. The fact is that no one in Ireland cares the last rattle of a dying damn for anything any longer, & they care less in the County Wexford than they do anywhere else. When you have time to write me a letter go to it (thats U.S.A.) for your letters are full to the lids with meat. AE was talking of you the other day & wondering would you come over here soon. I am not in Paris – yet.

Yours very truly
JAMES STEPHENS

To LADY OTTOLINE MORRELL

Dublin
[A/36] 27 December 1919

[Lady Ottoline Violet Anne Morrell (1873–1938) and her husband Philip (1870–1943) were members of the artistic circles in London and often entertained at their house near Oxford. William Ralph Inge (1860–1954) was Dean of St. Paul's in London; the first series of his *Outspoken Essays* was published in 1919. MacKenna's translation of the *Psychic and Physical Treatises* of Plotinus was published in 1921.]

Dear Lady Morrell:

Many thanks for your letter. It should have been pleasant having Yeats out. He, with AE, is one of the few men who are always in form, and, even when he is wrong, he is worth listening to. Everything over here is at sixes & sevens. It is impossible to write, or even to think with any ease. I think that great events do cast their shadows as a kind of mental inhibition & it is into dark shadows indeeds that the world seems moving. Not Ireland only, altho' we have had our 700 year-share of them. I'm no pessimist, & just as they say that a hard winter presages a fine summer, so I fancy that all this dis-ease & dilemma will be repaid. You mentioned Dean Inge. He seems a fine type, with a centre of his own, a self-loyalty that is better than all the loaned-loyalties we are trained to. Stephen MacKenna tells me his Plotinus (sec. volume) is well advanced, but the poor man is badgered and distraught with his own and his wife's illness. He is retreating further into himself & his concertina, & but for his wish to finish Plotinus I fancy he would let life slide off him as water off a duck. I wish you every good thing for the new year & all the years that come after it.

Yours sincerely
JAMES STEPHENS

To SIR FREDERICK MACMILLAN
(Macmillan & Company, London)

Dublin
[T/23] 20 February 1920

[Both the English and American editions of *Irish Fairy Tales* used the order listed here.]

Dear Sir Frederick Macmillan,

Thank you for your letter of 18th inst as to the Irish Fairy Tales, and the desire of your people in New York to vary the sequence of the tales. I sent a note to the printers some time ago suggesting the order in which these tales should run, and it is possible that the American Company do not know of this: here is the sequence:

The Story of Tuan Mac Cairill
The Boyhood of Fionn,
The Birth of Bran,
Oisin's Mother,
Becfola,
The Little Brawl at Allen,

The Carl of the Drab Coat,
The Enchanted Cave of Cesh Corran,
Becuma of the White Skin,
Mongan's Frenzy.

In that list there is no story of passion or jealousy until Becfola is reached, and, I think, the only story of the same tone would be Becuma and Mongan's Frenzy. The stories, as set out above, form a natural sequence, and to alter it would be to do violence to the book. It is, however, very likely that the sheets were sent to America in another order. None of these stories are younger than about fifteen hundred years ago, and much can be forgiven to such an antiquity.

If you would kindly convey these ideas to them they might reconsider their objections, but if they still consider that some rearrangement is necessary they have my fullest permission to act as they consider right.

Yours very truly,
JAMES STEPHENS

To SIR EDWARD MARSH

Dublin
[A/3] 9 March 1920

[Since Stephens did not contribute to *Georgian Poetry: 1918–1919* (1919), this cheque must have been for royalties on one of the earlier volumes. Hodgson's first wife had died in February 1920 after an extended illness. *The Golden Barque and the Weaver's Grave* by Seumas O'Kelly was published in 1919. Stephens was currently working on *Deirdre* (1923), having completed *In the Land of Youth*, and was planning to make the two novels part of a five-volume prose epic.]

My dear Marsh.

Many thanks for the Georgian cheque. I am sorry about Mrs Hodgson. I had met her a few times with Ralph; but, given all the circumstances, it is better that an intolerable state of things should end somehow. Perhaps in a little time he will get back to his old form again. Have you ever read a book (prose) called "The Golden Barque", by a lad from over here named Seumas O'Kelly – There is one short (hundred-page-long) story in it called "The Weaver's

Grave", and it is about as close to greatness as anything in our time. If you dont know the book I could get you a copy and, I think, a treat. I am writing away with, as it were, both hands: but I have undertaken the most monstrous job that a vain man ever measured himself against. If luck holds and if the gods are good I may pull it off.

Yours very truly
JAMES STEPHENS

To EDWARD MARSH

Dublin
[A/3] 15 March 1920

My dear Marsh.

I am send along by this post the Golden Barque. It is the first story in it "The Weavers Grave" that I referred to. I wonder will you think as highly of it as we do over here? Hodgson is happy when he has a dog round, & you speak of his dog "mooster". It was Jim when I knew him – a hill terrier with a mouth like a coal scuttle & the savagery of a rabbit. I do not expect much more from Hodgson – he is a "land-locked" man, & his sympathies or interests are not quite human. If he could be switched off to prose, even journalism & plenty of it there would be a new chance, but verse will only further concentrate & narrow him. This is rubbish I expect, and it is six years since I knew him. Good luck

Yours ever
JAMES STEPHENS

To SIR FREDERICK MACMILLAN
(Macmillan & Company, London)

Dublin
[T/23] 16 March 1920

[The £300 was an advance royalty on *Irish Fairy Tales*; Arthur Rackham (1867-1939) did the illustrations for the volume. The *Táin Bó Cuálnge* ("Cattle-Raid of Cooley") is the central epic in the Ulster or Red Branch Cycle of Irish tales. Stephens only completed the two volumes mentioned.]

Dear Sir Frederick Macmillan.

Many thanks for your letter of yesterday's date enclosing cheque for £100, and receipt showing £300 received. I return the latter duly completed. I note that all the first proofs were sent and completed by me, and hope that Mr Rackham is satisfied with the material.

I have been engaged for some time on a very lengthy work, "The Tain Bo Cuailgne" [–] It is a prose epic, possibly the most important in Europe, and, so far as I have gone, I am more than satisfied with the work. Although the subject is of vast antiquity I am handling it in the most direct and modern fashion. It will be in five volumnes. Each volumne will be a complete story in itself and can be read by itself, but each will yet form an introduction to the volume which succeeds it. The action will cover a period of about seventy years in time and the whole extent of Ireland in area. The first volumn "In the Land of the Young" is completed. The second volumn "Deirdre" is practically on its last chapter, but I would not wish to publish the first book until at least three books were actually finished. Do you think a work, such as I have sketched, would be of interest to you?

Yours very truly,
JAMES STEPHENS

Mr George Russell has read the greater part of "Deirdre", &, if you cared to write to him (I will not speak to him on the matter) he would give a very honest & competent idea of its workmanship and of the scope of the entire work that I am doing.

To JOHN QUINN

Dublin
[T/28] 12 May 1920

[Quinn had sent Stephens a copy of T.S. Eliot's *Poems* (1920); of his article on the American artist Walt Kuhn (1880–1949) in the *New York Sun* for 4 April 1920; and of his letter (untraced) in the *New York Sun* about Poland, which quoted the Polish-born writer Joseph Conrad (1857–1924). Auguste Rodin (1840–1917) was an important French sculptor.]

My dear Quinn,

I have just come back from a trip (3 weeks) in Paris and find your present, Eliot's poems, and the Sun with your letter, quoting Joseph Conrad, also your critical note on Walt Kuhn's pictures. Your note on the last makes me want to see the pictures. I have just been looking at some square miles of them in the Paris Salon, but there I saw so many bad canvases that I fancy I would not know a good one if it were presented to me. Practically every artist, every literary man, and, in this, more especially, the poets, are suffering from the same lack. They all have, and in particular the poets, bags of technique and cart loads of ingenuity, and one wonders why, with such equipment, they seldom bring anything off which one wants to remember. I dont know your later American poets so well, and so only speak for the English and French ones. They suffer, every damned man of them, from lack of sensibility. That is, they are not sensitive, and, whether in poetry or painting, this lack nullifies every other good quality they have. They see everything, but they dont feel anything, and, consequently, almost the whole of contemporary art is half-baked and indigestable, and, for they mostly know there is something wrong which they try to remedy by tricks, it is hypocritical into the bargain. Fantastic as it may seem I think that something of the masculinity of man has been submerged, and this "something" has rendered us all less sensitive and more touchy. I am inclined to call it feminism for want of a better definition. It began with Nietszche, a female voice squealing for strength and calling its squeal philosophy. Almost simultaneously Rodin began his female contortions, and he too and all his critics called it strength. In poetry Paul Claudel works in the same shapeless savagery, and his admirers call it strength. They all try to make up by violence the power which the Greeks got by repose. In Italy with cubists and vorticists and dadaists the exact same strain is at work, and in America – – – England seems to have escaped it, but it is only seeming. In other countries of Europe although the disease is radically social it has been expressed publicly in the arts, but in England the expression has been political, and the feminist movement differs in nothing but its vehicle of expression from that which is tormenting the rest of the world. You would know how to describe its effects in the political sphere, but in poetry I describe it thus: the male sensitive quality is dead. What has been wrong for so long a time in American literature, art and poetry? The artists are short in their brains & blunt in their feelings. As to Conrad & Russia I couldnt write about them under ten pages

Yours always
JAMES STEPHENS

To HERBERT EDWARD PALMER

Dublin
[A/36] 18 May 1920

[In his letter Palmer had requested "permission to quote certain appreciative sentences from your letter of last year"; eventually he included extracts from both Stephens's letter of 9 April 1919 and this letter in his *Two Foemen* (1920). "The song is to the singer, and comes back most to him" is from the second section of Walt Whitman's "Song of the Rolling Earth" (1881). W.B. Yeats had been awarded a Civil List pension of £150 per annum in 1910. Palmer's "To Certain Living Poets", an attack on the Georgians, was published in the *Westminster Gazette* for 12 January 1921.]

Dear Mr Palmer.

Print, or use in any way, anything of mine that you think will help. I am not sanguine, myself, that they will be of much assistance, and I would urge you not to let any (apparent) failure worry you. After all, the great thing is that you can write such good verse – that is, your part is faithfully performed. If publishers, or others, do not perform their part you cannot help it. You remember Whitman's phrase "The song returns to the singer" [–] I quote from memory, and always misquote. It is already a great thing to be a poet. Success lies simply in that fact. Even if recognition does not come to you the truth is unaltered, and you must bear, or, rather, be utterly careless of the whips and scorns of time, and all the other calamities which may seem to be piling on you. Some of us get into print more easily, but, after that, we are almost utterly neglected. Try, I beg you, to be content with your great gift; it is personal to you, and within your control, & all the rest is vanity. This may all seem priggish to you: but it is essentially true. I know no poet, on this side of the water, who does not live in poverty. Yeats has not three thousand readers, Russell has less, and I have less again. Yeats, of course, has a small pension, but the others of us, and another forty whom I could name, have to work for our living, and if we were condemned to live by our writings, we would all of us die of hunger. The poem returns to the poet – that is his, and your, reward, any other success than that is not his business. Is it nothing that you can walk along repeating the poems which you have actually made yourself, or that you can delight your friends with them! I think your work is excellent; you, I am sure, know that it is, and that certitude may be all the reward you will ever get, but it should be sufficient for a poet. You ought to be proud and happy, and you ought to let public success or failure go as they please.

Yours very truly
JAMES STEPHENS

P/S – I like immensely your verses "To Georgians & Some Others" [–] By the by, dont quote from this letter anything that is personal to me.

JS

To HERBERT EDWARD PALMER

Dublin
[A/36] 26 May 1920

[Palmer had asked Stephens to write a preface to *Two Foemen.*]

Dear Mr Palmer.

I will write as frankly as you did. I do not care to write a preface, not because I dont appreciate your verse, but because I dont like prefaces, &, in particular, I dont like writing them. Saving in the case of an actual beginner it savours too much of log-rolling, and one's actual freedom of expression is, forcibly, subordinated to other considerations. I do not feel a free man in a preface. Moreover, your work does not need any such first-aid. Please forgive my apparent ungenerosity, but it is a thing I do not wish to do.

Yours very truly
JAMES STEPHENS

To SIR FREDERICK MACMILLAN
(MACMILLAN & COMPANY, LONDON)

Dublin
[T/23] 18 June 1920

[Macmillan replied on 21 June 1920 that it was too late to change the title of *Irish Fairy Tales*. Although the volume is based generally on the Fenian Cycle, the characters of Tuan Mac Cairill, Becfola and Becuma are drawn from the Mythological Cycle of Irish tales.]

Dear Sir Frederick Macmillan,

Many thanks for your letter of yesterday. Please name the book exactly as you please.

In a way I am sorry that the book must be named in this fashion, for, instead of being a collection of Fairy Tales, it is really an original book, and is, in fact, the first half of the Finn Saga, sometimes called "the Ossian Cycle". There are two great Sagas in Ireland, the Tain Bo, and the Finn Saga. While the former is the more perfect, the latter is, many scholars think, vastly the more ancient – They are both pre-christian, but no kind of even approximate date could be put to the Finn stories, which you are now publishing.

I am,

Yours very truly,
JAMES STEPHENS

To JOHN QUINN

Dublin
[A/28] 30 July 1920

[Stephens is acknowledging payment for part of the manuscript of *Reincarnations.*]

My dear Quinn.

Many thanks for your letter & cheque for £35.10.8. It comes in very handy just now. I will do as you suggest about the missing parts in the ms, and hope to send these to you in a few days. About the few poems included in your ms, & which are not in the book. I thought you might like to have some work which has never been printed, & which, as you have the only copies, will never be printed by me. I am looking forward to getting your "personal" letter. Make it as long & full as you can, about yourself in the first place, &, then, please give me your opinion on "these present discontents" [–] What you think of conditions generally in America & the world – That's a tall order, but your letters interest me enormously. If you have printed anything recently please send it, or them, along also. My one idea at present is that the social order or scheme which we think of when we say "1914" is ended & that we are living in an interregnum out of which anything may come. You have a clear mind & are used to looking steadily at very complicated matters. Are we in for a bad or a good time? & is there any prospect that the mad race of wages & prices will cease. The reason I sent you that photograph was as a hint to you to send one of yours. If you have a spare one I would be very glad to have it.

Yours very truly
JAMES STEPHENS

To WILLIAM ROTHENSTEIN

Dublin
[T/15] 3 August 1920

[Stephens contributed the note on AE to *Twenty-Four Portraits* (1920) by the English artist William Rothenstein (1872–1945).]

Dear Mr Rothenstein,

I enclose a short note on George Russell (A.E.) [–] If it does'nt suit you tear it up and forgive me, for I am not very well just now and cannot interest myself in decent things.

I have seen only a little of your work, but that little I liked immensely. One lives very much off the track here in Dublin.

Yours very truly,
JAMES STEPHENS

Personally it is as a poet that I primarily conceive A.E.

To LADY GREGORY

Dublin
[A/3] 18 September 1920

[Lady Gregory sent Stephens a copy of *Visions and Beliefs in the West of Ireland* (1920). *Irish Fairy Tales* was published in October 1920.]

Dear Lady Gregory.

Your 2 volumes reached me today, and I have read about 50 pages already with delight. I am, indeed, very glad to have them, for the bathing in the past, in the strange & beautiful was never so necessary as in these horrible times. Macmillan tells me that my Finn stories will be published shortly. I will, if you permit, send you a copy when one is available.

With many thanks and all good wishes

Yours very truly
JAMES STEPHENS

To BEN W. HUEBSCH

Paris
[A/20] 24 September 1920

[Ben W. Heubsch (1876–1964) was the American publisher who had brought out Joyce's *A Portrait of the Artist as a Young Man*; Stephens was considering giving him the American rights for the five-volume prose epic, to include *In the Land of Youth* and *Deirdre*. Stephens was in Paris on holiday.]

Dear Mr Huebsch.

I have, unfortunately, left Dublin for a month, & am unable to let you have the ms you ask for. Boyd took away with him a type copy of each of the two volumes which are completed. I am not yet prepared to publish as I do not wish the first volume to appear until three complete books of the sequence are finished, so that there would be no delay in keeping the pot boiling as the children say & the publication of the five books would follow each other with sufficient regularity. The English Macmillans wish me to let them have both copyrights, but I do not wish to do this & am holding the matter over.

Yours very truly
JAMES STEPHENS

To W. T. H. HOWE

Dublin
[I/3] [October 1920 or later]

[The text is an inscription in the first London edition of *Irish Fairy Tales*. The quotation is from the epigraph to "The Boyhood of Fionn"; Stephens attributes it to S. Patrick. Howe had suggested a book of fairy tales in a letter which Stephens answered on 30 September 1913. The first 156 pages of *Irish Fairy Tales* includes "The Story of Tuan Mac Cairill", "The Boyhood of Fionn", "The Birth of Bran", "Oisin's Mother" and "The Wooing of Becfola".]

To W. T. H. Howe.
From his friend

JAMES STEPHENS

"He was a king, a seer, and a poet
He was a lord, with a manifold and great train – "

And, by the way, my dear Mr Howe, you may recollect that a few years ago you suggested I should write a book of Fairy Tales for children. Altho' that project did not come to anything. Yet, I would like you to know that it was your letter set me thinking of the subjects that later came to make this book – so, in a way you are the responsible grand-or-God-father of this volume. It is not a book for children at all, but, also, it would not have been a book at all, but that your letter switched my mind to your direction, & to the direction of these and such like tales. I think the first 156 pages of this book are as good as my best work, & I have to thank you heartily for switching me round to the writing of them. But I have to thank you for a lot of things. Seumas & Iris & Cynthia & this present James send or leave our love to you.

JS

To HENRY McBRIDE

Dublin

[A/42] 21 October 1920

["Mick" is Mildred Aldrich. The Biblical allusion is probably to Psalms 38:3: "Neither is there any health in my bones because of my sins." "Desire" had been published in *The Dial* for June 1920. *Plus ça change, plus c'est la même chose*, "the more things change, the more they are the same", is from *Les Guêpes* (January 1849) by the French writer Alphonse Karr (1808–90).]

My dear Henry

First, my love to you now & forever. I got your letter this morning, per Mick, and was gladder than if I had got tuppence. I am just a week back from my vacation in Paris, where I spent three weeks & saw the famous Mildred – Mick. She was in great form, & did a dance for us to the gramaphone. She has one, and she has five cats, a hairy dog that looks like a descent de lit, a mad bonne ["maid"], and tomatoes that weren't ripe enough for me to get at. The only sign of weakness about her is that she loves England. But we all have a soft spot, or a blind spot. But if Homer were alive today he wouldn't nod in the direction of that Angleterre, so why should she, or you? for I suppose you do too; and, as the Bible says, there is no health in us. I am glad you like "Desire", but a dozen times since I have licked that into a dozen cocked hats. A book of mine to be called (nonsensically) "Irish Fairy Tales" will be published the 29th of this month. Try to get a copy (for I can't send you one – its 15/- & I've no money) and read the first story in it called "The Story of Tuan mac Cairill", & say if "Desire" isn't licked out of sight. Then read the rest of it, and say if I am or am not It. After that & beyond that, & putting that completely out of memory, & out of joint I have written, finished, 2 volumnes of my 5 volume story "The Tain Bó [–] My dear Henry, words wouldn't talk about them. A dim, inadequate, totally misleading impression of those volumnes might be conveyed by a string quartette handled by Archangels. It is not only It, its the Goats Toe, & the best ever. That's that. When are you coming to Europe? Are you well now, and do you love Russia and hate Hell? "Plus ça change. . ." so far as your Republicans & Democrats are concerned, but the world is going to get a whoop on it. Ireland! We are about as happy here as an eel on a pan, or the burglar who had to open a Chubb safe with a piece of string. We are soused in misery to the chops & will duck in deeper before we let go that piece of string, but its all a long distance from New York, & I guess it doesnt matter very much! Write me when you find a lost minute, & remember me, not in your prayers, but in your dreams.

Mise go deó [*deo*]
["I am always"]
JAMES STEPHENS

To HERBERT EDWARD PALMER

Dublin
[A/36] 24 December 1920

[Stephens's operations were for a gastric ulcer. Palmer's book was *Two Foemen*; his manuscript poem was probably "The Wolf Knight", included in *Two Minstrels* (1921). Stephens had misquoted the same line from Whitman's "Song of the Rolling Earth" in his letter of 18 May 1920, in which he also gave permission for the use of extracts from his letters in *Two Foemen*.]

Dear Mr Palmer

Please excuse me for not replying to you sooner, but, since the last time you wrote to me, I have been very ill, & am not now but two days out of hospital after two rather severe operations. I have sent your book to AE. His address is: The Plunkett House, Merrion Square, Dublin: and I am returning herewith the ms poem which you so kindly let me read. There is no possibility of its being used by any of the Irish papers – It is too long for their purposes, and its matter would, I think, be much too occult for them. You remember Whitman's phrase

> "The poem is to the poet & comes back most to him"

So with this poem – It is deeply personal to yourself, & may not easily be understood by other people. There is, as in all your work, much good verse in it, but it does not appeal to me (perhaps I am too ill) and I think that its elucidation would require a whole volume. There are very few papers of literary merit in Ireland. Such as there were have been long ago suppressed, & of these none had any money to pay their contributors. I would suggest that you should try the better-class American publications with anything you wish to print. I take this opportunity of wishing you all the compliments of the season

Yours very truly
JAMES STEPHENS

P.S. Of course I do not mind your printing those extracts. I only hope they may be useful

To JOHN QUINN

Dublin
[A/28] 14 January 1921

[Quinn visited France, but not Ireland, in the summer of 1921; he did not meet Stephens.]

Mr dear Quinn.

Your advice was sound. My operation is well over, &, except for superficial wounds, I am ten times the man I was two months ago. I hope you will sometime write that medical essay you mentioned in your letter to me. Did you get my book of Fairy Tales? I sent you a copy. The first story in it "The Story of Tuan Mac Cairill" is probably the best I have yet published. And the Boyhood of Fionn is not bad. It is really not a book of fairy stories in the modern understanding of that term. But, I think, they are Fairy Stories in the ancient & authentic meaning. I claim that this is the first time real fairy stories have got into modern print, &, if the world likes them, there are plenty more where they came from. Have you started yet to think of a European visit? I will keep you advised of my movements so that if you tramp abroad you can tramp in my direction. I think you would like, say, Paris in the spring & Ireland in the summer. May all our woes be over by then, for we are having the devil's own time. All good things to you.

Yours very truly
JAMES STEPHENS

To W. T. H. HOWE

Dublin
[A/3] 2 February 1921

My dear Mr Howe,

I was delighted to get your letter, and your news, or, as Spicer-Simson used to put it, vos nouvelles ["your pieces of news"]. The cheque you sent I return herewith – I really sent you the book as a small present which it gives me great pleasure to make. Have we not been swapping presents for some ten years now. Your remarks as to what I really consider the best thing in the book made me chuckle. Indeed (and as you fore-told) I think it is all good. But when I advised you to read the first story, it is because I consider that one as especially excellent in a miraculously all-round excellence. You should know, by the way, that when I start bragging it means I am at work, and when I am at work I turn a most benevolent eye on the work, am in love with it, in short, and am apt to buttonhole strangers and confide to them my lauds on my own excellence. Still, the "Story of Tuan mac Cairill" is a collossal and terrific, and unsurpassable, top-hole story, and I shall expect to hear from you in parallel terms; for I am at work, and if an artist is not praised he gets the jigs and then the blues and next the dumps, and after that he becomes a patriot and is hanged to the tune of the Old Cow Died Of. Things are very various here, and it is no joke to be a patriot. We have discovered that there are an enormous number of guns in the world (they are all in Ireland now) and tanks and bombs, and, in particular, ubiquitous, sinister, abrupt, gruff-nosed revolvers. If I ever have to be shot I should prefer to be shot by a cannon: there is some dignity in that, but a revolver is a deadly nuisance, like a flea.

It is very difficult to surround and you cant prevent it from jumping. Well, the Lord and Ireland bide their time, and all will be very well in the heel of the hunt.

Remember me to the Spicer-Simsons if they are still with you, and believe me always,

Your friend,
JAMES STEPHENS

To W. T. H. HOWE

Dublin
[A/3] 10 February 1921

Dear Mr Howe.

I received your letter this morning. Punch Spicer-Simson in the eye for me, for suggesting that my youngsters are (or could be) anywhere else than in their own home. I send their photographs & their compliments to you. They order me to suggest that the "box" you speak of will be impatiently expected & uproariously received, & gratefully acknowledged. I am delighted with your appreciation of the Fairy Tales. But I implore you to read the first story twice. Read it aloud, if that can be done. It was meant to be so read. I swear it is a wonderful piece of work, & if nobody praises it but myself I'll burst with rage. I will look up my ms. Most of them are in my flat in Paris (I expect to be there in April next) but the Hill of Vision may be here, or some of it, & whatever I find I will send on to you.

Yours very truly
JAMES STEPHENS

To JOHN QUINN

Dublin
[T/28] 15 February 1921

[In a brief note on 3 February 1921, Stephens had promised to write "more fully tomorrow".]

Mr dear John,

I was after all unable to keep my word and write to you on the day following my recent note. A Board Meeting intervened from which a whole surge of business descended and swamped me. I have got my head up for a minute now and thought, not to whom do I owe, but to whom do I wish to write, and thats that. Barring a certain stiffness in the centre of things I am all right again and although I am not yet as strong as I was I am essentially a better man than I have been for years. I was greatly interested in what you wrote in your recent letters. All you said had been very keenly observed and, so far as I could control them, they were all medically and patiently true. I found that the really desolating part of the surgical operation is the ether. Not the going under but the coming out of ether: the stuff seems to hang about one, as it were, mentally and for many days. With me, it distorted time: my accustomed time-successions lost all their meaning so that the difference between an hour and twelve hours was not appreciable: my hours and days during that period lengthened abominably. I got breakfast at six o'clock in the morning, and at nine o'clock on the same morning nothing but two separately owned watches could convince me that it was not twelve o'clock at night. Just when I came out of the ether after the operation on Monday my wife came to visit me – she only stayed five minutes. Seemingly, during her stay, I closed and opened my eyes a few times. When she had gone I opened my eyes again and my mind was convinced that she had come to see me on three separate days, and that this day now was the fourth day since my operation. The thought cheered me immensely, for my doctor had told me that after four days the more searching part of my trouble would be over. I lay for some time thinking contentedly that now the pain and stiffness and general wretchedness would begin to diminish. When a nurse came by I asked her, how long was it since my operation? About three hours, she answered, and with her answer I got the most grisly surprise of my life: that condition of long-drawn, eternal, nothing-doing, endless, unhappy time remained with me for a week, and I remember it as the only unpleasant thing about my operation. Otherwise, I was cheerful. I went by preference into a public ward and made the acquaintence of seven farmerish kinds of people. Extremes in age, two were seventy and the others were seventeen. We all gossiped very cheerfully, and every now and then one or other of us would let three or four loud yells out of him, and when he had peacefully yelled his pain away we would take up the subject as if it had not been interrupted at all. A boy aged 19 or 20 came in during my second week and was put in the bed next to me. It was night time, about eight o'clock, mid-December. He had been shot through the stomach. In a few minutes a priest and a doctor arrived, having both leaped from their dinners to get there. They were in the Ward within five minutes of the sufferer's arrival. The poor lad moaned and cried dreadfully. He was laid on a bed and the priest took precedence of the doctor. I thought it unwise, but it is the custom, and the boy was given extreme unction and confessed: it was an eery, curious episode. One electric light only was lit in the Ward (all lights went out at eight o'clock) and the priest had arranged a little altar at the foot of the bed with two candles lit on it. His urgent whisperings to the lad and the lads whispers and groans struck terribly on the imagination. That ceremony must have taken twenty minutes. Then he was carried away to the operating room. "Take your hands out of your pockets, damn you", and as he was withdrawing his hands that person had rammed a revolver against his stomach and fired. He lived about thirty hours in great pain (after the operation) and then he died. We all in the Ward were chatting and joking about him, I mean round about him, we thought he was going on all right and the fact that he groaned a good deal did not trouble us, for we all gave a few roars every ten minutes or so. The nurse came from behind his screen and whispered to us in turn that he was dead. An extraordinary depression and misery came over the Ward at that news, not a sound was heard from any of the patients [and] the nurses went gravely on tip-toe and with downcast faces. That lasted for five minutes, and at the end of five minutes the whole Ward was shouting and laughing and making jokes, the nurses were as gay as so many thrushes in spring, every man had his cigarette or pipe going, and the ward was as jovial as if there was no death there, or as if death did not matter a damn. He lay there for three or four hours, and we missed him no more than if he had not been there at all. Then we grew downcast again, for his father arrived: an inarticulate man, bursting with his silent, difficult grief. He would walk up and down by the bed; every now and then he stood to look into his son's dead face – "Ah, you poor creature, you poor creature", he said no more than that, again and again he said it, until the desperate, dumb iteration almost broke one's heart. Or he asked an amazed and horrified question – ["] What would they shoot you for at all? What would they shoot you for"[?] He went away, and within three minutes we were all clowning and giggling and shouting again.

. . . . . .

I'll have to stop this letter, for its just closing time in the Gallery, and I've got to see to things. Until tomorrow or the next day, then, good bye.

Yours always,
JAMES STEPHENS

To P. E. LIMA

Dublin
[A/29] 18 February 1921

[Apparently P.E. Lima of Matawan, New Jersey, wrote to Stephens to congratulate him on *Irish Fairy Tales*. Only two of the "four books" were published: *In the Land of Youth* and *Deirdre.*]

Dear Sir.

Your letter gave me very real pleasure, and I hope my future writings (I have about four books nearly ready) will be equally liked by you. It is very good for an author to hear from someone that his work & care has been appreciated, and this is the more as in the case of an author like me, for I have not only to create my books I have actually to create my audience as well.

Yours very truly,
JAMES STEPHENS

To JOHN QUINN

Dublin
[T/28] 21 February 1921

Mr dear John,

Here is, what must seem to you inevitable, that is, a request. I want you to collect a ms (typed) for me from a publisher named Huebsch, and, if possible, I would like you to read it before you return it to me.

When Boyd was leaving here for America he took with him the above mentioned ms. There are, in reality, two ms, that is two complete stories, called "The Country of the Young", and "Deirdre". They are the first two volumnes of my five-volumned book "The Tain Bo Cuailgne". The Deirdre volumne is easily the best thing I have ever done, that is why I would like you to read it before returning it to me.

Boyd gave these mss to a firm calling itself Huebsch, and in October last while I was in Paris this Huebsch wrote asking for an interview. He was in a hotel on the rue de Rivoli (Place Jeanne d'Arc, I think)[.] I saw Mr Huebsch, and asked him if he pronounced his name with a button-hook? He said "No", but that he was very interested in my work, and would I have some tea. He then introduced me to his wife, who was from Scandinavia, and obviously didnt care a rap when one addressed her as Huebsch. I dont believe she knew about it, for I called her Huebsch several times, and she answered up like a pet lamb. She taught me how to say Huebsch in two lessons, but I never was any good at the piccolo, and I always hung fire at the bsch part, which my eye advised me ought to be pronounced biss-chich while my conscience protested that this sound meant chicken-food. I went away murmuring "Good-bye Mrs Eh, eh, Farewell Mr Um-m-m.["]

After all I am only five feet three high and cannot be expected to talk hard words like that, but you are a big fellow and I expect you can throw any word that was ever forged. Walk right in to him and say it quick, and then, while he is astonied and dismayed, you pinch my mss and get home by a side street. Thats that. If you wait you will forget the name, or you will mix it up with what it ought to mean, and you'll say "I want two buttered huebsche's on toast", and he'll think you are joking, and the kind of man who gets married in Scandinavia where the people live on sprats and can say worse things than Huebsch without spraining their ankles, that kind of man doesnt understand a joke unless he makes it himself, and then no one else understands it.

At that interview we talked very nobly to each other, but we did not talk any business, and I came away with the understanding that he would write to me about low monetary propositions as soon as he got back to America and was healed of newly-weddedness. I fancy he must be a man who gets more married than ever the more he thinks of it, for, to this day, and that is five months ago, he has never sent me a line. Maybe he is dead. Maybe his name grew inwards, like an ingrowing toe-nail, and he died of it; or maybe he has just retired into matrimony, and is telling everything else to go to hell. Maybe his wife is teaching him the American language. But I beg you to drive into that man's miseries, and elicit my manuscripts. I only ask you to pronounce his name once, but you can use any other reasonable violence on him that you care for.

I enclose a covering letter authorising every devilment you can possibly do to him.

I have just finished the lovliest story that ever was written by mortal man. But I'm in such a blue and wrinkled rage about that Huebsch that I'll keep it to tell of another time.

Yours always,
JAMES STEPHENS

The ms of "The land of the Young" is short & in one part. "Deirdre" is very long and is typed in *two* parts. So, the entire collection looks like *three* manuscripts, thus "Deirdre" part 1
"Deirdre part 2
"The Land ot the Young
JS

To BEN W. HUEBSCH

Dublin
[T/20] 21 February 1921

[The following was enclosed with the letter to Quinn on 21 February 1921.]

Dear Mr Huebsch,

You may remember our interview in Paris in late September of last year on the subject of my two stories "The Land of the Young", and "Deirdre". These stories were left with your firm by my friend Mr E. Boyd, late of this city.

I have decided not to publish these stories for some time, and will be very obliged if you will hand the mss to Mr John Quinn, 31 Nassau Street, New York, to whom this letter is being sent.

Yours faithfully,
JAMES STEPHENS

To ERNEST A. BOYD

Dublin
[A/12] 21 March 1921

[Boyd's review of *Irish Fairy Tales*, "The Irish Fairyland", was published in *The Freeman* (New York) for 9 March 1921 (Boyd was a general reviewer for *The Freeman* from the spring of 1920 to the winter of 1922). Although he did not like the illustrations by Arthur Rackham, Boyd was generally positive about the book: "these stories are the gold transmuted from the ore of traditional material." Boyd's French book was probably his translation of *The Opinions of Anatole France*, recorded by Paul Gsell (1922). The Boyds had settled in New York in early 1920.]

Mr dear Boyd.

The "Freeman" has just arrived with your article on my Fairy Tales. That is a good article & satisfies me in every part. I am sure it will round up a lot of the American readers that are now overdue. By the way, I saw your man Huebsch in Paris in September last, & we parted on the understanding that he was going back to the States & would write me about the mss which you had left with his firm. That is seven months ago & that Mr Huebsch has never ever written to say he had seen the mss, or even that he has the mss. I did not know your address & so I write to Quinn a month ago asking him to unbury my stories from that Huebsch & to send them back to me. I wont publish with such a man. Send me a note sometime to say how you are getting on. Is the French book progressing? And are you consolidating & planning & commencing the conquest of America? Our greetings to you & to Mrs Boyd. Dublin is very different from the one you knew. There is the devil to pay, & everyone is at the top of form.

Toujours à vous
JAMES STEPHENS

To ANDRÉ BRULÉ

Dublin
[A/19] 28 May 1921

[André Brulé (1879–1953) was a French actor. The article in the *Times Literary Supplement* for 26 May 1921 was "Pure Music" by the English critic Arthur Clutton-Brock (1868–1924). Clutton-Brock made a reference to the "*Voi che sapete*" aria in Act II of Mozart's *The Marriage of Figaro*.]

Dear Mr Brulé

This is just a note to ask how you and Madame & the bambino are. MacKenna has just been in with me asking for your address. Everytime (about three times a week) that he has met me in the past month he has asked passionately for your address. But this time he wrote it down in his pocket book, and I expect you will get his nouvelles ["pieces of news"] before you get this letter. Things here are not only bad; they are damn bad, and there does not seem to be any break in our clouds. I got quite a lot of the music you told me of and I and MacKenna play it gently to ourselves during Curfew hours, & even if we make no music, we make time pass. I enclose the front page of the present Times Literary Supplement. There is rather a good article in it by one Clutton Brock. I wonder do you know the piece by Mozart which he quotes. MacKenna would chide me for wondering thus ignorantly, for he contends that you know everything worth knowing. Do you consider the song to be as heavenly as Clutton Brock states it to be. I marvel that you & Madam, having progressed so far in music, should permit that inappreciable blessing to rust for lack of use. As you see from this letter I haven't anything to say, and am merely writing you to say so. All good things to yourself, to your gracious Madame & the babe. I expect you are being baked into a piecrust in Paris. Here it is delightfully cool, but I expect we will pass that on to you in a few days.

Yours very truly
JAMES STEPHENS

To JOHN QUINN

Dublin
[T/28] 3 June 1921

[Quinn had prepared his *Memorandum Against the Imposition of Any Duty on Original Works of Art* (1921) for presentation to a sub-committee of the Ways and Means Committee of the House of Representatives on 10 May 1921.]

My dear John,

Thanks for sending me your "Memorandum against the imposition of any duty on original works of art". I have read it with great interest, and, both as an artist, and as (for seven years now) the Registrar of a very important Art Collection, I agree absolutely with every word you have written. Your wise and witty pleading at the top of page 21 should be framed in the Entrance Hall of every Gallery in America, and it would do no harm if they were exposed in

Europe also. Too many people think, mainly because there is no one to tell them or teach them the contrary, that the artist is a lazy and often immoral vagabond who has discovered a royal road to easy money, and I am glad that on the same page you have so finely uttered the truth about them ". . . Artists are the true educators, and for that reason we must guard against any prejudice against artists. Artists are diligent men, none more diligent, and all the more so because, like men of science and learned students, they love their work . . . "

Ask any man or woman who has sat for a portrait whether they or the painter got tired first. I have had the experience with some sculptors and several painters, and I know that their tendancy is not to quit soon and early, but to work their unfortunate sitter to death; and I think that the average artist's capacity for work is one of the most extraordinary facts I know in the whole realm of labour. There are few enough occupations in this sad world the basis of which is actual love and reverence for one's material. The older world which had that saving grace has almost vanished, and, but for the artist, it might be said to have completely vanished, and with it one of the most profound and irreplaceable elements in our humanity goes also.

You say again, page one, that ". . . The art of every age is the fine flowering of all the scientific and all the philosophic thought of its own day and time. It quickens vitality and intensifies the love of beauty and the love of country, and increases the joy of life – "

These are incontrovertable dicta, and I think that a better definition of art and its function could not be made. There is no such thing as spontaneous combustion, or spontaneous art or spontaneous anything, but an endless sequence and interrelation of all things, and it is true that art is "the fine flowering" wherein all the complexities of environment and thought and action are resolved and generalized. If our statesmen were as wise as our voters think they would give much more loving and reverent heed to the artist than the artist will ever ask for.

After all, it is not stupidity or malice that stands in the way of progress or reform, it is that a number of people think along prescribed lines, and they require to be told that there is another and better way of looking at things than the way they are accustomed to. The artist does his duty, and he does it with his whole soul; let the others do their share of the universal obligation, that is, if they cannot love one another, to love something, and work for it.

But your brief has said the whole thing. Good luck to the brief and to you. You didnt answer any of my recent letters. I was in Paris a fortnight ago for three weeks: it was very pleasant there. I marched out resolutely during the curfew hours, and did gloats towards my poor friends in Dublin. Things here are particularly and poignantly interesting.

Yours very truly,
JAMES STEPHENS

To JOHN QUINN

Dublin
[T/28] 14 June 1921

[*The Arts* (New York) for May 1921 contained reproductions of some paintings which Quinn owned by Paul Gauguin (1848–1903), André Derain (1880–1954), Odilon Redon (1840–1916) and Pablo Picasso. Nathaniel Hone (1831–1917) was an Irish landscape painter.

Mt dear John,

Thanks for your present of "The Arts". It is an interesting production, and has reproduced your pictures very nicely. Why dont you publish an illustrated catalogue of your collection, with a running commentary by yourself? You must have a quantity of treasure which art lovers everywhere would be glad to get in touch with. We are having an exhibition here (in this Gallery) of part of our Nathanial Hone bequest. We have been left some fifteen hundred pieces, and have shaped an exhibition of about one hundred pictures and water colours out of that vast collection. The water colours are especially delightful. In spite of Hone's great qualities I find a certain lack of variety in him and a sadness of mood which is also too frequent. We are all, or should be all, fire-worshippers, and these Hone pictures show the fire burning low, or even burning out. But what about your illustrated catalogue?

Yours always,
JAMES STEPHENS

To JOHN QUINN

Dublin
[T/28] 22 June 1921

[The "blasted Act" was the Government of Ireland Act (1920).]

My dear John,

Your letter of the 5th June came in this morning. I am glad that bothersome business with Huebsch is ended, and am more than delighted that you liked the stories.

We are existing here under most extraordinary conditions. There is an endless, intensive military occupation over the country, and one would imagine that it would be impossible for as much as a fly to move without detection, but the whole country seethes and goes still in the most startling alternations. As you say, the Irish do not quit easily, and I can nowhere discover any sign that anyone is tired or even beginning to think of quitting. From all over the country the story is the same. Ireland is stiff as an iron bar, and, short of absolute decimation, she will never give in. And, with that, there is no hysteria, no excitement: there is nothing but the will to win, and to outlast anything. I am quite in agreement with your definition of what we might accept. Personally, I do not care a rap by what name we go adventuring in time, let it be kingdom or republic or colony – it is immaterial – the one actuality for me is – are we to be given the unrestricted control of our own money? That control is government, is freedom, and without it anything else that is given is nonsense. The permission to a number of elected Irishmen to make public speeches in a Parliament House in Dublin is not good enough. We have gone far beyond the desire to hear any person making a speech in or out of a Parliament House, and that is all the English offer us under the name of freedom. The English politician must descend to reality in dealing with us henceforth, and the reality is, that we know what we want and we wont be happy until we get it. Indeed we are not demanding freedom to control their money: it is our own three halfpence we are after. Nor do we consider it just that the scheme of taxation under which England lives should be applied to us. England, a large and wealthy nation, can manage, although with inconvenience, on that scale, but we, a small and less than moderately wealthy country, cannot afford to cut our cloth after the pattern of our millionaire neighbour. The money raised in England by taxation goes to relieve England, the money raised in Ireland also goes to relieve England, none of it (after necessary services) comes our way, and the result to us is exactly the same as if we loaded our surplus capital into a tug and dumped it into the middle of the sea. We are forcibly, and by a thousand channels, made to export our capital, and, in consequence, we are forced to export an important percentage of our population. Their blasted Act obliges us to first pay all our own services per year, and then to pay them eighteen million pounds per year. We will be taxed for our own purposes and for their purposes. If they asked us to sink that eighteen millions in the vasty deep it would do us just as much good as the sending it to them will do. For, with the eighteen millions, there must leave our shores the percentage of our population which these eighteen millions would enable to live here. Anyhow, the future is always only half a minute away, and we will just wait for it, and grin when we can and grunt when we cant.

Always affectionately yours,
JS

A thousand thanks for all you have done for me.

To HAROLD LOEB

Dublin

[A/1] 12 July 1921

[The writer and economist Harold Loeb (1891–1974) was the founder and editor of *Broom: An International Magazine of the Arts.* Stephens's "Hunger", published in booklet form by the Candles Press in Dublin in 1918, was the opening short story of the first issue of *Broom* (November 1921). No other work by Stephens appeared in the magazine. Shaw's play was *Back to Methuselah* (1921). A truce between the British and Irish forces was proclaimed on 10 July 1921. Loeb gave Stephens a gramophone in September 1920.]

Mr dear Loeb.

Well, you are getting into the job! I'm sure you'll make a success of it. Anyway, I'll be curious to see how your work is shaping since we last met. About "Hunger". The copyright is mine. The firm that published it has ceased to exist, and you may go ahead without any acknowledgments or care. I have another story. I dont know if you will like it. But its my best yet. I was thinking of sending it away, but if you care to read it I'll post it to you instead. I can, of course, send you an occasional column in literature, art & Irish matters if you desire such. Did you read Shaw's new play. Its great stuff. I'd like to review that for you. It is Shaw reborn & a mighty fine young Shaw. We will leave for Paris on 5th September for three weeks. Things are quiet here. This is the 2nd day of our truce, & all last night we had bonfires in the middle of the streets, & a good deal of bad singing. We are none of us over hopeful, but are all interested, & wondering what will happen next. That gramaphone of yours has made me a musician. I play the concertina, but may slide from it to the fiddle.

Mis go déo [*deo*]
["I am, always"]
JAMES STEPHENS

To ALICE HENRY

Dublin
[A/26] 23 July 1921

[Alice Henry was the wife of Augustine Henry (1857–1930), Professor of Forestry at University College, Dublin. The quotation from *The Bacchae* is taken from *Euripedes* (1902), translated by Gilbert Murray.]

Dear Elsie.

I never thanked you for copying out the extracts from the Bacchae. They are all great and beautiful; & have that stamp of beauty that they are true at all times, and are applicable everywhere. It is hard to speak of absolute truth in a world where all values seem relative: But for me, I snigger benevolently all to myself at that so terrifying relativity, for I know that life itself is absolute & not relative, & that the essential qualities of life, beauty and truth, are also absolute; & are real & similar in all places & at all angles. When a thought or emotion has been actually felt & uttered, altho' two or three thousand years ago, or twenty thousand years ago, it applies to our modernity in actual fact & tissue, & not with any relative curtailments or contingencies. I blink (benevolently) at one lovely phrase in one of the choruses.

"Dreams of the proud man making great
And greater ever
Things which are not of God . . . "

And would amend or remind, being temerarious:

That which is not of God is not at all,
God is, and God is all, & all of Him.

Matter may be in the wrong place & become dirt. So may action or thought get strayed & reappear as a villiany; but the proof of all things is just that they Be, & Being so they are God; good or bad, in focus or out of it, to Be is to Be God: & there we reach an end which begins always; or appetite comes be ["by"] eating; or we live by living. Fountain pens never know when to stop. Cuss them! They just fountain. Think of an essay on "The Fountain-Penness of Things[".]

Mise go deó [*deo*] agat
["I am yours always"]
JAMES STEPHENS

To HAROLD LOEB

Dublin
1 August 1921

[A/1]

[Shaw's book was *Back to Methuselah.*]

Dear Loeb.

I got your letter all right, & note you will be in Paris in September. We hope to get there (11 rue Campagne-Premiere) on 6th September & will stay there for three weeks. I dont understand why you wont put some of your own stuff in the Broom. Perhaps you feel a bit diffident yet. From the play I saw I predict that you have the goods, and all you have to do is to go to it. The really important thing about Shaw's book is, that he has got a new lease of life. He is, in a curious manner, reborn. There will always be, as you say, a good deal of "loose thinking" in anything he writes. He writes too easily, & is inclined to play with his talents instead of working with them. But he is surely a tophole man.

Yours always
JAMES STEPHENS

To HERBERT EDWARD PALMER

Dublin

[A/36] 26 September 1921

[Palmer's book was *Two Minstrels* (1921). Stephens had been in Paris for three weeks on holiday.]

Dear Mr Palmer.

A thousand thanks for your book which I have read with delight. I have only just returned from Paris where I spent my vacation, & so did not get the book until yesterday. This accounts for my delay in acknowledging your kindness. In this, as in your other books, there is no doubt of your poetry or of your power. The whole seems as though dashed off at a white hot speed, & is of a most remarkable intensity. Self-expression is a great thing, but self-mastery is a better, & you are still beating against bars which, to a gift like yours, should be imperceptible. As far as victory is concerned, you have already won, for the things you may lack are not of much consideration beside the thing you have. I will not enter into counsels of perfection, but would merely draw your attention to the riches & powers you have, & to the comparative worthlessness of anything else. I cannot criticise your poetry, that would be an impertinence, for you know as much about it as any man. But your work is so intensely individual that, as well as poetry, you offer yourself to your reader, &, without a certain amount of "transmutation" this is not always wise.

Yours very truly
JAMES STEPHENS

To SIR FREDERICK MACMILLAN
(Macmillan & Company, London)

Dublin

[T/23] 3 December 1921

[Neither of these books was published, though Stephens later was a co-editor of *English Romantic Poets* (1933).]

Dear Sir Frederick Macmillan,

I have lately been reading Shelley, and with so great an admiration that I wish to write about him.

I would like to publish a book that would include his Prometheus Unbound, the Adonais and the Epipsichidion, with a long preliminery essay.

I think that a new book and a new view on Shelley might be welcomed by quite a large public, and if the idea appealed to you I would like to undertake it.

I hope shortly to go ahead with other original work.

If the above suggestion meets with your approval I would like to do a similar selection and essay on Keats. Neither of these poets have, I think, been adequately (altho' plentifully) anthologised or criticised.

Yours very truly
JAMES STEPHENS

To EDWARD MARSH

Dublin
[A/3] 6 December 1921

[Stephens apparently received another royalty payment for his contributions to Marsh's *Georgian Poetry* volumes.]

My dear Marsh.

Many thanks. These books of yours are the wonder of the world. I am doing rather good stuff now & have just discovered Shelley & Keats.

Yours always
JAMES STEPHENS

To W. T. H. HOWE

Dublin
[A/3] 3 January 1922

[Stephens's poem was "Minuette: On the Freedom of Ireland/To Eamonn de Valera", published in *Poblacht na h-Eireann* (Dublin) for 3 January 1922. The poem was included in *Little Things* (1924); the fourth stanza was retained, becoming the last two stanzas of Part II of the poem. *Little Things* contained six poems.]

Dear Mr Howe,

There has just come in a box with a beautiful vase which my wife has immediately decked with flowers, & a parcel of books for signature. I am returning these by separate post. I enclose a newspaper. You may remember that I sent you a new poem before Christmas. I have published it in the first issue of this paper, which will only run during the (our) peace negotiations. &, as there are several changes in this later version, I send it to you. I still think that in a final printing I will omit the fourth verse. I think I will take advantage of your kind offer to print a little book of about five poems, &, so, I may send you in a few more days a small manuscript.

All good things be with you in this New Year, & in all years

Yours very truly
JAMES STEPHENS

To JOHN HOUSTON FINLEY

Dublin
[T/28] 16 February 1922

[The educator and author John Houston Finley (1863–1940) was currently an Associate Editor of the *New York Times*.]

My dear Mr. Finley,

Your letter of January 25th duly received.

I also am very sorry that we were unable to meet while you were over here, and hope we shall both have better luck next time. My stay in Paris was very short.

If you should see John Quinn again will you please greet him for me. I am glad you liked "The Demi-Gods", but I think the first hundred pages of the "Irish Fairy Tales", which I published about a year ago, lick the Demi-Gods to nowhere. The first story, anyhow, "The Story of Tuan Mac Cairill", is one that makes me feel that one of these days I'll turn out some fine writing.

Yours very truly,
JAMES STEPHENS

To OLIVER ST. JOHN GOGARTY

Dublin
[A/9] [1–4] May 1922

[Stephens left for a two-week visit to Paris on 5 May 1922. This letter must have accomplished its purpose, as Theodore Spicer-Simson did make a medal of Yeats in 1922.]

My dear Oliver:

This is to introduce my friend, Theodore Spicer-Simson. He has sculped everybody except Yeats, & you could help to hold down that great man for him, if anyone can. Anyway, he would love to see your treasures & yourselves.

go deó [*deo*] agat
["yours always"]
JAMES STEPHENS

To W. T. H. HOWE

[A/3] Dublin
26 June 1922

[The book was published in 1924 as *Little Things*. "Nachiketas and Death" was dedicated to Howe.]

My dear Mr Howe:

Do you remember saying you would like to bring out a tiny booklet of poems. Here are the poems, if you are still of that mind – I think they are among the best I have written. I would like you to read, in particular, "Nachiketas & Death". It is rather a feat to put the whole of the Upanishads & the Vedanta into verse, & to put it so shortly. I might say that it took me fifteen years to write that poem, although I actually did write it in ten minutes. The *third* verse of the Pit of Bliss is rather curious. I there try in the first nine lines to give a tumble through all space, & these nine lines should be said in one sole mouthful. Write me that you have no objection to the line under the Title of "Nachiketas & Death". We are just back from Paris, where I go again on 1st September for a month.

Yours always
JAMES STEPHENS

Iris was enchanted with the Dolls – They stand most coquettishly on my bookcase as guardian angels over the Revue Celtique – While in Paris I let the Spicer Simsons have my flat, & they have done a lot of work here. Iris & Seumas & my wife & I send our most affectionate greetings to you.

To HAROLD LOEB

[T/1]

Dublin
14 July 1922

[Up to this point Loeb's contributions to *Broom* (which sold for 50¢ an issue) were several translations and the "Comment" section in at least two issues. Stephen's "Hunger" was included on the "Roll of Honour" published in *Best British Short Stories of 1922*, ed. E. J. O'Brien and John Cournos (1923). "Clair de Lune" is either an unpublished story or an early version of "Etched in Moonlight". Charles Garvice (1833–1920) was an English writer.]

Dear Loeb,

Your note reached me in full tide of war. By the Lord, if we dont stop having wars soon we'll get sick of them. What are you doing yourself? Are you writing? I have only seen one thing of yours in Broom. It is still miles and away the best of magazines. I think you give far too good value for the money, and, in these days, that is a very curious thing to say.

Are you still in love with Italy? or is the first fine edge of appreciation wearing off. For my part, I would give anybody's right leg to be able to stay in Rome for a year or so, but I am rather tied up and tied down. Nothing's doing; that's not a complaint or a growl, just a statement. One of these days, when we get through with our wars, I'll go off with a bang and I'll bust royalties off someone.

What do you mean by writing that Hunger was elected the best British Short Story for 1922? First I've heard of it. Of course its the best, but I dont expect anyone else to spot that until you and I have been very comfortably dead for about ten years. More than that, for I feel like bragging, the first story in my Fairy Tales, "The Story of Tuan Mac Cairill", is the best short story in English also; and further, for at this mortal minute I am just chock full of brags, the next 100 or so pages of the Fairy Tales are the best short stories in the British or any other old language, and to continue I did a 17,000 word tale called (provisionally) Clair de Lune which is the only white man's hope that is. And beyond that there is Deirdre. Best Short Stories – I am the only man that writes em. I have em patented, and some day if people will go on praising other fellows I'll get right up and I'll start praising myself so loudly that someone will hear. My real curse is modesty, and actually-applied modesty will make a pauper of a Thug. Dont you do it ever. If you ever feel modest or modestish grow a moustache, and if it continues play for the movies.

All the same we are still at war here, and not a soul cares a kick about the best short story in the world, two scores of which I have written. They just go heaving bombs as if there was nothing worth buying. They havent the brains. They buy Garvice and Shaw. God help them, for if He wont help me he must help someone.

You must remember that you didnt write me a letter. You wrote me a curtailed note, and it doesnt count.

From this grave gallery in which I sit-a-ly
I send fond greetings to thee in Italy.

Mise
["I am"]
JAMES STEPHENS

Memories would scan better than "greetings" [–] We will change it in the second edition

To SARAH PURSER

Dublin
[A/26] 22 July 1922

["Frank" is Dr. Frank Purser (1876–1934).]

Dear Miss Purser:

I got your card, & send herewith a note to Miss Stein. If you go to see her you will enjoy not only her pictures but herself. She is a very good sort. We are still at war, & every night the old guns that you are so used to start their cursed row from half twelve onwards, & upwards I suppose for if they hit anything it must be the sky. Last night I went into Frank & had my share of an Irish lesson & twice my share of a gargantuan dish of raspberries & logan-berries with

Cream distilled from gentler cows
Than in Elysium do browse,
And dulcet as the Irish tongue
We were not taught when we were young.

All good luck for ever

Mise
["I am"]
JAMES STEPHENS

To GERTRUDE STEIN

Dublin
[A/42] 26 July 1922

[This note, written (like so many others) on National Gallery of Ireland stationery, was enclosed with the above letter to Purser. Marie Bashkirtsev (1860–84) was a French diarist and painter.]

Dear Miss Stein:

I would like very much to introduce Miss Sarah Purser to you. As well as being a Governor of this Gallery Miss Purser is a distinguished artist, & is a very particularly great friend of mine. She can tell you all about Marie Baskertseff (how does one spell her) for she was a pal of that nice girl in the days of yore. I hope to be in Paris in September, 11 rue Campagne-Premiere, & will be very glad to see you again

Yours very truly
JAMES STEPHENS

To JOHN HOUSTON FINLEY

Dublin
[A/28] 11 August 1922

[I have not located a contemporary publication of Finley's article or poem, but the latter was included in the posthumous *Poems* (1941). Stephens may have forgotten his letter to Finley on 16 February 1922.]

Dear Mr. Finley:

You will perhaps be astonished at receiving a letter from me: but the facts are: – You wrote to my friend John Quinn sending him a nice little article entitled "Good News", and a poem on "Tuam". John kept these to send on to me, & he has asked me to write you acknowledging their receipt, & apologising for his not having replied to you himself. Tis a roundabout business, but tis a roundabout world, & here are you & I, whether we will it or whether we dont, introduced to each other and buying postage stamps we never dreamed of. Will you drop a line to John telling him he is forgiven, for he thinks that perhaps you think that he has been rude which he was and isn't. Look at the way my style is going to pieces, but when one is called upon, at a moment's notice, to apologise across half the earth to a man whom one doesnt know & hopes to know better for a misdeed in which one had no part, style wilts. In his letter to me John said a number of the nicest things about you that one man could say about another. If he had just written these things to you like an honest man (he is a lawyer isn't he) he wouldnt have me overworking an already jaded pen on apologies that I am innocent of. Here is one good thing out of it all – I read your verse on "Tuam", and I have read no verse recently that moved me so poignantly or that has seemed to be written from so deep & clean an impulse. With that I'll apologise no more. Let John Quinn go suffer for his own sins and not be sticking them on me who never did him or you any harm. Hoping you will acknowledge receipt of John Quinn's apologies by return of post, whereupon (my God!) I shall immediately forward same to him, & apologising to you most profoundly for having apologised to you.

I am,
dear Mr Finley
Your obliged and obedient servant
JAMES STEPHENS

To HAROLD LOEB

Dublin
[A/1] 12 August 1922

[Loeb's article was "The Mysticism of Money", published in *Broom* for September 1922.]

Dear Loeb:

I return the article. It is fine, and I read it with the greatest interest. The writing, after three pages or so, as soon as you really get to grips with your subject, gets continually better. Quite in the beginning it tends to be a trifle difficult, but afterwards & for the whole of what is a long essay it is limpid & easy & expressive. As to the ideas – I think they are quite sound, even when they are most ingenious. I have no doubt that you will find people agreeing & disagreeing with you violently. Let 'em. Just you go ahead and spill yourself out in every subject that comes under your notice. But dont go in, too exclusively, for philosophy. There are plays to be written by your pen, & it is much greater fun to turn ideas into people than to turn people into ideas, which is what philosophy does. All these blessed movements are men whether we call them social ideas, or economic laws, & I think they can be better (both) expounded and examined in the human guise than in the abstract one. Anyhow, & notwithstanding I am very pleased with the article & will look forward to rereading it in Broom

Yours always
JAMES STEPHENS

To JOHN QUINN

Dublin
[T/28] 15 August 1922

[*Ulysses* had been published in Paris on 2 February 1922, Joyce's fortieth birthday. *Beyond Good and Evil* (1891) is a work by Friedrich Nietzsche.]

My dear John,

Your letter of July 30th was delivered here on the 12th inst, and I was delighted to get it. I had been wondering what had swallowed you up, or, rather, in what new interest you had adventured and disappeared. What with law, literature, painting and the criticising of all these you manage to get ten men's interest into and out of life, and one never knows at any moment in which of them you are to be sought.

I did not read Ulysses – It is too expensive to buy, and too difficult to borrow, and too long to read, and, from what I have heard about it, altogether too difficult to talk about. Of course, I know Joyce's work pretty well, and I intend to go on thinking that his little book of verse "Chamber Music" is the best work he has ever done, or is ever likely to do. He is certainly a man who can "write": I am not so certain that he is man who can live, or that he is a man who can initiate a story, or a man who can do any more than remember very sharply anything that has ever happened to him. The great writer is not one who can remember an experience, altho' he must be able to do this – He is one who can make many bricks out of very little straw, and he can, so, transmute many experiences out of one experience. He (Joyce) may have carried his matter "beyond good and evil" [–] We may admit that he has carried it beyond evil, for one can see the (God save the mark) evil, and admit that it has been carried somewhere. As for the good, it is to seek, and I do not know that the "good" end of the criticism is justified.

That one should be able to talk freely on all kinds of subjects is an excellent desire, and the artist who craves to talk to the top or bottom of his bent on the subject of sensuality in general cannot be blamed for so desiring. But the fact is, that these same artists have nothing whatever to tell us on this subject that we dont know. The world swims in unwritten, verbally-recorded, tales of this ilk: many of them of an amazing excellence and wit, and we all, from the age of fourteen have received a fairly intensive education on the subject of sex in general and in particular. The cravings and aberrations of a human being on this subject are so well understood by us all that I consider it a mark of mediocrity of talent in the artist who will write of this when a world that is teeming with interest and newness and originality is there for him to fathom if he can. If he can . . . When you cannot be modern there is nothing left for you but to be ancestral, and when you are incapable of a new experience there is nothing left for you but to be interested in the memory of the old ones. This is the crime of Joyce, that he is incapable of any current impression, and that, at the age of about twenty five, he ceased to live either as a man or an artist. He has written, say, three books in prose – they are all the same book, and the man that he is at forty five or six is only and merely the boy that he was at nineteen and twenty five. If a tree doesnt grow it is no good, if a man does not grow he is no good. If a man does not continue to collect and digest experience he is next door to a dead man, or is, at his best, only an example of arrested animation.

I have written to your friend, Dr John Finley. I liked his poem on "Tuam" immensely. I note you are going to Westport which, you say, is on the west shore of Lake Champlain, and from which, you say, one can see the Green Mountains of Vermont. You cannot fool me that way. I know all about Westport. I was there. It is the next station before you get to Galway, and you couldnt see Vermont from it unless you climbed right up on the Moon and thence telescoped Vermont, and even then I dont know if you could see Vermont from Westport. As to Lake Champlain – All I will say about it is, that it is not "a very pictueresque and large lake", and that there is no such lake near Westport. Now . . .

Yours always
JAMES STEPHENS

To THOMAS MOULT

Dublin

[T/36] 7 January 1923

[The English critic Thomas Moult (1895–) was preparing an edition of *The Best Poems of 1922* (1923). "Green Weeds" had been published in *The Nation and The Athenaeum* for 14 January 1922. Stephens's book was *Little Things*.]

Dear Sir,

Thanks for your letter of the 1st instant, which has been forwarded to me by the Editor of the Nation.

I am sorry that I cannot give permission to include "Green Weeds" in your forthcoming anthology. I am preparing my later stuff for publication, and, as there is not very much of it, I would not like it to appear elsewhere before I published it myself.

Please forgive me, but my book will be a very little one, and will not bear dilution.

Yours very truly,
JAMES STEPHENS

To THOMAS MOULT

Dublin

[A/36] 19 January 1923

["Green Weeds" was included in Moult's *The Best Poems of 1922*.]

Dear Mr Moult:

Thanks for your letter & suggestion. You may use the poem "*Green Weeds*" in your Anthology. I do not know when I shall publish my small book, &, in the circumstances, you need not delay your publication on my account. I hope the Anthology will be very successful.

Yours sincerely
JAMES STEPHENS

To W. T. H. HOWE

Dublin
[T/3] 24 March 1923

[Zane Grey (1875–1939) was an American writer of western stories. Since the *Collected Poems* of the American poet Vachel Lindsay (1879–1931) was not published until May 1923, Stephens would have read "Aladdin and the Jinn" in *The Congo and Other Poems* (1914) and "A Negro Sermon: – Simon Legree" (Part I of "The Booker Washington Trilogy") and "The Chinese Nightingale" in *The Chinese Nightingale and Other Poems* (1917). An edition of *The Crock of Gold* with illustrations by the English artist Wilfred Jones (1890–) was published in 1922. "Brinsley Macnamara" was the pseudonym of the Irish playwright and novelist John Weldon (1890–1963).]

My dear Mr Howe:

Thanks for your letter – The little parcel came by the same post, and I have no doubt that Iris and Seumas will be delighted with their presents. We, [(]their mother and I) are going to England at Easter to see them – they are at school there – and we will dutifully present the red necklace and the toy, leaving it to them to express their own contentments.

Things here are much as they were. Guns go off every night, and bombs are thrown, or, which is a newer delight, land-mines are exploded. It has all come to seem rather meaningless, and I expect it will stop shortly. For my part I begin to feel the wanderlust again, and would like to pull up my stakes and go to America for a few years – to see how it is, and what it is. I know America (most of us here do) largely from the novels of Zane Grey. I think he is rather fine of his kind, and I know he wiled away long hours for me lately in hospital. In the matter of poetry – I have been delighted with some of Vachell Lindsay's work – If you havent read Aladdin and the Jinn, Simon Lergree, and, in especial, The Chinese Nightingale, you ought to read them quickly. There is nobody among the younger school of English poets half as good as he is: his energy is terrific, and he seems to have everything in his make up for the largest kind of success, he has energy, humour, tenderness, drama – He is really rather a wonder.

In the matter of our little book – I will not be in the least dissatisfied if you cannot get anyone to illustrate it. The art of illustration is lost. Look for example at those that some one done to my Crock of Gold. They are the vilest example of bad art that I have ever come across, and I would much rather have had to shed tears over that man's grave than have had to sloush them over my poor pages. This typewriting machine has gone off its chump. It has a kind of fit every three lines, and in a minute or two it will begin to misspell me. Over here McNamara's books are not taken very seriously. A drab mind will note that the glistning gates of heaven are drab coloured. It is generally a sign of low vitality in the author or artist, for this is always true, that we project ourselves into every bit of creative work we do. Lord, if there is a drab creator what but a dull creation can one expect. Still, it is unfair to criticise without having read the books, but you have read them for me. All that is perhaps easily said, but I have been watching this typing machine with such curiosity that I dont know any longer what I am saying.

All good luck to you.

Yours very truly,
JAMES STEPHENS

To W. T. H. HOWE

Dublin
[T/3] 3 May 1923

[Stephens would have read Lindsay's "The Congo" in *The Congo and Other Poems*; "The Devil" is a character in "A Negro Sermon: – Simon Legree". The book was eventually entitled *Little Things* and began with "Little Things".]

My dear Mr Howe:

Our best thanks for your kind invitation, and, if we get to America, you may be sure that we shall remind you not to forget it.

Thanks, too, for the candies – They brought out the very worst side in me and my wife. We had intended sending them to the children; but, unfortunately for them, we tasted them first – Then we tasted them again. Then we decided that we would eat another one; and then we ate the lot – and packed off an entirely spurious, native candy to those deluded infants, and did not say a word to them about Pecan candies. I dont believe you can beat us, however, in dough-nuts. My wife builds a dough-nut that is more remarkable than the Woolworth Building. She made some for our guests the other night – some painters and writers; and they behaved towards the dough-nuts exactly as we did to your candies.

About Vachell Lindsay – He has written quite a lot of stuff that is no good. The poems that I praise him for are – The Chinese Nightengale: Aladdin and the Jinn; and, some way afterwards, The Congo. I dont think he bears examination in his mass-production. Oh, there is also, Simon Legree and the Devil.

About the poems – Whatever you say on this matter goes: and I shall do exactly as you instruct me, and say, thank you, into the bargain. I fancy that the first poem in the little collection is called "Green Weeds" [–] No, that would not do, for I have already published a booklet called "Green Branches", a lovely title, I think. Let us get a title that never has been used before. Here is one

"W. T. H. H."

I think that will do – Let us name the book then,

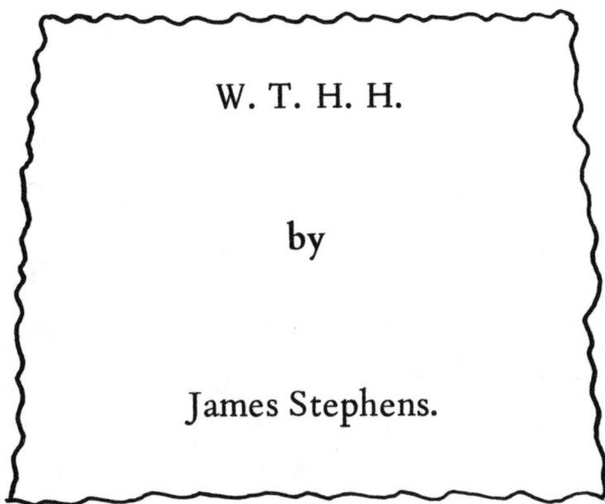

And, as you are responsable for the booklet, you shall take some of the cover-risk.

You consider that we will want about fifteen original couplets. I'll start at once thinking out nice ones: that shall each say a lot in little.

Yours very truly,
JAMES STEPHENS

By the way – I am dispatching today, by parcels post, the two books which you sent me for signature. I took the occasion to reread them while they were here, and, upon my word, there are very nice things in them. I am doing the proofs of Deirdre: so I suppose it will be published in the autumn. It is the best ever, and, more than that, it is better than the best ever.

To SIR FREDERICK MACMILLAN
(Macmillan & Company, London)

Dublin
[T/23] 9 May 1923

[Macmillan declined to publish this work.]

Dear Sir Frederick Macmillan:

I enclose a short book entitled "The Storyteller" [–] It is really an endeavour to examine the psychology of the novel and the novelist. I think it is of interest at the moment. I would be glad to know if you will care to publish it?

Yours very truly,
JAMES STEPHENS

To IRIS STEPHENS

Dublin
[A/1] 29 May 1923

[Douglas was a friend of Iris at school; Miss Smith and Miss Slater were her headmistresses. Rowena is the heroine of *Ivanhoe* (1819) by Sir Walter Scott. George Eliot's *Adam Bede* was published in 1859. Stephens's speech was probably in connection with Trinity Week, which began on 28 May.]

My dear little Iris:

Thanks for your nice letter & for the photo of Douglas. Yes, I read "Ivanhoe" – three times, I think; and, in those days, I thought it lovely! Somehow, I never cared a very great deal about Scott, but I did like Ivanhoe, & for long after reading it I longed to be a Crusader, and to perform deeds of chivelry, & rescue lovely damsels from other fellows. But, on the whole, I think I prefer these days to the days of yore; & I prefer Iris to any Rowena (or whatever her name was) of them all. I read Adam Bede, too. George Elliot, the author, was you know a woman. In these days I was a small boy in knickers, and, like your friend, I also thought her very nice: But, really, she was much too wise for me, and if I had told the truth, which I never did in those days, I would have admitted that I thought her very dull – In fact I only really enjoyed real bad books – Deadwood Dick, and Montezuma the Merciless (please spell that word for me) and Alligator Ike, or the Terror of the Plains. I loved bluggy stories, where someone was always shooting someone else, & people were being slung down precipices, & searching for buried treasure, and all that kind of thing, which I suppose you will think of as rot. However, there is no doubt that Adam Bede is a very good book, & George Elliots masterpiece – Her other books I could not read at all. We have had the beastliest weather here for months: rainy, sleety, east-windy weather, and we are looking forward to our vacation in Paris in September. Mammy will go before me to get you, I suppose at the beginning of August, & will bring Noiro with her. He asked me this morning to send you his love. He asked me this morning to let him into your room, I did so, & he took a long smell at one of your boots, & then he asked me to send you his love & a long purr – I can't enclose them, but I send them. He is really the nicest thing that ever was except you, & you are the nicest thing that ever was except me. I think the girl whose portrait you sent this morning is a good sort, & am glad you are friends with her. You can give her half of Noiro's love & some of his purr. Please remember me to Miss Smith & Miss Slater, & give my kind regards to the 3 squirrels & the Kingfisher. Here is Noiro's love [drawing] & this is his purr [drawing].

T'Athair
["Thy Father"]
JS

I have to make a speech tonight at Trinity College. Hate making speeches. Pray for me.

To ANDRÉ BRULÉ

Dublin
[A/19] 30 May 1923

[*The Orissers* by the English writer Leopold Hamilton Myers (1881–1944) was published in 1922. *Children of the Dead End: The Autobiography of a Navvy* (1914) is by the Irish writer Patrick MacGill (1890–1963).]

My dear Mr Brulé:

I delayed answering your welcome letter until I should hear from MacKenna as to his new address – I have now got it

"Chine Hall, Boscombe Spa Road
Bournemouth, England.

And I expect that he will be very glad indeed to have a letter from you. Thanks for the cutting. It is a somewhat doubtful joy to be realistically studied, or threatened with that fate. However, I dont care, & could write much worse things about myself than any one else can. I shall have a book out this autumn "Deirdre", the first of a five-volume series to be called "The Táin Bó Cuailgne" – The epic of nous autres Irlaindaises ["we Irish"] – and I tend to be very pleased with it: but, in all. I have six books completed – I publish lazily, being more content to get a thing done than to see it in print. There has recently been published a very remarkable book called "The Orissers", by one L. Myers. For an English book it is extraordinary – It has no morals, immense psychology and a most beautiful style. It seems to me that, with this book English fiction has come of age. Thanks for telling me about your lecture at Rouen – I am sure you treated me in the friendliest fashion. Dont bother about the "Children of the Dead End", or give it away to someone. My movements are terribly at sea, for the Director here is not able to make up his mind as to when he can come over here and release me. All our good wishes to you both.

Yours very truly
JAMES STEPHENS

To SIR FREDERICK MACMILLAN
(Macmillan & Company, London)

Dublin
[T/23] 1 June 1923

[Macmillan had declined to publish *The Storyteller.*]

Dear Sir Frederick Macmillan:

I received your letter of yesterday's date this morning, and, just now, the typescript of The Storyteller.

I am very sorry indeed that you did not care for the matter; and am somewhat bewildered also, for it seemed to me to be good stuff, and, at the moment, exceedingly apropos; the entire of the ms was not forwarded, but enough to let the scope of the work be visible – It is really an examination of changed conditions, and of the universal artistic and technical unrest that is prevalent in every part of the world. There is such an universal unrest, and it is of prime importance.

To provide a working psychology for younger novelists was my aim, for literature and all the arts are now in a transition period; and to overrun, in however generalised a form, the whole of the material of the story-teller is the plan of this small book. I hold that I have done this, and, even if the treatment does not gain sympathy, it is something that should be done, and I contend, despite your advisers, that I have done it well.

I shall send you something else very shortly.

Yours very truly,
JAMES STEPHENS

To W. T. H. HOWE

Dublin
[T/3] 8 June 1923

[Edith Tranter was Howe's secretary. *Little Things* contained an etching by the Irish artist Power O'Malley (1876–1946); O'Malley was currently living in the United States. "Little Things" had been published in *The Nation and The Athenaeum* for 13 January 1923. Lucius O'Callaghan succeeded Captain Robert Langton Douglas as Director of the National Gallery.]

Dear Mr Howe:

Please congratulate Miss Tranter for me. The title "Little Things" will do excellently. And Power O'Malley's idea for the etching is fine. The poem "Little Things" has never been published, except in a weekly paper, "The Nation", so it can be used as you please.

About "Deirdre". I think it is the best thing I have done – It is the first book (complete in itself) of a story in 5 volumes to be called the "Tain Bo", and although it is as old as time, it will be as modern as tomorrow's newspaper. It will be published the coming autumn.

We are all at sixes and sevens over here. We are being reorganised in every department, and this place (the Gallery) is wondering who will be its master, and is working like the deuce for the one they want, and is shudderingly certain it will get the one it doesnt want. But we are all in the middle of politics, for the first time in our modern history. It is interesting, but wareing. A world of jobs and jobbers has appeared, and the late gun-men are nowhere, or are wondering what it was they gunned for anyway. All good wishes to you,

Yours always,
JAMES STEPHENS

To JAMES SULLIVAN STARKEY

Dublin

[A/18] 16 June 1923

[Starkey sent Stephens a copy of his *Nicolas Flamel: A Play in Four Acts, from the French of Gérard Nerval*, published in 1926 along with *Common Adventures: A Book of Prose and Verse*. Stephens is correct as to the location of the Tower of St. Jacques but mistaken about its height (172 feet, only 53 feet less than the Towers of Notre Dame). Starkey kept the setting of Scene III of his play at the Tower of St. Jacques: the Devil tells Flamel that "you know, from tradition, that I rule there all night". In the published play Starkey used "fool's bargain". Starkey was editor of the *Dublin Magazine*, which was first published in August 1923.]

Dear Starkie:

I have read the little play – it is delightfully done, and reads straight through – I should not try to stage this in the ordinary way – it lacks stage substance, & its interest is apart from the modern demand, but as a Noh play without scenery or any accessories, & perhaps played with masks, it would be wonderful. By the way, I think the Tour St Jacques is a rather lowish, one storied thing. Isnt it the little gingerbread ornament besides Sarah Bernhardts theatre? The towers of Notre Dame would suit. They are very high, & from their tops the view down is terrific. On page 20 would the words "fools march" be fools "marché" [–] fools "business"? The play is beautifully written, and interesting from the first to the last word. Why not think over the writing of a series of Noh Plays. You have the technique for it, & could make a great success. This play should surely be published in your new paper, to which, & to you, all good luck

Yours
JAMES STEPHENS

To [L. A. G. STRONG]

Dublin
[A/36] 12 July 1923

[The Irish writer and critic Leonard Alfred George Strong (1896–1958) was preparing an edition of *The Best Poems of 1923* (1924). "The Last Word" had been published in *The Dial* for March 1923. The poem was not included in *Little Things*; it was published, with revisions, as "The Crest Jewel" in the enlarged edition of *A Poetry Recital* (1926).]

Dear Sir,

Please excuse my delay in replying to your letter. The fact is, that if you can do without "The Last Word" I would be pleased, as I wish to bring it out myself in a book so small that even one poem published elsewhere would be felt. If, however, you must have the poem why I give you permission to use it, but in that case you must let me have a proof as I have made some alterations since it appeared in the Dial

Yours truly
JAMES STEPHENS

To [L. A. G. STRONG]

Dublin
[A/36] 16 July 1923

["The Golden Bird", reprinted from *The Nation and The Athenaeum* for 14 October 1922, was included in Strong's *The Best Poems of 1923*.]

Dear Sir:

Many thanks for your letter. If the "Golden Bird" would suit your Anthology of course you can have it – I think it is a quite pleasant piece, & that it will not require alteration

Yours very truly
JAMES STEPHENS

To THOMAS MOULT

Dublin
[A/36] 13 October 1923

["Little Things" was included in Moult's edition of *The Best Poems of 1923* (1924), with minor revisions from the text in *The Nation and The Athenaeum.*]

Dear Mr Moult:

I have pleasure in giving permission to use the poem "Little Things" for your Anthology. Will you let me have a copy as I think a few words should be changed

Yours very truly
JAMES STEPHENS

To CLEMENT SHORTER

Dublin
[T/3] 28 October 1923

[*The Immortal Hour* (1900) by the Scottish writer William Sharp (1856–1905), who used the pseudonym "Fiona MacLeod", had opened at the Regent Theatre in London on 13 October 1922. Stephens contributed "Tochmarc Etainé: 'The Immortal Hour' ", a discussion of the legendary basis of the play, to *The Sphere*; the article was published in two parts on 1 December and 8 December 1923. Stephens's *Deirdre* had been published in September 1923.]

Mr dear Shorter:

Of course: I would always be delighted to do anything you wished. Send the book along, and I'll let you have the articles as early as is possible.

I am sending you, by this post, a copy of my last book, "Deirdre". Not to bother you to read it, but just as a hand across the sea.

I am, my dear Shorter,

Yours very truly,
JAMES STEPHENS

To FREDERICK B. EDDY

[A/12]

Dublin
6 November 1923

[Frederick B. Eddy's "When Magic Ruled", a review of *Deirdre*, was published in the *Literary Review* (New York) for 13 October 1923; Eddy suggested the possibility of reading the novel as an allegory of Irish politics. Although Stephens may be thinking of "An Adventure in Prophecy", published in the *Atlantic Monthly* for May 1922, a more detailed discussion of literature and war is found in "Ireland Returning to Her Fountains", published in the *Survey Midmonthly* (New York) for 26 November 1921; neither article appears to have been published in England.]

Dear Mr Eddy:

Many thanks for your letter & for the copy of your very pleasant review of Deirdre. My intention in writing Deirdre was to keep as closely as possible to the recorded facts; and while making the story as old as time to make it at the same moment as modern as tomorrow. The article on Literature & War was published in both America & England. The Atlantic Monthly, I think, in the States. I return your list of my books & have added a few of the latest items. I think it is quite full.

With all good wishes to you

Yours very truly
JAMES STEPHENS

To ANDRÉ BRULÉ

Dublin

[T/19] 16 November 1923

[Brulé was working on his "James Stephens", published in the *Revue Anglo-Américaine* for June 1924. Brulé had asked: "Do you Irish mean by crock any piece of earthenware, or has a crock a special shape, and what is it? Would 'Pot d'Or' translate it?" In the article he used *Le Pot d'Or. Beasts, Men and Gods* by the Polish writer Ferdinand Ossendowski (1876–1945) was published in America in 1922 and in England in 1923.]

Mr dear Mr Brulé:

I was very glad to hear from you, and I send our best remembrances to you and to Madame Brulé.

Now as to your letter – Of course, you may translate all such extracts as you please. My latest book, Deirdre, is now published about a month. I shall send you a copy.

I return the list which you made of my books, amended.

As to the title "Crock of Gold". The actual sense of this phrase is – Crock filled with gold, or Crock used to keep gold in. A golden crock would be a crock made of that metal. What would Pot d'Or mean.

Chez nous autres [*auteurs*] irlandais [i.e. "to we Irish"] a crock is a rather deep earthenware vessel, much the shape of a flower-pot. I am sure you will do your article beautifully, and I hope you will let me have a copy of it when it appears, so that I may fittingly applaud it. By the way, two rather remarkable books, lately appeared, are "Beasts, Men and Gods", by one Ossendowski, published, I think, firstly, in America. The other a novel called "The Orissers" by L. H. Myers.

Yours very truly,
JAMES STEPHENS

Copy of "Deirdre" posted to you today –

To W. T. H. HOWE

Dublin
[A/3] 2 January 1924

[The twenty-five-copy vellum edition of *Little Things* contained special inscriptions by Stephens. The story of Etain forms the second part of *In the Land of Youth* (1924). "That chap" was Edmond Byrne Hackett (1879–1953), President of the Brick Row Book Shop in New York; Howe told Stephens that he was asking $250 for the manuscript of *Irish Fairy Tales* and $75 for the manuscript of the play *The Demi-Gods*.]

My dear Mr Howe:

I have just returned from London where I passed the Christmas holidays. I brought over the pot*een* which you sent for Iris, & she was delighted. She says that no other girl in her school will have so pretty a machine to keep her pins and other diamonds in. But her mother thinks that the jug*een*, which we got as a present, beats Iris's pot*een* into fits, and so say I. We also brought over a (moderate) share of the candies. London has good sweets, but nothing to touch Texas. That is good news about "Little Things". I will be impatient to see a copy; and will scratch my head until the proper inscriptions come. Did you like "Deirdre" [–] I think it is the best thing that I have yet done, except (thank God) the story of Etain, which I am now doing, and which is a gem of storytelling and beats the band. I must look you up some manuscripts. No! The prices that chap gave me dont come within shouting distance of the prices he is getting. May the devil boil him in tar, and then tear his hide off and make him eat it. The best of all New Years to you from

JAMES STEPHENS

To *THE DIAL*

Dublin
March 1924

[The text is from *The Dial* for April 1924. The article is a commentary on George Moore's *Conversations in Ebury Street* (1924), which Stephens had also reviewed in the *Observer* for 3 February 1924.

Moore's *A Mummer's Wife* (1885) and *Esther Waters* (1894)

were naturalistic novels; the autobiographical *Hail and Farewell* was published in 1911–14. The artists Henry Tonks (1862–1937), Walter Richard Sickert (1860–1942), Philip Wilson Steer (1860–1942) and Lawrence Alexander ("Peter") Harrison (1866–1937) were all members of the New English Art Club. The poet and critic John Freeman (1880–1929) wrote *A Portrait of George Moore in a Study of His Work* (1922). Walter de la Mare (1873–1956) was a poet and novelist; Edmund Gosse (1849–1928) was an influential literary critic and the author of *Father and Son* (1907); Robert Bontine Cunninghame Graham (1852–1936) was best known for his travel literature. Moore had previously published his Conversations with Gosse, the Shakespearean critic Harley Granville-Barker (1877–1946), and Freeman in *The Dial.* The slightly misquoted line from Whitman is from "So Long!", first published as the concluding poem to the 1860 *Leaves of Grass*. The playwright Edward Martyn (1859–1924) was one of the founders of the Irish Literary Theatre. In the early part of his career Moore had published poems in both English and French.]

IRISH LETTER

We can say, almost with certainty, that a given picture must have been painted at Siena, and such another at Florence, or Venice or Perugia, and when the reasons for these distributions are given it is quite evident that the several pictures came from these and could not have been painted in any other localities. But in the craft of writing our literary senses have not been so minutely trained in critical examination. The authors of all considerable stories, poems, and essays are well known, and the Mother of Invention has had no necessity for exploring, and no market to reward her curious diligence. But locality does not only influence one's accent: it subtly shades all our perspectives and preoccupations: it should be found in every book, so that, after a few lines of any author, one should exclaim – a Dublin book, a Connemara book, as one says, at a taste or a smell – a Cheshire cheese, a Limerick ham, a Dublin Bay herring. When a criticism of origins becomes as remunerative, or as fashionable, in literature as it is in painting the timely critic will not only be ready for his obol, he will be clamant.

Whenever it may be published, or wherever he may live, a book by Mr George Moore is an Irish literary event. His prose is English, for it is written in English, but it is all the more Irish for that. One who knows the West of Ireland – and what better knowledge is there! should recognize, if he heard it in his sleep, that this is Connaught prose; and, than the County of sweet-tongued Raftery, there is no place upon earth so lovely, as there is no prose being written by any one but Mr Moore so limpid, so modest, so certain to be overlooked by the vulgar, the hasty – by those who do not know the West of Ireland.

Two years ago Ireland burned down Moore Hall, the residence of Mr Moore's ancestors (he has lived there so rarely that it cannot properly be called his residence). But in return Ireland (not England or France) has presented him with a prose style that is lovelier that any mansion he could forget to live in, or that even the County Mayo could sacrifice to the gods. This is to be said, Mr Moore's present style is not English or Continental: it is not Catholic – he would sleep ill if he found it to be so: it is not Protestant – he should never sleep at all if that were hinted: it is West of Ireland, and, so, classical in the finest sense; which is to say, that it can best be enjoyed by a gentleman who has not entirely neglected to be somewhat of a scholar also. Irish saints are exported chiefly from Dublin, but her scholars are drawn mainly from Kerry and Mayo.

The matter of this book is in the form of Conversations, but by a feat of legerdemain which nobody but this author could contrive, they are really stories, and the book is actually a new kind of novel. In the Mummer's Wife and Esther Waters Mr Moore brought a new element into English literature. In his remarkable three-volume book, Hail and Farewell, he created a new form for the novel, and in this book he has again gone adventuring in form. After a few pages the reader can forget that the Moore of this book is a real person who can be rung up on a real telephone; and that one could criticize, and give his hat to, and shake the hands of, the pictures, the maids, and the visitors, that one reads of.

It is an achievement which only real skill and knowledge could save from degenerating into a feat. Skill can often astonish and distress one, but knowledge is as satisfying as bread. There are violinists we do not care to listen to – their technique is too good, and there are passages in any man's writing where the virtuoso performs his natural function of astonishing without convincing. Criticism, dealing with this or this other book, may sometime query whether Mr Moore is mostly a writer or mainly a literary man, but when his total work is considered it will be found that he was doing his job much oftener than only talking about it.

In these Conversations Mr Moore introduces us to a selection of his visitors at Ebury Street. – There are painters, such as, Tonks, Sickert, Steer, Harrison. His poets are Messrs Freeman and Walter de la Mare, and we must frown on this stint of the best that genius can attract. His literary men include Messrs Gosse, Cunningham Graham, and St Paul.

He has been really interested in making all these gentlemen talk, but it is mainly as a means of eliciting, not so much his own ideas on the various subjects raised, but his own personality and reactions. These subjects are of great variety, and Mr Moore's ideas do not triumph over those of his friends – he is much too courteous, too accomplished for that: but they are vastly more interesting to him, and to us, than are those of his various vis-à-vis.

Readers of THE DIAL are familiar with some of these Conversations.

Mr Moore's literary interests lie mainly in the immediate past. He has not given us his opinion on Messrs Wells, Bennett, Shaw (I cannot recollect any other present-day authors myself). He would surely have opinions on these great men, but while they may be ready they might not be fit for utterance. Alas! we can only talk with enthusiasm about a very young writer or a quite dead one: for, except Mr Moore, the writer who does not die on attaining the age of forty-five lives doggedly on but to bore his unwilling contemporaries.

Mr Moore issues a magnificence of praise to Balzac that he accords to no one else. It would be interesting to find, or to search for, the reason why we may only praise in fiction by the spoon where we laud in poetry by the bucket. Mr Moore could do this for us masterfully, and he has wooed so many enmities already that an odd dozen more could not inconvenience him. I should like (for I have remembered a name) I should like Mr Moore to make a bet that he could praise Mr Conrad for twenty minutes without stopping for rest or refreshment, and I should like to secrete a dictaphone in the studio of 121 Ebury Street while he was doing it.

A criticism of English fiction, and of English praise [prose?] generally might be made on the following lines: There are authors who surrender themselves totally to their subjects – they are, usually, not very good writers. There are others to whom the subject totally surrenders itself – these are the rare powerful artists: the

Balzacs, Tolstoys, Dostoevskys. These great writers have engraved themselves into their works as into mountains. In England, and in poetry, Shakespeare and Shelley are continuous with and inseparable from their matter. It is generally true that the bulk of English verse responds to Whitman's line – "Who touches this book touches a man", and it escapes anonymity by sheer individual vigour.

It is peculiar that the race which could in so decided and masculine a manner conquer poetry should have so submitted and surrendered to prose. There can be no style in prose unless prose be loved as verse has been loved, and be hammered as verse has been hammered. But, excepting a few names (and leaving the ideas aside) any ten English novels might have been written by any of the hundred and ten authors that did not write them. The vice of English fiction is not that it is romantic or sentimental, but that it is ill-informed. It has never grown up. It is written on the playing grounds of Eton. It is eternally a boy's tale, and the authors of it are naturally ashamed and anonymous.

Prose must be as mature, or as immature, as is the story it tells, for the subject controls the style, and the English novelist's evasion of the purple is justified by his inability to carry it. In another branch of the art – the vice of English criticism is not that it is ill-informed, it is that it will be clever, and it is clever as a means of avoiding the writing of good prose. Let the reader beware when he sees an epigram: 'tis the last refuge of an inferiority complex.

One could write a book on Mr Moore's book and that proves its soundness, for the book that cannot have children has been serialized in vain. There are, too, the books that won't have children – the Tempests, the Prometheuses Bound and Unbound. These gestate in geologic periods, or they leave a world not lusty enough to remain in, and come back to it no more. Mr Moore has always done better than his best, and kept always a little ahead of his record, but a great author is a champion and one lusts to match him with another, and to dare him be greater still. If he has a real weakness it is that he likes difficult tasks – it is the great artist's way to do so: but the great writer has always hated difficult tasks as a saint hates sin. The great writer does not write artistically, he does not need to – he writes gaudily and trails his purple. One cannot help beseeching the canary to be a crow, or the classical writer to have a try at romance.

A number of the most entertaining of these Conversations are with painters whom Mr Moore has long striven to love. Does he love these gentlemen as he once loved Yeats and Russell and Martyn? And, can a literary man love a painter? Can any one? I do not think that Mr Moore has ever been frightened of a literary man – he knows them too well. But he seems actually terrified of painters, and he treads among that ill sect as warily as his own cat would tread among tin tacks, while in the company of literary men and story-telling matters he is brazen and murderous and unabashable.

Mr Moore does not perceive that painters are unfriendly people – they are the strayed cats of art as musicians are the strayed dogs, and architects the missing links, and the most excellent prose is as wasted on them as kindness would be.

To the poets he extends an instinctive hospitality and mistrust. He is not hostile to them: they live in his attic with the pigeons or in his outhouse with the mushrooms: he gives them place and freedom, and he can delight in and doubt their testimony on any subject. It may be that his adoration of prose prevents him from giving more than a margin of his mind to verse: and, if a questioner, a painter, advanced it, he might agree that verse was merely prose mishandled and, perhaps, devitalized. Literature to Mr Moore is narrative first and prose afterwards. Were one (none but a painter could ask it) to demand what fiction was he might reply, that it is people and the things they do. He would conceal from a painter that there is the third, unknown quality to be added, which has made of him a great artist. The painter would try to see this, as every other statement, as a landscape, and would lose it, where he loses everything else, in the middle-distance.

Mr Moore loves ideas that transfer into action. He might be a more sympathetic, attentive listener to the village shrew with a load of gossip than to another Plato with an up-to-date Absolute. Freud in love would fetch a giggle from him that Freud on love could never unloosen. We are all citizens of the realm of humour, and Mr Moore is a veritable man-of-the-world there. It is the quality most to be dreaded of the literary man, and Mr Moore has mastered it as thoroughly as all his other material.

But, however expert we may be, or become, every man preserves, usually as a secret, his private joke. Love is Mr Moore's joke. He sees it as an exquisite idiocy that is peculiarly visible in painters, and as peculiarly rare among poets. He cherishes the poets because they are the only normal beings he has ever met – they do not fall in love: they visit there. He frequents painters, whom he loathes from the soul out, because they give him copy, and the copy he has gathered here is excellent. But what trash painters talk! All about pictures and Exhibitions!

He does not believe that writers fall in love. He knows that they pretend to: he sees the literary cause behind the enormous pretence, and believes in it only as he believes in comedy.

He has won success in every branch of prose, and has valiantly ill-treated poetry in two languages, but, for this scribe at least, his most remarkable achievement lies in the domain of Comedy. Comedy is the human art, the folk art, the household art: for, if Mr Moore is an aristocrat by birth, he is a humourist by nature, and a wit by education. When his wit is as dusty as his aristocracy his humour will still be alive, and will embalm him a memory as lasting as we need hope for in these hasty days.

There are still Conversations with Mr de la Mare, Mr Gosse, Mr Granville Barker, all men who hate painters, and space forbids to tell how good these are.

Every criticism that has been written on a book by Mr Moore has degenerated after ten lines into a discussion of the author himself. It has happened also in these pages. He is even more interesting than his books. It is the harshest thing that will ever be said of him.

JAMES STEPHENS

To *THE DIAL*

Dublin
May 1924

[The text is from *The Dial* for June 1924. The article is a review of *An Offering of Swans* (1923) by Oliver St. John Gogarty and *Salt Air* (1923) by the Irish writer Frederick Robert Higgins (1896–1941).

Colum and Boyd had settled in America in 1914 and 1920, respectively. Yeats took office as an appointed member of the Irish Senate on 11 December 1922; the first issue of the (second) *Irish Statesman*, which Russell edited, was published on 15 September 1923; Moore had settled in London in 1911; Gogarty had spent a year in London in 1921–2 after he had been kidnapped by members of Sinn Féin; Magee had moved to Wales because of his opposition to the Irish Free State. Stephens discussed the Irish playwright Seán

O'Casey (1884–1964) in his "Dublin Letter" in *The Dial* for August 1924.

Robert Herrick (1591–1674) was an English poet; of the various Fletchers, the English dramatist John Fletcher (1579–1625) is most noted for his use of rhythm. The quotation from the Irish poet Sir Samuel Ferguson (1810–68) is from "The Fairy Thorn" (1832). The first Yeats quotation is from "The Lover Speaks to the Hearers of his Songs in Coming Days" (1896); the other two are from "The Withering of the Boughs" (1900). The lines from Russell are from "The Voice of the Waters" and "Twilight in the Cabin", both included in *The Divine Vision and Other Poems* (1904). Gaius Valerius Catullus (*ca*. 84–54 B.C.) was a Roman poet. Other than "Perfection" and "Golden Stockings", the Gogarty poems quoted are "Non Blandula Illa" and "To a Lady"; the poem on page 10 of Gogarty's volume is "Virgil". The final quotation is from Higgins's "The Old Wine".]

IRISH LETTER

Our dramatist, Colum, from whom we expected great things, has become an American; our critic, Boyd, has become an American; and to be an American is at least as difficult an occupation as those they hurried from in Dublin. And now, for woe falls on woe, Yeats is a senator, Russell is an editor, Moore is a Londoner, Gogarty is a demi-absentee, and Magee a foreigner. Once more Ireland is exporting her saints and scholars, and is but ill-comforted in retaining her senators, her republicans and sinners – her kittle cattle. The arena is being left to the young folk, and some of them are writing verse that one must be even younger to read. Five years hence, or even next year under the stimulus of O'Casey, our new dramatist (about whom more next month) they may be less tenuous.

As an interlude in hectic adventures Oliver Gogarty has produced a book of verse, An Offering of Swans, with a foreword by Mr Yeats (the Cuala Press, Merrion Square, Dublin). Mr Yeats uses words delicately but definitely. He considers that Dr Gogarty's adventures and enforced absences in London have brought him "a new sense of English lyric tradition, and changed a wit into a poet". Or, that Dr Gogarty's muse is more distinctly English than Irish. When he continues, that "Oliver Gogarty has discovered the rhythm of Herrick and of Fletcher, something different from himself and yet akin to himself', he emphasizes the first statement, and indicates in the "something different" a thought that he has not had space, or has not cared, to pursue. Mr Yeats ends with the statement:

> "Here are a few pages that a few months have made, and there are careless lines now and again, traces of the old confused exuberance. He never stops long at his best, but how beautiful that best is, how noble, how joyous."

Used by Mr Yeats, such a sentence is more memorable, more to be cherished by an author than many a column of flattery in a magazine. Mr Yeats names in special commendation three poems of this little collection: Non Dolet, Begone Sweet Ghost, and Good Luck. Only an amateur of bad luck or one who forgets his own unhappiness will disagree in poetry with Mr Yeats, and yet there are poems in this book which I prefer to those he has chosen. In Irish verse the native critic looks for a singing quality inside the words used. This is a subtle vowel quality which is rarely found in English poetry. English poetry sings in the line, Irish sings in the word. Ferguson's

> "Away in milky wanderings of neck and ankle bare"

is Irish. So too is Yeats's

> "O Colleens, kneeling at your altar rails, long hence,"

or:

> "I cried when the moon was murmuring to the birds,"

or:

> "The honey-pale moon lay low on the sleepy hill,"

or George Russell's

> "Where the Greyhound River windeth through a loneliness so deep,"

or:

> "Fades the eve in dreamy fire."

When this quality of easy melody is not found in verse, the native critic is inclined to give the poetry to England. In the case of Dr Gogarty this seems to be both right and wrong. His poetry is not breathed in the Irish manner. It is more carved than flowing, but his master is Catullus rather than Herrick. I prefer his Perfection to any of the poems already named. In it his Latinity is fairly evident:

> "By Perfection fooled too long
> I will dream of that no longer!
> Venus, you have done me wrong
> By your unattainable beauty,
> Till it seemed to be my duty
> To belittle all the throng.
> I have found attraction stronger;
> I have found a lady younger
> Who can make a hard heart stir:
> Like an athlete, tall and slender,
> With no more than human splendour;
> Yet, for all the faults of her,
> Than Perfection perfecter.
>
> Though she guards it, grace breaks through
> Every blithe and careless movement;
> What shall I compare her to?
> – When she takes the ball left-handed,
> Speed and sweetness are so blended
> Nothing awkward can she do,
> She whose faults are an improvement!
> – If only she knew what Love meant
> I would not be seeking now
> To describe the curved perfection
> Of all loveliness in action –
> Perfect she would be, I vow
> With the mole above the brow."

In lines like

"But far off on the margin of the West
A sea-grey house whereby the blackbird sings"

the Celt in Dr Gogarty is already promising that if he can forget his scholarship he will remember his ancestors, and sing like a lark instead of like a musician.

His work in this small volume only fails when, as in Dunsany Castle, he remembers Wordsworth, or, on page ten, he remembers Milton, or when, as in Amor he shadows two beautiful verses by remembering that he is a wit in the third. Wit becomes a scholar, but it is a mark of ill-breeding in a poet; and the poet who can write

" . . . timeless like a shrine
Upon the margin of a Grecian town
Where there is calm"

need not condescend to sparkle.

Dr Gogarty is still a little the slave of his vast memory of Latin verse, English lyric, and Scotch ballad, and a little more he is the sport of a desire to assert his scholarship by remembering it. When he forgets these small matters he writes Golden Stockings, and writes himself into every anthology of poetry that is to come:

"Golden Stockings you had on
In the meadow where you ran;
And your little knees together
Bobbed like pippins in the weather
When the breezes rush and fight
For those dimples of delight;
And they dance from the pursuit,
And the leaf looks like the fruit.

I have many a sight in mind
That would last if I were blind;
Many verses I could write
That would bring me many a sight:
Now I only see but one,
See you running in the sun;
And the gold-dust coming up
From the trampled butter-cup."

He is the stoniest in form and the tenderest in heart of our poets.

Mr F. R. Higgins has published Salt Air (The Irish Bookshop: Dawson Street, Dublin). This young poet has still to strain from his ancestors or his contemporaries the poetry that is his, and which he undoubtedly has. The best poem in his tiny booklet is the one that is authentically his own – Connemara:

"The soft rain is falling
    Round bushy isles.
Veiling the waters
    Over wet miles
And hushing the grasses
    Where plovers call,
While soft clouds are falling
    Over all.

I pulled my new curragh
    Through the clear sea
And left the brown sailings
    Far behind me,
For who would not hurry
    Down to the isle,
Where Una has lured me
    With a smile.

She moves through her sheiling
    Under the haws,
Her movements are softer
    Than kittens' paws;
And shiny blackberries
    Sweeten the rain,
Where I haunt her beaded
    Window-pane.

I would she were heeding –
    Keeping my tryst –
That soft moon of amber
    Blurred in the mist,
And rising the plovers
    Where salleys fall,
Till slumbers come hushing
    One and all."

His other poems must be taken as very interesting experiments of his muse, and as promise of good poetry to come. It is not so much that this singer is a disciple of any one, but that he is dwelling in moods of languor and wistfulness that are out-moded. But the poet who can write

"... cold men herding swine
By wasted seas,
Was captured in his singing –
But where's Beauty's joy,
While Beauty's dust is clinging
To a lonely cairn in Connacht
And a burning wind from Troy"

can learn to discover himself, and can learn to leave Helen and Troy where they belong, to the studio, that is.

JAMES STEPHENS

To SIR FREDERICK MACMILLAN
(Macmillan & Company, London)

Dublin
30 May 1924

[A/23]

[*In the Land of Youth* was the second and last volume of Stephens's "Táin Saga".]

Dear Sir Frederick Macmillan:

On receiving your letter of May 19th I started at once to put the ms of the 2nd vol of the Táin Saga into final shape, & have it now almost completed: I hope to post it to you on Saturday – I have added more than double the material which you had accepted. The entire second part gives the story (now I think fully told for the first time) of Midir and Etain – a version of which is, at present, playing in London under the title of the "Immortal Hour". It is a very wonderful story, but Fiona McLeod only had a scrap of it.

Yours very truly
JAMES STEPHENS

P.S. The title is "In the Land of Youth".
Part I The Feast of Samhain
Part II The Feast of Lugnasad

To JAMES SULLIVAN STARKEY

Dublin
[A/16] 10 June 1924

[Starkey sent Stephens a copy of Thomas MacDonagh's *Lyrical Poems*. The poet Roy Campbell (1902–57), who was born in Durban, South Africa, had just published his first book, *The Flaming Terrapin* (1924).]

Dear Starkie:

Many thanks for your note & for MacDonagh's book. I remember that poor Tommy went through it with me & ticked off the poems that he did not much like. I suppose that (when I was going away to Paris) I sold or gave away the book – Now, I am very glad, indeed, to have it. I send you a rhymed scrap. Lord! with what anguish one sought for verse in the days of yore, & with what ecstacy one got it! I get both still – in prose, and now only neighbour poesy but do not live with her. I – &c &c. It is a nice little rhythm. There is a new man called Roy Campbell who seems worthy of keeping an eye on. You ought to write to him, demanding verse. He writes with such energy that it seems to me he must have Irish in his ancestry, if it be only a bar sinister.

Yours very truly
JAMES STEPHENS

To W. T. H. HOWE

Dublin
[A/3] 16 June 1924

[W. F. Nihart was the agent for the American Book Company in Columbus, Ohio. Although all three of the Powys brothers wrote novels, the reference here is probably to Theodore Francis Powys (1875–1953),whose *Mark Only* (1924) had recently been published. "Lepanto" by the English writer Gilbert Keith Chesterton (1874–1936) was included in his *Collected Poems* (1915).]

Dear Mr Howe:

I waited for Mr Nihart's book to come in before replying to your letter of 29th May. The book came in today, & I am dispatching it to you by this post. Mr Power O'Malley was in with me a day or two ago. He had it all his own way, for he is deaf and I amn't. But in revenge I took the hide off two Oxford professors who came in shortly afterwards. By the way, there is an English fictioneer named Powys who is worth watching. For a limited time that is; I fear he wont be able to get out of the particular trench he is digging himself into. But, in that, he is marvellously lively. I shall drop his book along to you tomorrow. It is unpleasant, but it lives and moves and has a being. There is also a poet named Roy Campbell, a whale of a lad. He seems bigger than the war. Do you know a ballad of Chesterton's called "Lepanto"? It is fine stuff. I have found some more of the Here Are Ladies ms, & will unload them at you some day.

Yours always
JAMES STEPHENS

To *THE DIAL*

Dublin
July 1924

[The text is from *The Dial* for August 1924.

William Congreve (1670–1729) was educated in Ireland; Richard Brinsley Sheridan (1751–1816), Oliver Goldsmith (1730–74), Wilde, Shaw and Synge were all born in Ireland. However, William Wycherley (1640–1716) was neither born nor educated in Ireland, and Stephens appears to be unique in claiming him as Irish. In addition to Jack B. Yeats and George Russell, the painters mentioned are John Lavery (1856–1941), William Orpen (1878–1931), (probably) Sir Gerald Festus Kelly (1879–1972), Charles Hazelwood Shannon (1863–1937) and Arthur Ambrose McEvoy (1878–1927). To describe the last three as "Irish" is rather tenuous.

The scores of the rugby matches which Stephens mentions, all played in 1924, were as follows: on 26 January at Dublin: Ireland 6, France 0; on 9 February at Belfast: England 14, Ireland 3 (a close game despite the score); on 23 February at Inverleith: Scotland 13, Ireland 8; and on 8 March at Cardiff: Ireland 13, Wales 10.

Yeats received the Nobel Prize for Literature on 10 December 1923. O'Casey's *Juno and the Paycock* (1925) was first performed at the Abbey Theatre on 3 March 1924. John L. Sullivan (1858–1918) and William Harrison ("Jack") Dempsey (1895–), both Americans, were heavyweight boxing champions of the world. Terence MacSwiney (1879–1920) was Lord Mayor of Cork and one of the organizers of the Irish Volunteers in Cork; arrested on 12 August 1920, he refused to acknowledge the authority of the British court and died in Brixton prison, London, after a seventy-four-day hunger strike.]

DUBLIN LETTER

Trade returns can tell the physical fact that a nation is or is not active, but they will not reveal a psychological or spiritual fact, nor enable nations to know each other except as rivals and possible enemies. Trade is not individual, it is scarcely even national: it is anonymous and international, and the very important information that we glean from it ends largely with itself. We may say, from business data, that Ireland or Spain or America is or is not lazy, but we cannot say that one of them is intelligent and another not, nor that they are or are not contented or ambitious or quarrelsome.

Certainly, a nation with a low mental content will have a low export trade. This could, however, be as true of a country that was largely self-sufficing and was not overpopulated. Psychological facts, that is, truth regarding the energies of a nation, must be sought elsewhere. Politics will not teach us much. They lie in the almost elemental region of self-preservation: they are daily matters, and almost three parts automatic; and the religion of a country is too largely habitual to be a gauge of energy. A nation's sports and arts are all that is left to consider, and these are her true interpreters, or are the only interpreters that tell the truth about her.

Every fake that is known is possible in the realms of business and politics, but games must be won by winners, and art can only be produced by artists. There are no synthetic champions in running or jumping, and if the dud-artist does not get his label by return of post, he yet will get it in fairly good time.

The contention here is, that games and art are not individual energies. They are national.

In games the chance of a freak or sport is possible, but it may be generalized that no second-rate country produces champions in a game that calls for endurance and speed. Speed is intelligence. And in art, it may be completely stated that no second-class country has ever produced a first-class artist.

When England was great so were her literature and her sports. When France was great she produced great painting. When Germany was great she produced great music. One or another of these nations might be essentially the greatest: but, in their spheres, the supremacy of each was unquestionable, and the nations about them, whether prosperous or not as traders, were merely satellites, sharing in, but adding little to the arts they revolved about.

Within the last hundred years Ireland has taken part in whatever games were within reach. Nationally she may not have made any great show, but she has scattered champions broadcast to England and America and elsewhere: and in literature she has made a more than respectable contribution to the general stock. Up to quite recently Irish painting, poetry, and fiction were not of grave importance, but the history of Irish drama is extraordinary. It is the truth to say that since Shakespeare almost every first-class name in English drama is that of an Irishman, or of a person who was born or educated in Ireland – Congreve, Wycherley, Sheridan, Goldsmith, Wilde, Shaw, Synge – the tale of champions comes to our own day, and is not yet finished. We are now doing better work in poetry; and in painting – witness, Orpen, Lavery, MacEvoy, Kelly, Shannon, Yeats, Russell. And in fiction also we are settling into our stride. Whatever our commercial energy may seem like, our national form is good.

In games we are doing better than one should have dared to prophesy. Last season, in the football matches, we were beaten by England and Scotland: but we gave the victors a run for their money, and took the last ounce out of them. We beat Wales and France, and are considering, with a certain bashfulness, that we may lick the universe next year.

In the same season we captured the Nobel Prize, and we crowned a play by Mr Sean O'Casey.

On the strength of these deeds Dublin is taking the air with a dignity that is engagingly modest, but she may shortly be enquiring as to the grounds on which London and New York consider themselves to be Capital cities.

Mr O'Casey's play is called Juno and the Paycock, and it is in every way worthy of that delicate and delightful title. Never was a Peacock so iridescent or with such a spread of tail as our Paycock. Never was a Juno such a dote as our Juno. The play is Irish in every word of it, but it is magnificently more. – It is Dublin, and how wonderful a thing is that to say! Dublin flocked to see itself at the Abbey Theatre. It packed the little building nightly, and was turned, in morose multitudes, away from the too-crowded house, and from the finest acting that has ever been seen in Ireland, or perhaps, that has ever been seen anywhere.

Will another audience get this play as we do? Will they get the terror, the tragedy, the trickery, the tenderness, the laughter and happiness of it, as we do?

Perhaps they won't. Time must tell if its appeal is more than local. But we know that a great play and a great playwright has come. He does not empty words and actions on to a stage. He spills life there, and spills it with a gleeful exuberance that bodes well for him, and for us.

Any man named Casey should do great deeds as naturally as a man named Dempsey or Sullivan packs an upper-cut; but it was Dublin herself that wrote this play. Ireland has used Mr Yeats to write her lyrics, but she adopted the gentle poet with a certain formalism, as of one who should lament kings only and should make love only to a queen. So, royally, she chose poor Terence MacSwiney to starve to death for her, which is almost the same thing as making love to a queen. She is a man-killer, is Ireland. But Dublin has used Mr O'Casey for her purposes simply, cleanly, civically, cordially. She is his favourite aunt.

We may mark time a little in order to get our wind back after the alarums and battlings that we have been through during the past ten years, but our form is all right – Sean O'Casey has proved it; or, rather, for there is a distinction, Dublin has proved it.

JAMES STEPHENS

To W. T. H. HOWE

Dublin

[A/3] 26 July 1924

[The front page of the vellum edition of *Little Things* contained special inscriptions by Stephens. The manuscript dealer was Walter M. Hill, a bookseller in Chicago. Stephens left on his first American tour on 28 January 1925.]

My dear Mr Howe,

Your letters buck one up like a cocktail. I suppose by now the front pages of "Little Things" have got to you. They were the devil's own going, & I did them in a day. If the sale comes off as you predict (But not being a poet you are an optimist) it will make my record. I dont know whether I'll buy a farm or a bank, or a pair of boots. However we'll worry when the time comes.

I sent out the ms of three stories thinking someone might like to buy 'em. You spoke of someone in your parts who sells ms. Nothing has been arranged yet about my visit to the Great Country. It lies with the agent. I'm expecting to see Colum in about a month, & he'll put me wise as to whether its for this Autumn or next Spring. I shall be greatly delighted to meet you at last.

Yours always.
JAMES STEPHENS

To CYNTHIA STEPHENS

Dublin
[A/1] 6 August 1924

[The rest of the Stephens family had gone to Paris in anticipation of his one-month vacation there. The "huge bustle" was caused by the Dublin Horse Show, which opened on 5 August, and the revived *Aonach Tailteann* festival, held in Dublin from 2 to 18 August. The main judges in the literary competition, which was open to works published in the last three years, were Yeats, Russell, and the Irish playwright Esmé Stuart Lennox Robinson (1886–1958); Stephens assisted Russell in deciding the poetry prize. There was no award for drama. The scholarship prize was given to MacKenna for his edition of Plotinus's *Psychic and Physical Treatises* (1921), the second part of his five-volume translation of Plotinus; the English writer Compton Mackenzie (1883–1973) accepted the award for MacKenna. The award for poetry was shared by Gogarty's *An Offering of Swans* and *We Have Kept the Faith* (1923) by the Irish writer Francis Stuart (1902–). The fiction prize went to Stephens's *Deirdre.* One of the four medals was co-sponsored by the Royal Irish Academy; all the awards were presented by Yeats on 9 August.

Lady Wheeler was the wife of Sir William Ireland de Courcy Wheeler (1879–1943), a Dublin surgeon; Lady Mary O'Connell was the wife of Sir John Robert O'Connell (1868–1943), a Dublin lawyer. Dr. Frank Cahill was a Dublin physician; his wife, formerly Mrs. Frances Baker (1873–1944), was an artist.]

My darling Cynthia.

I got the Passport this morning, & am so glad to know that you have all arrived safely. Seumas wrote me: he is a good man. Iris didn't, she isnt a man at all. I have a cubicle in the Arts Club. It is comfortable enough, but I envy the Colum's my nice flat. They say that Noiro is very nice to them, & that they like him greatly. There is a huge bustle over here, & I have dined with Lady Wheeler, then, last night, with the Cahills, & tonight with Lady O'Connell. Tomorrow eve Yeats & Russell & Compton MacKenzie & I go to the Abbey Theatre to give prizes for novels, plays, poems, & essays. So we are all dining together at the Moira. It is said that the horse Show this year is better than it ever was, & that there are huge crowds. I may go this evening. Gogarty and Yeats are in their glory, & Yeats has bought a tall hat. I think I am to get a prize on Saturday from the Royal Irish Academy for the best novel, but am not certain. If it is a medal I shall bring it over. I would like to kiss you at this moment. More than that, too, I would like – I would like – but you know what I would like – Write me again at once & say what you would like. The thought makes my pen shake.

Your lover
JAMES

To JOHN HOUSTON FINLEY

Dublin
[A/28] 16 August 1924

[Quinn had died on 28 July 1924. Finley sent Stephens a manuscript copy of his "In Memory of John Quinn". *In the Land of Youth* was published on 21 October 1924.]

Dear Mr Finlay.

Many thanks for your letter. I was so sorry to hear John Quinn had died. I had been corresponding with him for years, and always hoped that he would come to Ireland to meet me, or should I go to the States I should meet him. He was, I should fancy, an extraordinary man with energy enough for twenty. That was a nice little verse you did for him, and I marvel at the beauty of the print in which you did it. I think you are just in placing of my books the "Demi-Gods" first. But I also think that the book I will publish this autumn "In the Land of Youth" beats it hollow. That is, the second part of it The Story of Midir & Etain does

Yours very truly
JAMES STEPHENS

To HERBERT EDWARD PALMER

Dublin
[A/36] 22 September 1924

[Palmer sent Stephens a copy of *The Unknown Warrior and Other Poems* (1924), which included a poem from *Reincarnations* as the "frontispiece verse".]

My dear Mr Palmer:

I have just returned from a month's vacation in France, & find your book and letter waiting for me here. I have had, as yet, only the time to look through the book – not properly to read it, but I think it is full of fine stuff, & that in each book you excel yourself. There is gallant singing here and speed and beauty. I feel assured that with this book your reputation will be more firmly established & that your long tramping of the wilderness must be nigh its end. Forgive me that I can do no more than write heartningly to you. The idea of getting anybody a job on this side of the world is so remote that it is nearly laughable. My crown is of paper: my success is on paper, and, without the job that luck brought me, my literary revenues (one likes big words) would not keep me living for four months out of a year – But neither I nor you need too much repine. I am certain, of myself, for the future, and I think yours is just as stable, and I think we have both worked well. Keep your courage up as well as you can. I'dd dare to prophesy that things will soon change for you.

Yours very truly
JAMES STEPHENS

To STEPHEN MacKENNA

Dublin
[A/19] 13 November 1924

[The first part of this letter concerns *In the Land of Youth*. Marie MacKenna had died on 4 July 1923.]

My dear Stephen:

That (the criticism part of your letter on my book) is not illness, nor illusions, nor idiocy – it is sound critical sense. & I take off my hat to you. Personally, & in especial, I detest those pigs, but there they were, & I did my real best with them. The whole first half of my book is as God permitted it to be. I count it as part of the inescapable drudgery of the Táin, & I worked it to the very limits of my ability. But I pin myself all over with medals & I put cock feathers in my hat about the second part. There the story gripped me, and, let who will say me nay, there I gripped it, and made of it a great, a noble and a wonderous tale. Viola, and thus it is! Everybody except you, & God forgive them all & reward you, has praised that first part. Russell has praised that first part, & has, not mispraised, so much as faintly damned my second part. But I know what I know, and tho' not another soul shall ever mention the second half of the book I praise it myself and shall never cease praising it. I know you cant (or wont) write these things yourself, but your taste, tact, knowledge, whatever is the quality in literature, is better than anybody's that I know & I am delighted that we agree in this matter. I'm glad you are going to leave the wilds and get to people and things & movements. Those Dark Nights of the Soul are to be borne, but not, I think, to be courted. If they could be shared I would apply for a modest parcel of your trouble. Whatever ones heaven maybe one's hell is one's very own, & must be worn out of, if it cant be won out of. It isnt poor Marie is the trouble, Stephen MacKenna is your trouble as James Stephens is mine. One can be too intelligent to be anything but a fool, but I do think that an applied interest in the devil can destroy him, and can liberate if that is to be liberated, and I do think that one hasnt got to go through certain experiences more than once. If that Dark Night is on you are you not to be congratulated, being so close to the Dawn, & so nigh to God itself.

That thing was with you when Marie was with you – its usefulness must be nearly worn out, & in a minute, or an hour, or a day you may be the most joyous creature under the sun.

Go deó [*deo*] agat
["Thine forever"]
JS

1925 - 1938

> I wonder has anyone heard of Jamesy Stephens, whether he likes America, succeeds as a lecturer, etc.: he looked to me very ill when he was here, tho' he talked with immense animation and showed every way vitality. I secretly feared the strain of travelling, grinning, roaring in halls, would be too much for him – tho' I notice he doesn't take eagerly what he has to take – he has nerve placidity with intellectual agitation, a very enviable conjunction.
>
> Stephen MacKenna to Edmund Curtis, 1925 (*Journal and Letters of Stephen MacKenna*, ed. E. R. Dodds)

In January 1925 Stephens went on his first American lecture tour. In the years from 1925 to 1935 he would make no fewer than nine trips to America, spending the equivalent of almost four years there. Three of those trips were primarily lecture tours (1925, 1926 and 1935). On the other occasions he would give a few lectures but spent most of his time at Freelands, the Kentucky estate of W. T. H. Howe of the American Book Company. Howe gave Stephens various tasks to do, such as preparing a catalogue of his Thackeray collection or writing an introduction to an anthology of Romantic poetry he was publishing. Their relationship seems to have been based on a sometimes uneasy combination of friendship and patronage.

When not in America, Stephens stayed at either Eversleigh, his house in the Kingsbury suburb of London, or his flat in Paris. It was in Paris in July 1927 that Stephens and James Joyce began to develop a close friendship; a few months later, Joyce proposed that Stephens should complete *Finnegans Wake* if he were unable or indisposed to do so. In the spring of 1928 Stephens substituted for Joyce as a lecturer at the Third International Book Fair in Florence; in 1929 he went to Rumania, where he met Queen Marie.

Stephens's basic mood during this period was one of depression, and his literary activity was relatively small. After his first American tour he published the poems he had read as *A Poetry Recital* (June 1925). In October 1926 he issued *Collected Poems*, which contained only a very few new poems. Early in 1928 he published *Etched in Moonlight*, the stories in which had been published between 1918 and 1923. Most of his original activity during this period was in verse. In 1930 he published *Theme and Variations*, expanded with a few additional poems as *Strict Joy* in September 1931. His last separate volume was *Kings and the Moon*, published in November 1938. This late poetry is heavily influenced by Stephens's study of Buddhism.

During this period Stephens witnessed the death of two of his closest friends, Stephen MacKenna in 1934 and AE in 1935; closest to home, his son, James Naiose, was accidentally killed on Christmas Eve in 1937.

To *THE DIAL*

[New York]
March 1925

[The text is from *The Dial* for April 1925. Stephens wrote this letter during his first American lecture tour.

The slightly misquoted line is from an anonymous ninth- or tenth-century Irish poem, usually called the "Song of Summer"; Stephens might have read it in Kuno Meyer's *Four Old Irish Songs of Summer and Winter* (1903). O'Casey's new play was *The Plough and the Stars*, first performed at the Abbey Theatre on 8 February 1926.]

DUBLIN LETTER

Our tendency, for 'tis a time of mechanics, is to be interested in the distributions and periodicities of things: and we ask, fruitfully or not, if there is a geographical distribution of talent, and if there are times in which talent is available, and periods again in which it is reserved. We instinctively agree that the argument by analogy is about the only valid argument we possess, and that time and space are our most easily manipulated concepts. The year and its seasonable changes stand behind a vast content of human thought, and the north and south of space translate for us to a north and south of things, and to a north and south of our thinking about them.

Certainly a most curious polarity is developed by every nation. Whether it be Ireland or England, France or Germany, or Italy, these countries have all developed a northern and southern temperament quite irrespective of geography, for the north of any country is merely the south of its neighbour. A law of the national being seems to demand that one extreme of the nation shall be hard and reserved and competent, and that the other end shall be softer, more confiding, more careless; and, with this idea in mind, a geographical distribution of talent may be reasonably looked for.

We might even consider that science and painting, the exportable arts, are to be expected from a national-north, while literature and music, the home arts, would be properly produced from the south. No government can be a good one that is not faced by an effective opposition, and it is perhaps as true to say that no country is stable or effective to its fullest extent that has not developed its true internal antagonism or polarity. In Ireland, and in this respect, we are most happily provided for. We have a stern, unbending, highly moral and competent north, and we have in the south the extremes of those virtues. If it be remarked that there is an east and west in every country, and that these points ought to be considered, I should assume this to be inexact. East and west are merely geographical expressions: they have no national significance, for the east of a country is merely a prolongation of the north, and the west is as characteristically southern.

These ideas are true I think of a small country. In a huge country such as the United States they may seem unproven; but as time goes on it may be found that America will resolve each of her vast states into a temperamentally separate entity, and that each of these sub-nations may evolve the northern and southern characteristics that appear to be inherent in, or to pass from the soil to, the group that inhabits it.

I do not think that there is any true centre to a country. I conceive it to be only north and south, and that the central or steadying or home-holding tendency in a land is southern, while the explosive, externalizing, adventurous tendencies are northern. The sum of these, the total tendency or aptitude, is the nation, and is a different quality for every land.

A place-distribution of talent may thus be conceived, but as to whether there is a time-distribution is also a question. The mechanical argument, the argument, that is, by analogy, is always an enticing one. The reaction of the earth to the great seasonal changes is continuous. This happens inevitably, and these and those as inevitably follow with summer, autumn, and winter. A very ancient Irish poet wrote of the spring:

"A wild longing comes upon one to race horses."

The same longing still comes with the spring. It is not only that the earth thrills anew to a promise to the sun – the mind is equally thrilled, and does seem to awaken, and to look as adventurously abroad as the body does, or as the still withered, but hopeful trees and clay and animals do. If all that is, is but a mode of mind, then the seasonable changes are most competently true in a mental than in a material realm, and a winter and summer of the mind itself should be discoverable.

One would like to know from various artists if they write or paint more easily in the summer than in the winter, or if they merely experience and mature in the summer that which they harvest in the autumn and record in winter. Is there a winter or hibernating-period for a man and, by extension, for his nation? No country wants to fight in winter, the ancient tendency was for opposing armies to tuck themselves into winter quarters and fall asleep on a truce. Is there a national desire to abstain from business in winter, and do employers notice that industrial production, irrespective of lack or abundance of raw material, has a seasonable ebb and flow?

In the Spring a Young Man's Fancy, *et cetera* – Proverbs occupy themselves greatly with young men and love: they say curiously little about young women and love. Will some female novelist tell us if loves comes in for them also with the first daisy and the long-looked-for sprout? Winter has set on us in Ireland, and, so far as I know, no writer is meditating a new book, nor is any painter dreaming, with a red and rolling eye, of the canvas that he hopes to make glowing and astonishing and profitable. Sean O'Casey, our new dramatist, whose Juno and the Paycock was our great national event, has written a new play. 'Twas an autumnal harvesting, and is possibly now finished.

In the winter we must live by bread alone – The Master of Arts has withheld his sunlight, and the lesser artists must reserve theirs also. Only the politicians work, gloomily, coldly – 'tis a wintry trade, and might rightly be forbidden for the other three seasons of the year. . . . . How sweetly a blackbird's pipe, or a lyric note from poor dead Ledwidge now would take the ear. But now we could dislike either of these. They do not belong to the chill day, and might do uncalled for wrong to the snow, and to the round red berries of the haw.

JAMES STEPHENS

To DOROTHY CANFIELD FISHER

[T/40]

Cincinnati
23 March 1925

[*Rough Hewn* by the American writer Dorothy Canfield Fisher (1879–1958) was published in 1922. Fisher was living in Arlington, Vermont.]

Dear Mrs. Fisher,

I was more than delighted to get your letter, not because of the compliments that were in it, for between us compliments are neither here nor there. It was because of the agreeable writing that was in it and the sense I got that you really did like my stuff. I have still a lot of pleasure in store because there are books of yours which I have not read. I have only read one so far – "Rough Hewn" and found in it so many well-seen and well-told things that delighted me and rather astonished me. I had not thought that any American writer, or that any woman writer anyhow, had observed life on the Continent so closely, so finely, so humourously or so poignantly, so that although I had practically given up the reading of novels this one was finished by night where most books are finished at the 50th page and I found myself again for the first time curious about the writer of another country.

I remember mentioning your name to somebody in Paris. Unfortunately the day after I was leaving Paris for Dublin. And that person, whoever it may have been, told me that you were then in Paris and that he could have arranged an interview between us if I were staying. Now that an interview is also as it were available I find that it is almost as far away from Cincinnati or Chicago or Charleston, whither I am bound, as it was from Dublin to Paris.

Believe me that if there is anybody in this country in my own class of work whom I should really like to meet it would be yourself. And believe also that I will read your other works and hope to find the qualities that I found in "Rough Hewn".

Will your please convey my compliments to your husband and to your daughter and, although it will not mean anything, to Jimmy. Tell him that another Jimmy sends him his very best wishes.

Excuse my writing in type to you but I have almost lost all hope of answering any letter whatever if I do not get it off this way.

In fact, any letter whatever will remain unanswered by me unless somebody writes it for me.

Yours very truly,
JAMES STEPHENS.

To EDWARD GROFF CONKLIN

[A/12]

Chicago
18 April 1925

[The American critic Edward Groff Conklin (1905–) was currently a student at Dartmouth College.]

Dear Mr Conklin:

Please forgive me for keeping your two pieces of prose so long, and for leaving your letter so long unanswered. I was really waiting for the leisure to reply to you, and have now made up my mind that while I am touring the United States I will not have any leisure, or an opportunity of really bringing my mind to bear to any subject whatever. So I now return your articles. You have certainly a fine prose sense. Indeed, you seem to me to have that rarest of all literary gifts a prose style. All you need is to give it as much work as can be managed. Work means to me a patient vigilent attention to the thing that one is doing. Only yourself can impose these three qualities on yourself, patience & vigilence & attention; but unless they are present to the very extreme of their possibilities the whole value of yourself and your art will not be elicited. A letter such as this, any letter of advice, must seem priggish, for one is placed in the superior position of being able to advise, & advice is much easier & better conveyed orally than by letter. Your trouble (or your joy) will come what ["when"] you decide what it is you desire to write about. You will not waste good prose on inferior matter. An artist is always writing about himself, about his nature seen as desire; & it is the claim, or postulate, of such an one that he is more self-conscious than are other people. Before you become a writer you must become the master of your own moods or modes, & you must always tell all the truth about yourself. Style is truth-telling, but you must know the truth to tell it, and truth can only be known as onesself. If you can avoid it dont write for a while for newspapers, or for money, or for any other purpose than your own pleasure. All counsel is, of course, a counsel of perfection, and useless. You have a prose-style, and all the rest is up to you – You'll win out if you play the prose game as you would a ball-game, that is to play it with all your heart. If you dont put that much into it you wont win and wont deserve to. Every good wish to your work

Yours very truly
JAMES STEPHENS

Ideas can run away with one – Be more interested *in the writing* of an idea that in the idea itself. So with action or passion or whatever else. Be more interested in the writing of these than in these; for writing is your art, where ideas and actions & what not else is any man's or everyman's. Art is any idea in itself, and is easily superior to any other idea.

To W. T. H. HOWE

Eversleigh
[A/3] 12 August 1925

[Stephens had returned from his first American tour on 18 June 1925. After a visit to MacKenna in Bournemouth and a three-week stay in Paris, he settled into "Eversleigh", the house in the Kingsbury suburb of London which became his final home.

Howe had sent Stephens a Gibson guitar. John Good ("Long John") Reilly (1858–1937) was a former professional baseball player in Cincinnati. The Irish actor Dudley Digges (1879–1947) had moved to New York in 1904. The press cutting was probably about *A Poetry Recital* (1925). Stephens's *Collected Poems* (1926) was divided into six sections: "In Green Ways", "A Honeycomb", "In the Two Lights", "Heels and Head", "Less than Daintily" and "The Golden Bird".]

My Dear Mr Howe:

Here we are settled for a spell. Any letters you send to the above address should come right through. The guitar has arrived, & I am now negotiating with the Customs people for it. I shall start lessons immediately I get it. Wasn't it rotten that we did'nt make John play for us, when you had him, & the guitar, & the place, all set. Still, even a guitar manhandled by Long John Reilly could scarcely have wooed (or weaned) me from the fireflies on that lovely night! I wonder did you write to Dudley Diggs? I spoke to him, lyrically, about Freelands, and he hearkened to me with fervour. I enclose a press cutting that has just come in. You are one half its hero! We must do another little "buke", as you say, in John's story, that belonged to Colum, who pinched it from – an hundred ancestors. I'd like to do it really in order that I might put your name on its title page in token of my liking for you – For I wont say anything about gratitude. I am working at my Collected Poems. Tis a troublesome, but entertaining, job; and there are so many poems that it is difficult to make a sequence. I'm trying it in genres & species – A bunch of grotesque-verse, tapering into "ideas"-verse. Another swathe of pastoral poems (& jolly good they are!) [–] Then a crowd of verses showing People – Next verses in the Irish mode, & then Thought-verses (the style of your Nachiketas & Death) [–] But verse is a nimble matter – It doesnt stay "put". They lap, & overlap, & overflow: They become "grotesques" that has been "pastorals", and, if I may say so, vice-verses. It is, I think, about as easy to organise a Sodality of Fleas, as a book of verse. Here endeth this letter. Write you me one; & remember me, with both hands, to Miss Tranter. Are there any books over here that I can send you!

Mise go deó [*deo*]
["I am, forever"]
JAMES STEPHENS

To STEPHEN MacKENNA

Eversleigh
[A/19] 17 August 1925

[AE's book was *Voices of the Stones*, published on 5 June 1925. "Curtis" is probably a reference to Edmund Curtis. In *The Gramophone* for May 1925, Compton Mackenzie had announced a new invention to increase the volume of a record player (as explained in *The Gramophone* for November 1925, the gadget was a "Lifebelt", a piece of rubber tubing).]

A c[h]ara Stíopháin ["Dear Stephen"]:

My blessing to you for the music, & for your letters, & the Homestead, & the Crescendos. I wrote AE, & he has written me, decent man, sending on a copy of his book. He is a wonderful man volcanoing poetry out of him, & avalanching prose. I'll swear, on my honour as a second-hand Englishman, that all them lads he writes for, & that Curtis curses, & that you love not at all, will wither on the bough, & will be trodden under foot, & be forgot of Ireland. The patient land. Patienter than ever an ass was! But the land that sticks tight to her idea, & that never lets go of it. Back Tadg [*Tadhg*, i.e. "Timothy", a typical Irishman] against Ralph, & go happy to heaven for your money. Oh Lord! Oh Lord! She smells sweet to me from here, & she smelt sweet to me as far as Kentucky is, that wraps herself in little hills, as the County Cavan enwraps herself in little lakes. I have not played any music yet, nor thrummed a thumb of my thumbs, and I with two fists full of them, on a string – I havent got my Gibson guitar. God knows when I'll have my Gibson guitar! Maybe I never will have etc – The Customs people are writing me, & wiring me, & postcarding me, & telephoning me but that by God his Grace I havent got a telephone – saying that I'm liable for duty & gaol, & cruel indignities & forfeitures, and mulctings; & that I'm a bloody smuggler of the bloodiest kind, & that I'm robbing the widows & orphans of the English blood – When I get my Gibson guitar, me being still alive, & owning a penny I'll present you with a waxish candle, & let you burn it on the atrium of your house in your own honour & to the confusion of Customs Houses. I haven't met one Soul here yet. What did Compton MacKenzie say in his Gramaphone about epoch-making inventions that he had up his sleeve – or was he just MacKenzying out of him. I am still moving, & desolate, and de-toothed, & with nothing to play, & nothing to read, & nothing to write, & no one to talk to, except our black cat, the son of your grey cat, whom may God eternally bless

Mise
["I am"]
JAMES STEPHENS

To STEPHEN MacKENNA

Eversleigh
[A/19] 4 September 1925

[Below the inside address Stephens wrote "And on the fourth day of September in the year One Thousand Nine Hundred and Twenty Five after the Birth of Christ".]

Dear Stephen:

Here is a bookeen that fits in the pocket, & is of the right size to make cigarette papers, or to twist for lighting them, or to read a page of every month, or to give me an excuse for writing to you. I say that, on the whole, this world of a desolateness to astonish and enrage every son of God, and God Himself. It should be happiness just to feel the sun shining, or to see it shine. It should be happiness just to be in a backyard all laid in ashes but where one daisy grows. It should be an inexhaustible bliss and delirium just to be – and nothing else whatever but to be being – But it isnt. I say that I love nothing in the world but our black cat, & that nothing in the world loves me but our black cat, and that if I loved God half as well as I love our black cat, or if God loved me half as well as our black cat loves me I'd be so, and thus, and that way. Hereto is my hand on the day and date above written

JAMES STEPHENS

To SEÁN O'CASEY

London
[A/1] 21 September 1925

[O'Casey's play was *The Plough and the Stars.* Major W. Van R. Whitall was a bibliophile whom Stephens met on his first American tour; he must have died within the next few months, as his library (including many books inscribed by Stephens) was sold in February 1927 at the Anderson Galleries. Like Dudley Digges, J. M. Kerrigan (1885–1964) had acted with the Abbey in its early days and was now working in America. O'Casey did not undertake the proposed lecture tour.]

My dear Sean:

As is to be expected, I have mislaid your letter & (so) your address, & have been waiting for it to turn up, which it hasnt. I am delighted to know that you are pleased with your new play. Tis all rubbish what people say – that an author isn't a good judge of his own work. Given that he *is* a writer he knows better than anyone else will ever know, and if the rest of the world is against him then the rest of the world is an ass. After all, my dear lad, you are the White Man's hope, in drama anyway; & tis the very deuce and the very devil, & the very diamond-point and pinnicle of responsibility (not to have that said of one but) to have that to say to oneself when the times seem meagre & the winds at the east.

A friend of mine in America (Major W. Van R. Whitall, Pelham, New York) wants you to go out there on a (modified) lecture trip.

He thought (in conversation with me) that he (with Dudley Digges & Kerrigan & a few others helping) could see to it that you got enough "speeches" to pay your way there & back & leave something over, & that it would be a bit of a change, & a bit of an experience for you. If you can do it you ought to go. Twould be interesting. And, I assure you, can depend on Van Whitall – He is Allwhite. He wants you to stay with him, & he is the decentest soul, & the generousest that you could stay with. As for Digges – There are few men I like better, or would trust farther, and I dont think there is any man whose word is so authorative, or wise either, in theatrical America than Dudley Digges' is. It would be a stimulating holiday for you; and, if Whitall has written you – He arranged with me that he would do so – don't baulk or jib at the well-meant offer – Just go to it, and do it. America is really wonderful, when you get a bit into it. And New York is the wonderfullest kind of thing that is on the globe, except the simple kindness of Americans, & that, in every part of America & in New York, is the principal thing that beats New York. You should send Whitall, or Digges a copy of your new play with a view to American production. Digges can advise you as to this, & I am certain that his advice would be as honest as your own. If you see AE (lucky man to be actually able to see AE whenever you want) give him my love, & say that I do never forget him.

Mise
["I am"]
JAMES STEPHENS

To W. T. H. HOWE

Eversleigh

[A/3] 29th September 1925

My dear Mr Howe:

The guitar has just arrived – It was held up by the Customs people at Southampton – It is the most magnificent instrument that I ever saw; and I wont try to say how much (or half of how much) I am obliged to you & Miss Tranter for sending it. Is all well with you over there? Do you still run out to Freelands, or is the weather moving off from you? We have here a little houseen with an hundred-foot garden: and when I think of the work that this hundred-foot garden demands, I start wondering what calls must be on you with a reservation as big as a county. Did Spicer-Simson finish the little statue, & (if so) does it come up to its promise in the rough? Also, did you have steps let into the little pond? You remember the poor toad that got in & couldnt get out. & the way he kept right tight for you to rescue him. Poor little devil – he was all in it up to the neck that day. I would give a bob any minute for an hours chat with you & Miss Tranter & Long John whose decency is even larger than he is. By the way, I am accumulating mss for you, & will start sending you batches of it (Hill of Vision) shortly. Dont you dare say a word about money and these mss. I want you to have them, & I owe you more than I can count, & I feel a considerable pig about owing so much. I am getting a collected edition of my poems together at this moment, and have just, last night, finished deciding what is to go in, & what is to stay out. I think it will be a decent book. I had to rewrite quite an amount of verse. Good luck to you.

Mise gó deó [*go deo*]
["I am, always"]
JAMES STEPHENS

Can I do anything over here for any of you?

To STEPHEN MacKENNA

Eversleigh
[A/19] 28 October 1925

[Thomas MacGreevy (1893–1967) was an Irish poet and critic. The Irish writer and politician Darrell Edmund Figgis (b.1882) had committed suicide on 26–27 October 1925.]

My dear Stephen:

Its rotten to think that you are not well. I just hate that anything should be wrong with you or out of joint. Maybe you are better now, or getting all right. As soon as you feel like it send me a post card. I have not heard from McGreevy. He would, of course, have lots to do in London, & not too much time to look for people at the circumference. Poor old Figgis. I just saw this morning's paper & his death. You know, everything that unfortunate man ever did went wrong on him, every single thing, &, when all the other things are said, he had qualities & energies that could have made the fortunes of ten others. He'll possibly have better luck next time, the luck not to be born too vain, & I surely wish him every good thing.

Your room is waiting for you when you can come. I want you to give me guitar tips, & to play my Gibson. I begin to think that it can be done (be played) in a way, with evasions & subterfuges. Good man

JS

To STEPHEN MacKENNA

Eversleigh

[A/19] 31 October 1925

[I have not identified the guitar music. "Darrell" was Darrell Figgis.]

Dear Stephen:

You are better anyway, & thats something in a dull world. I just hate to think you dont feel like twenty-five years. About the guitar music – I have Leonards Tutor, Ellis Tutor, & 18 guitar journals, which 18 latter are for you to take away when you come here. As to the other stuff that you have – Twould be an idea if sometime, going through your stocks you set aside any things that you have two copies of, & you could then let me have the odd copies, & in that way we would all be quits. The music I got in Paris, thanks to the exchange, cost next door to nothing and a ha'penny, so dont worry about that – it wouldnt all come to half a crown. You know German languages and such. When you feel well and happy & have nothing to do but eat could you write some or many German music-shops asking for their guitar music lists, likewise Spanish music shops. There must be bee-utiful things, musics worth living for, written for & transcribed for guitar. If we dont get these (& Georgian & masses guittarred) we have lived in vain.

Mise go deo, do c[h]ara, Amen.
["I am forever, your friend"]
JAMES STEPHENS

Still, & for all that, I plains [*je plains*, "I pity"?] Darrell. The dice was loaded against him, by Fate, by Time, by his own self. He must have gone out as bitterly as any man ever did. We can only blame a man for his accidents, not for his temperament. He was Darrell as a cat is a cat, & the harms he did were all done to himself. He never had a cats chance.

To HAROLD LOEB
[A/1]

Eversleigh
10 November 1925

[Loeb sent Stephens a copy of his *Doodab* (1925).]

Dear Loeb.

Thanks for the book. I have been in Paris and did not get it until my return here. I am rereading it, & it is all bettered by your later work. You know how much I liked it in the raw, & now I like it better. It does strike quite a new note in the American literary mode, but for me the chief thing is the admirable prose that it is written in. I am sure, if you will stick to it, that you will go on from power to power. There is eager, vivid writing, & artistic as well as human understanding in this book, & I wish it, and its successors all the good luck that it deserves. You have humour & style and brains – all in plenty. Add courage to that little lot & you will do one good man's work. Dont be disappointed if recognition is slow – it must be; or if the reward is slower – these things are certainties for any virginal artist, but his real success is just as certain & worth working for. Goodbye for a while

Mise
["I am"]
JAMES STEPHENS

To SEUMAS STEPHENS
[A/36]

Eversleigh
18 November 1925

[Mr. Brine was Seumas's school headmaster. Stephens left on his second American tour on 30 December 1925. "This is my own, native land" is from Sir Walter Scott's *The Lay of the Last Minstrel.*]

Mr dear Man:

I havent had a letter from you for a world of ages, and am beginning to wonder why this thusness. Here things slide along, each day very like the last one, the garden being a little gardened, and the meals all being ate as soon as they are cooked. Mr Brine dined with us a few evenings ago, & had a lot to say about you. He really is a nice chap, & very fond of you. Iris came out but only for the afternoon. She looked very well, and, mirab[i]le dictu ["wonderful to be told"], I think she is beginning to skin down a bit. Then we gave dinner a few days, maybe a week, before that to a Mr & Miss Hill, whom we met in Chicago. He is over here buying rare editions of books for America, & he has collected some of mine. I sold him some manuscripts also that he said he wanted after dinner, so things are a trifle easier just now than they were just then. When I get to town, tomorrow or the next day, I will drop you a small, mean, postal order as your share of the swag. We are lunching tomorrow with Bernard Shaw, whom I havent seen now for quite a while. And I have signed a contract to go to America after Christmas, so that is certain. I look forward to it with a kind of horrified pleasure. If it were not for all the jaw I have to give I should like the journey, & the seeing of strange places and strange people. I should like to do a tour in America with you, & then run round Ireland, so that you should get to know it better [–] "thine own, thy native land", as the bard says, & then I should like us to go to Venice and Florence and Rome where the maccaroni grows and the great red sausage blooms. If you can find a pen with a nib in it, & a piece of paper without a hole in the middle, and a little grim determination you might be able to manage a note in return for this long one. How is the Latin getting on? I sympathise with you about it, but there it is, & there you are, & you must just worry away until it or you caves in. Are you beginning to buckle down to your work? Its not easy, but nothing that is worth doing is easy, and when it becomes easy it should be dropped for a tougher job. You are almost a young man now & must learn to go for things whether they are tiresome or disagreeable or the reverse of these. You see I'm advising you to be a Spartan Youth – not bad advice either. I'm beginning to preach, so I'll shut off right now, Have you read anything decent lately? I havent.

Mise, t'at[h]air.
["I am, thy father"]
JS

The above fairy-finger-prints are Noirro's paws. He keeps walking on this page & asking me to stop making black marks on paper, & to pet him instead

To W. T. H. HOWE

[A/3]

New York
8 January 192[6]

["Mr. Glass" was Stephens's agent from the lecture bureau founded by Lee Keedick (1879–1959). The manuscript poems are those from *The Hill of Vision* sent to Howe on 29 September 1925. Howe had purchased from E. B. Hackett the manuscript of *Irish Fairy Tales*, which apparently was lacking "The Story of Tuan Mac Cairill". Howe had privately printed Stephens's "Christmas in Freelands" as his "Christmas Greeting for 1925"; Russell published it in the *Irish Statesman* for 26 December 1925.]

Mr dear Mr Howe:

I got in yesterday, & have your letter. I had been looking forward so much to seeing you & Miss Tranter, & am so disappointed to think we may not, perhaps, meet for quite a time. Mr Glass (Lee Keedick Co) has told you our itinerary. I start in on the 11th here in New York, & on the 17th go to Chicago, & thence westwards away, & will not be New Yorking again until March. We have arranged to return to Europe on 31st March. Still you are a great traveller, and somewhere our routes may coincide. Dont bother about poems (mss) I sent you [–] we can discuss them when we meet. I have not said anything about them to anyone, & would like to keep the matter between ourselves. I have a couple of small matters in my pocket that you will like. About the first of the Irish Fairy Tales. Of course I will write it for you. But I want to see first the sort of paper I wrote the others on (your ms) so that I can make the first story in the same form as the others. I am full of curiosity about the "ideas" you have, & which you want me to partner. Our last partnership was a remunerative one for me, but not for you. I thought Your Christmas Card was a beauty & just loved our poem in it. Did you get a copy of the "Irish Statesman" from AE (George Russell) [–] He promised to send it to you, & wrote me that on receipt of "Christmas in Freelands" he had jettisoned all the poems of his friends over there in its favour. I have to thank you for the opportunity you gave me of writing that poem, &, were justice done, I should be paying you £20 for giving me a poem instead of you paying me £20 to materialise your inspiration – But isnt it a little beauty! I laughed with joy when

I got your royal command, & sat right down at the job, saying, if my friend W.T.H.H, wants a poem he is sure going to get one if it bursts every button I've got. I hope Daisy is pleased, but I expect she would say, were she fronted with it, "poem about me! I should worry, I'm a poem myself! Besides", she might continue, "none of these humans can create real poetry, only cows can do that – Bull-cows that is", she would amend it, & get again to her muncheon. Well, until we meet I'm not happy, so its up to you. Every good wish for the New Year to you & to Miss Tranter, & to John Reilly, & to Daisy, & to Freelands, where all these & those are at home as well as this present well-wisher to them-those well-wished.

JAMES STEPHENS

To [S. K. RATCLIFFE]

New York
[A/30] 12 January 1926

[The English journalist and lecturer Samuel Kerkham Ratcliffe (1868–1958) was currently a lecturer at the Bromley Foundation, Yale University. The story of Fionn and Saeve is told in "Oisin's Mother". The main characters in the second part of *In the Land of Youth* are Midir and Etain.

Russell's poem was "Ideal Poems: J__s St___s", which begins "Hi God! Get off that throne/You've had your turn & turn about/' S fair play you know." Although a French version of the poem appeared in Simone Téry's *L'Ile des Bardes* (1925), the only extant copy in English appears to be one written on the back flyleaf of a copy (in the University of North Carolina Rare Book Room) of *Secret Springs of Dublin Song*, edited by Susan Mitchell (1918). Russell had included two "Ideal Poems" in *Secret Springs*: "S.O'S." [Seumas O'Sullivan] and "Y__s" [Yeats]. In "J__s St__s", Russell is imitating Stephens's attitude towards God in poems such as "The Lonely God", "Mac Dhoul" and "Who'll Carry a Message?"]

Hail, Brother, & Farewell!

I'm off tomorrow for Holyoke, & thence to Chicago, & thenceforward away, westward away – I dont know where. My manager is set deep in a cogitation as to whether he should post me there or yon, and I lie on his knees. So far as it is settled-unsettled I dont touch New York until mid of March. So, tis a blue outlook for our meeting. As for the information desired by your sweet lady – Behold! To think it out I should have to think, & I shall not be able to think until the last day of March when I quit lecturing, & these shores. All that I can call to mind at this moment, (made sunny by getting a note from you) is my own work. Other folks rhapsodies are descended, for me, to their appropriate limbos. Let you tell her from me and from us, that there is a chapter in Deirdre that unbores God when He gets bored, & remembers who He ought to read. Tell her that the whole *second* part of in the Land of Youth will never be surpassed even by me. In the (my) Irish Fairy Tales, there is the Story of Fionn and Saev – a masterpiece twice over, & then some. If she can stand verse let her read in The Poetry Recital, (& let you read it too, & go wild again) "The Coolin", & "Geoffrey Keating", & "Green Weeds["]. Dear God. Dear S.K! All that she can desire, of that especial ilk, she will find chez moi. She may swim there to Paradise. Look you, & may Heaven save me from the sin of modesty! In that second half of Land of Youth, there is the sole & only desirable woman in modern fiction, she__enough! And there also is the only male person for whom, or in despair of whom, any lovely lady may honourably mourn. God made man, But I made this man & that woman. There is a distinction in my favour. George Russell (AE) once made a poem beginning:

> God get off that throne!
> Stephens wants it!

Twas a good poem (altho' not written by me) and well-grounded. If your delicious lady misses Saeve out of Faery, let her grave it on her tomb, in the cold years to come

> "I missed Saeve – How can I
> R.I.P.?"

Henceforth, let no man praise me. I shall praise myself, & this is my first essay in that delectable life-work.

I wish I had known you were coming to my Show. I should have made up a lecture all for yourself, & altho the lecture I gave was a corker, your lecture would have been twice as cork. Dont forget my address in London is

"Eversleigh",
Queen's Walk
Kingsbury. N.W.9

Cri de coeur ["Cry of the heart"]
Away from home I get the willy!
O Regent Street! O Picadilly!

There is a "c" or a "d" left out of that there dilly – I know not which. I am adrift in a far land, & a lady wants to know from me about the love affairs that I didnt write

O God! O High Holborn!

Good hunting, & love to S.K.R from

JAMES STEPHENS

To W. T. H. HOWE

Chicago
[I/3] 18 January 1926

[The text is an inscription in a copy of the 1925 New York edition of *A Poetry Recital*; beginning with the second paragraph, the material was used as the "Foreword" to the enlarged edition of *A Poetry Recital*, published in March 1926. The enlarged edition contained seven additional poems: "Little Things", "The Snare", "The Merry Music", "The Fifteen Acres", "The Crest Jewel", "Thy Soul" and "Christmas in Freelands". The Byron quotation is from *Childe Harold*. "Away! Far Away!" ended with the following note: "Accented letters are to be sounded for as long as is possible. Two beats of this duration are to be held at the end of each line, four at the end of each verse. Unmarked words and phrases are to be said quickly, and ended sharply. All line endings and verse endings, or silences, are to be well held."]

My dear W. T. H. Howe.

This book will show you what is going in its second edition. I took it that you would let me include your Freeland poem, &, as the publishers were in great haste, I could not get the permission from you that I bet myself you would give.

There has been some misconception as to my purpose in publishing this book, and I would like to explain in this second edition that the title "*A Poetry Recital*" exactly indicates the purpose of this volume. The poems given are those which I selected for recitation during my lecture tour in the United States in 1925. In order to be audible in the large halls & theatres in which I spoke poems of a certain quality of sound had to be used. This book is, therefore, not to be taken as a final selection from my work in verse but as containing the poems which I consider to be best adapted for public utterance.

I have made many experiments in verse, and many of the poems in this book are experimental[.] In "The Paps of Dana", for example, there are six lines which should be repeated on one breath (from the words "peak to peak" to "into the clouds") [–]The poem is about a mountain, and, on repeating the lines indicated a speaker should be as out of breath as if he had actually climbed the hill[.] "The Centaurs" tries to reproduce the beating of a horses hooves[.] In "The Fur Coat" I tried to capture something of the delicate impertinence of a cat. In "The Coolin" I sought to represent that state which is almost entirely a condition of dream, wherein the passion of love has almost overreached itself, and is sinking to a motionless langour. "The Rose on the Wind" seeks to reproduce a swaying and balancing that would be slow enough & gentle enough and limited enough to justify that title[.] In "The Voice of God" I tried to give an immense quantity and quality of sound, and in "The Main Deep" I sought for a rhythm and a motion that would convey the roll, & march, & rush of great waters. A critic, commenting this poem, wrote that it should not have been published "even as an experiment" [–] It may be regarded as an experiment, but it is also a thing done. Generally, in dealing with the sea, in dealing with any external thing the poet will desert his non-human subject (the sea, or the air, or a bird, or what not) and hedge himself, after the first explanatory line, behind the thought or action of a human being – thus in

"Roll on thou deep & dark blue ocean roll
. . . Man marks the earth with ruin . . ."

Byron gave one line to the sea, & the remainder of his poem to intellections, or even platitudes on the futility of ambition. In singing about birds almost all poets, even the very greatest, evade their manifest duty to their matter – They will not sing or fly – they philosophise – They do an injustice on the one hand to philosophy, and, on the other hand, to their bird, and their readers, and themselves. A bird sings over and over one phrase, but the poetic bird sings a dictionary

Another poem in this collection which has been ill-interpreted is "Away Far Away" [–] In this poem I tried to mould the rhythm which I think of as Death. It is properly, if not a Funeral March a Keen, and to get its quality at all it should be uttered in the manner indicated by the footnote. This foot-note has earned for me a series of critical exclamations that includes all the shades between kindly commisseration for another good man gone wrong and the desire to kill one who was ill-treating the English language. It is commonly believed that in verse only vowel sounds can be held or prolonged – this is not so. Most of the so-called consonants can be held for as long as one pleases, and in especial the letter-sounds l. m. n can be held for as long a period & uttered as loudly as any vowel of them all. There is vastly more sound in the English language than the English poet permits himself to use.

In "The Pit of Bliss" I tried to give in the 3rd verse the effect of an eagle tumbling violently through all of the space that he had previously climbed, and by a curious sympathetic action the 4th verse repeats in the mind the tumble that had previously been in the air.

I have added a few poems for this second edition. "Little Things" is a variation on the Lord's Prayer[.] The "Crest Jewel" & "Thy Soul" are both founded on the Vedas. In the first I have taken it that there are only two systems of Philosophy – the Philosophy of Pessimism, and the Philosophy of the Soul. I have tried in the first verse to give the normal pessimistic statement, & in the second verse to raise that to an absolute utterance. The 3rd verse seeks to convey the accepted doctrine of the Soul, & the fourth verse to raise that to its absolute utterance.

It is a proper rule that a writer should not reply to criticism. The examination of any artist's work during his life-time is bound to be tentative and experimental, & he cannot do anything to assist it. These remarks merely embody suggestions that I made to my audiences as to the reasons or emotions that shaped these poems.

JAMES STEPHENS

To HARRIET MOODY

New Orleans
[A/11] 5 February 1926

[Mrs. Harriet Brainerd (1857–1932) married the American writer William Vaughn Moody (1869–1910) in 1909; Mrs. Moody maintained her house as an artistic salon. *Those Not Elect* by the American poet Léonie Adams (1899–) was published in 1925. *The Fire-Bringer* (1904) was a poetic drama by W. V. Moody.]

Dear Harriet:

This is but a note to say we are still alive, and, like Felix, walking still. I begin to feel that I should be developing some kind of wheel-system where my legs are, we have wheeled so much & so far. It was curious to waken up from Chicago into Texas, & to find our vanished summer – The population of Fort Worth were all sauntering about in their shirt-sleeves, & the sun was doing itself proud. Naturally, and, of course, I caught a fifty sneeze-power cold, & have been sneezing myself into and away from lectures ever since. Very miserable this person was, & very frightened that he wouldnt be able to talk in loud and rotund noises, & very desirous of being back in Chicago, and very much better now. Now we are away far away by the Gulf of Mexico, a name I had seen before on a map & maps, but never dreamed I should neighbour. Tis an un-American-looking City, and tis dressing itself up for Mardi Gras. Bunting in the streets, and congregations in the ten-cent stores; and all the neighbouring territories are sending in hourly contingents to swell the crowds. On the 16th (I think) all of these people will clamp red-plaster noses over their own noses, & will blow blasts on tin whistles. But we, thank God, will be back in Chicago by then, unwhistled and un-nosed. I think that public happiness is about the unhappiest – But that is to carp, which the Lord forever save me from. I talk here on the 8th & we hope to quit these parts on the 9th and on the straight route for Chicago. We will wire you as to this.

I talked to all kinds of reviewers about your Léonie Adams, & hope that some of them will give her a mention. But when I get back you must read the Fire-Bringer to me – We will make a special evening for that. It will be good to be with you again. Love to you from us both, & twice from me.

go deó [*deo*]. do c[h]ara.
["forever, thy friend"]
JAMES STEPHENS

To STEPHEN MacKENNA

Eversleigh

[A/19] 4 October 1926

[MacKenna sent Stephens a copy of William Foden's *Guitar Lessons* (1904). MacKenna's *The Divine Mind*, the fourth in his five-volume translation of Plotinus, was published in 1926.]

Biggest & Best of all the
Stephens that have that for a first name:

I should have written you earlier, & have been daily meditating it, but hadnt your new address – Iris having it, & she *at* the school! Thanks for that Foden. God will deal with him as he merits. I put down here for the first time that the G^r cannot be played, & that I have proved that judgement upon its body. Angels who are also octapuses may play it, & the main body of music that has been written for it is detes-damnable & in waltz-time. AE came to Paris for his first visit. I was (we were) there for his entry, & for his next day. What he thought of it I dont know. Con Curran & he Louvred possibly per day. I introd^d him to ces Spicèrs, who brought him to artists & cafès, & the sun shone every day. I wish I had, but I didnt hear that Brahms or any Brahms that could "make Beethoven sound like a musical box", & even if I listened to such a Brahms I should not be able to hear such a Brahms as that, for there aint no such. I am reading French stuff. They are as clever as all the devils, & stupid as pigs – In fact they are pigs. If you do send Plotinus I shall read you both with delight. My own pen has gone rusty. I dont *want* to write any more. Three quarters of all writing anyhow is an indecent exhibition of onesself. Nothing, furthermore, is worth writing about. The French hold that real life is conducted in bed. The English hold that you'r not alive unless you'r committing murder. The Americans say that life is robbery, the Germans that it's work. They are all, without exception, Pigs.

Mise, muc, mar a gceadhna [*an gcéadna*]
["I am, a pig, likewise"]
JS

To DANIEL MACMILLAN (Macmillan & Company, London)

Eversleigh

[A/23] 16 October 1926

[Daniel Macmillan (1886–1965), a nephew of Sir Frederick Macmillan, sent Stephens a copy of *King Goshawk and the Birds* (1926) by the Irish writer Eimar Ultan O'Duffy (1893–1935). Five hundred copies of the *Collected Poems* were signed by Stephens; the 1926 edition of *The Crock of Gold* was illustrated by Thomas MacKenzie.]

Dear Mr Macmillan

I delayed acknowledging receipt of Eimer O'Duffy's book "King Goshawk & the Birds" until I could read it. I think it is exceedingly clever, & shows that Mr O'Duffy has a much greater talent than I had suspected. I knew him a little in Dublin but only as a clever, satiracle writer. There are parts of this book that no one could better; an ease & clearness of expression and a generous rage and humour that is unusual. He will, of course, outgrow his models, &, from this book, I should be inclined to prophesy good future work by him. I read the book with delight, & am greatly obliged to you for sending it.

Yours very truly

JAMES STEPHENS

By the way, I wrote asking Sir Frederick to reserve six of the signed copies of my poems, & six of the Illustrated Crock of Gold for me. Perhaps *three of each of these* will do for me.

JS

To W. T. H. HOWE

[October 1926 or later]

[I/3]

[The text is an inscription in one of the five hundred signed copies of the *Collected Poems*. "Christmas at Freelands" did not contain a dedication.]

Dear Mr Howe:

Here, at last, are all my poems, or all those that I care much for. I think you know them better than anybody, not excepting myself. I write here that, dedication or no dedication, the poem "*Christmas in Freelands*" was dedicated to you, & is & always will be your poem, & that I have to thank you for, in a manner, giving it to me.

Mise, go deo, agat
["I am, always, yours"]
JAMES STEPHENS

To [W. T. H. HOWE]
[I/3] [October 1926 or later]

[The text is an inscription in Howe's copy of the 1926 New York edition of *Collected Poems*.]

There is a reason for everything. There is even a reason why this writer has never written blank-verse. A very lazy writer can write blank-verse with ease. A writer of another type of laziness cannot write blank-verse at all. Certainly to produce a good lyrical poem requires a vast mobilizing of energy. But even the double of that energy is not good enough for blank-verse. And, while this writer was (isnt now) was quite capable of that effort, he just wouldnt do it. Not because he didn't want to, but because he wouldnt do it. Mystere! as the French say.

[drawing]
Astral portrait of this writer
making up his mind that
he wont write blank verse.

To W. T. H. HOWE
[I/3] [October 1926 or later]

[The text is an inscription in one of the five hundred and twenty-five copies on hand-made paper of the 1926 *The Crock of Gold*, illustrated by Thomas MacKenzie.]

To W. T. H. HOWE

with remembrance of all the good times we had with him, & with hopes for all the good times to come.

JAMES STEPHENS

And Postscriptum:

I expect that an author always wants to strangle or suppress his illustrator. There are no illustrators with the brains of a louse, or the tact of a hyena – This illustrator is thoroughly in his tradition. He has given me for the Philosopher a low-comedy comedian, which is precisely what my Philosopher isnt: and he has imagined for my girl a bleak, blank, blasted ham-bone. Just pipe me that girl of his, & invent for me out of the goodness of your heart the proper & necessary curses to hit the case. His landscapes belong to the well-known school of Pseudo-Pseudo. They werent, arent, wont, & oughtnt. Me Miserable! But I'm not as miserable as all that. No writer is as miserable as the brainless boobies that undertake the illustrations of books, & paint the pictures of the world. They were damned before they were born, and they act according. I pray earnestly & in three languages that Heaven may not treat him & them as they deserve. When I consider that illustrators & painters are credited with immortal souls I get the pip, the whole pip, & nothing but the pip. Amen!

JS

To STEPHEN MacKENNA

Paris

[A/19] 16 November 1926

[The French historian and critic Abbé Henri Bremond (1865–1933) had published *Prière et Poésie* in 1925 and *La Poésie pure* in 1926. Paul Valéry (1871–1945) was a French poet associated with the doctrine of "pure poetry". *Les Faux-Monnayeurs* by the French writer André Gide (1869–1951) was published in 1926. Yeats's remark – about G. B. Shaw, not H. G. Wells – was made in *The Trembling of the Veil* (1922).]

My dear Stephen:

Just a mot ["word"] to accuse reception of your letter. It gave me delights & d[´]elices ["delights"] to know you reading and liking the verses of this One. I have sent you on odds & ends of things. What do you think of Bremond. He is an Abbé by the way, & is on all the bookstalls with two present books. Poesié, Pure and Poésie et Priére. There is, c'est mon avis ["it is my opinion"], a literary & religious movement forward here. The literary one almost purely critical. They say immense good of Valéry. He is good, but not, I'd say, quite so good as that & all that. He is conferencing at the moment in Allegmagne of the Germans & being adored there as the new god. Gide is still applauded on bended knees. His book (I'm sending it to you) "Faux Monnayeurs" is called the biggest & best (Yeats said that Wells has the mind of a sewing-machine – that apropos of nothing) [–] I am discovered & found out by the French nation. They all speak English & want to feed me, or even to pelt me with apples. Give me your nouvelles ["news"]

Mise
["I am"]
JS

I have met, as I went out & he came into a house, & shaken hands with Andre Brulé. His address is 42 Avenue Mozart, 16e [–] I shall see him again.

To STEPHEN MacKENNA

Eversleigh
[A/32] [1927?]

[The date of 1927 is conjectural, having been faintly added in a hand which does not seem to be that of either MacKenna or Stephens; however, it is consistent with internal evidence.

Though grammatically incorrect, the coined "fear na villy-co" is based on Irish expressions such as *fear na héadála*, "man of the profit" (i.e. "money-maker"). Stephens apparently intends "man of the billy-cock [hat]", followed by "men of the billy-cock[hat]".

The three postscripts are written at the bottom of the letter. The first gives directions for playing the tango on a guitar: "The first motions are made by stroking; the letter S indicates raising the hand, the B lowering it, trying to give the true sound of Tangos." The third postscript means roughly: "Get on your way."]

Dear Stephen:

I got & rejoiced at your letter. As to the query in it – God help us all! And. in especial, help me. I have never had any brains. I could never follow an argument. I disguise (successfully I think) that sad fact, because I can make rapid & gyratory movements, & thus I lure my vis-a-vis (?) away from his subject and start one of my own; & there I am, & there he isnt. I would say with you, that there is a vast & a huge difference between the Lord C's [Christ's] statement that God is my father, & my statement that I am God's son. I dont mind the Lord C. saying the first, but I'll be damned if I say the second: if it be but on the ground that He knows what He's talking about, & I dont. There is something comic and sad in the spectacle of a clergyman, a fear na villy-co, hopping about, & twittering at other feara na villy-cos that he & they are sons of God, billy-cock hats & all. All that in the Christian tongue & doctrine, but if you tackle me on the Veda I'll uphold to the death that the "great sentenses" are true, or are nothing, & that the greatest of the great sentenses "Thou Art That" is exactly so and thus. Thank all the goodnesses there is no God in the Vedanta – There is a That, & I feel natively capable of being a That where I should hesitate long & shrink from the possibility of being a child of God. Anyone can be and enjoy being a That: and every Relative can tumble to its Absolute in the twinkling of an eye, as it were. Observe that in the Vedas every statement that can possibly be made is qualified by the words "as it were" [–] I like the Vedanta, & I dont like Christianity. The sun is shining herewards this evening. Will you be coming to London again ever?

Mise. An Rud siud [*súd*]
["I am. that there Thing"]
JAMES STEPHENS

Can you translate this here Spanish [–] "Los primeros compases se hacen rasqueando; la letra S. indica subiendo la mano la B. bajando, procurando dar el verdadero aire de Tangos["]

Do you want any music? I've got some doubles

What do the words "Salta al Paseo" mean?

To STEPHEN MacKENNA

Eversleigh
[A/19] [26 January 1927]

[I have not identified the book by D. H. Lawrence (his most recent major work was *The Plumed Serpent* of 1926). The concert by the Spanish guitarist Andrés Segovia (1893–) in Wigmore Hall was on

29 January 1927; "Tessarech" was Stephens's guitar teacher in Paris. I have not traced Stephens's lectures in Scotland. The work by the French writer Georges Duhamel (1884–1966) was "Journal de Salavin", published in the *Nouvelle Revue Française* from September to December 1926; Stephens was doubtless disappointed with the conclusion, in which Salavin returns to his unsaintly self.]

Dear Stephen:

Thanks for the Lawrence book. He is very clever, & that's all, Treats surfaces, for he isnt steady enough to hold his stuff steady enough to work at. God help every artist who cant put his stuff into a vice, so that it cant move until he is done with it. Look you, my dear – Or, rather, dont, for why should you indeed, & why should I – Amen.

You are right about the Foden – Given a small, preliminery, knowledge, he is the best of the whole lot. He knows the actual fingering difficulties, & gives lessons that easily and gently dissolves those difficulties. I can see that when I have (which I now have) gone over his exercises in C. G. D. A Major, and then (which I now havent but am at) tackle their respect[v] Minors, progress will have been made. That Segovia (violently hated by my Tessarech & thus hated dutifully by me, & virtuously conspued) is to be in the Wigmore Hall on Saturday, & I shall be there. Alas that you shant – I mean wont.

On Monday, & for four days afterwards I'll be in Scotland lecturing at Universities, God help us all: I see by a paper that one of my lecture places will (without as much as a by-your-leave) broadcast me on its radio, but whether Bournemouth can hark intil Scotland I don't know. Nor do I even know that it would if it could. Iris & Seumas have gone back to School, & I have started a story – wonderful – if I can do it – Wonderful even if I cant. The courage needed to write such a story as this one is greater than has hitherto been known to man. I say it. The mind, the spirit, must arrive at an incredible dilation to begin it, & must then dilate itself incredibly and dutifully [–] per blooming day, mind you!!!!! [–] till the deed be done & over –

Pray God, that He
Be good to thee,
And good to me
Jamesie Ste-
phens

P.S.

By the way – there is running through the Nouvelle Review Francaise a story – study, by George Duhamel about a man, aged 40, who examined his conscience to see what he could attempt & do. He hadnt courage enough to be a hero, nor brains enough to be a philosopher, nor skill to be an artist. Nothing. He decided then to be a Saint, and took up that profession, much as, I, say, you, say, might take up the profession of plumbing & gasfitting, or tailoring. Two numbers are out, & with one: one is still to come. Tis very good, I misdoubt me that in the last instalment the good man will go bankrupt, but if he does twill be Duhamel's banqueroute ["failure"], & no one else's. There is a right-mindedness, but there is deja [*déjà*. "already"] a sarcasm cachée ["hidden"]. If, I say it, there be a sarcasm hidden in the soul of an artist, twill out, & there is his good-night, & his light-that-failed. No writer should give board & lodging to a spot of sarcasm that is as big as half the head of a small pin. It will rot a head or a hogshead. If the Duhamel dares to create a Saint, what a dare that will be! & how one should have to revise all one's ideas of France & the French language! It has never been done – I could do it. It never will be done, unless I do it. Loud cheers from hell. Hears-hears from Heaven. Sniggers from Duhamel in his fourth-dimension form. Wild applause, mingled with At-a-boys from MacKenna –

[drawing]
Extra-dimensional
ME ready to take
it on.

To DANIEL MACMILLAN (MACMILLAN AND COMPANY, LONDON)

Eversleigh

[A/23] 6 March 1927

[Macmillan sent Stephens a copy of W. B. Yeats's *Autobiographies* (1926).]

Dear Mr Macmillan:

Many thanks for your kindness in sending me Yeats's Autobiographies. I feel a little ashamed at taking them from you in this way, as it had really been my intention to buy them, & thus help the good work. I wish you had put your name in the volume as it is, of course, a book that I shall cherish. I have already dipped deeply into it, & find it everywhere excellent.

Yours very truly
JAMES STEPHENS

To GEORGE W. RUSSELL

Eversleigh
[A/12] 3 June 1927

[Abel Chevalley (1868–1933) translated *The Charwoman's Daughter* into French as *Mary Semblant* (1927). Humbert Wolfe (1886–1940) was an English poet and civil servant. Stephens's book was *Etched in Moonlight*, published in February 1928. *Chopin: ou le poète* by the French critic Guy de Pourtalès (1884–1959) was published in March 1927. "Ichabod" probably refers not to the literary character but to the Hebrew name, generally translated as "no glory" (see 1 Samuel 4:21, "And she named the child Ichabod, saying, The glory is departed from Israel . . . ."). Thus "delind est" seems intended for the Latin *delenda est*, "must be destroyed" (as in Cato the Elder's *Carthago delenda est*). William Ewart Gladstone (1809–98) and Stanley Baldwin (1867–1947) were both Prime Ministers of England, the latter the current one. "Wallis" is doubtless an error for Edgar Wallace (1875–1932), a popular English writer of detective fiction. "Janey" is Janie Stewart (d. 1940, aged 87), AE's hostess in Donegal; Osborn Joseph Bergin (1873–1950) was the Professor of Early Irish in University College, Dublin; James Winder Good (d. 1930, aged 53) was one of AE's assistants on the *Irish Statesman*.]

My dear AE:

I have been in Paris: I had to give a lecture there. Had to, is the proper expression. A friend, you may have met him, Abel Chevalley has just published a translation (his own) of the Charwoman's Daughter, & I had to be there to give the book a send off. I had, that is, to be seen & heard before I could be bought. I should have thought that the simple view of me would put people off buying any book of mine. As for my news – I dont have any. In now a year, I have dined once with Drinkwater (at whose house I met H. Wolff) & that is all the dissipation that can be quoted against me. Actually I have not met anyone for over a year, until yesterday, when Captain

Douglas (whom I hadnt seen for 2 years [)] came out here thinking to get sunlight & a drink, & we out of both. He got, poor man, tea and rain. I am preparing a short book of short stories for this autumn. It is all old stuff, for virtue has gone out of me, & I havent written a line for ages & times. I dont want to. Wish I were rich – richish, & didnt ever have to work. News for me is news of Ireland. All that I get of that is from the Irish Statesman wherefrom, weekly, I reconstruct you, & as much of it as can get into notes. I dont admire Wolff too much: & I dont admire anybody much. He has energy & intelligence, & the one is apt to tangle the other up. I warned a little, delicately, at him, but he may not be able to take a hint; there is a vanity – he is not too vain, but there is a self-protective vanity that will refuse advice, or that cannot afford to consider itself lacking: & there is a very pleasant mind to which that particular vanity is native, & unpartable. I am a modest bloke, & were it put to me I could agree that I must forget everything I now know – But Wolff, perhaps, could not – would not grasp that this is a prime necessity for him. Like all the other lads, he prefers being clever to being a poet. I am writing round & about: actually he (& the rest) does all that he can, & leaves undone what he cant. I, who to this day, yesterday, hated biographies, & have never read any, am reading a life of Chopin by Guy de Portalés: very curious, interesting too – You see, my dear, even if the poets are bad, the novelists are worse. The only fiction-stuff worth reading is in American magazines. It is curious how good these are, & how the world-fiction has turned to violence as the only subject that has interest. In pre-war Europe violence came in as a philosophy, or a theory. In after-war America violence is used on a lower grade: it is for everybody's, everyday use. I think the American over-soul, as Emerson called it, is meditating doughty deeds. Anyhow, so far as English fiction goes, I cant read any of it; & find also that I dont want to write any of it. My Muse has the pip. Do you know, when I had read the verse in, say, a dozen of your Statesmen, I said to me – These may or may not be fine verse – but – they are the only verse worth reading these days & in these climes. In all these poems there is actually some poetry – So I said & say. Our young men may not have sacks full, but they have not sacks empty; & the sacks of this here land are all empty. Ichabod for England, and delind est for her, & the devil & all to pay for her. Do you remember tracing her decline & fall through the d & f of her Statesmen from Gladstone down through the lawyers to end in Baldwin & his pipe. Writing (even fiction) was also levelling down, & now Edgar Wallis is their only It. We had all better learn Irish & escape the rot to come. I've been interrupted about forty times trying to write this screed; & as you may gather from it I havent a thing to say – which, also is a lie for me, for I have a million things to say, or to urge you to say, & me to listen peaceable. One doesnt write anything if it matters: life & God & victory – all of those & these that fill the mind, but wont write themselves. Do you recollect meditating an anthology of Sacred passages? If you dont get it done twont be done, & it worth all the doing that may be. I spent a week two months ago with MacKenna. He is unchanged, or more musicalish, more in love with small things, babies, birds, & as bent on teaching any English boys that come near him – the carpenters son, the grocers boyeen, how not to be English, & how to be good Irishmen, rebels to wit:

And you in Donegal. I wish I were there now that you are there. Sandhills & sea & the bushes, & the small path running from Janeys to where you paint; & the great cakes of bread; & the great noggins of buttermilk; &, were we together, the great talking you'd have, & the great listening that'd be mine. I think of packing a toothbrush, & a ms book & going there, or westwards away to Connemara, or Southward Ho towards Dingle, & try there for a month to write my soul out or in; I havent even scratched the surface of my soul, & it a hefty one. Adieu, but why should I wish God to you, & he nowhere else.

Mise
["I am"]
JAMES STEPHENS

If Janey remembers me, which she doesnt, remember me to her, & give my love to Bergin, & to Jimmy Good.

To ANDRÉ BRULÉ

[Eversleigh]
[A/19] 2 October 1927

[Brulé had written on 17 September 1927; he mentioned that his mother had recently died and also promised to write an article on Stephens's poetry.]

My dear Brulé:

I was delighted to hear from you, but did not reply as I thought that, from day to day, I might be going over, & found that, from day to day, I wasnt going. I may be in Paris for a few days in about a fortnight, but will write you again as to this. You & Mrs Brulé have certainly been having a poor time lately, & I am glad that your suspense is ended, & that you can be single-minded in all your plannings. I went for three days with Chevalley to Touraine, & had a delightful time. He is a first-class man, & a companionable. He has all sorts of knowledges that I lack and covet, as you have too. I've been doing nothing except to make myself adept in the art of not being a literary man – i.e., not writing, & not wanting to write. However, the wolf will begin to howl shortly, & I shall have to write again to stay his clamours. I am going to be curious & impatient about your article on my poems. Eureka! At last I shall be adequately praised. Laud me with Oceans. Trumpet me with Planets, for thus I do deserve. And where you must blame me, then curse me with Comets & with Milky-Ways, & give me something to cuss back at. All good to ye all, from

Mise
["I am"]
JAMES STEPHENS

To HARRIET MOODY

Eversleigh
[A/11] 2 October 1927

[*Beasts, Men and Gods* is by Ferdinand Ossendowski. Edith Kellogg was Moody's secretary; "Bessie" was Elizabeth O'Neill, her housekeeper-companion; the "little girl" was Alice Harriet Tilden, her niece.]

Dear Harriet:

I was delighted to get your letter, & to know you are all right. About the Paris flat which someone has lent you for the winter – I do hope that you will be able to come over & use it: if not immediately & in the winter, at least in the spring. You tell just the bare truth when you say that time & change & fate & the devil did not really intend you to be a businesswoman. There are lots to do that, but there are not lots to be you. Naturally I (or we) have nothing against business. Tis only when we enquire how deeply it can interest a person (like you) that we see that it has much of poverty.

Tis great to initiate & to bring to its success, & to quit; & that I hope you'll be able to do.

I see you have been reading Beasts Men & Gods. What a singular book! And what a singular author! He is an adept at personal evasion. After reading his book one has undergone many physical & mental adventures but the sense of intimacy that should subsist between a writer & a reader has not been given. One knows nothing, at the end of the book about Ossendowsky – If he is dark or fair, or amorous or gluttonous or timid or not – or anything. This only comes, and it comes without being "given", that he is more determinedly and darkly, & (perhaps) fretfully, hunting God than any other modern we know of. God seems to be less his hope than his quarry. He consorts with "miracles", the sign always of a man whose God is power. I'm not blaming, not even criticising. We all go for what we want, & we all want what we can; & we all get what we are equal to. I am prepared to hope for every creature that is that it gets what it wants to the limit.

Anyhow, you write that you may be able to come over: t'will brighten the winter. You like winter, God bless you. That do not I. Climatically – I am a Mr Facing Both Ways. I rejoice in the summer when winter's in it: & I laud the winter when summer is here. Padraic & Mary Colum are here, & I have been seeing something of them this week. Padraic is one excellent person, & so is Molly in her different way. Remember me to Edith & to Bessie, & to your little girl.

Mise, go deó [*deo*]
["I am, forever"]
JAMES STEPHENS

To JAMES RAYE WELLS

Eversleigh
[T/42] 19 October 1927

[James Raye Wells was President of the Bowling Green Press, publishers of Stephens's *On Prose and Verse* (1928). "On Prose" was a re-writing in English of the preface which Stephens had composed for *Mary Semblant*; "La Poésie Pure" was written especially for *On Prose and Verse*.

Wells had sent Stephens a copy of *Frontier Ballads* (1927) by the American writer Charles Joseph Finger (1869–1941).]

Dear Mr Wells,

Thanks for your letter of 11th inst., and for the book Frontier Ballads, which has just come in this morning. I have browsed for an half hour over it, and it seems full of excellent things.

I am sending on the prose copy with this letter. The original copy, which you read, only contained six pages. I have now added extra matter of ten pages, making 16 typed pages in all, and I think that the bookeen will be of quite respectable size.

I am pushing on about the verse copy as quickly as I can, and will write you again about this.

Every good wish to you from this side,

Mise,
["I am"]
JAMES STEPHENS

By the way – This stuff has never yet been printed in the present, English, form. The original form in fact.

To HARRIET MOODY

Eversleigh
[A/11] 24 January 1928

[Russell did visit Moody during his lecture tour of America in January–March 1928. "William" was one of Moody's servants. The book by the American writer Carl Sandburg (1878–1967) was *The American Songbag* (1927). Stephens prepared the *Edmund Spenser* (1928) and *Byron* (1928) volumes in "The Augustan Books of English Poetry" series, the general editor of which was Humbert Wolfe.]

My dear Harriet:

There is a thing you could do for me, & get my blessing – you having that already[.] Could you order for me the "*Modern Album for Guitar*" *by Vahdah Olcott Bickford*, from the American Guitar Society 2280 West 23rd St. Los Angeles, Calif – I'd order it myself, but I cant believe they'd get my letter; or, that getting it, they'd bother to reply; or, that replying, I'd get the reply. Please get their *catalogue also* for me; & we'll settle all the finance of the transacting when you come over. May that be soon. I wrote to AE lauding Chicago & you, but he could not come to London, & I dont know if he had already made his plans. You will see him anyhow. Tell him to let me know the date of his return to Dublin, so that I can run over there, & hear his stories of the States. I do hope he will be able to stay with you, & for a long time, & that he will love William & the big dog, & the sea-saw bed in the dining room. I would give a lot to be able to trot myself into that dining-room this mortal minute, & to see you cuddling the telephone on your chest, & beaming wild or wicked or wonderful beams according as the bloke or blokeen at the other end of the phone deserved or looked these. All my thanks for Sandbergs big book, & for the cake that weighed a ton but tasted feathery. There is none of it left. There is not nany whatever. Twas a vast & satisfying gateau ["cake"], but liable to time, diminution & disappearance. Alas! It Was! It Aint. It Wont again. I'm doing a tiny Anthology from Spencer. Lovely! And another from Byron. Lovely. These two chaps are more wonderful than ink can tell, saving that its ink used by themselves. I'll send you the booklets when they appear. I've another thing to send you, but will say naught of it till I send it. Meanwhile, come over to Macedonia. Dont come until you send me that guitar thing – But come then that same minute. All good wishes to Edith & Bessie. Tell me how AE strikes you, & how he seems to others, & if he does or doesnt succeed & how greatly he does or doesnt, & everything.

Mise, do c[h]ara,
["I am, your friend"]
JAMES STEPHENS

To AN ANONYMOUS CORRESPONDENT

Eversleigh
[A/19] 2 March 1928

[The letter is about *Etched in Moonlight.*]

Dear Sir:

Thanks for your letter, & for your "felicitations". I am sorry I cannot give you the dates of these stories. You may notice that there is a depression of mood common to most of them. All of these (except Etched in Moonlight) were written at the one moment, & that was about the 2nd year of the war (When writing the above I was called away, & could not again find your letter with the address. Will you please excuse me)

Yours very truly
JAMES STEPHENS

To WALTER H. PARKER

[A/3] Eversleigh
12 March 1928

[Walter H. Parker was a librarian in London.]

Dear Mr Parker:

Many thanks for your kind letter. I hope you may find something to like in "Etched in Moonlight". It is not, however, a likeable book, but it does represent, on my part, quite a lot of work

Yours very truly
JAMES STEPHENS

The title story may seem dull: the excuse is, that I wanted to do a certain kind of thing in a certain kind of way, & perhaps that thing can not be done in that way: to dispense with action, or to transfer action into the mind itself is not an easy thing.

To CYNTHIA STEPHENS

[A/1] Eversleigh
10 April 1928

[Jocye wrote to Stephens on 5 April 1928, enclosing a letter from the Italian writer and journalist Paolo Orano (1875–1945) inviting him to lecture during the "Cultural Weeks" segment of the Third International Book Fair in Florence. Joyce had declined to lecture and had suggested Stephens as a substitute, telling Orano that Stephens had "much more experience in that line than I have" and knew "more about the Irish literary movement than I who have been abroad from Dublin for nearly a quarter of a century". Stephens accepted the invitation and took Joyce's place in Florence.

"Lady Ottoline" was Lady Morrell. Louis Untermeyer (1885–) is an American poet and critic.]

My dear girl:

I enclose a letter in Italian written to Joyce, & which he has sent on to me. He suggests that I should give the lecture in Florence instead of him, & says he has written to those people about it. Joyces address in Paris (shd you wish to see him) is 2 Square Robiac, 192 rue de Grenelle – You will see from the letter that they offer 2000 lire "non enormo certo" ["indeed not large"] !!! The people here were working very busily, & they have put the front door on & painted all front of the house & part of back. Mr Jones was speaking to me, & he lamented & mourned over the colour that you had chosen – primrose – He claimed that it was the world's worst colour, & begged me to stop it. But I said, put it on; my wife will change it when she comes back, if she wants to. Mr Healy has dug & dug, & will plant potatoes tomorrow in his dug. It was very fine here over the holidays, but today it rained off & on. Lady Ottoline, whom I rung up at N. ["Nursing"] Home, is no better. I dined last night with Untermeyer, & will see him again tomorrow. Iris is going to the Post with her letters & yowls for me to finish this one. Good bye & all love to you.

JAMES

To CYNTHIA STEPHENS

Eversleigh

[A/1] [13 April 1928]

My dear girl:

We got your letter. Make what arrangements you please about the lecture. After all, they have not yet asked us: Tis as yet a question of Joyce's being asked. Give him & his people my compliments. I had a row with Moore. No, I told you that. Just now I've been talking on the phone with Morrell. He tells me that Lady Ottoline was very bad; had two operations, & that for some time her life was despaired of. By the way, the whole street is hating the colour scheme of your house. Its not bad at second sight. But it startles at first. Simmonds men were here ten minutes ago looking at the sitting room grate & at the back fence. They will set these right when you come back, & will tackle the stair-passage wrinkles later on also. James has the car ready to go to town; & is yelling at me. So good bye & all my love to you.

JAMES

You make all the Italian arrangements as seems best to you

To GEORGE PLATT BRETT (Macmillan Company, New York)

Eversleigh

[A/28] 28 June 1928

[Brett wrote on 1 May 1928, telling Stephens that he had become General Manager of the company and that *Etched in Moonlight* had sold about 14,000 copies.]

My dear Mr Brett:

I am the rottenest correspondent on earth. I beat my breast, & yowl – mea culpa, mea maxima culpa – But, & in exculpation, I have been very much away from home, in France & Italy, & bothered, and not too well. I should like so much to see you, instead of only writing, and thus getting all your news in a huge mouthful. All my congratulations on your new position. I'm certain that nobody else would be half as good in it as you, & I wish you every other success that you care for. I still remember the lovely time you gave me in New York, & wish I were there again. The news about "Etched in Moonlight" is very good, & pleases me greatly. It did well here, but nothing like as well as with you. Please remember me to Mrs Brett.

Yours always
JAMES STEPHENS

To W. T. H. HOWE

Eversleigh

[A/3] 21 January & February 1929

[This letter is inserted in Howe's copy of *On Prose and Verse*, apparently the book referred to; possibly "Colum's story" is the anecdote about mice in "On Prose".]

Mr dear Mr Howe:

What a delay I've had in writing to you, & worse, in thanking you for the load of lovely things you sent to make our Christmas happy. It did that same. I have been waiting for the publishers to send along the copies of a "little buke" – You remember Colum's story, bequeathed by him to Long John, & told me by Long John & by nearly-as-Long-You. I expected the books daily – but something happened, either the 6 books were not posted, or they went astray or they were pinched in the post – So I'll wait no longer but will send on the two that James R. Wells (he is publishing it) gave me when he was here last week, and which I was keeping for MacKenna and Russell. The others will come in, perhaps, sometime. I loved your letters, but there were not enough of them. One of these days Spring is going to come and Freelands will be again all that we remember. Ah me! Twas lovely there! I am (for a week now) writing poetry like one gone lunatic. I write it in my sleep: and think that a nice thing is coming from it. Here is all love to you. I'm sending one of the books to our Miss Tranter.

Mise go deo agat.
["I am yours always."]
JAMES STEPHENS

I open to say: forgive! This got "not posted" under a pile of papers. Tell Miss Tranter too. I hope you like it. Will write again.

Feb. 1929

To LADY OTTOLINE MORRELL

London
[A/36] [29 April 1929]

[Morrell sent Stephens a cutting of "A Violin Prodigy", an article on the violinist Yehudi Menuhin (1916–) from the *Observer* for 26 April 1929. The portraits of Albert Einstein (1879–1955) and G. B. Shaw which Stephens mentions were included in William Rothenstein's *Twelve Portraits* (1929).]

Dear Lay Ottoline:

Thanks for the cutting, which I return. Isnt it a blessed thing to know that genius is born into the world. Ease and precision, but in especial that some one finds the difficult way easy, and the complicated way simple. I see this youngster is a Jew. In a few more years we shall be forced to acknowledge that all the first-class people we know, or hear of, are Jews. You know it is part of my modern-theory that the Jew is in renaissance after how many thousand years, & that it will be worth while watching everything that happens in Jewry. They are still dreadful vulgarians, but that will cease immediately they become race conscious in a nobler form. There is never a first-class artist in a second-class country; & never a first-class man in a second-class race. Einstein alone will lift his whole nation, or, rather, his whole nation has lifted Einstein. Ah me! The world of the immediate tomorrow – America, and the Jews. On[e] sighs to think that we are out of it, and that cricket, & playing cricket will no longer matter a rap. I went last night to supper with Rothenstein; & he showed me a portrait that he had made of Einstein – It was a radiancy – ! The lovliest portrait, the lovliest face, that I have seen in ten years. Something to thank God & Rothenstein for. He had also finished a portrait of Shaw, very fine; full of colour & character, but his Einstein was ["is" written above line] adorable. He promised to give it & the Shaw to me. I hope he will. I shall miss my Thursdays. for I, who keep myself severely away from people and friendships find that I do really like yourself & Philip. Good luck!

Yours very truly
JAMES STEPHENS

To JAMES JOYCE

Eversleigh
[A/35] 23 July 1929

[Joyce was currently vacationing in Torquay. Joyce and Stephens had met earlier in the month, probably in London; Joyce had by now proposed that Stephens complete *Finnegans Wake* if he were unable to do so. Stephens went to America in August 1929 to write an introduction to a catalogue of Howe's collection of Thackeray items.]

Dear Joyce:

Its too bad; but we find that its not possible, in the time, to make a trip to Torquay. I'll be off to the States in two weeks, & we find, so many engagements have been made, & so much business must be done in that short time, that all the dates are filled. I fancy you will still be in England when I come back, or, if in France, we'll be going there, & will have that talk.

Mise
["I am"]
JAMES STEPHENS

To S. S. KOTELIANSKY

[A/6] [New York]
12 August 1929

[Samuel Solomonovitch Koteliansky (1880–1955), who translated numerous Russian works into English, became one of Stephens's closest friends at this period. Stephens enclosed in his letter the foreword to Koteliansky's translation of *Fallen Leaves, Bundle One* by the Russian writer Vasili Vasilyevich Rozanov (1856–1919). The "above address" was Howe's office in Cincinnati.]

Dear Kot:

Here is the Foreword. I hope you will like it. I had intended writing a different kind of introduction. But, on the boat, my pen went off in another way, & this is the result. Will you drop a note to the above address merely to say that the ms arrived, & that you are or are not disappointed. If your publisher doesnt care fot it he need not print it.

Getting off the boat.

Mise
["I am"]
JAMES STEPHENS

To ROBERT FLEMING RATTRAY

[A/12] Cincinnati
26 September 1929

[Robert Fleming Rattray (1886–1967) was currently Principal of University College, Leicester. In May 1929 Stephens had gone to Bucharest and Budapest; this letter is the only indication I know of a trip to Greece and Turkey.]

Dear Dr Rattray.

I am away, not in the wilds but in the distances. I fear I shant be back in time to accept your kind invitation. I had a delightful time in Leicester the last time I was there. I have been travelling far & fast (as far as Roumania & Greece & Turkey during now a number of months, & your two letters have caught on me here

Please remember me to Miss Vincent. I hope she got (& is getting) great pleasure from her garden this year.

Yours very truly
JAMES STEPHENS

To LADY OTTOLINE MORRELL

London
[A/36] 28 April 1930

[AE's *Irish Statesman* ceased publication with the issue for 12 April 1930. Augustus John (1878–1961) was a British artist. Stephens was going to America to continue his work on Howe's Thackeray collection.]

Dear Lady Ottoline:

I was away longer than I had intended. Dublin looks nicer than I had thought, after so long an absence, it would. AE does not know whether to be depressed at loosing his weekly paper, or to jubilate at being quit of a weekly job that might have been looked on as a daily misery. His unfortunate pen has had to run, all of 25 years in blinkers, where the political nonsense of the week forced him to write the necessary political or economic article to match it

I got your letter. John is ridiculous, which is nothing new nor wonderful, but he makes a chambermaid ridiculous also; a sin against both church & state. The chambermaidery of certain types is, I suppose, just a kind of inverted snobism: I should hate to write like Thackery, but the distinguished artist, enamoured & vociferous about his c'maid is a subject that a Thackeray could bore a whole swathe of posterity about. There is a yellow streak in every painter: God loves them not, & the devil flies them; & a middle-being called Iggerance claims them for its own. Bad and "rather-good" poets are pretty abominable, but the abominablist thing that life & fate has ever dreamt of is the bad painter, for he is bad even when he is good; & he is to be entheusiastically conspued. On the day after tomorrow, Wednesday, I set sail for Kentucky, & will be there, or not back here, for about 6 weeks. Alas! I grieve to know that you are not yet quite well. Let us hope that you are having all of the evils that you will ever have in the one fell bout: & that you will never know ache or ill again. My address in the States will be c/o Mr W. T. H. Howe,

American Book Co. Cincinnati Ohio. Goodbye, & good luck, & love to you & Philip from

JAMES STEPHENS

To JAMES RAYE WELLS

[A/32]

Cincinnati
1 June 1930

[*Theme and Variations* was published by Wells's Fountain Press (New York) in 1930. Stephens remained in America through July 1930.]

Dear James Wells:

Salute, and a blessing. We pulled out of New York on the same evening that we pushed in; &, so, I saw no one that I wanted to say ["see"]: & by my own poor management I had not your address with me. If Theme and Variations are ready it would be nice to get a few copies here. I dont know how you will handle those royalties: but if you can rustle up some, why I'll pick them off you, as berries are picked from the hedge, when I'm going home in a few weeks. I cant put a date yet to my return, but should be ready to veer and tack homewards in about a fortnight. Remember me, with all good wishes, to Hilda. You never hunt in this direction, I suppose?

Mise
["I am"]
JAMES STEPHENS

To JAMES RAYE WELLS

[A/42]

Cincinnati
July 1931

[Stephens had gone to America in late April 1931 and stayed there through September. The "new tome" was *Strict Joy* (1931). Wells did not include any work by Stephens in the only issue published (December 1931) of his *Gentle Reader: A New Monthly Magazine about Books and Authors, also Arts and Artists, and Other Topics of General Interest* (New York).]

Dear Jimmy Wells:

Arent you a terrible fellow for making a fellow write letters when a fellow doesnt want to; & it all of Hades its hotness. I cant write letters: I can only sweat and moult and swear. Anyway, herewith is a set of verses that I've cut out of proofs, from my new tome thats to be published by Macmillan in September. Make your choice, or use what you will from "Theme & Variations[")]. The (projected) new paper looks interesting. All good luck to it, & to Madame, & to you. I'll be here for another two weeks, & then: & then I'll go where men is men, & gin isnt synthetic, which it isnt here either.

Mise
["I am"]
JAMES STEPHENS

To L. A. G. STRONG

Eversleigh
[A/36] 24 December 1931

[Strong sent Stephens a copy of the manuscript of *A Letter to W. B. Yeats*, published very early in 1932 (the British Museum copy has the date-stamp of 5 January 1932).]

Dear Strong:

I am a dreadful person about answering letters. But here, at least & last, is your Yeats returned. There isnt anything to say about it, except that I hope soon to see it in print. From about page 8 right to the end it is fine. As to those first seven pages you hadnt got into your stride, & they seem to me a bit too introductory, or too casting about as if to see how you could come upon what you wanted to say. I am sure Yeats was pleased with your appreciation, and all the kind & comprehending things you said of his lovely verse. Happy Christmas, or if thats too late Happy New Year.

Mise
["I am"]
JAMES STEPHENS

To MAURICE BROWNE

Eversleigh
[A/24] 10 January 1932

[Stephens had asked his friend Maurice Browne (1881–1955), a theatrical producer, for help in finding employment for his son. Seumas Stephens was interested in both writing and the theatre.]

Dear Maurice Browne:

I am greatly obliged to you for the trouble you took about my son, and for giving him a start. It isnt easy these days to do anything with a youngster: but he is a willing boy, and, as his heart is in this work, I feel sure he will be satisfactory. Sometime, when you are not too busy, (if such a sometime ever comes to a busy man) I should greatly like to meet you again.

Yours very truly
JAMES STEPHENS

To LADY OTTOLINE MORRELL

London
[A/36] 6 April 1932

["Barbara Rich" was the pseudonym used by the American writer Laura Riding (1901–) and the English writer Robert Graves (1895–) in publishing *No Decency Left* (1932). "The Centenary of Goethe" was published in the *Times Literary Supplement* for 24 March 1932. The article by John Middleton Murry in the April 1932 *Adelphi* was "Goethe: 1749–1832". *The Near and the Far* by L. H. Myers was published in 1929.]

Dear Ottoline:

I havent been too well – all hot and cold: and tired, and so-forth: but am now all right-ish, or thereabouts. I'll bring back the Barbara Rich book on Thursday. You are, I think, always right about books, and, perhaps, also, about pictures. This book is almost the worst rubbish I've ever read. Properly it should even be unwritable as well as unreadable. I will also bring you the Times Litt. article on Goethe. It is likely, as you say by Murry. There is matter in it, but the writing is so wooly that a dozen times my mind was not catching on to the meaning of the sentenses. I also got a copy of the current Adelphi with another long Goethe article by Murry, this time signed. There is the same wooliness of statement. I should say that Murry has written far too much, and that he is, unconsciously, out of love with all philosophical subjects, and unable to grip them.

My real reason for writing you has nothing to do with these. I have just, yesterday, finished reading Leo Myers "The Near and the Far". He sent it to me in 1929, and I never opened it. It is even wonderfully good. There is no moment in this long book in which Leo's mind is not thoroughly focussed on his matter. There are all kinds of curious things in it which invite the severest criticism, but which also, being temperamental and Myerish, repel the critic as though he had come against a wall. I am inclined to think that there is no more "interesting" mind at work in the *Art of* fiction these ten years past than Myers. He goes his way as the great ones do, and does not compound with his time or with anything. Tis a very honourable writer, and I laud him with trumpets (no, with fifes and a kettledrum) [–] In a way it is a sad thing to be unique, to be that is, an artist, – He shall lack readers wherever he goes. The "Near and the Far" is, of course, unreadable: it is too intelligent, and holds too closely to its game. Am not I a perverse being! I never write letters, and here I am inflicting pages and pages of one on you. Poor Myers, and poor everyone who tries to give his best, and has a best to give: he shall eat his words, for no one else will, and Piccadilly will keep on dillying. Good bye until tomorrow.

JAMES STEPHENS

To S. S. KOTELIANSKY

Eversleigh
[A/6] 15 April 1932

["Ralph" refers to Ralph Hodgson; Walter James Redfern Turner (1889–1946) was an English writer and critic. *New Signatures: Poems by Several Hands* (1932), edited by the English poet and critic Michael Roberts (1902–48), contained work by W. H. Auden (1907–73), Cecil Day-Lewis (1904–72), Stephen Spender (1909–), and others.]

Dear Kot.

I am off to Paris in the morning, & will be there for a week, at least. So I shant see you on Wednesday. If there is a letter for me please keep it until I get back. I am sorry to miss even one of our meetings, for I think, as time goes on, that they get better & better. I got the book Ralph was talking about & Turner [–] It is really very good. "New Signatures" is the title.

Mise
["I am"]
JAMES STEPHENS

To JAMES JOYCE

Eversleigh
[A/35] 9 May 1932

[On 7 May 1932 Joyce sent Stephens translations of "The Wind" (entitled "Stephen's Green" in *The Adventures of Seumas Beg*) into German, Latin, Norwegian, Italian and French. Joyce asked that Stephens write an Irish version, which he did not do.]

Dear Joyce:

I got your letter this morning. With the original English, my squib is now crackling in six tongues. How many languages do you know, and how many more are you learning? In that, at least we are different. I know English and no more. I tried to break into Irish and French, but got not much further than the front-door-mat in either. All good wishes.

Mise
["I am"]
JAMES STEPHENS

To S. S. KOTELIANSKY

Eversleigh
[A/6] 22 May 1932

[Koteliansky, a close friend of D. H. Lawrence, sent Stephens a copy of *Lorenzo in Taos* (1932) by the American writer Mabel Dodge Luhan (1879–1962); the book is a recounting of her relationship with Lawrence.]

Dear Kot:

Highbrow! You quote at, or toward me, from the Torah. It is good to be able to quote from one's own race, even, as it were, from one's own marrow: and to be not as the gentiles are, who, when they would quote, must surely misquote: and must still depend for their wisdom on another effort than their own. You see, I am writing nearly as cryptically as you did. I have finished all that I shall read of the Dodge Lawrence book. It is a fundamentally dishonest piece of work. Not dishonest by intention, but by temperament. What weak idiots are these vanity-ridden people! And by what shifts do they disguise weakness and semi-idiocy! And how they do seek, as in a frenzy, for values, where they so poignantly know that no value is. Once people were hag-ridden: now even the hags are bed-ridden: and, with their tonsils out: their appendixes gone, their wombs removed, their bladders bust, & their guts in decay, they seek to woo & to be wooed! Only in bed is there hope, they say: only in bed is life. God help us all. Forgive

JS

To S. S. KOTELIANSKY

Cincinnati
[A/6] 5 October 1932

[Stephens had gone to America in August 1932 to work on *English Romantic Poets* (1933) and *Victorian and Later English Poets* (1934), anthologies prepared in collaboration with Edwin Long Beck (1874–1957) and Royall Henderson Snow (1898–), both English professors at Ohio State University. "Coleridge" (1888) by the English critic Sir Leslie Stephen (1832–1904) was included in the third volume of *Hours in a Library* (1879); the article discusses Coleridge's friendships with Lamb, Wordsworth, and others. The article by John Middleton Murry may have been an unsigned review of John H. Muirhead's *Coleridge as Philosopher* (1930), published in the *Times Literary Supplement* for 16 October 1930; The *T.L.S.* writer stated that "the weakness of Coleridge's philosophy is the weakness of the man". *But for the Grace of God* by the English writer J. W. N. Sullivan (1866–1937), a reviewer for *The Times*, was published in 1932.]

Dear Kot:

I got your letters, and was very glad to get them too. Also I got the papers you sent. You are the best of men. I am the busiest of men. I'm making a large-scale Anthology, for my friend, here of the poetry of the 19th Century. I never knew there was so much verse written until I began reading for this work. There are heavens knows how many thousands of writers in that epoch, and while some of them are responsable for about three thousand close pages, none, I think, fall below one thousand. They used all to write in their sleep as well as in their wake. But I have been (and still am) enormously interested, and have been (and still am) working at the rate of at least eight hours a day. I have all the big ones done (and what big ones they were!) Wordsworth, Shelley, Keats, Arnold, Swinburne, Browning, Tennyson: and the littler one (most of whom are done also) are big enough for anyone today. By the way, and apropos des bottes [*à propos de bottes*, "irrelevantly"] – I read an article in *Hours in a Library*, or *Among my books*, or some such title by Leslie Stephen Vol 3. I've looked for, and found it "*Hours in a Library*" it is. There is an article there on Coleridge which you should read in order to offset the article you got me to read in the Times Lit. Supp. by Murry. Taken by itself Murry's article is a piece of dreadful unfairness, and you should get to the antidote as quickly as may be. Coleridge was such and such and so, not a doubt of it, as also am I & you and Murry, but beyond all such suchness, and before them, and away from them, he was Coleridge – one who was respected and beloved by Lamb & Wordsworth, and by man[y] another leal soul and wise. I miss enormously our meetings, and, in especial, I miss Kot. The news you gave about Sullivan was not of the best. I brought his book here with me, & a dozen people now have read it with acclamation. I wrote, just a noteen of a note, to Ottoline a few days ago; and as I have nothing to write about (this letter being the proof) why I had nothing to tell her. Eight hours a day of 19th Century poetry is, believe me, a grueller. Heigho, I'll get a book out of it and a penny, and live happy ever after.

Mise, go deo, agat, do c[h]ara
["I am, always, yours, your friend"]
JAMES STEPHENS

To IRIS & SEUMAS STEPHENS

Paris
[A/1] 2 February 1933

[Joyce always made a point of celebrating the "mutual birthday": in 1935 and 1936, for instance, he sent telegrams to Stephens to celebrate the event. *La Coupole* is a restaurant in the Montparnasse section of Paris.]

Les Enfants:

Many thanks for the birthday cards. I didnt think you could have remembered that most noble of dates. There are all sorts of things about this date in the papers today. Tis Candlemas, and it is also the end of most things, and the beginning of everything. We are now, 5. o'clock, sitting in the Coupole: and will go home to dine; & will go thence at 8.30 to the Joyces where a party of some kind is to be held to celebrate our mutual birthday. I've seen nobody and went nowhere: but will be home on Sunday. So, dont send on any more letters to me. It was bitterly cold here until three days ago, & I had a cold – your mother has it now, but I didnt need it anyway, and she can keep it if she wants to. Goodbye: Tis her turn to write.

JS

To ALICE HENRY

Eversleigh

[A/26] 17 March 1933

[Stephens gave a poetry reading at the Abbey Theatre on 5 March 1933. "Loneliness" is a poem by Susan Mitchell, included in her *The Living Chalice* (1908).]

Dear Elsie:

I got your letter & have delayed answering it largely because there is nothing to be said. Do you remember one of the poems I said at the Abbey Theatre – "*Lonliness*" [–] That is one thing that is sure; & on the instant that we get into either joy or sorrow the lonliness that is central, & is us, is evident. You are a brave little lady, as well as a good one – God knows, that perhaps every man & woman, & every cat and dog and beetle is brave and good; and we all, and they all, learn, if we learn nothing else, to carry on. It was delightful to see you again, and, when you come over here, it will again be delightful to see you again. All love to you.

Mise
["I am"]
JAMES STEPHENS

To AUSTIN CLARKE, OLIVER ST. JOHN GOGARTY, SEUMAS O'SULLIVAN [& OTHERS]

London

[T/36, 9, 16] [29 June 1933]

[In collaboration with the English critic Colin Summerford (1908–), a reader for Methuen & Co., Stephens was planning to publish an anthology of writings by members of the Irish Academy of Letters. The project was never completed, partially due to the difficulty in obtaining material from all the writers involved; although a manuscript was submitted on 6 September 1935, by 9 March 1936 Stephens and Summerford were still lacking the contributions from Shaw, Yeats and Liam O'Flaherty (1897–). The death in 1938 of E. V. Lucas, the Methuen Director who had sponsored the project, was another reason why the volume was never published.

Stephens wrote personal greetings on each of the letters, as follows. "Dear Austin Clarke: I hope you will take part in the under Anthology [–] If you will send something of your own especial choice the book will be enriched." "Dear Oliver. Send four poems that you love [–] Only four of your wealth and your loves." "Dear Seumas: Four of your own choice, and your blessing with them." The date of 29 June 1933 is supplied by O'Sullivan on his letter. The letters are written on Methuen & Co. letterhead.]

You will remember the conversation with Colin Summerford and myself about getting together an Anthology that would, in however small a measure, be representative of the Irish Academy, and would be a gathering together of the first Academicians. Apart from the literary value disclosed such an Anthology would finally be of real historical importance. I am suggesting that each artist should personally select the item which he would like to be represented by. Generally, the selection should not exceed 1,500 words, if in prose, or, say, four short poems if the choice should be for verse. I beg you will let me have your contribution at the earliest possible moment, as Messrs. Methuen & Co. have intimated their willingness to publish, if the matter is promptly dealt with. I should also like a list, as complete as possible, of all your published, or shortly to be published, work, for inclusion at the end of the book. It would be a very great advantage if you would obtain your publisher's consent for any passage to be reproduced. Please reply to me at the above address.

Yours always
JAMES STEPHENS

To JOHN HOUSTON FINLEY

Cincinnati
[A/28] 27 August 1933

[Stephens had gone to America in late July 1933 to work on an anthology, never published, to be entitled *The Reader's Byron*. He sent Finley a copy of *English Romantic Poets*.]

Dear Dr Finley:

This is mainly to say, that I'm in the States: and to ask if I may see you when I am going home, in about a month. About a book (an Anthology) that may reach you. I feel so diffident about sending a book to a friend who is connected with a great paper that I have never before done it in my life. Please take the volume as merely in return for the great book you gave me at our last lunch together, and as a private symbol of my esteem for you. By the way, I feel rather pleased with my preface to it; and, should you ever get to reading it, I would like to know if you approve of my ideas or not. All good wishes to you from

JAMES STEPHENS

To CHESTER R. HECK

Cincinnati
[A/3] [3?] and 1 September 1933

[Chester R. Heck was Editor of the College Division of the American Book Company. Heck asked Stephens to submit a report on *The Reader's Browning: Selected Poems*, edited by Walter James Graham (1885–1944), an English professor at the University of Illinois. The book was published early in 1934. Graham clearly accepted one of Stephens's suggestions – the change from "nineteenth century" to "Victorian period" – and may have been led to include more of *The Ring and the Book* (almost 100 pages of extracts) through Stephens's final comment. However, Graham retained the material on Browning and Whitman and did include "A Toccata of Galuppi's" as one of Browning's best works.]

Dear Mr Heck

I enclose "note" on the Reader's Browning, which you sent me: and hope that it is what you want. My bothering you in the matter was due to the fact that I did not grasp as from what angle you wished the work done. It is quite a good selection. Hoping to see you soon again

Yours
JAMES STEPHENS

There are two examinations now to be made upon Browning's work, and these depend on the class of reader which is to be addressed. If an analysis is to be made for an audience trained in poetry, and interested as to final criticism such an analysis must be undertaken in a fault-finding spirit; and it is likely that as from this date, a more rigorous enquiry will be made into the technical resources, and, more especially, into the underlying ideas of Browning than has hitherto been devoted to this poet. The sense that a large amount of "slag" lies in Browning's work is one that cannot now be evaded: and the suspicion that his wisdom is too easy and man-of-the-worldly to be satisfying to another generation than his own is one that criticism has still to pronounce upon as well or ill-founded. It is possible that a very large, (and, hitherto considered, important) part of the Browning oeuvre will be winnowed from this poet's work, and that his reputation will finally rest on slighter matters than he, or his generation, would have considered possible.

There is another examination, however, the aim of which is to make available to students and the larger public the Browning who was not only a poet, but was also a man and a period. "*The Reader's Browning*", selected and edited by Walter Graham, does precisely this, and it may be said at once that the work could scarcely be bettered. One who knows the book can be said to know his Browning, and can follow intelligently the further evaluation which is to come, and take part in disputes which will be among the most interesting that modern poetry makes possible.

In his preface Mr Graham submits to the reader the salient facts about Browning, his life, and works. These are treated rapidly but with great clarity. In addition he has supplied "a summary of the scholarly findings of the last thirty years", and a bibliography of Browning studies which has been published within this period. The notes elucidating the meanings of poems are very compact and yet full, and there is added a useful list, with indicated pronunciation of the most troublesome Italian names which are met with in the poems.

In the second part of his prefatory essay Mr Graham does consider Browning from the critical standpoint, and it is evident that he is critically as apt in this part as he was, in the first part; historically cogent and swift. But when he writes that "Tennyson and Browning are now usually regarded as the two considerable poets of the nineteenth century", it would, perhaps, be as well to have written of the "Victorian period" rather than of the "nineteenth century["]. His identification of Browning and Whitman as markers out of "the main course which poetry is to follow in our time["] is very interesting, was true, but is now debateable; as is his finding that Whitman sang only of the body where Browning sang of the soul: a finding that can be held in transposition just as neatly as in position. These, precisely, are points upon which future criticism will be busy. Even the question whether Browning ever had a soul could arise; although this could scarcely arise in the case of Whitman, who had soul enough for twenty: but all this is treated persuasively and eloquently in Mr Graham's pages. It is very interesting that Mr Graham should choose (but merely en passant) as among the greatest of Browning's work "A Tocata of Galuppi's" "Abt Vogler", "Love Among the Ruins", and "the Ring and The Book". Lovely as the Toccata is it cannot stand at ease among these greater poems: and, so great or strange, whether as fact or freak or "stunt" is " the Ring and The Book" that Mr Graham might have found space for further extracts from it to supplement the few he has (excellently) chosen.

JAMES STEPHENS
1st Sep. 1933

To LADY OTTOLINE MORRELL

Cincinnati
[A/36] 25 September 1933

[For his work on *The Reader's Byron*, Stephens was reading *Byron* (1930) by the French critic André Maurois (1885–1967) and *The Pilgrim of Eternity: Byron – A Conflict* (1925) by John Drinkwater.]

Dear Ottoline:

All thanks for the photoes. Kot came out excellently, as did you. I havent any kind of news. I havent seen anybody nor read anything of interest. Just now, however, I have a job: am making an Anthology of Lord Byron; and for that purpose am reading him: or, rather, am reading his life and lives. Have just finished Maurois Life of Byron. That man (M) should be suppressed. He would vulgarise a Life of Christ. Now I am reading Drinkwater's Life of B. He is curiously good, readable an[d] obviously deeply caught by his subject. I never knew anything about Byron except his poetry, and am greatly surprised at the undergraduatish life which yet so matches his undergrds letters. The virtue of that kind of writing is to astonish one, and Byron can always do that. But, truly, he is wonderful: I'll be getting to his verse next week, & will reread him with quite another understanding. I havent written Kot. I havent his address. I wish I could drop round to see you.

Mise
["I am"]
JAMES STEPHENS

To JOSEPH HONE

Eversleigh
15 March 1934

[A/3]

[Mackenna had died on 8 March 1934. Hone wrote to Stephens that "I think he led a satisfying life in spite of all his protestations and a coherent one in spite of all his changes of opinion"; Hone also asked if Stephens would give a lecture next winter under the auspices of the Irish Academy of Letters, of which Hone was an "Associate Member".]

Dear Hone:

I am all bothered about MacKenna's death. Unconsciously, it must have been to me that no person in whom I was truly, that is affectionately, interested could die; and my mind keeps conceiving that I have been played a dirty trick, mainly by MacKenna. When he went to hospital in November I was in the United States. I got back a week before Christmas. I wrote him four times at the Cornwall address. But he never received those letters, for his house was shut up, and I did not (and dont) know the name of the hospital he was hospitalised in. His few notes to me were simply headed "In an hospital". Well, that's that: and the game is short a player – You are right about him – He protested – but he was an happy man:

Indeed his protestations were happier than are the expressed satisfactions of many a contented person. If he were looking over the shoulder & read that statement his would be an outraged ghost, and he would asseverate, in a very luxury and superabundance of wit and reason and laughter, that he was the crowned with thorns, and the mainstay of woe from the cradle to the grave. He was singularly personal to me: and is the first person who has quitted our ways that I miss. I blame him, and, if his ghost be overlooking, I tell it so.

About a lecture away in the January of another year – Tis too far off to be imagined. Dont take any notice of it, nor nothing prepare. I dont credit distant Januaries nor believe in them. Adieu

Mise
["I am"]
JAMES STEPHENS

of course he was, as you say, "coherent" in all his changes of opinion. He was a thusness, and lived accordingly: and if ever he seemed wrong twas in the right way. Nor did he ever "change", for he was of a piece.

To LADY OTTOLINE MORRELL

London
[A/36] [19 March 1934]

Dear Ottoline

Thanks for your letter. However you divined it, the truth is, that the fact of MacKenna's death has been lying greatly in my mind and, even, to a small extent, on my conscience. I expect that the feeling is usual enough, that one should take or make more opportunities to see and hear and know all that may be of a friend before it is too late. He was a very wilful man, and had to go his own way, and do his own deeds: a very social, lonely, soul. He was nearer to me intellectually, and even temperamentally, than any other man I have ever known. Indeed, we were singularly intimate, so much so that we could neither shock nor astonish the other, altho' we could each give to the other much and continuous delight: even that word is not excessive. A nobler, or better-furnished, and more fantastic, and generous mind than his I have never known. Strangely, I am still expecting that, if he can get a word across to me from wherever he is, he will or ought to attempt it, and that if he does not he will be treating me badly, which is something he never did do.

Mise
["I am"]
JAMES STEPHENS

To FREDERICK CLARKE PRESCOTT

Cincinnati
[A/13] 2 October 1934

[Frederick Clarke Prescott (1871–1957) was an English professor at Cornell University and the author of several critical studies. Stephens had gone to America in late August 1934 to continue his work on *The Reader's Byron*; later in the year he went on a brief lecture tour. Byron's marriage to Anne Isabella Milbanke (1792–1860) lasted for only a year. "Harriet Godwin" is a combination of Harriet Westbrook (1795–1816), Shelley's first wife, and Mary Wollstonecraft Godwin (1791–1851), his second wife. Claire Clairmont (1798–1879) was one of Byron's mistresses and bore him a daughter, Allegra.]

Dear Dr Prescott:

Mr Howe tells me that you have kindly consented to read the Preface I am doing for him on Byron. It struck me that, perhaps, (not being an expert on the Byronic people) I might be, unconsciously, unfair to some of them. The last chapter is still unfinished: this will deal with Lady Byron. By a curious lapse of memory I have written the name Harriet Godwin for Claire Clairmont in the copy which you will get.

Yours very truly
JAMES STEPHENS

To S. S. KOTELIANSKY

Cincinnati
[A/6] 4 October 1934

[*Descent from Parnassus* by the English critic Dilys Powell (1901–) was published by the Cresset Press (with which Koteliansky was associated) in 1934. The *Observer* for 12 August 1934 carried an advertisement stating that Eiluned Lewis's *Dew on the Grass* (1934) was in its third impression. Hyman Levy (1889–   ) was a Professor of Mathematics in the Imperial College of Science and Technology, University of London.]

Dear Kot

You are an angel for sending me the papers: they have been a blessing. I didnt write because I have nothing to tell. Day follows day, & thats that. I got Dily's book: but there is nothing doing in the way you suggest. My friend would not even look at it. Their shelves are packed with mss they can't print, &, because of the depression they will never print. I do hope that the book has a success in London for the Cresset, & for her. I should like both the partners to be surprised & delighted. I see by the Observer that Miss Lewis is third impressioning. I hope Miss Dilys twentieths. I am reading it: have just finished the first essay – Lawrence – and she made me want to read the Lawrence poems, which I shd have thought an impossible thing to make me want to do. Give her all my best hopes. I am going to lecture here and there about, & will stay for a week at (N) Carolina University taking classes. My Byron is finished. Tis wonderful & beautiful, & strange, & marvellous. I look forward to getting back. Am writing this in a huge hurry

Mise
["I am"]
JAMES STEPHENS

Give my love to our Sullivan & every pleasant remembrance to Turner & Levy.

To FREDERICK CLARKE PRESCOTT

Cincinnati
[A/13] 12 October 1934

[Countess Teresa Guiccioli (1800?–73) was one of Byron's mistresses.]

Dear Dr Prescott:

Thanks for your letter. I hope I am not being a bother to you. It is really the matter of being, possibly, unfair to the Byron personages that troubles: and if you give me your o.k. on this I shall be happy. Of course, also, I should be more than glad of your opinion on the general case if you have time to give it. As you noticed I have omitted the Countess Guiccioli from the group discussed. My idea is that this lady, (in so far as Byron is considered as writer or lover) was of no importance either to Byron or to his reader. If one were writing, say, a novellette about Byron she could easily and properly be the centre of the tale of adventure. But critically, or artistically she seemed to me to be of even singular unimportance: I am still flinching from the Lady Byron chapter. Do not wait for this, for you already know everything that can be said about her. With many thanks

Yours very truly
JAMES STEPHENS

To S. S. KOTELIANSKY

Cincinnati
[A/6] 17 October 1934

[The book by the English writer Ruth Pitter (1897–) was *A Mad Lady's Garland*, published in 1934 by the Cresset Press. Stephens had just finished *Not I but the Wind* . . . (1934), the autobiography of Frieda Lawrence (1879–1956).]

Dear Kot:

Thanks for the Ruth Pitter book. Are not you glad to publish so beautiful a thing. I have written to Kind Ruth Pitter, but have not the address of your firm, so I send you the letter, & you send it to her. I have just finished reading Frieda Lawrence's book: and find it not bad, tho' scrappy. She does give a sense of herself & he. Give my love to Ottoline.

Mise
["I am"]
JAMES STEPHENS

To RUTH PITTER

Cincinnati
[A/1] 18 October 1934

[In the preface to *A Mad Lady's Garland*, Hilaire Belloc had commented that he preferred the version of "The Kitten's Eclogue" which appeared in the *New English Weekly* "spelt in the old seventeenth-century fashion with redundant e's, and I confess regret to see it transmuted into modern spelling". In his note on the back of the dust-jacket, AE had stated that "every now and then these grotesques carved with such skill, glow into a pure beauty as in 'Fowls, Celestial and Terrestrial' ". AE had added, however, that he could not "altogether forgive the poetess's irony which led me to see portions of my own nature in the undesirable forms of earwigs, cockroaches, and coffin-worms". The other volume by Pitter which Stephens had may have been *Persephone in Hades* (1931), her most recent book before *A Mad Lady's Garland*.]

Dear Ruth Pitter.

Koteliansky sent me your book. It came at 4 o'clock: and now at 8 o'c I have twice read it through. In spite of what Belloc says, I am glad you modernized the spelling. Everyone will agree with what AE says on the back wrapper about "Fowls, Celestial & Terrestrial". It is purely lovely; but one need not lament with him about your general subjects. They are all lovely, and strange & satisfying. Leaving Yeats aside, I suppose that you are the finest poet writing today: and easily the most original. I have another volume of yours unread. I went to France when it arrived, & went to Ireland, & went to America: and was then unwilling to read anyone else's verse, being suspicious that nobody else was willing to read mine. But I am as delighted with your Garland as tho' I had woven it myself and will be more pleased with your fame than you will be

Mise
["I am"]
JAMES STEPHENS

To FREDERICK CLARKE PRESCOTT

Cincinnati
[A/13] 22 October 1934

[Byron repented his harsh treatment of his mother, Catherine Gordon of Gight (1765?–1811), after her death; Stephens probably knew Byron's letter to Dr. Pigot on 2 August 1811 and the commentary on it in the *Life, Letters, and Journals of Lord Byron* (1830), edited by the Irish writer Thomas Moore (1779–1852). "Claire" is Claire Clairmont. Byron's *Don Juan* was published from 1819 to 1824.]

Dear Dr Prescott:

Many thanks for your letter. That was exactly what I wanted to get, & wanted to know. I'll look over my stuff again, with your extra suggestions in mind. I dont think that Byron's post mortem penn'orth of tears will alter my ideas as to his treatment of her [(] his mother[)] : and I am still inclined to hold that his "dislike" of Claire differed in quality & intensity from that he showed to others. You & I are on opposite sides regarding La Guiccioli, and perhaps could only settle our opinions with half-bricks at a dozen paces. I can only see in that affair an affair, without beauty, or gallantry, or reason, or aught else but the lazy man's load of love. My point is, that Byron knew nothing whatever about love (Who does? you may ask, and shant be answered by me) & that he plus the Guiccioli knew less of it than did he plus any of his other inamorati. My "last word" re the Byron and the Juan is that neither of them knew anything about love, or, perhaps, that they both knew as much or as little about it as tom-cats do. But I'm not wise in it myself; and as I should not be censorious I am.

Your greatly obliged,
JAMES STEPHENS

To S. S. KOTELIANSKY

New York
24 October 1934

[A/6]

[Powell's book was *Descent from Parnassus*.]

Dear Kot.

Thanks for your note. Believe that I am just hungering to see you. I am off tomorrow lecturing around New York & places and shall then go to London of the Saxons. I enclose a letter for Dilys Powell. I dont know her address. Would you mind sending it to her. Her book is actually the best thing that I have read by any of the immediate critics: and I do hope she gets some encouragement.

Mise
["I am"]
JAMES STEPHENS

To DILYS POWELL

New York
[A/41] 24 October 1934

["Advance Guard", the last chapter of *Descent from Parnassus*, was a study of Auden, Day-Lewis and Spender. Edith Sitwell (1887–1964) was an English poet. The poems by T. S. Eliot (1888–1965) in the *Virginia Quarterly Review* for April 1934 were "Words for Music: New Hampshire; Virginia".]

Dear Dilys:

This is just a note to say I have now read your book. Finished it today under forced draught. I was told last night that I was wanted to lecture today on, of all subjects "The trend of modern poetry". Something I know nothing about. And there were no books here. I didnt know what to do, and then I remembered your book: read the last chapter, & lectured on that, with huge success. By the way, I read it, that chapter, with extraordinary interest: and agreed with every word as tho' it had been written by God. I have now read the whole book, except the Sassoon chapter. I think it is really a fine work, especially fine in the Sitwell & the younger poets chapters[.] I greatly admired also your work on Lawrence, but, as I dont know his poetry, I cannot properly write about it. We dont agree about Eliot: that may be my fault. I am not in sympathy with his verse, &, therefore, not fair, perhaps, to him. You may be right: but, if his future works holds up to his stuff in the Virginian Quarterly, then, even in my opinion, there will be hope for his poetry. All that as it may be, it is a fifty per cent better book than even I had looked for.

All good to you.
JAMES STEPHENS

To S. S. KOTELIANSKY

[Buffalo, N.Y.]
[A/6] 25 October 1934

[Stephens's lecture tour included stops in Buffalo, Boston, Durham, N.C., and New Orleans. Stephens sent Koteliansky two articles from the *Reader's Digest* for October 1934: Arthur L. Mayer's "Why Hollywood Goes Wrong", and Ann Morse's "Writing for a Living".]

Dear Kot:

Leaving this evg. for New York: I enclose a few pages from a paper: they are interesting. I have a new mascot for you, to replace the one you lost: so, now, you will have no more luck until you [for "I"] get back. O Kot, get me a job, so that I dont have to do idiotic travellings.

Mise
["I am"]
JAMES STEPHENS

To W. B. YEATS

Eversleigh
[A/1] [24 July 1935]

[AE had died on 17 July 1935. Yeats was asking for a poem to be published as one of the new series of Cuala Press *Broadsides*.]

Dear Yeats:

I am so sorry for the delay. I was in France, & returned on the day of AE's death, & have been bothered. You may use any dozen of my poems, but the music cannot be used. There are arrangements being made about this. I hope you will be over here shortly.

Yours always
JAMES STEPHENS

To W. B. YEATS

Eversleigh
[A/1] 26 July 1935

[Stephens's "The Fifteen Acres" was published as a Cuala Press *Broadside* in August 1935. The "Irish Academy Anthology" was never published. Yeats's *Collected Plays* appeared in 1934; Stephens was probably referring to works such as *The Resurrection* (1931). The "Mandookya Upanishad with an Introduction by William Butler Yeats" was published in *The Criterion* for July 1935. The book which Yeats borrowed from Stephens was probably *The Mândûkyopanishad, with Gaudapâdas Kârikâs and the Bhâshya of S'ankara* (1894).]

Dear Yeats:

I hope you got my letter giving permission to use the Fifteen Acres, & any other dozen of my verses that you wish. I couldnt give the tune, as it is already contracted for to a gramaphone & music company.

But this letter is on another matter. Colin Summerford tells me that Methuen wants to put the Irish Academy Anthology into proof, & that they hope Shaw will write a preface to the book. They want to send proofs to Shaw. You will remember that the matter required from each author is very short, about 1500 words in prose, or a few pages of verse. Choose as you please. By the way, I should like to say something about your later little plays. They are as astonishing as your later verse. There is nothing like them in English. Tis a new art. You are the first man to write "pure" drama, using that word as in pure poetry, or pure music: and I hope that you will write huge lots of it.

I saw an essay by you today in a quarterly on the Manduka Upanishad. I think I lent that to you years ago. Tis a wonderful Upanishad. My copy had the Guadapada and Shankara commentaries. It is strange to think that an Upanishad can be enriched – but these enrich that. I am stricken about AE – I didnt see him often enough. All greetings to Mrs Yeats

Yours always.
JAMES STEPHENS

To HAMLIN GARLAND

[Cincinnati?]
[A/31] [September–November 1935]

[Stephens went to America in September 1935 for another lecture tour, the only one which included California. Stephens met with the American writer Hamlin Garland (1860–1940) in Los Angeles on 16 November 1935.]

My dear Mr Hamlin Garland:

I was delighted to hear from you. Of course, I have read, most appreciatively your books, & know of you very well. Many thanks for your kind invitation to meet you. That must be for a date to be settled later on. At present, as you will easily understand, I am the slave of a Manager; and act & move, as it were, without volition. Believe me, dear Mr Hamlin Garland, to be

Yours very sincerely
JAMES STEPHENS

To S. S. KOTELIANSKY

[A/6]

Syracuse, N.Y.
5 December 1935

Dear Kot.

This is but a note to say that the end of my adventurings is nigh. I take ship (the Acquitania) on the 12 or 14th & shall be about Picadilly three days before Christmas. All my thanks for the papers you sent. It is bitterly cold up here, & will be 40 below zero in Maine when I get there. Moving about the way I am now (17,000 miles in six weeks) there is nothing to write about; just places & they are all the same place, & people who are always the same people: and lectures by me, which are always the same lectures: and trains, & trains, & trains, & now snow, & snow, & snow. All love to you.

Mise
["I am"]
JAMES STEPHENS

To RUTH PITTER

[T/1]

Eversleigh
April [1936]

[Stephens wrote the Preface to Pitter's *A Trophy of Arms: Poems 1926–1935* (1936).]

Dear Miss Pitter.

I brought the preface in to you some days ago, but, when near your district, I grew dissatisfied, and brought it home again, and wrote it again; and it does seem to me that I could keep on rewriting it for the next few years. You may not care for it as a preface, and you have my fullest permission not to use it if it dissatisfies you.

I have not criticised any of your poems, as perhaps I should have done, but have taken your talent as in the lump, and this preface is the result of taking it that way.

Yours very truly,
JAMES STEPHENS

To S. S. KOTELIANSKY

Paris

[A/6] [12 June 1936]

[Ridgeway's in London was the site of a regular Wednesday meeting of a group of literary people, including among others Stephens, Koteliansky, Hodgson, Turner, Sullivan and Murry. Stephens and Koteliansky also had a standing arrangement to have supper at Pagani's Restaurant on Wednesday nights. "Tib's Eve" is an Anglo-Irish expression meaning "never". Joyce went to Copenhagen instead of London in August 1936.]

Dear Kot:

I am returning the Ruth Pitter Preface. Will you handle the proof, & not send it any more to me, for I could go on writing it until Tib's Eve & the morning of the pealing of the last trump. We expect to be home on Tuesday, &, so, will meet on Wednesday at Ridgeways. We dined last night with James & Mrs Joyce. They may be coming to London in a while. I should like you to meet them. In case we dont return until Wednesday, then I'll see you at Pagani's about 7 o'c. All love to you.

Mise
["I am"]
JAMES STEPHENS

To JAMES JOYCE

Paris

[A/35] 20 September 1936

[On 18 September 1936, Joyce delivered to Stephens's flat a copy of *Little Eyolf* (1894) by the Norwegian playwright Henrik Ibsen (1828–1906); he wrote Stephens that "if you read it you should not interrupt any act of it". The other Ibsen plays which Stephens mentions are *The Wild Duck* (1885) and *The Master Builder* (1892).]

My dear Joyce –

There are two things about you which are unchangeable: you are the most subtil man, and the most continuously kind male creature I have ever known. All that merely apropos des bottes [*à propos de bottes*, "by the way"]. I got the Ibsen book you left with my concierge – To think of you, with your poor sight, navigating the wildernesses of Paris merely to give me a book, scandalises me, and makes me proud. I send you my love in return, but that is so easy to send by a postman that it is not worth signing a receipt for at the other end.

I take it that you sent me this book because of the remarks I made to you upon Ibsen. I will agree, with any man who cares to be agreed with, that Ibsen is a more than competent stage-manager. If a character of his sneezes in the first-act he will have a cold in the second-act, and will die of pneumonia in the third. My criticism (fault-finding) goes deeper than his handling of a selected matter in a first, a second and a third act. It is this: that of all those who have come to (deserved) eminence in drama, or, generally, in literature Ibsen is the most thorough-going liar, or falsifyer of the truth, that ever attained such eminence. His idealist in (was it?) the Wild Duck was no idealist, He was a mere, uncomplicated, commonplace swindler. His Master-Builder man was, similarly, an ordinary, and exceedingly-mere ass.

Now I have read, at your behest, his Little Eyolf – and, again, I take off all my hats to that exceedingly skilful presentation, and withdraw every demi-semi-quaver of my soul from his tale, and the truth of it.

The catastrophe he so cogently engineers is everywhere unmerited: has not, by a single one of his characters, been worked for, or earned, or deserved. The man is a pestilent dramatist, and all his works are framed with the desire to make those pay who do not owe, and to make those suffer who have not merited it. If ever there was in literature a sadist such an one was Ibsen, and that anyone could ever have been taken in by him, critically or morally, remains for me as an inexplicable enigma. This play is, for me, an effect without a cause – which is ridiculous: and equally ill-founded, and as equally ridiculous are all his other triumphs. To hell with that dark man of the black north, for that is where he came from, and his literature is as nigh to hellish as the complete–bourgeois can possibly manage.

Mise agat-sa, do c[h]ara go deó [*deo*]
["I am your own, your friend forever"]
JAMES STEPHENS

To S.S. KOTELIANSKY

[A/6]

Paris
23 September 1936

[Koteliansky had recently been in hospital. Stephens's dinner with Joyce was apparently on 17 September 1936.]

My dear Kot:

This is merely a note, to say, first, that I have nothing to say, & to say, second, that when one has nothing to say, or to do, one can still have something to hope: therefore, I hope you are 99¾% better than you were two weeks ago. We may be here for another week: so, if you find time – No: dont write, for we may be back within the week, & I'll then give you a ring. From this part of the world there is no news. The newspapers are, even designedly, dull: they tell, in a lower tone, all that the Daily Mail, et all, squawks. But this city is unhappy, & is waiting for the problematicalist morrow. Personally, I think, in every despite, that the world-weather is "set fair", & that if we can merely weather the next two years we shall have weathered a whole lot of weather. Of my own self I have nothing to say. A sense of "interim" is so pronounced within me, and without, that almost I dont exist, or am merely a semi-suspended animation. Three nights ago we dined with Joyce at the other (the wrong) side of the city.

There is a man who is almost happy! He bothers, that is, if he bothers at all, about his own botherations, and, in so far as I can see it, he doesnt bother one smallest part of a demi-damn about the world and its waggings. But he is nice – which, perhaps, is no great virtue, but is assuredly nowhat whatever of a vice. We argued, & quarreled, and made up on a Reissling wine, all about Ibsen – Joyce and Kot are of an equal weakness there, for Kot and Joyce do both applaud that one who is deplored by this one. Next day Joyce left in at my taudis ["hovel"] an Ibsen book "Little Eyolf &c", & I have just replied to him that, on the strength of this alone (buttressed by all his other works) Ibsen is the only example of the literary sadist that western literature has known. As you see, I am writing you about nothing, having nothing to write about. Joyces opinion, & mine, & yours, about Ibsen! If that isnt the very inner non-being, & non-guts of nothing believe me mistaken even in science & mathematics, which twain, knowing nothing of I cant be mistaken in. My Hebrew also cannot be attacked, but my Irish is bad.

JAMES STEPHENS

To OLIVER ST. JOHN GOGARTY

Eversleigh
[A/8] 25 December 1936

[*The Oxford Book of Modern Verse*, edited by W. B. Yeats, was published on 19 November 1936. Yeats included seventeen poems by Gogarty and called him "one of the great lyric poets of our age".]

Dear Oliver.

I have only today got Yeats' Anthology, & read his preface. I am writing to you because of our long friendship, & because it is good to say, right out, what one wishes to say. I think that, after Yeats himself, you are the best poet of our land: and that, outside of our land, & in the English-speaking mode, you are the sole example of the classical poet writing anywhere today. It may be that, perhaps, you will not be praised as you should be until about fifty years after you are dead: but I will write now to you, secretly as it were, for every letter is a secret, to assert, all in your own ear, that no poet whatever writing at this moment is so good as Oliver St John Gogerty

This all is rather out of the blue:
Take it as meant, as friendly, as true,
Good poet! tis good to do hommage to you.

Mise["I am"], your own friend
JAMES STEPHENS

To S.S. KOTELIANSKY

Eversleigh
[A/6] [5 June 1937]

[Koteliansky sent Stephens a copy of *Encounter in April* (1937) by the American writer May Sarton (1912–). There are fifteen sonnets in the book; the first is "Love, fall as lightly on his lids as sleep". Sarton included a verse "Letter to James Stephens" in *Inner Landscape*, published in 1939 by the Cresset Press.]

Dear Kot.

I'm sending back Miss Sarton's book. I ran right through it in one reading. It is all good, &, at times, more than that. In especial I liked "On the Atlantic". The Trees. Evening Landscape. Portrait of the Artist. Portr of Three Women. Slight Death. Song for Drought, which I liked better than anything else. To the Weary, also, is lovely. So for Keats & Mozart. The first sonnet in especial, but all the sonnets. I expect on further reading I might like others more, but for an impression there is my just & mere impression. Tis a good book by a good writer.

Mise agat-sa
["I am your own"]
JAMES STEPHENS
to Kot

To ROBERT FLEMING RATTRAY

Eversleigh
[A/12] 2 September 1937

[Rattray, now Minister of the Memorial Church (Unitarian) in Cambridge, was arranging for individual lectures under the Hibbert Trust, to be preceded by a talk at the church. Stephens gave his lectures on 24 and 25 October 1937. Stephens had probably recently returned from Paris; I have not traced his lecturing at University College, Leicester.]

Dear Mr Rattray.

I have been away for a little time. I remember very well the pleasant time I had when I lectured at the University College. I wonder could you let me know – are there any newspaper or other reports of previous lectures for the Hibbert Trust? which I could see as a guide to how other speakers handled their matter. Mainly, my kind of talk is on poetry, or literature in general. If you could let me know as to this I would reply at once

Yours very truly
JAMES STEPHENS

To FREDERICK CHARLES OWLETT

Eversleigh
[A/35] 16 September 1937

[The English critic Frederick Charles Owlett sent Stephens a copy of his *The Spacious Days and Other Essays* (1937). The first essay is entitled "The Spacious Days".]

Dear Mr Owlett.

Many thanks for your book "Spacious Days" [–] I read it all as between last night & this morning. You have certainly a most gallant prose of your own. It is a pleasure, these days, to read matter that is not dispirited. All these essays are very good, but I doubt if anyone can beat your opening essay for high spirits and "spaciousness.["] I wish you all good luck in your (hinted at) coming visit to the States.

Yours very truly
JAMES STEPHENS

To ROBERT FLEMING RATTRAY

Eversleigh
[A/12] 21 September 1937

[Rattray had sent Stephens reports of the Hibbert Lectures.]

Dear Mr Rattray:

I return the newspaper reports you so kindly lent me. They were quite helpful. I think the titles of my talk might be, one, as you suggested, "Religion and Poetry" & the other "Pure Values".

Yours very truly
JAMES STEPHENS

To RUTH PITTER

Eversleigh
[A/1] [10 or 17 October 1937]

[Pitter sent Stephens a copy of Nora Kennedy MacCausland's *The Legendary Shore* (1937).]

Dear Ruth Pitter.

Many thanks for sending me the McCausland book. You are certainly right, & it is treasure. It's rarely that we come on anything so good, so lovely. The two poems you praised are very good, but there are ten others that enough couldnt be said of. Salutations, & thanks

Mise
["I am"]
JAMES STEPHENS

To LORD DUNSANY

Eversleigh
[A/3] 6 November 1937

[The production by the Habima Players of *The Dybbuk* (1920) by the Yiddish writer "S. Ansky", the pen name of Shloyme Zaynvl Rappaport (1863–1920), opened at the Savoy Theatre on 15 November 1937. *The Dybbuk* had previously been produced at the Royalty Theatre on 4 April 1927.]

Dear Dunsany:

It was delightful meeting you both again, & when I come back from Paris, at the end of the week, I give your house a ring. This note is to say that the Habima Players will be in London, & on the 15th they will be playing The Dybbuk. If you havent seen this play it might interest you. When I saw it a few years ago I thought it one of the most remarkable pieces of dramatic work that had ever come my way.

Yours very truly
JAMES STEPHENS

To W. K. MAGEE

Paris
[A/1] 9 November 1937

[Stephens's lecture in Cambridge was not a Hibbert Lecture but the one arranged by Robert Fleming Rattray. Cyril Clemens (1902–), a kinsman of Mark Twain, founded the Mark Twain Association; on 26 September 1936, Clemens wrote Stephens and offered him the Mark Twain Medal for *Irish Fairy Tales.* Not receiving an answer, Clemens tried to contact Stephens through Magee.]

My dear Magee:

I was delighted to get your letter, but only because it was from you. Also it has only now come to me. I had been in Cambridge giving the (or *a*) Hibbert lecture, & had stayed there a week. Lovely place, & lovely people, & lovely the lecture I gave: & then I beat it here where business (my wife's) called. Now about that person who writes presenting unwished & uncalled for, & unworked for medals. He has written me a dozen times, about I could never make out what, & I have honourably never replied to him, and I intend to rest in that state of grace. I deserve many medals, each as big as a barn door, & each composed of massy ore enriched with diamonds: but – so metaphysical am I! – I also want to know who has the right to give 'em, & what I am getting them for. I should love to see you whenever you are in town. Alas! And Alas! And Alas! Our Mackenna, our AE!

Yours always
JAMES STEPHENS

28 Queen's-walk. London N.W.9 [–] *where I return in a week*

To DANIEL MACMILLAN (Macmillan & Company, London)

Eversleigh
[A/23] 5 September 1938

[Stephens enclosed the manuscript for *Kings and the Moon*, his last book, published in November 1938.]

Dear Mr Macmillan.

Here, at last, are the poems. I hope you will be pleased with them. It is curious the enormity of work they took, but I don't believe I can better one line more. I have sent the ms on to America.

Yours very truly
JAMES STEPHENS

P.S. Perhaps I should bring to your notice the poem on page 26 "Flowers of the Forest"[.] It is, in a way, political.

To GEORGE PLATT BRETT (Macmillan Company, New York)

Eversleigh
[A/28] 5 September 1938

Dear Mr Brett.

Here is the book of verse which I have promised you for so long. I found it very difficult to let go of them: there was always a word to add, & another word to query. But, as it now stands, tis finished. I hope we shall sell a million copies of it the first week, and thereafter in reasonable proportion.

Yours very truly
JAMES STEPHENS

To SIR WILLIAM ROTHENSTEIN

[A/15] Eversleigh
17 October 1938

[In *Since Fifty: Men and Memories, 1922–1938* (1939), William Rothenstein identifies the book he had commented on as *Deirdre* (though *Etched in Moonlight* seems more likely). Stephens's edition of the *Mahabharata* in twelve volumes was translated by Pratap Chandra Roy and published from 1883 to 1896. The "Twins" are Nakula and Sahadeva.]

My dear Rothenstein.

Your letter from the blue bucked me up. Tis a good book, but that is the first time since it was published that anyone said so. Twas stillborn of the war. I'm in the mid-sea of the vast Mahabharata, on my 9th volume, with three more to go. There is a book to thank the Dragons for! All the names, ten thousand, Bhishma, Drona, Yudhishthira, & the Twins, are of my household. I've some niceish poems coming out soon. All good wishes to you, & to you all.

Mise
["I am"]
JAMES STEPHENS

To LORD DUNSANY

[A/3] Eversleigh
[24 November 1938]

[Dunsany sent Stephens a copy of *Mirage Water* (1938). The poems which Stephens mentions are "On the Death of a Mohammedan Friend", "Geography", "To a Spirit Seen in a Dream", "To a lost Spirit", "To a Dog Dreaming", "The Banker and the Broker", "The Debate", "On the Safe Side", "Vox Populi", "The Path", "The Faithful" and "The Lost Poet" (the second poem on AE).]

Dear Dunsany.

Just a note to see which are the poems I prefer on a first reading

"May you go safe, my friend["]
Geography p. 10
And so dishonest Ghost, and If Dogma errs

Both pages 14 & 15
The Debate
On the Safe Side & Vox Pop.
The Path (24) I liked very much, & every line of it [–] So did I with Faithful.

I'll leave the others for another letter (as I've got to go out) & merely say that your second poem to AE is quite one of the loveliest things that has ever been writ for a friend.

Yours always
JAMES STEPHENS

1939 - 1946

James Stephens has read the *Tain* in the light of the *Veda* but the time is against him and he is silent.

W. B. Yeats, *Pages from a Diary Written in Nineteen Hundred and Thirty* (1944)

The state of depression which characterized Stephens's third period was only deepened during the last twelve years of his life. His literary activity in these years consisted basically of an introduction and some scattered reviews; he also worked at the autobiography which he had contracted for in 1938 but published only a small section of it as "A Rhinoceros, Some Ladies, and a Horse". However, in the face of his adversity (not the least of which was ill-health) Stephens in fact did begin a new career; if lecturing in America had been his second career, broadcasting on the B.B.C. became his third. Between 1937 and 1950 Stephens gave over seventy B.B.C. broadcasts, on topics ranging from reminiscences of his old friends to evaluations of particular poets. As with his lecturing, he is remembered as being excellent in this art.

In 1940 Stephens moved to Woodside Chapel in Gloucestershire to escape the Blitz, remaining there until 1945. His closest friend during the last years of his life was S.S. Koteliansky, whom he would regularly meet in London for dinner. Late in 1947 Stephens was awarded an honorary D.Litt. degree by Dublin University (Trinity College).

On 11 June 1950 Stephens gave his final broacast – "Childhood Days" – on the B.B.C. He died at his home in London on St. Stephen's Day in 1950.

To THE EDITOR OF THE *SPECTATOR*

[London]
23 June 1939

[The text is from the *Spectator* for 23 June 1939. Stephens is responding to a discussion of the differences between northern and southern temperaments by the English writer Harold George Nicolson (1886–1968) in the "People and Things" column of the *Spectator* for 9 June 1939. Stephens's remarks parallel those in his "Dublin Letter" in *The Dial* for April 1925. Nicolson did not comment on this letter.]

NORTH AND SOUTH

Sir, –

I was very interested reading Mr. Nicolson's note on the curious northnesses and southnesses which have evolved in every land, for this reason. Some years ago, lecturing in America, I spoke of this strange social climate which reproduces a geography that never was on sea or land. I held that in every country there is a hard-headed, businesslike north; and, in balance, an easy-going, artistic south. That the east of a country is socially, and even physically, a simplified prolongation of the north, and the west is always as southern as it can manage to be. I also held that no nation is stable until it has evolved these natural temperamental poles. (I foolishly thought that I was the only person who had spotted this oddity.) I continued, that every country I knew of had established itself upon a north and south line, with one exception, that the United States of America had departed, geographically and temperamentally, from the world-rule, and was organising itself along an eastern and western axis; and that, consequently, the U.S.A. citizen must, in time, be psychically different from every other human being; and be, indeed, foreign, and perhaps even incredible, to all the world. I hope Mr. Nicolson will comment on this addition to his riddle.

– Yours faithfully,
JAMES STEPHENS'

To THE EDITOR OF *THE TIMES* (London)

Eversleigh
19 June 1940

[The text is from *The Times* (London) for 19 June 1940.]

Sir –

There is, after all, something in loving God and the neighbour as yourself. These three are all the loving, all the living, we can ever know: and, if it comes to that, are all that is worth dying for also. In these searching days little care need be taken of what any Irishman thinks. One Irishman wishes to elect himself an Englishman for the duration: and, in our vernacular, he wishes to God that he could be of some use. Other Irish people will, of course, do as they can as long as they can, and will then do as they must.

I am, Sir, your obedient servant,
JAMES STEPHENS

To S.S. KOTELIANSKY

[A/6]

Woodside Chapel
25 October 1940

[Stephens had just moved into a vacant chapel at Tunley, a small village near Sapperton and Cirencester in Gloucestershire. The B.B.C. broadcast which Stephens was working on was probably "Books and People", transmitted on 8 November 1940.]

Dear Kot.

Apologies to you for not having written, but I am about six miles from a town, and the getting of a bottle of ink was a whole job. I am living in a disused Chapel, which has nothing whatever in it, except a fire-place, & we live like the people of the primitive and the prime. One goes out every day to draw water, and to pick up sticks for the fireplace, but I dont doubt that we shall be the chilliest people of earth when the winter comes. Already this place, it is on the topmost reach of the Cotswolds, is as cold as winter does be in London, & will be colder. I was in town about ten days ago, went up with Rothenstein, got there at 12.30, rehearsed at the B.B.C. till one, had lunch, returned B.B.C. at 2, spoke at 2.30[,] had to meet R'stein at 3, & catch, with him, the 4.30 for Stroud, & drive back here. So I was unable to see you, or even try to. I'm going up again shortly to speak but dont know when; and doubt that I'll be able to get in touch with you during the, perhaps, half hour that I'll have free. Bombs fall here every night, same as elsewhere, & it seems that we protect the Port of Bristol. I havent seen one newspaper since I left London, but we've a small portable wireless thing which gives the exact same news every time we turn it on. All love to you, my dear, send me an occasional letter.

Yours
JAMES STEPHENS

Damn it – I miss our talks!

To E.R. EDDISON

[A/4]

Woodside Chapel
18 November 1940

[The English writer Eric Rucker Eddison (1882–1945) wrote Stephens on 26 October 1940 and asked him to do an introduction to *A Fish Dinner in Memison* (1941). Stephens had previously written an introduction to the 1926 New York edition of Eddison's *The Worm Ouroboros* (1924).]

My dear Eddison.

I am so pleased, & so desolated. Desolated because your letter went to Macmillans, & thence to my London address, & stayed there. I being then addressable as above. Tis only by the chance of our going up to London to B.B.C. that I got the letter. As to my being pleased – I'm pleased because I'm honoured. If you can forgive a delay that I could never be part[n]er in where you are concerned will you have the script sent me, and I'll do the best that remains to me, for I'm beginning to suspect that I'm not as good as I used to be. But I shall love to read you. We were practically bombed out of our district a few days before you wrote – hence the miserable delay. Believe me always your admiring

JAMES STEPHENS

To E.R. EDDISON

Woodside Chapel
[A/4] 14 December 1940

My dear Eddison.

I enclose my chattering on your book. I think you will recognize that a work like this Fish Dinner just cant be written about by anybody else than its writer. For myself, I should need a full month of scratching out and scratching in to "do" merely a review of it. I beg you will be friendly – That is, if there is anything that you (your publisher rather) care for in my writing let it go at that, but if there is anything which you, personally, dont care for please delete it. My only wish in the matter is to know that the greatly strange book gets to easy publication, be it only that you will then feel free to get on with your next. It is a blessing in these days to read something that has been written by a man.

Yours (meaning what I say about "delete")
very truly,
JAMES STEPHENS

I sometimes think that no one is worthy except the writer of it to read a book.

To S.S. KOTELIANSKY

Woodside Chapel
[A/6] 15 December 1940

[Angus Morrison (1902–) is an English pianist. Stephens did not publish in the *Sunday Times* (London) again until a 1946 review. "D" probably refers to Dilys Powell. The preface was that to Eddison's *A Fish Dinner in Memison.*]

Dear Kot.

The postman came this morning with your parcel. What a mighty lot of cigarettes! I smoked ten of them one right after the other; and, as God looking on the world thought it good – the only silly thought He ever had – so, smoking them, I knew them good. Cigarettes get more & more difficult to get, even Woodbines; so you may guess how astonished I was to see your hundred thousand. I'll try to make them last a long time. A very nice chap, named Angus Morrison, owns this Chapel. He is a musician, plays a lot on B.B.C. programmes (piano) [–] He & his lady called in the other night to see us (from Bristol) [–] Do you know him at all? I havent seen a Sunday paper, or a weekly, since I left London. The only daily is the Daily Mail, & it doesnt always get here. I'll be glad to Sunday-Times-write if they want me to. Morrison told me that the B.B.C. had been badly bombed again. There are always bombs about these parts, but the parts are so wide, and hilly and valley that one doesnt mind them. I wish we were back in London. I wish we had never left it. I wish I was getting the every night bombing that London, and you, is getting. I wish I could see you every Wednesday. I wish I could see you every day of the week. I wish that U and I, and D, and whatever other alphebeticals you would elect for, could be meeting together once a week, and lunching together once a day, and dining together every night; and that, thereon, we all went to bed together. How delicious t'would be, then, for us all to breakfast together: and, thereon, to start getting ready to lunch, and dine, and bed and board with ourselves, and with none others whatever. As far as the world is concerned I am indifferent – but, I like my loves! From these parts there is no news, nor ever will be – There is nothing whatever here except Cotswolds, and the almost nightly bombing of them. But there are imperceptably (I saw them) squirrels in the trees, looking for nuts that dont exist: and foxes in the hinterlands looking for hens that are triply wired in. God blast the Allemands; but God help the squirrels, and the foxes, & the strayed cats, & the good, brave, diligent, hungry, masterless dogs – And the crows that look for something where nothing is, and U, and I, and D, who have only got a bit, where we, perhaps, hoped for a piece. I have just finished, and sent off to him, (you dont know him) a preface, or prefatory writing to his new book. If the book ever comes out I'll direct him send it to you. Other than that I am merely a lost soul, wishing to die, or to be back in London. Give my love to our loves! But what is that? Philosophically, and annualy, I begin to be querlous about wisdom and love, and to be interested only in whoso I like; and in the craft of verse. You wont read this.

Always, my dear,
JAMES STEPHENS

To E.R. EDDISON

Woodside Chapel

[A/4] 1 January 194[1]

[Lord Morville is a character in *A Fish Dinner in Memison*. The "Morville note" refers to a passage in an early draft of Stephens's introduction. Stephens wrote that "he does not see how Lord Morville deserved this blame, these cuckoldings, this 'unpaunching' which are measured immeasurably to him by Fiorinda and Mr Eddison. Whoever is responsible for this, be it even the Queen of Heaven, she acted like a bad barmaid worthy of being sacked from the Old Bull and Bush, or, if she casts the blame on Mr Eddison, let him reply to the dreadful accusation as best he may – One reader is outraged!" The passage was not retained in the published version.

Eddison's *Mistress of Mistresses: A Vision of Zimiamvia* was published in 1935. The quotation is from Shakespeare's *Two Gentlemen of Verona*, IV. ii. 44–5.]

My dear Eddison:

Thanks for your letter, & for copy of the Introductory stuff.

I think that it is now not so bad. The small, wise, alterations do pull it together, and it reads as writ with a flowing hand that was writ as with a wooden leg. Your remarks are all just. There should not be anything within a book that even resembles criticism of it – That truly would be to poison life at the source. Criticism anyhow is the job of the blasted reviewers.* (N.B. I really put in the Morville note as a bait and tantalization to the possible reader – That good person who died twenty years before we were born – but I did recognize that it was unplaced) [–] As to your friend's curiosity anent my thought about your treatment of your women [–] Well – There is the Mistress of Mistresses *and* The Mother of Life. When one of these is in residence the other is in the Poor House. Perhaps either of them is left out at some peril. I wonder, instead, how you stand about your ladies yourself!

> "Is she kind, as she is fair?
> For beauty lives with kindness!"

I think there is a devil as big as a duck in all your dames. But, God help us, they are very attractive.

Yours always –
JAMES STEPHENS

*I couldnt criticize a book of yours except in a whole book
A Happy New Year to You.

To S.S.KOTELIANSKY

Woodside Chapel
16 March 1941

[A/6]

[*Twenty-three Tales* of Tolstoy, translated by Louise and Aylmer Maude, was published in 1936.]

Dear Kot.

Just a line, and an enquiry. Do you remember telling me, some time ago, that you had been rereading Tolstoi; & that some particular short story of his, which you had already read twenty times, had quite suddenly revealed itself to you, so that you saw a new story, & a new Tolstoi, & a new Kot. Well I've just got a book "*Twenty Three Stories*["], by Tol. published Oxford Un. Press. trans Louise & Aylmer Maud. I think you said (or imagine) that your story was in such a Collection. Could you tell me its name again. I've read a few of these – How good he is! And how he makes our story-writers seem mean & unfortunate! All love to you from

Yours always
JAMES STEPHENS

To E.R. EDDISON

[A/4]

Woodside Chapel
31 March 1941

[Eddison wrote that E.P. Dutton & Co. would pay Stephens $50 for his introduction to *A Fish Dinner in Memison. Du côté de chez Swann* (1913) is the first volume of *À la recherche du temps perdu* (1913–27) by the French novelist Marcel Proust (1871–1922). The volumes which Stephens did not complete were *Sodome et Gomorrhe* (1921–3) and *Le Temps retrouvé* (1927).]

My dear Eddison.

Your letter surprised me. Imagine anyone in this world paying money that wasnt asked for, or expected, or even dreamt of! What an imaginative and original publisher you have! I'll bet he goes to heaven when he dies, and thats something else that no publisher ever did. So you are going after Proust. There isnt any doubt at all that, so far as we moderns are concerned, he is the top of all our writings. What patience the man had, and his reader has to have as much! The greatest modern vice is reading too quickly: I expect that writing too quickly is conditioned by it, and I think that, barring half a dozen good pen men, writers are just spewing books out of themselves instead of planting and sowing and reaping 'em as should be. Some of Proust (much) is astonishingly painful. The first volume, Chez Swann, is surely the most dreadful recreation of physical jealousy that ever came from a pen. I read all of him some years back (except the last two volumes which I kept on keeping by me for a rainy day, or an illness.[)] I wonder shall I ever get to those two, & will you? Someone told me they are the best of the lot. All good to you

JAMES STEPHENS

To E.R. EDDISON

[A/4]

Woodside Chapel
8 April 1941

[Stephens's son-in-law was Norman Wise (1907–), who married Iris Stephens in 1937. The English translation of *Marcel Proust: sa vie, son oeuvre* (1925) by the French critic Léon Pierre-Quint (1895–) was published in 1927. *À la recherche du temps perdu* was translated by the Scottish translator C. K. Scott Moncrieff (1889–1930) and the English novelist Stephen Hudson (1869?–1944) between 1922 and 1931.]

My dear Eddison.

I was up in London yesterday, poking about among my books, and I found two Proust'ish books, which remembering you, I asked my son in law to post away to your Dark Lane – What a lovely address yours is! But I think my "Chapel" which truly is a chapel, beats you. I've met an ancient who preached in it, & an antique who played its harmonium – Anyhow, returning here I got your letter, and write to hope that the book and bookeen do get to you; for while one can trust a son-in-law to marry your daughter we cant trust him to go to the post with a packet. The critic chap of one of the books, Paul Louis (?) Quint, is very well worth reading, if my memory of some fifteen years back is reliable. I think you are right in reading the Proust in English. The Moncrieff translation is excellent, and, in French, the Proustian prose is often as rebutting as prose can manage to be. I've seen a sentence of his run over three pages, & at the end of some of these I was as befogged & bedevilled as though I had swam through soup & sulphur. This is only to acknowledge yours, & to hope that mine reaches you.

Yours
JAMES STEPHENS

A chap I dont know has, by the same post, written me that he has translated one thousand eight hundred French poems into English, & will I read them? Do you get oddities like that addressed at you?

To E.R. EDDISON

Woodside Chapel
[A/4] 1 August 1941

[The review of *A Fish Dinner in Memison* by Henry A. Lappin, an English professor at D'Yourville College for Women in Buffalo, was published in the *Buffalo Evening News* for 17 May 1941; the review by the English critic Richard Ellis Roberts (1879–1953) was published in the *Saturday Review of Literature* (New York) for 7 June 1941. Stephens had contracted with Macmillan for his unpublished autobiography in 1938.]

Dear Eddison.

I am an abominable person about letters, & have been also a good deal away, in London. By the way I was there two days ago, B.B.Cing, & brought back your Mistress of Mistresses (I have only a few of my books in these wilds) [–] Yes I got the Fish Dinner, & lovely it looks, & the notice that Lappen wrote. Tis a good lad, & I hope he writes more. I met him in Dublin years ago, & then I stayed several times in his house when I was lecturing at his College away up at Niagara Falls. I return the Ellis Roberts notice. It is very good, and tis evident that he likes this book, & your books in general. I got also the Proust books. I made an almost vow that I would finish the reading of that vast work. I halted somewhere in Sodom & Gomorrah. I suppose it is the greatest prose lump of our time. But some old how I cant get down to real reading, or real writing for that matter, in these dull days. I write only those fifteen minute jaw-scraps for broadcasting, & there is no health in them. It is a new Journalism, & I think one airs oneself at some peril. My publishers keep on asking me for a contracted-for, &, long ago, half-paid-for autobiography-thing, which I cant write.

O Lord! I wish I had some mon,
And then I'd only write for fun

Do you know, when one comes to years of discretion, after fifty, one hasnt got an autobiography any more. Only memories, all erroneous, and all no good.

All good luck to you, anyway.
JAMES STEPHENS

To S.S. KOTELIANSKY

[A/6]

Woodside Chapel
[26] August 1941

[Stephens had just bought a copy of Koteliansky's edition of *Russian Short Stories* (1941). "Captain Ribnikov" and "The River of Life" are by Aleksandr Ivanovich Kurpin (1870–1938); "The Gentleman from San Francisco" is by Ivan Alekseyevich Bunin (1870–1953). Stephens had probably read the Bunin story in either the 1922 or the 1934 edition of *The Gentleman from San Francisco and Other Stories*, translated by Koteliansky, D.H. Lawrence and the English critic Leonard Woolf (1880–1969). Sir Julian Sorrell Huxley (1887–) is an English biologist and writer.]

Dear Kot.

I got your letter, and have now, 12 o'c of tonight, read the first story, Ribnikov. Its very good. I'll start the River of Life tomorrow. I read the Gentleman from San Francisco years ago, but fancy that it may have been someone else's transl^{n}, so I'll read it again in yours. When I was in town B.B.C'ing there was never an opportunity of getting in touch with you. I'd get in at one o'c. Begin rehearsals at 2. Keep at it till six. have a drink. Rehearse again at 7. o'c. Give the stuff at 8. o'c. Get away at 8.30. Get some food. Get home before Blackout at 9.30 or 10. & be away next morning by the 10. o'c train. And I couldnt tell you I was coming, for I never knew if the 1 o'c train got in at 1 or at half 2. And there was always the devil in it, and the devil of a fag in it too. Those 3 to 4 hours of crowded travelling are tiresome, but I like to do them because I like the fee, and need it too. Down here we never see one soul in a month. We are far away in the wilds, 8 miles from a station. Every now & then we see Wm & Alice Rothenstein, & thats about all our seeings. Grub is scarce, cigarettes are even scarcer, but the countryside, (immediately outside our door, that is) is interesting, even lovely. The weather rotten. A bosche, or two, or five, groans over us every night. And life's not worth living. I cant write, & wish I never had to write again; and wish, too, that we had never left London. I carried back with me a bag full of books, mostly Buddist things. Are you keeping well? We had good talks together. Remember me to Mrs & Julian Huxley if you see them, & to who ever else remembers me.

All good to you
JAMES STEPHENS

To H.O. WHITE

[A/38]

Eversleigh
18 November 1946

[Herbet Martyn Oliver White (1885–1963) was Professor of English Literature in Dublin University (Trinity College). White wrote to tell Stephens that he had been awarded an honorary Doctor of Literature degree.]

Dear White:

It was nice to get your letter. I dont believe I'll be able to get over. I'm as sick as the devil: head & heels sick! I'd love to get over there, but, whatever the jigs are, I've got em. All my good wishes to you, & to Trinity, & to a Mulberry Tree that used to be in front of the Provost's House, or thereabouts.

Yours,
JAMES STEPHENS

To H.O. WHITE

[A/38]

Eversleigh
27 November 1946

[Despite this letter, Stephens did go to Dublin in 1947 to receive his D.Litt. degree. "King Billy" refers to a statue of William III. In the confusing final sentence, Stephens probably intended references to three Englishmen not occupying a favourable position in Irish history: Henry VIII (1491–1547), his daughter Elizabeth I (1533–1603), and Lord Arthur Grey of Wilton (1536–93), Lord Deputy of Ireland in 1580–2 and best remembered for his massacre of Spanish troops at Smerwick. Neither Lady Jane Grey (1537–54), nominal Queen of England for nine days in 1553, nor her father, Henry Grey, Duke of Suffolk (d. 1554), had any important role in Irish affairs.]

My dear White:

I got your letter – the nicest letter I think that I've ever got: and this is just to say that I shant be able to go. You may easily understand how abominable this is to me for I'd give a couple of toes just to walk down a Dublin street. I'd salute King Billy with all my hat! All because of Trinity I forgive Queen Elizabeth[,] Lady Jane Grey, & even her Papa.

Yours
JAMES STEPHENS

Appendix A: The Date of James Stephens's Birth

There are very few facts about Stephens's childhood which can be established with any certainty. Stephens was constantly reticent about that period of his life; his typical response to a request for information can be seen in the letter to Henry McBride on 27 August 1914 (pp. 140–1). Moreover, he did little to counteract the various apocryphal tales about his youth which circulated in Dublin and indeed seems to have encouraged them.

In the matter of his date of birth itself, we are faced with at least three distinct possibilities:

A. A birth, most likely illegitimate, at a time and place which Stephens himself did not know.

B. 9 February 1880 in Dublin. This suggestion was first made by Oliver St. John Gogarty in the *Dictionary of National Biography: 1941–1950* (1959); it was apparently arrived at independently by Hilary Pyle in *James Stephens: His Work and an Account of His Life* (1965). The evidence for this suggestion would seem to be the following: (1) the birth on that date of an "unnamed male child" to Francis and Charlotte Stephens of 5 Thomas Court in Dublin; (2) the fact that Stephens's age was given as six when he was entered into the Meath Protestant Industrial School for Boys in June 1886. According to Alan Denson in the *Irish Times* for 22 January 1965, p. 9, Cynthia Stephens stated that Gogarty "had evidently guessed, and his 'facts' were not proven."

C. 2 February 1882 in County Dublin. This was the time and place announced by Stephens himself. The year and place were first given in a list providing such information for ten writers which appeared in *Sinn Féin* for 11 January 1913. Although three of the other dates given are wrong, it seems only reasonable to assume that Stephens personally provided his friend Arthur Griffith, the editor of *Sinn Féin*,

> with the information on himself. (It is interesting to observe that even at this early point Stephens was vague about his birth, listing only "County Dublin" when an exact locality was given for the nine other writers.) The earliest written document stating the day of his birth known to me is his passport, issued in 1924 (probably August – see p. 316), on which he gave his birth as 2 February 1882 in Dublin. The same information appears on his resignation from the National Gallery of Ireland at the end of 1924. Although the application papers from 1915 are apparently lost, it seems obvious that Stephens must have established his birthday by then, if not before (his stepdaughter, for example, has assured me that her father's birthday was always 2 February).

In my opinion there is not enough evidence to make a firm choice among these three alternatives. I suspect that Stephens probably did not know when he was born and certainly did not care much about it: when he was married in 1919, for example, he gave his age as thirty-six when by his own reckoning he was thirty-seven (Cynthia Stephens gave her age as thirty-two when she was in fact thirty-six). This lack of interest in his birth may be paralleled by the fact that he published or acted under six different names – James Stephens, James Esse, Stephen James, Seumas James, Samuel James and Shemus Beg.

Thus, the purpose of this Appendix has been not to resolve the issue but simply to refute the suggestion that Stephens somehow changed the date of his birth so that it would coincide with the 2 February 1882 birth of James Joyce. This possibility was suggested by Gogarty and then considerably elaborated on by Pyle; it has most recently been accepted as gospel by Eavan Boland in "The Secret of James Stephens", published in the *Irish Times* for 26 January 1971, p. 8.

However, it is clear from numerous passages in these *Letters* that prior to 1927 (when their friendship developed), Stephens's evaluation of Joyce as both a writer and a person was consistently quite low (see, for instance, the letter to W.T.H. Howe on 24 April 1917, pp. 208–9). Indeed, it might be said that Stephens was harsher on Joyce than he was on any other person. And from what has been said above, it is equally clear that Stephens had established

2 February 1882 as his birthday long before he changed his mind about Joyce. Thus, the suggestion that Stephens rearranged his birthday must be categorically dismissed, and the coincidence of the Stephens/Joyce birthday must be accepted as being just that, a coincidence.

Appendix B: Printed Writings by James Stephens

This list of Stephens's published work is based on Birgit Bramsbäck's *James Stephens: A Literary and Bibliographical Study*, Upsala Irish Studies, IV (1959), supplemented by the following sources: Richard Cary's "James Stephens at Colby College", *Colby Library Quarterly* (March 1961); the Appendix in *James, Seumas and Jacques*, edited by Lloyd Frankenberg (1964); and the Bibliography in Hilary Pyle's *James Stephens: His Work and an Account of His Life* (1965). No attempt has been made to replace Bramsbäck's work in terms of bibliographical descriptions of the books, listing of reprints, translations, reviews, secondary material, and so forth.

This list includes over 130 items not cited in the above sources; in addition, numerous entries have been corrected and a few spurious items eliminated. Of the new citations, over sixty are additions to the canon, representing work published by Stephens but nowhere reprinted.

Items included in this edition from a printed source (all from Part III) are preceded by a †.

PART I: BOOKS

This list includes first editions and revised editions but not reprints. I have annotated only those items which are inadequately described in Bramsbäck. In addition, three volumes listed in Bramsbäck were not, to my knowledge, actually published.

The Lonely God and Other Poems (Bramsbäck 284) was printed by Macmillan (New York) for copyright purposes but was never published. The only copies known to me are the two which were entered at the Library of Congress on 29 October 1909. The contents of the book, with the next printing of the poems if any, are as follows:

"The Lonely God" – published in *The Open Window*, March 1911

"Astray" – published as "Little Lady" in *The Open Window*, November 1910
"In the High Court of Justice" – published as "The Last Judgment" in *Poetry Review*, June 1912
"Change"
"Who'll Carry a Message?"
"Secrets" – published in *The Hill of Vision*
"Light O' Love" – published in *The Hill of Vision*

The only source for *Dublin Letters* (Bramsbäck 318) is its listing in Will Ransom's *Private Presses and Their Books* (New York: Bowker, 1929), p. 421, as "in preparation". The book was to have been printed in an edition of 75 copies by the Slide Mountain Press in Gaylordsville, Connecticut; the contents would probably have been the "Irish Letters" and "Dublin Letters" which Stephens published in *The Dial* in 1924–5.

The Symbol Song (Bramsbäck 301) is also listed as "in preparation" in Ransom, p. 284; in addition, there are typescripts in the Yale University Library (Bramsbäck 46) and in the Stephens Papers. The book was to have been published in an edition of 1000 copies by the Fountain Press in New York. The work consists of poems on the numbers 1 to 12, to be sung to the tune of "Green Grow the Rushes, O".

The Yale typescript of *The Symbol Song* appears to have been used by a printer; and since Professor Bramsbäck has informed me that she recalls having seen a printed copy (but cannot recall where), it is possible that the work was printed. On the other hand, the typescript in the Stephens Papers has a note asking Stephens to "extend this introduction to as many words as *possible*"; the fact that this typescript is still in the Stephens Papers indicates that he failed to meet that request, thereby frustrating the planned publication.

It is, perhaps, finally impossible to demonstrate conclusively that a certain book does *not* exist. Obviously, neither *Dublin Letters* nor *The Symbol Song* is listed in any of the standard catalogues or mentioned in any of the letters I have read. Moreover, there is not a copy of either work in, for example, the British Museum, the National Library of Ireland, Trinity College Library, the Library of Congress, Colby College Library (which has the collection of Ernest A. Boyd), the New York Public Library, or the Berg Collection. This last is especially significant because it contains the library of W.T.H.

Howe, to whom Stephens customarily sent at least one inscribed copy of any new book which appeared during the time that *Dublin Letters* and *The Symbol Song* would have been published.

Insurrections. Dublin: Maunsel, 1909. New York: Macmillan, 1909.
The Charwoman's Daughter. London: Macmillan, 1912.
Identical with *Mary, Mary.* Boston: Small, Maynard, 1912.
The Hill of Vision. New York: Macmillan, 1912. Dublin: Maunsel, 1912.
The Crock of Gold. London: Macmillan, 1912. New York: Macmillan, 1913.
Before the American rights were transferred to Macmillan, at least three copies (dated 1912) were printed by Small, Maynard in Boston. There are two copies in the Library of Congress and one copy in the Berg Collection.
Here Are Ladies. London & New York: Macmillan, 1913.
Five New Poems. Flying Fame Chapbooks, Second Series. London: printed by A.T. Stevens for *Flying Fame*, 1913.
The Demi-Gods. London & New York: Macmillan, 1914.
Songs from the Clay. London & New York: Macmillan, 1915.
The Adventures of Seumas Beg/The Rocky Road to Dublin. London & New York: Macmillan, 1915.
Green Branches. Dublin & London: Maunsel, 1916. New York: Macmillan, 1916.
The Insurrection in Dublin. Dublin & London: Maunsel, 1916. New York: Macmillan, 1916.
James Esse. *Hunger: A Dublin Story.* Dublin: The Candles Press, 1918.
Reincarnations. London & New York: Macmillan, 1918.
Irish Fairy Tales. London & New York: Macmillan, 1920.
Arthur Griffith: Journalist and Statesman. Dublin: Wilson, Hartnell, [1922].
The Hill of Vision. Third Edition. London: Macmillan, 1922.
Textually a second edition, eliminating eleven poems and all but part I of "Said the Young-Young Man to the Old-Old Man" (printed as "I Wish").
Deirdre. London & New York: Macmillan, 1923.
Little Things. New York: Brick Row Book Shop, 1923.
Printed as a Christmas Card.

Little Things. Freelands, Kentucky: privately printed by W.M. Hill, 1924.

In addition to the contents listed in Bramsbäck (295, title incorrect), this volume contained "Minuette: On the Freedom of Ireland/to Eamonn de Valera".

In the Land of Youth. London & New York: Macmillan, 1924.

A Poetry Recital. New York: Macmillan, 1925.

This edition has a different order of poems from that listed in Bramsbäck (297) and does not include "His Will" or "Besides That". Cited in Part III of this list as *A Poetry Recital.*

A Poetry Recital. London: Macmillan, 1925.

Cited in Part III of this list as *A Poetry Recital* (London).

Christmas in Freelands. Freelands, Kentucky: privately printed by W.M. Hill, 1925.

Printed as a Christmas Card.

A Poetry Recital. New Edition. New York & London: Macmillan, 1926.

To the order and contents of the 1925 American edition, this edition adds a "Foreword" by Stephens and seven additional poems: "Little Things", "The Snare", "The Merry Music", "The Fifteen Acres", "The Crest Jewel", "Thy Soul" and "Christmas in Freelands". Cited in Part III of this list as *A Poetry Recital* (1926).

Collected Poems. London & New York: Macmillan, 1926.

Etched in Moonlight. London & New York: Macmillan, 1928.

On Prose and Verse. New York: Bowling Green Press, 1928.

Julia Elizabeth: A Comedy in One Act. New York: Crosby Gaige, 1929.

The Optimist. Gaylordsville, Connecticut: Slide Mountain Press, 1929.

The Outcast. London: Faber & Faber, 1929.

Theme and Variations. New York: Fountain Press, 1930.

The date of 1929 (Bramsbäck 302) is incorrect.

How St. Patrick Saves the Irish. Privately printed, 1931.

Strict Joy. London & New York: Macmillan, 1931.

Stars Do Not Make a Noise. Los Angeles: Deux Magots Press, 1931.

Consists of a photographic facsimile of an inscription in a first edition of *The Crock of Gold* and a printing of that inscription. The material in the inscription comes from the novel itself.

Kings and the Moon. London & New York: Macmillan, 1938.

Collected Poems. Second edition. London & New York: Macmillan, 1954.

James, Seumas and Jacques: Unpublished Writings by James Stephens. Edited by Lloyd Frankenberg. London & New York: Macmillan, 1964.

Consists primarily of scripts for B.B.C. broadcasts.

PART II: CONTRIBUTIONS TO BOOKS

With one exception (a review which became an introduction), this list includes only material published for the first time in book form. Reprints of published items in anthologies, yearbooks and similar works have not been listed.

Posthumous volumes have been included only when they contain at least one complete item (in each case, a letter or inscription). Complete letters not included in this edition have been indicated.

[Preface] to *The Poetical Works of Thomas MacDonagh.* Dublin: Talbot Press, 1916.

"George Russell (A.E.)", in William Rothenstein, *Twenty-Four Portraits.* London: Allen & Unwin, 1920.

"Introduction" to E.R. Eddison, *The Worm Ouroboros.* New York: Albert & Charles Boni, 1926.

First published in the *Irish Statesman* for 19 July 1924.

"Preface" to Neely McCoy, *The Tale of the Good Cat Jupie.* New York: Macmillan, 1926.

The Notable Library of Major W. Van R. Whitall. New York: American Art Association, 1927.

Inscriptions containing unique material of interest at items 1196, 1202, 1204, 1206, 1208, 1209, 1210, 1215, 1216.

"Preface" to *Edmund Spenser.* The Augustan Books of English Poetry, Second Series, No. 25, ed. Humbert Wolfe. London: Ernest Benn, [1928].

"Preface" to *Byron.* The Augustan Books of English Poetry, Second Series, No. 26, ed. Humbert Wolfe. London: Ernest Benn, [1928].

"Preface" to Roger Chauviré, *The Sword in the Soul*, trans. Ernest Boyd. London, New York & Toronto: Longmans, Green, 1929.

"Foreword" to V. V. Rozanov, *Fallen Leaves: Bundle One*, trans. S.S. Koteliansky. London: Mandrake Press, 1929.

"Introduction" to Darrell Figgis, *The Return of the Hero*. New York: Charles Boni, 1930.

Catalogue Twenty-Six: A Catalogue of Original Manuscripts, Presentation Copies, First Editions, and Autograph Letters of Modern Authors. Philadelphia & New York: The Rosenbach Company, 1933.
Inscriptions containing unique material of interest at items 227, 229, 231, 234, 239, 240, 242, 244, 247.

"The Poets and Poetry of the Nineteenth Century: An Estimate", in *English Romantic Poets*, ed. James Stephens, Edwin L. Beck and Royall H. Snow. New York: American Book Company, 1933.
Also printed in *Victorian and Later English Poets*, ed. Stephens, Beck and Snow. New York: American Book Company, 1934. This essay was Stephens's sole contribution to the anthologies.

"Preface" to Josef Kastein, *Jews in Germany*, trans. Dorothy Richardson. London: Cresset Press, [1934].

The Royal Literary Fund: Annual Reports: The Anniversary Meeting. St. Albans: by William Cartmel & Sons, 1935. Contains Stephens's speech at the Royal Literary Fund Dinner on 2 May 1935.

First Editions, Autograph Letters and Manuscripts and Original Drawings, Sale Number 4253. New York: American Art Association/Anderson Galleries, 1936.
Inscriptions containing unique material of interest at items 578 and 580; facsimile of manuscript page at item 573.

"Preface" to Ruth Pitter, *A Trophy of Arms: Poems, 1926–1935.* London: Cresset Press, [1936]; New York: Macmillan, 1936.

Authors Take Sides on the Spanish War. London: Left Review, [1937]. Stephens wrote: "I am for Spain, and hope, with all my heart, for the defeat of her rebellious military men and their Italian and Germanic abettors."

"Preface" to Fitzhugh Lee Minnigerode, *Arrows in the Twilight.* Freelands, Kentucky: privately printed, 1938.

"About Love Songs", in *The Saturday Book, 1941–42: A New Miscellany*, ed. Leonard Russell. London: Hutchinson, 1941.

"Introduction" to E.R. Eddison, *A Fish Dinner in Memison.* New York: E.P. Dutton, 1941.

Olivia Howard Dunbar, *A House in Chicago*. Chicago: University of Chicago Press, 1947.

Contains one letter and excerpts from four letters to Harriet Moody.

[C. F. McLoughlin], *Command*. Under the Mushroom at Tara: privately printed, 1948.

Contains an excerpt from a letter to Norah Hoult on 14 October 1948.

"Doffing the Bonnet", in *First Time in America*, ed. John Arlott. New York: Duell, Sloan & Pearce, 1948.

Printed in *Collected Poems* (1954).

Richard Ellmann, *James Joyce*. London & New York: Oxford University Press, 1959.

Contains a letter to Joyce on 20 September 1936. Also printed in *Letters of James Joyce*, vol. III, ed. Richard Ellmann. London: Faber & Faber, 1966; New York: Viking Press, 1966.

Birgit Bramsbäck, *James Stephens: A Literary and Bibliographical Study*. Upsala Irish Studies, IV (1959).

A 1948 inscription to C.F. McLoughlin in a copy of *Here Are Ladies* reproduced opposite p. 46; also contains summaries and brief excerpts of letters to various correspondents.

Hilary Pyle, *James Stephens: His Work and an Account of His Life*. London: Routledge & Kegan Paul, 1965; New York: Barnes & Noble, 1965.

Contains letters and excerpts from letters to various correspondents. Complete letters not included here: to Mrs. Sleith, 25 July 1906; to S.S. Koteliansky, 6 August 1932, 15 November 1934, 11 January 1937, 29 August 1941.

Letters to Macmillan, ed. Simon Nowell-Smith. London: Macmillan, 1967; New York: St. Martin's Press, 1967.

Contains two letters to Sir Frederick Macmillan.

PART III: CONTRIBUTIONS TO PERIODICALS

This section lists items first published in periodicals and indicates the first volume (if any) in which they were reprinted. The British Museum Catalogue has been followed in treating the Cuala Press *Broadsides* as a periodical publication. Periodical items which are reprints from another source (such as those in *The Living Age* or the *Literary Digest*) have not been included. Items reprinted by Stephens (see, for example, "Midnight" in *Sinn Féin* for 29 May

1909) have been listed and cross-referenced, as have been items published in both British and American periodicals without any indication of reprinting being involved.

For work published in both *Sinn Féin Daily* and *Sinn Féin*, the title used is that of the earlier publication. Generic titles such as "Eight Poems" or "Three Sketches" have not been included. Items published at the same time have been listed in alphabetical order.

Posthumous works have been cited only when they include at least one complete item (in each case, a letter or inscription). Complete letters not included in this edition have been indicated.

In most instances, items first published in a periodical and then included in a volume have undergone revision; except in a few cases, there has been no attempt to indicate the extent of this process. However, any major change in the title of a work has been cited by listing the first volume in which the new title was used.

1905

THE GREATEST MIRACLE
United Irishman, 16 September

1907

THE SEOININ
Sinn Féin, 20 April
BUILDERS
Sinn Féin, 11 May
PATRIOTISM AND PAROCHIAL POLITICS
Sinn Féin, 25 May
IRISH ENGLISHMEN
Sinn Féin, 1 June
POETRY
Sinn Féin, 22 June
NATURE AG LABHAIRT
Sinn Féin, 29 June
Printed as "Nature" in *Insurrections*
THE SONG OF OSSIAN
Sinn Féin, 3 August
MRS. MAURICE M'QUILLAN
Sinn Féin, 17 August
THE STRANGER
Sinn Féin, 7 September

TATTERED THOUGHTS
Sinn Féin, 5 October
MRS. JERRY GORMAN
Sinn Féin, 2 November
Printed as "Three Angry People: II" in *Here Are Ladies*
MISS ARABELLA HENNESSY
Sinn Féin, 21 December
Printed as "Three Women Who Wept: III" in *Here Are Ladies*

1908

MRS. LARRY TRACY
Sinn Féin, 4 January
Printed as "Three Women Who Wept: II" in *Here Are Ladies*
TO MR. GEORGE BIRMINGHAM'S "ASSES": AN EPISTLE
Sinn Féin, 4 January
THE REBEL
Sinn Féin, 18 January
Printed in *Insurrections*
ANOTHER REBEL
Sinn Féin, 1 February
OLD MRS. HANNIGAN
Sinn Féin, 29 February
Incorporated in *The Crock of Gold*, pp. 115–22
THE INSURRECTION OF '98
Sinn Féin, 21 March
SUCCESS
Sinn Féin, 28 March
MISS KATHLEEN RAFTERY
Sinn Féin, 10 October
Printed as "Three Young Wives: II" in *Here Are Ladies*
SO EARLY IN THE MORNING O
Sinn Féin, 24 October
Printed as "The Fifteen Acres " in *The Adventures of Seumas Beg*
WHERE THE DEMONS GRIN
A Broadside (Dundrum: Cuala Press), November
Printed in *Insurrections*
WINDY CORNER
Irish Homestead, December (Christmas Number)
Printed in *Insurrections*

AS AUTUMN ENDS
Sinn Féin, 19 December
Printed as "This Way to Winter" in *Songs from the Clay*
THE WATCHER
Sinn Féin, 26 December
Printed in *Insurrections*

1909

WHY TOMAS CAM WAS GRUMPY
A Broadside (Dundrum: Cuala Press), January
Printed in *The Hill of Vision*
A NOVEMBER RIDE
Sinn Féin, 9 January
Printed as "Etched in Frost" in *Songs from the Clay*
ON WASHING
Sinn Féin, 16 January
Incorporated in *The Crock of Gold*, pp. 24–6
ON GOING TO BED
Sinn Féin, 30 January
Incorporated in *The Crock of Gold*, pp. 33–5
ON SHAVING
Sinn Féin, 6 February
Incorporated in "There is a Tavern in the Town: XI" in *Here Are Ladies*
ON EATING
Sinn Féin, 13 February
Incorporated in "There is a Tavern in the Town: XII" in *Here Are Ladies*
TRANSLATIONS (SAPPHO): MIDNIGHT
Sinn Féin, 29 May; revised as "Midnight: After Sappho", *New Yorker*, 25 May 1929
Included in *Collected Poems* (1954)
TRANSLATIONS (SAPPHO): TO A RICH LADY
Sinn Féin, 29 May
Printed as "Roses of Pieria" in *Collected Poems* (1954)
TRANSLATIONS (SAPPHO): AFTERWARDS
Sinn Féin, 5 June
Printed in *The Hill of Vision*
TRANSLATIONS (SAPPHO): QUERY
Sinn Féin, 19 June
Printed as "Women Shapes" in *Songs from the Clay*

TRANSLATIONS (SAPPHO): SNOW TIME
Sinn Féin, 19 June
ON DRINKING
Sinn Féin,26 June
Incorporated in "There is a Tavern in the Town: V" in *Here Are Ladies*
TRANSLATIONS: PATIENCE AT THE LOOM
Sinn Féin, 10 July
LOVE'S MENDICANT
Sinn Féin, 17 July
Review of Susan L. Mitchell, *The Living Chalice*
THE OLD PHILOSOPHER: JAMES STEPHENS' MENTOR DISCUSSES SMOKING AND INCIDENTALLY THE BUDGET
Sinn Féin Daily, 24 August; *Sinn Féin*, 4 September
Incorporated in "There is a Tavern in the Town: III" in *Here Are Ladies*
THE OLD PHILOSOPHER: THE THOUGHTS OF ENGLISHMEN
Sinn Féin Daily, 25 August
Incorporated in "There is a Tavern in the Town: VIII" in *Here Are Ladies*
THE OLD PHILOSOPHER: CONSIDERS LEGS AND WHEELS
Sinn Féin Daily, 26 August
Incorporated in "There is a Tavern in the Town: IX" in *Here Are Ladies*
THE OLD PHILOSOPHER: TALKS OF THE ABSURDITY OF MARRIAGE
Sinn Féin Daily, 27 August
Incorporated in "There is a Tavern in the Town: I" in *Here Are Ladies*
THE OLD PHILOSOPHER: DISCOURSES ON EDUCATION
Sinn Féin Daily, 8 August; *Sinn Féin*, 18 September
Incorporated in "There is a Tavern in the Town: IV" in *Here Are Ladies*
THE OLD PHILOSOPHER: DISCOURSES ON THE VICEREGAL MICROBE
Sinn Féin Daily, 7 September; *Sinn Féin*, 11 September
THE OLD PHILOSOPHER: DISCOURSES ON THE NORTH POLE
Sinn Féin Daily, 8 September; *Sinn Féin*, 25 September
Incorporated in "There is a Tavern in the Town: X" in *Here Are Ladies*

IN THE COOL OF THE EVENING

The Nation (London), 11 September; *Sinn Féin*, 1 October 1910

Printed in *The Hill of Vision*

NOTHING AT ALL

The Nation (London), 11 September

Printed in *The Hill of Vision*

WHAT THE DEVIL SAID

The Nation (London), 11 September

Printed in *The Hill of Vision*

THE OLD PHILOSOPHER: DISCOURSES ON POLICEMEN

Sinn Féin Daily, 18 September; *Sinn Féin*, 25 September

Incorporated in *The Crock of Gold*, pp. 204–7

THE OLD PHILOSOPHER: DISCOURSES ON LANGUAGE

Sinn Féin Daily, 25 September; *Sinn Féin*, 2 October

Incorporated in "There is a Tavern in the Town: VI" in *Here Are Ladies*

THE OLD PHILOSOPHER: DISCOURSES ON GOVERNMENT

Sinn Féin Daily, 29 September

NORA CRIONA

The Nation (London), 2 October

Printed in *The Hill of Vision*

THE OLD PHILOSOPHER: DISCOURSES ON POETRY

Sinn Féin Daily, 2 October; *Sinn Féin*, 9 October

Incorporated in "There is a Tavern in the Town: VII" in *Here Are Ladies*

IMAGINATION

Sinn Féin Daily, 9 October; *Sinn Féin*, 16 October

MR. ALOYSIUS MURPHY

Sinn Féin, 23 October

Printed as "Three Lovers Who Lost: III" in *Here Are Ladies*

GRIERSON'S DISCOVERY

Sinn Féin, 6 November

Incorporated in *The Crock of Gold*, pp. 255–64

THE MAN WHO WAS AFRAID

Sinn Féin, 6 November

Incorporated in *The Crock of Gold*, pp. 245–53

MRS. BERNARD NAGLE

Sinn Féin, 13 November

Printed as "Three Young Wives: I" in *Here Are Ladies*

1910

A NEW BOOK BY SEÚMAS O'SULLIVAN
Sinn Féin Daily, 7 January; *Sinn Féin*, 15 January
Review of Seumas O'Sullivan, *The Earth-Lover and Other Verses*

FROM THE GOLDEN BOOK [I]
The Nation (London), 22 January
Printed as "Eve" in *The Hill of Vision*

MR. JOHN MONROE
Sinn Féin, 29 January
Printed as "Three Heavy Husbands: III" in *Here Are Ladies*

KING GUAIRE
Sinn Féin, 12 February

OISIN AND NIAMH
Sinn Féin, 26 February

THE GUESTS
Sinn Féin, 12 March

THE FULNESS OF TIME
The Nation (London), 19 March
Printed in *The Hill of Vision*

THE ADVENTURES OF SEUMAS BEG: IN THE ORCHARD
A Broadside (Dundrum: Cuala Press), April
Printed in *The Adventures of Seumas Beg*

THE ADVENTURES OF SEUMAS BEG: THE VISIT FROM ABROAD
A Broadside (Dundrum: Cuala Press), April
Printed in *The Adventures of Seumas Beg*

MISE FEIN
The Nation (London), 16 April
Printed as "Everything That I Can Spy" in *The Hill of Vision*

PEADAR OG GOES COURTING
Sinn Féin, 16 April
Printed in *The Hill of Vision*

IRISH IDIOSYNCRASIES
Sinn Féin, 7 May

HAIL AND FAREWELL
Sinn Féin, 14 May
Printed in *The Hill of Vision*

RUS IN URBE
Sinn Féin, 14 May
Printed as "Charlotte Street" in *The Adventures of Seumas Beg*

GOOD AND EVIL
Sinn Féin, 21 May
OCTOBER
Sinn Féin, 21 May
Printed as "The College of Surgeons" in *The Adventures of Seumas Beg*
THE ADVENTURES OF SEUMAS BEG: TREASURE TROVE
A Broadside (Dundrum: Cuala Press), June
Printed as "The Coral Island" in *The Adventures of Seumas Beg*
CHARITY
Sinn Féin, 4 June; *Collier's Magazine*, 22 May 1915
Printed as "York Street" in *The Adventures of Seumas Beg*
THE LADY IN RED
Sinn Féin, 11 June
SUMMER [I]
Sinn Féin, 18 June; as "Day and Night", *Harper's Monthly Magazine*, August 1913
Printed as "Day and Night" in *The Adventures of Seumas Beg*
DOWN BY THE MOAT
Sinn Féin, 25 June
CROOKED-HEART
Spectator, 9 July
Printed in *The Hill of Vision*
THOMAS MUSKERRY
Sinn Féin, 16 July
THE BREATH OF LIFE
Sinn Féin, 6 August
Printed in *The Hill of Vision*
THE FAIRY BOY
Sinn Féin, 20 August
Printed in *The Hill of Vision*
TIRED
Sinn Féin, 27 August
Printed as Part I of "Said the Young-Young Man to the Old-Old Man" in *The Hill of Vision*; as "I Wish" in the 1922 *The Hill of Vision*
THE GIRL I LEFT BEHIND ME
English Review, September
Printed in *The Hill of Vision*

THE SPY

A Broadside (Dundrum: Cuala Press), September; as "The Scout", *Rhythm* (London), July 1912

Printed as "The Apple Tree" in *The Adventures of Seumas Beg*

THE TINKER'S BRAT

English Review, September

Printed in *The Hill of Vision*; as "Soft Wings" in *Collected Poems*

WOMEN

English Review, September

Printed as "George's Street" in *The Adventures of Seumas Beg*

NEW PINIONS

Sinn Féin, 17 September

Printed in *The Hill of Vision*

ON POLITENESS

Sinn Féin, 17 September

SHAME

The Nation (London), 17 September

Printed in *The Hill of Vision*

FACTS

Sinn Féin, 1 October

IN THE COOL OF THE EVENING

Sinn Féin, 1 October; *The Nation* (London), 11 September 1909

Printed in *The Hill of Vision*

LOVE

Sinn Féin, 1 October

DECADENCE

Sinn Féin, 8 October

Review of Rachel Annand Taylor, *The Hours of Fiametta*

A GAELIC LEAGUE ART EXHIBITION

Sinn Féin, 15 October

CARICATURES

Sinn Féin, 22 October

HOLIDAY

The Open Window, November

LITTLE LADY

The Open Window, November

Included as "Astray" in *The Lonely God and Other Poems*

†A REPLY TO AN OPEN LETTER

Sinn Féin, 5 November

EPITHALAMIUM
Sinn Féin, 26 November
THE QUEEN OF BEAUTY
The Nation (London), 17 December
THE UNWORTHY PRINCESS
Irish Homestead, 17 December (Christmas Number)
Printed as "Three Lovers Who Lost: II" in *Here Are Ladies*
BOOKS FOR CHRISTMAS
Sinn Féin, 24 December
Review of Ella Young, *Celtic Wonder Tales*, and Thomas MacDonagh, *Songs of Myself*

1911

IN THE POPPY FIELD
Irish Review, March
Printed in *The Hill of Vision*
THE LONELY GOD
The Open Window, March
Included in *The Lonely God and Other Poems*; printed in *The Hill of Vision*
BESSIE BOBTAIL
Irish Review, April
Printed in *The Hill of Vision*
MARY: A STORY
Irish Review, April 1911–February 1912 (eleven parts)
Printed as *The Charwoman's Daughter* in England and as *Mary, Mary* in America
ON DANCING
Sinn Féin, 29 April
Printed as "There is a Tavern in the Town: II" in *Here Are Ladies*
ON LAWYERS
Sinn Féin, 10 June
SUMMER [II]
Sinn Féin, 22 July
Printed as part of "A Prelude and a Song" in *The Hill of Vision*; as "No more of woeful Misery I sing" in *Collected Poems*
DUTY
Nash's Magazine, October

1912

MAC DHOUL
Irish Review, January
Printed in *The Hill of Vision*

A WESTERN AWAKENING
Sinn Féin, 3 February
Review of Bligh Talbot Crosbie, *A Western Awakening*

THE WISDOM OF THE WEST
Irish Review, April
Review of James H. Cousins, *The Wisdom of the West*

†PRESENT-DAY CRITICISM
The New Age, 9 May

AN ADVENTURE OF SEUMAS BEG
Irish Review, June
Printed as "The Devil's Bag" in *The Adventures of Seumas Beg*

THE DAWN
Poetry Review, June

FROM THE GOLDEN BOOK [II]
Poetry Review, June
In *The Adventures of Seumas Beg*: stanza 1 printed as part of "Custom House Quay"; stanza 2 printed as part of "O'Connell Bridge" (as "When You Walk" in *Collected Poems*); stanza 3 printed as "The Patriot's Bed"; stanza 4 printed as "Donnelly's Orchard"; stanza 5 printed as "The Dodder Bank"

INCOGNITO
Poetry Review, June

THE LAST JUDGMENT
Poetry Review, June
Included as "In the High Court of Justice" in *The Lonely God and Other Poems*: printed as "The Tramp's Dream" in *Songs from the Clay*

MADAME SECRET
Poetry Review, June

PESSIMIST
Poetry Review, June

THE SINNER
Poetry Review, June

WHEN I WAS YOUNG
Poetry Review, June
Printed in *The Adventures of Seumas Beg*

THE POPULACE MIND
Irish Citizen, 1, 8, 15, 22 June
POEMS OLD AND NEW
Sinn Féin, 15 June
Review of A. H. Beesly, *Poems, Old and New*
TWO ADVENTURES OF SEUMAS BEG: AT THE TURN OF THE ROAD & THE SCOUT
Rhythm (London), July; "The Scout" printed as "The Spy", *A Broadside* (Dundrum: Cuala Press), September 1910
Printed as "The Turn of the Road" and "The Apple Tree" in *The Adventures of Seumas Beg*
AN ADVENTURE OF SEUMAS BEG: BEHIND THE HILL
Rhythm (London), August
Printed in *The Adventures of Seumas Beg*
HOW THE HUSBAND OF THE THIN WOMAN LOST HIS BROTHER
Irish Review, August
Incorporated in *The Crock of Gold*, pp. 3–21
THE IRISH YEAR
Irish Review, September
Review of Padraic Colum, *My Irish Year*
POEMS OF LOVE AND EARTH
Poetry Review, September
Review of John Drinkwater, *Poems of Love and Earth*
A HEAVY HUSBAND
The Nation (London), 7 December
Printed as "Three Heavy Husbands: II" in *Here Are Ladies*
THE APPOINTMENT
Sinn Féin, 21 December
Printed in *The Adventures of Seumas Beg*
DECEMBER
Sinn Féin, 21 December
Printed as "The Bare Trees" in *The Adventures of Seumas Beg*

1913

THE DAISIES
Irish Review, January
Printed in *Here Are Ladies* and *Songs from the Clay*

THE YOUNG MAN OUT OF A BOOK
The Nation (London), 4 January
Printed as "Three Women Who Wept: I" in *Here Are Ladies*
NOT AT HOME
The Nation (London), 22 February; as "The Woman Who Thumped Her Lap – A Sketch", *Current Opinion* (New York), July
Printed as "Three Angry People: III" in *Here Are Ladies*
†A POET IN DEFENCE OF HIS ORDER
Irish Homestead, 22 February
†THE HUMBLE PLEA OF THE POETS
Irish Homestead, 1 March
THE TRIANGLE [I]
The Nation (London), 8 March
Printed as "Three Heavy Husbands: I" in *Here Are Ladies*
THE STONE-MAN
The Nation (London), 12 April
Printed as "Three Angry People: I" in *Here Are Ladies*
THE REASON
Irish Review, May
THE MORNING ROAD
The Nation (London), 3 May
Printed as "Three Happy Places: III" in *Here Are Ladies*
BY FIRE LIGHT
The Nation (London), 7 June
Printed as "Three Young Wives: III" in *Here Are Ladies*
WITH THE DAISIES
Harper's Monthly Magazine, July
UN BOCK BRUN
The Nation (London), 26 July; as " 'Un Bock Brun': A Story in Which Nothing Happens", *Current Opinion* (New York), November
Printed as "A Glass of Beer" in *Here Are Ladies*
DAY AND NIGHT
Harper's Monthly Magazine, August; as "Summer", *Sinn Féin*, 18 June 1910
Printed in *The Adventures of Seumas Beg*
JEALOUSY
Irish Review, August
THE HORSES
The Nation (London), 16 August
Printed in *Here Are Ladies*

THE THREE-PENNY PIECE
Irish Review, September
Printed in *Here Are Ladies*; also incorporated in *The Demi-Gods*, pp. 167–83

THE TRIANGLE [II]
The Nation (London), 6 September
Printed in *Here Are Ladies*

BY THE CURB
Harper's Monthly Magazine, October
Printed as "The Horse" in *The Adventures of Seumas Beg*

THE BLIND MAN
The Nation (London), 4 October
Printed in *Here Are Ladies*

†THE SIROCCO!
Irish Homestead, 4 October

†ENTER MR. JAMES STEPHENS
The New Age, 20 November

IN SHINING ARMOUR
Saturday Review (London), 22 November

†RE-ENTER Mr. JAMES STEPHENS
The New Age, 27 November

A WINTER REVERIE
Harper's Monthly Magazine, December
Printed as "Donnybrook" in *The Adventures of Seumas Beg*

COME OFF THAT FENCE!
Irish Worker, 13 December

A TUNE ON A REED
The Sphere, 27 December
Divided into "The Rivals", "A Reply" and "A Tune on a Reed" in *Songs from the Clay* (one stanza omitted)

1914

GOING TO WORK
The Nation (London), 3 January

THE NODDING STARS
Saturday Review (London), 17 January
Printed in *Songs from the Clay*; as "The Devil" in *Collected Poems*

THE WHITE WINDOW
The Sphere, 24 January
Printed in *The Adventures of Seumas Beg*

A SONG FOR LOVERS
The Sphere, 28 February
Printed in *Songs from the Clay*; as "Lovers" in *Collected Poems*

THE CENTAURS
Irish Review, April
Printed in *Songs from the Clay*

DEIRDRE
Irish Review, April
Printed in *Songs from the Clay*

AN ESSAY IN CUBES
English Review, April

IN THE DARK
Irish Review, April
Printed as "The Snare" in *Songs from the Clay*

THE VOICE OF GOD
Irish Review, April
Printed in *Songs from the Clay*

BREAKFAST-TIME
The Sphere, 4 April
Printed in *The Adventures of Seumas Beg*

THE CROWN
The Sphere, 25 April
Printed as "The Crown of Thorns" in *Songs from the Clay*

THE MESSENGER
Saturday Review (London), 2 May
Printed in *Songs from the Clay*; as "To the Queen of the Bees" in *Collected Poems*

†THE MAN ON THE BOG
Irish Homestead, 27 June

DARK WINGS
Poetry (Chicago), August
Printed in *Songs from the Clay*; as "A Bird Sings Now" in *Collected Poems*

HAWKS
Poetry (Chicago), August
Printed as "From Hawk and Kite" in *The Adventures of Seumas Beg*

THE LIAR
Poetry (Chicago), August
Printed in *Songs from the Clay*
THE WASTE PLACES
Poetry (Chicago), August
Printed in *Songs from the Clay*; Part I as "In Waste Places" in *Collected Poems*
IN THE RAIN
The Nation (London), 10 October
Printed in *The Demi-Gods*, pp. 111–14
CANON HANNAY IN AMERICA
Daily News and Leader (London), 13 November
Review of George A. Birmingham, *Connaught to Chicago*
SIR RICHARD BURTON
Daily News and Leader (London), 29 December
Review of Sir Richard Burton, *The Kasîdah of Hâjî Abdû el Yezdi*

1915

CHECK!
Harper's Monthly Magazine, March
Printed in *The Adventures of Seumas Beg*
GEORGE BORROW, CHARLATAN
Daily News and Leader (London), 17 March
Review of George Borrow, *Welsh Poems and Ballads*
†AFFIRMATIONS
The New Age, 18 March
THE OLD WOMAN'S MONEY
Century Magazine, May
LORD DUNSANY'S TALES
Daily News and Leader (London), 5 May
Review of Lord Dunsany, *Fifty-One Tales*
CHARITY
Collier's Magazine, 22 May; *Sinn Féin*, 4 June 1910
Printed as "York Street" in *The Adventures of Seumas Beg*
AUTHORS AND EDITORS
The Author (London), June
Letter to the Editor
THE SAD SHEPHERD
Collier's Magazine, 3 July
Printed as "The Piper" in *The Adventures of Seumas Beg*

THE PROUD MOUNTAINS
Collier's Magazine, 14 August
Printed as "The Paps Of Dana" in *The Adventures of Seumas Beg*

THE FUR COAT
New Ireland, 2 October
Printed in *The Adventures of Seumas Beg*

†THE END OF "ROMANTICISM"
The New Age, 7 October

PEACE IN WAR TIME
Collier's Magazine, 11 December

1916

A CENTENARY APPRECIATION OF THE AUTHOR OF "JANE EYRE"
The Sphere, 22 April

GOD BLESS THE WORK
New Ireland, 22 April

†TO MR. SHAW
The New Age, 4 May

†AN APOLOGY TO MR. SHAW
The New Age, 18 May

GARLANDS
New Ireland, 1 July
Printed as Part I of "Spring 1916" in *Green Branches*

LEADERS OF THE IRISH REBELLION
New Republic, 1 July
Printed in *The Insurrection in Dublin*, pp. 87–92

THE SPRING IN IRELAND, 1916
The Nation (London), 8 July
Printed as "Spring 1916" in *Green Branches*

THE DUBLIN INSURRECTION: THE FIRST DAY
New Ireland, 15 July
Printed in *The Insurrection in Dublin*, pp. 1–20

JOY BE WITH US
New Ireland, 15 July
Printed in *Green Branches*

IN THE INTERVAL
New Ireland, 12 August

IN THE SILENCE
New Ireland, 19 August

CONSCRIPTION AND THE RETURN OF THE DOG
New Ireland, 23 September

1917

TO HIMSELF YEARS HENCE
New Ireland, 5 May
ANTHOLOGY: MARY HYNES
New Ireland, 7 July
Printed in *Reincarnations*
ANTHOLOGY: NANCY WALSH [I]
New Ireland, 7 July
Printed in *Reincarnations*, p. 8
ANTHOLOGY: ANTHONY O'DALY
New Ireland, 14 July
Printed in *Reincarnations*
ANTHOLOGY: MARY RUANE
New Ireland, 14 July
Printed in *Reincarnations*
ANTHOLOGY: PEGGY MITCHELL
New Ireland, 21 July
Printed in *Reincarnations*
ANTHOLOGY: WILLIAM O'KELLY
New Ireland, 21 July
Printed in *Reincarnations*
ANTHOLOGY: THE COOLUN
New Ireland, 28 July
Printed in *Reincarnations*
ANTHOLOGY: EILEEN, DIARMUID AND TEIG
New Ireland, 28 July
Printed in *Reincarnations*
ANTHOLOGY: NANCY WALSH [II]
New Ireland, 4 August
Printed in *Reincarnations*, pp. 11–12
ANTHOLOGY: THE RED MAN'S WIFE
New Ireland, 4 August
Printed in *Reincarnations*
ANTHOLOGY: CLANN CARTIE
New Ireland, 11 August
Printed in *Reincarnations*; as "The Wave of Cliona" in *Collected Poems*

PAMPHLETS
New Ireland, 25 August
TO JOACHIM DU BELLAY
New Ireland, 25 August
ANTHOLOGY: EGAN O'RAHILLY
New Ireland, 27 October
Printed in *Reincarnations*
ANTHOLOGY: RIGHTEOUS ANGER
New Ireland, 27 October
Printed in *Reincarnations*; as "A Glass of Beer" in *Collected Poems*
ANTHOLOGY: THE GERALDINE'S CLOAK
New Ireland, 3 November
Printed in *Reincarnations*
ANTHOLOGY: BLUE BLOOD
New Ireland, 10 November
Printed in *Reincarnations*
ANTHOLOGY: PLUS ÇA CHANGE . . . !
New Ireland, 17 November
Printed as "The Gang" in *Reincarnations*
ANTHOLOGY: INIS FAIL
New Ireland, 1 December
Printed in *Reincarnations*
ANTHOLOGY: ODELL
New Ireland, 8 December
Printed in *Reincarnations*
ANTHOLOGY: THE COUNTY MAYO
New Ireland, 22 December
Printed in *Reincarnations*
ANTHOLOGY: SKIM-MILK
New Ireland, 22 December
Printed in *Reincarnations*

1918

DESIRE
The Nation (London), 26 January; *The Dial*, June 1920
Printed in *Etched in Moonlight*
HONORO BUTLER AND LORD KENMARE
New Statesman, 9 February
Printed in *Reincarnations*

DARLING
Smart Set Magazine, June
Printed in *Etched in Moonlight*

CRÊPE DE CHINE
Smart Set Magazine, July

SAWDUST
Century Magazine, September; *Everyman* (London), 23 August 1919

SCHOOL-FELLOWS
Century Magazine, September
Printed in *Etched in Moonlight*

THE WOLF
Century Magazine, September; *Everyman* (London), 3 May 1919
Printed in *Etched in Moonlight*

THE BIRTHDAY PARTY
Novel Magazine (London), December

1919

THE WOLF
Everyman (London), 3 May; *Century Magazine*, September 1918
Printed in *Etched in Moonlight*

THE STORY OF TUAN MAC CAIRILL
Irish Statesman, 28 June–12 July (three parts)
Printed as part of "The Story of Tuan Mac Cairill" in *Irish Fairy Tales*

SAWDUST
Everyman (London), 23 August; *Century Magazine*, September 1918

DUBLIN: A CITY OF WONDERFUL DREAMS. SILENT AND VOLUBLE FOLK
The Times (London), 4 November (Irish Number)

MYTHOLOGY: QUAINT TALES OF ORIGINATION. THE CULT OF DEATH
The Times (London), 4 November (Irish Number)

1920

THE BOSS
The Dial, April
Printed in *Etched in Moonlight*

DESIRE

The Dial, June; *The Nation* (London), 26 January 1918

Printed in *Etched in Moonlight*

THE THIEVES

The Dial, August

IN THE BEECHWOOD

London Mercury, November; *The Dial*, December

Incorporated in *In the Land of Youth*, pp. 93–111

1921

IRELAND RETURNING TO HER FOUNTAINS

Survey (New York), 26 November

FROM THE KATHA UPANISHAD

The Nation and The Athenaeum (London), 10 December

Printed as "Nachiketas and Death" in *Little Things*; as "Thy Soul" in *A Poetry Recital* (1926)

1922

MINUETTE: ON THE FREEDOM OF IRELAND

Poblacht na h-Eireann (Dublin), 3 January

Printed in *Little Things*; as "Minuette" in *Collected Poems*

GREEN WEEDS

The Nation and The Athenaeum (London), 14 January

Printed in *A Poetry Recital*

ARTHUR GRIFFITH: PRESIDENT OF DAIL EIREANN

Review of Reviews (London), March

Printed in *Arthur Griffith: Journalist and Statesman*

THE PIT OF BLISS

The Nation and The Athenaeum, 8 April

Printed in *A Poetry Recital*

AN ADVENTURE IN PROPHECY

Atlantic Monthly, May

[A SECTION OF " THE GOSSIP SHOP"]

The Bookman (New York), May

Contains part of a letter to Grace Wallace

ARTHUR GRIFFITH

Studies (Dublin), September

Printed in *Arthur Griffith: Journalist and Statesman*

THE OUTLOOK FOR LITERATURE: WITH SPECIAL REFERENCE TO IRELAND
Century Magazine, October

THE GOLDEN BIRD
The Nation and The Athenaeum, 14 October
Printed in *A Poetry Recital*

ON A LONELY SPRAY
The Nation and The Athenaeum, 23 December
Printed in *A Poetry Recital*

1923

LITTLE THINGS
The Nation and The Athenaeum, 13 January
Printed as a Christmas card by the Brick Row Book Shop, Inc., in New York; included in *Little Things*

THE LAST WORD
The Dial, March
Printed as "The Crest Jewel" in *A Poetry Recital* (1926)

ETCHED IN MOONLIGHT
Dublin Magazine, August–October (three parts)
Printed in *Etched in Moonlight*

THE GHOST
New Republic, 1 August
Revised text in *The New Republic Anthology: 1915–1935*, ed. Groff Conklin (New York: Dodge Publishing Company, 1936)

IN TIR NA N-OG
Irish Statesman, 15 September–8 December (thirteen parts)
Incorporated in "The Feast of Samhain" in *In the Land of Youth*

AN INTERVIEW WITH MR. JAMES STEPHENS: BY OUR SPECIAL CORRESPONDENT [JAMES ESSE]
Irish Statesman, , 22 September

TOCHMARC ETAINÉ: "THE IMMORTAL HOUR"
The Sphere, 1 and 8 December

THE NEW JAPAN
Irish Statesman, 22 December
Review of James H. Cousins, *The New Japan*

THE ROVER
Irish Statesman, 22 December
Review of Joseph Conrad, *The Rover*

BESIDES THAT
Green and Gold (Waterford), Christmas 1923–March 1924
Printed in *A Poetry Recital* (London)

1924

CONTEMPORARY BRITISH ARTISTS [I]
Irish Statesman, 2 February
Review of *Augustus John* in "Contemporary British Artists" series

CONTEMPORARY BRITISH ARTISTS [II]
Irish Statesman, 9 February
Review of *Sir William Orpen* in "Contemporary British Artists" series

†IRISH LETTER[I]
The Dial, April

THE NOVELIST AND FINAL UTTERANCE
Irish Statesman, 12 April

GROWTH IN FICTION
Irish Statesman, 17 May

†IRISH LETTER [II]
The Dial, June

HIS WILL
Dublin Magazine, July
Printed in *A Poetry Recital* (London); as "Arpeggio" in *Collected Poems*

THE WORM OUROBOROS
Irish Statesman, 19 July
Review of E. R. Eddison, *The Worm Ouroboros*; printed as introduction to the 1926 New York edition

†DUBLIN LETTER [I]
The Dial, August

CONTEMPORARY BRITISH ARTISTS [III]
Irish Statesman, 2 August
Review of *Ambrose McEvoy* in "Contemporary British Artists" series

DEATH
The Dial, November; *Dublin Magazine*, February 1925
Printed in *Collected Poems*

THE MAIN-DEEP
The Dial, November; *Dublin Magazine*, February 1925
Printed in *A Poetry Recital*

THE ROSE IN THE WIND
The Dial, November; *Dublin Magazine*, February 1925
Printed in *A Poetry Recital*

CONVERSATIONS IN EBURY STREET
Observer, 3 November
Review of George Moore, *Conversations in Ebury Street*

1925

DEATH
Dublin Magazine, February; *The Dial*, November 1924
Printed in *Collected Poems*

THE MAIN-DEEP
Dublin Magazine, February; *The Dial*, November 1924
Printed in *A Poetry Recital*

THE ROSE IN THE WIND
Dublin Magazine, February; *The Dial*, November 1924
Printed in *A Poetry Recital*

†DUBLIN LETTER [II]
The Dial, April

CHRISTMAS IN FREELANDS
Irish Statesman, 26 December
Privately printed as W.T.H. Howe's Christmas Greeting for 1925; included in *A Poetry Recital* (1926)

1926

MR. GEORGE MOORE
Observer, 1 August
Review of George Moore, *Ulick and Soracha*

1927

MON PREMIER LIVRE DE PROSE
Europe (Paris), 15 March
Printed as the preface to *Mary Semblant* (1927), a translation of *The Charwoman's Daughter* by Abel Chevalley; revised English version printed in *On Prose and Verse*

POEMS FROM THE GREEK ANTHOLOGY
Observer, 18 September
Review of Humbert Wolfe, *Others Abide*

TRYING TO FIND THE STRAND
Evening News (London), 22 December

LONDON WOOS A MAN!
Evening News (London), 23 December

1928

FOR ST. PATRICK'S DAY
Radio Times (London), 9 March

HOW ST. PATRICK SAVES THE IRISH
New York Times, 11 March
Printed as *How St. Patrick Saves the Irish*

I REMEMBER J. M. SYNGE
Radio Times (London), 23 March
Included in *James, Seumas and Jacques*

FAMOUS WOMEN
Observer, 6 May
Review of Beatrice Curtis Brown, *Elizabeth Chudleigh*; Clifford Bax, *Bianca Capello*; Geoffrey West, *Mrs. Annie Besant*; V. Sackville-West, *Aphra Behn*; and Martin Armstrong, *Lady Hester Stanhope*

1929

IN MEMORIAM
New Yorker, 13 April
Printed in *Strict Joy*

THE ROSE
New Yorker, 13 April
Printed in *Theme and Variations* (variation 13)

SPRING [II]
New Yorker, 13 April
Printed in *Theme and Variations* (variation 15)
WINTER
New Yorker, 13 April
Printed in *Theme and Variations* (variation 8)
THE SILVER CAR
New Yorker, 20 April
Included in *Collected Poems* (1954)
THE OPTIMIST
Harper's Monthly Magazine, May
Printed as *The Optimist*; included in *Collected Poems* (1954)
INVOCATION
New Yorker, 4 May
Printed in *Theme and Variations* (variation 3)
REVERIE ON A ROSE
New Yorker, 11 May
Printed in *Strict Joy*
MIDNIGHT: AFTER SAPPHO
New Yorker, 25 May; revision of "Midnight", *Sinn Féin*, 29 May 1909
Included in *Collected Poems* (1954)
RED BERRIES
New Yorker, 25 May

1930

AMERICA'S PLACE IN HISTORY: AN IRISH DIALOGUE
Forum (Philadelphia), February
STRICT CARE, STRICT JOY!
New Statesman, 11 October
Printed in *Strict Joy*
THE APPLE BLOSSOM
New Statesman, 18 October
Printed in *Strict Joy*

1933

A POETRY READING WITH COMMENTS
MS. (New York), May

[THAT IS A YOUNG TREE GROWING IN THE WOOD!]
Dublin Magazine, July–September
Printed as "Trumpets in Woodland" in *Kings and the Moon*

THE MIGHTY MOTHER
Observer, 28 July
Printed in *Kings and the Moon*

1934

AN IRISH PROPHECY: THE NEW SOCIAL ORDER IN 1916
Forum (Philadelphia), August
Part of a letter to Warren Barton Blake on 22 February 1916

1935

THE ROOT AND THE FLOWER
Now and Then (London), Summer
Review of L. H. Myers, *The Root and the Flower*

THE PASSING OF "A.E."
Observer, 21 July

1936

THE MOON HATH NOT
Dublin Magazine, April– June
Printed as part of "Gathering the Waters" in *Kings and the Moon*

1937

A YOUNG MAN IN OLD NEW YORK
Sunday Times (London), 21 February
Review of Stephen Hudson, *The Other Side*

THE AMERICAN LITERARY SCENE
Sunday Times (London), 7 March
Review of Carl Van Doren, *Three Worlds*

MR. FROST'S NEW POEMS
Sunday Times (London), 4 April
Review of Robert Frost, *A Further Range*

MEMORIES OF DUBLIN
Sunday Times (London), 18 April

Review of Oliver St. John Gogarty, *As I Was Going Down Sackville Street*

POET, PAINTER AND CRITIC

Sunday Times (London), 4 July

Review of *The Collected Works of Isaac Rosenberg*, edited by Gordon Bottomley and Denys Harding

THE ART OF CHEKHOV: BOREDOM MADE EXCITING

Sunday Times (London), 12 September

Review of Princess Nina Andronikova Toumanova, *Anton Chekhov*

IRISH WIT AND WISDOM: ONE MAN'S LIFE

Sunday Times (London), 24 October

Review of Gerald Griffin, *The Dead March Past*

1938

ESSAYS ON AUTHORS: SWINBURNE AND OTHERS

Sunday Times (London), 27 February

Review of Ford Madox Ford, *Mightier than the Sword*

GHOSTS OF DUBLIN

Sunday Times (London), 15 May

Review of Stephen Gwynn, *Dublin Old and New*

THE HUMAN COMEDY: WONDER AND THE ARTIST

Sunday Times (London), 28 August

Review of Lennox Robinson, *Three Homes*

THE POET'S WORKSHOP: JOHN DRINKWATER'S LAST BOOK

Sunday Times (London), 25 September

Review of John Drinkwater, *English Poetry: An Unfinished History*

TANSIT

New York Times, 30 October

Printed in *Kings and the Moon*

BIDDING THE MOON

New York Times, 8 November

Printed in *Kings and the Moon*

MAGIC OF IRISH FOLK-TALES

Sunday Times (London), 20 November

Review of Pat Mullen, *Irish Tales*

1939

HERE'S WISHING!
The Listener, 5 January
B.B.C. broadcast

THE END OF A CHAPTER
Sunday Times (London), 8 January
Review of Maud Gonne MacBride, *A Servant of the Queen*

A DUBLIN FROLIC
Sunday Times (London), 12 March
Review of Oliver St. John Gogarty, *Tumbling in the Hay*

A NEW POET'S SUCCESS
Sunday Times (London), 16 April
Review of May Sarton, *Inner Landscape*

BORDERS OF SLEEP: MR. WALTER DE LA MARE'S NEW ANTHOLOGY
Observer, 14 May
Review of Walter de la Mare, *Behold, this Dreamer!*

†NORTH AND SOUTH
Spectator, 23 June

THE HARVEST OF POETRY: ANTHOLOGIES GOOD AND BAD
Sunday Times (London), 27 August
Review of *Modern Poetry*, edited by Robert Lynd

1940

†TO THE EDITOR OF THE TIMES
The Times (London), 19 June

IRISH JOURNEYS
Sunday Times (London), 7 July
Review of Richard Hayward, *Where the River Shannon Flows*, and Seán O'Faolain, *An Irish Journey*

HOMAGE TO W.B. YEATS
Spectator, 12 July
Review of *Scattering Branches*, edited by Stephen Gwynn

1941

HOW SHOULD POETRY BE READ?
The Listener, 22 May
B.B.C. broadcast

MUST POETRY MAKE SENSE?
The Listener, 5 June
B.B.C. broadcast

IS VERSE-SPEAKING A LOST ART?
The Listener, 12 June
B.B.C. broadcast

DOES IT STICK IN YOUR THROAT?
The Listener, 24 July
B.B.C. broadcast

1942

YEATS AND THE TELEPHONE
The Listener, 22 January (excerpt)
B.B.C. broadcast; included in full as "W.B. Yeats" in *James, Seumas and Jacques*

HARDY THE UNHAPPY
Spectator, 13 March
Review of Edmund Blunden, *Thomas Hardy*

"A.E.": A WONDERFUL AMATEUR
The Listener, 9 April
B.B.C. broadcast; included as "A.E. [I]" in *James, Seumas and Jacques*

1943

VILLAGES I REMEMBER
The Listener, 18 March
B.B.C. broadcast; included in *James, Seumas and Jacques*

"HE DIED YOUNGER THAN HE WAS BORN"
The Listener, 18 March
B.B.C. broadcast; included as "Yeats as Dramatist" in *James, Seumas and Jacques*

TWO GREAT TALKERS
The Listener, 16 September (excerpt)
B.B.C. broadcast; included in full as "Bernard Shaw" in *James, Seumas and Jacques*

1944

"NOTHING MUCH"

St. Martin's Review (London), April

B.B.C. broadcast; included in *James, Seumas and Jacques*

THOMAS MOORE: CHAMPION MINOR POET

The Listener, 8 June

B.B.C. broadcast

1945

AN IRISHMAN'S DAYS

The Listener, 22 February

B.B.C. broadcast; included in *James, Seumas and Jacques*

A STORY OF A GOOD DOG

The Listener, 28 June

B.B.C. broadcast; included in *James, Seumas and Jacques*

"THE 'PUREST' POET OF THEM ALL"

The Listener, 6 September

B.B.C. broadcast; included as "William Blake" in *James, Seumas and Jacques*

1946

POETRY FOR FUN

The Listener, 7 February (excerpt)

B.B.C. broadcast; included in full as "On His Poems [II]" in *James, Seumas and Jacques*

PRAISE OF LADIES

Sunday Times (London), 17 February

Review of Clifford Bax, *The Beauty of Women*

THE CHINESE WERE IMPRESSED

The Listener, 28 March (excerpt)

B.B.C. broadcast; included in full as "St. Patric" in *James, Seumas and Jacques*

A CHINESE POET

Spectator, 10 May

Review of Gerald Bullet's translation of *The Golden Year of Fan Cheng-Ta*

NOVELS – DEAD OR ALIVE?

The Listener, 13 June

B.B.C. broadcast

TALK AND TALKERS
The Listener, 4 July
B.B.C. broadcast; included as "Talk" in *James, Seumas and Jacques*

THE " PERIOD TALENT" OF G.K. CHESTERTON
The Listener, 17 October
B.B.C. broadcast

THE JAMES JOYCE I KNEW
The Listener, 24 October
B.B.C. broadcast; included in *James, Seumas and Jacques*

A RHINOCEROS, SOME LADIES, AND A HORSE
Irish Writing, No. 1 [November?]
Included in *James, Seumas and Jacques*

1947

ABBEY THEATRE ECHOES
Spectator, 10 January
Review of *Lady Gregory's Journals, 1916–1930*, edited by Lennox Robinson

A CONVERSATION WITH GEORGE MOORE
The Listener, 16 January
B.B.C. broadcast; included as "First Meeting with George Moore" in *James, Seumas and Jacques*

"THE PRINCE OF WITS": AN APPRECIATION OF JOHN DONNE
The Listener, 23 January
B.B.C. broadcast; included as "John Donne" in *James, Seumas and Jacques*

LIVING – WHATEVER THAT IS
The Listener, 19 June
B.B.C. broadcast; included in *James, Seumas and Jacques*

MEMORIES OF THREE CITIES
Spectator, 24 October
Review of Mary Colum, *Life and the Dream*

1948

A MEMORY OF "A.E."
The Listener, 22 January
B.B.C. broadcast; included as "A.E. [II]" in *James, Seumas and Jacques*

STEPHEN MacKENNA: TALKER AND PHILOSOPHER
The Listener, 29 January
B.B.C. broadcast; included as "Stephen MacKenna [I]" in *James, Seumas and Jacques*

NO MORE PEASANTS
The Listener, 26 August
B.B.C. broadcast; included in *James, Seumas and Jacques*

W. B. YEATS: A TRIBUTE
Observer, 19 September

THE POEMS OF RICHARD CHURCH
Spectator, 8 October
Review of Richard Church, *Collected Poems*

1961

JAMES STEPHENS AT COLBY COLLEGE
Colby Library Quarterly, March
A listing by Richard Cary of Stephens material at Colby College; contains some interesting inscriptions (principally in books from the library of Ernest A. Boyd) and summaries of letters to various correspondents

1970

LETTERS FROM LADY GREGORY AND JAMES STEPHENS
Bibliotheca Bucnellensis (Lewisburg, Pennsylvania), New Series, vol. VIII
Two letters to Oliver St. John Gogarty, edited by James F. Carens; the letter of 12 April 1930 not included here

THREE UNPUBLISHED LETTERS FROM JAMES STEPHENS
Papers on Language & Literature (Edwardsville, Illinois), Spring
Three letters to Lewis Chase, edited by Richard J. Finneran

1972

["WELDON SUBSCRIPTION FUND"]
Seamas O Saothrai, "Brinsley Macnamara", *Irish Booklore*, Spring
Stephens was one of several writers to sign a circular, dated 18 December 1923, in support of Brinsley Macnamara; the Circular is reproduced on p. 78 of this article

Index to Correspondents

Index to the Writings of James Stephens

General Index